W9-CBM-901

TELL IT LIKE IT IS

Chuck Stone

TELL IT LIKE IT IS

TRIDENT PRESS · NEW YORK

The publisher wishes to acknowledge permission to republish material from the Afro-American, ©, *1960–1963; and from the Chicago* Daily Defender, ©, *1963–1964.*

Library of Congress Catalog Card Number: 68–13435

Published by Trident Press, a division of Simon & Schuster, Inc., 630 Fifth Avenue, New York, N.Y. 10020.

Third Printing

Printed in the United States of America

Contents

Preface

Tell It Like It Is took six years to write.

And what a swinging six years it was!

From 1959 to 1964, I was successively editor of the New York *Age,* the Washington *Afro-American* and the Chicago *Daily Defender.* And I wish to acknowledge with thanks permission to reprint material copyrighted by them within these pages.

During those editorships—before the era of black power, before the black rebellions in American cities and before the present nitty-gritty confrontation between whites and blacks in America—I tried to tell it like it was in my column, "A Stone's Throw."

Ignoring (and frequently offending) middle-class "house Negroes" I was more concerned with "rapping" with the true "soul brothers" who understood so well that "the man" was "running a game on them." Reaching them, involving them in the newspaper's crusades at the risk of alienating the white power structure or, for that matter, the captive "Negro leader," was far more important to me. And you know something? It kept me in constant trouble. But, baby, I had a ball!

Some of the columns may seem tame against the harsh crucible of today's racial tensions. I wrote about "Negroes" and "colored people" from 1959 to 1964. Today, in 1967, I would write about "black people." This is because we have rediscovered our blackness and its beauty is pleasing to our senses.

I realize now more than ever in re-reading these columns that I have always been an advocate of black power—I just didn't call it that. But all through these columns, a single thread runs—the advocacy of black power—black power at the ballot box, black power in controlling black communities, black power in developing black businesses, black power in educational excellence, black power in racial pride, black power in top-level government positions, black power in personal achievement, black power in civic responsibility, and black power in love for our fellow man.

During those years, I was understandably known as a "rabble-rouser," a "racist" and an "irresponsible newsman." (I take enormous pride in my rejection by the National Press Club for membership because of my outspoken views on race relations and phony white liberals.) But today, next to the splendid militancy of today's young black leaders, those columns sound almost moderate. (I never could quite understand how anyone could be a "moderate" about injustice, poverty, and racism. But that's why we have Urban Leagues and National Conferences of Christians and Jews—to allow people to postpone the immediate eradication of racial injustice by being moderates.)

Tell It Like It Is is a philosophy of life. It slashes and pokes fun, but at all times it's in there "wailing" for "the brother." When the need arises it can "put down" black folks, and when the occasion warrants it can "put on" white folks. At all times, it gives the white power structure an unmitigated hard time.

And peeking through that wall of unrelenting anger are occasional words of love and endearment for all of mankind.

Isn't that what it's all about?

CHUCK STONE
Washington, D.C.
August 26th, 1967

TO THE FOUR LADIES IN MY LIFE WHO REPRESENT THE PAST, THE PRESENT, AND THE FUTURE OF BLACK WOMANHOOD: MY GRACIOUS MOTHER, MADALENE; MY "TOGETHER" WIFE, LOUISE; AND MY DELIGHTFUL DAUGHTERS, KRISHNA AND ALLEGRA.

1963: The Year of No Quarter

A Prologue, December 27, 1963—This column, "1963: The Year of No Quarter," was written on April twentieth 1963, while I was working in Washington, D.C. At that time, the "Negro Revolt" was a suspicion, a creation in the minds of the civil rights writers and a hoped-for thing. Birmingham had not exploded yet. Philadelphia, Chicago, Danville, Cambridge, St. Louis were all relatively quiet. But there was a tense excitement and an expectancy of all-out action in the air. Many Negroes felt it. I felt it and wrote about it on April twentieth, 1963. Now, eight months later, December twenty-seventh, 1963, the "Negro Revolt" is a fierce part of American history. In summing up the year 1963, in civil rights, I can add nothing to those thoughts of April twentieth, 1963.

"I will not yield to kiss the ground before young Malcolm's feet and to be baited with the rabble's curse. . . .

"Before my body, I throw my warlike shield. Lay on, Macduff, and damn'd be him that first cries 'Hold enough.' "

Macbeth's militant quotation—which is perhaps not the most appropriate to use, since Macduff wiped the floor with the Scottish king—nonetheless most succinctly and fittingly describes how many Negroes and virtually all Africans feel toward the struggle with white people for full equality.

After inviting Macduff to a personal confrontation, Macbeth was swiftly dispatched.

I am supremely confident that neither colored Americans nor Africans will be dispatched and will, in fact, be magnificently victorious in their historical battle with the white race.

The black man's two-centuries-old struggle for human dignity has suddenly and cataclysmally achieved a new dimension.

It is the new dimension of fearless and open confrontation.

It is the new dimension of "no quarter."

Negroes no longer run from the fray. They stand and they fight. And a few die.

Into such a pattern of social conflict composed of elements first introduced by the majority race, the inevitable voices of "moderation" and "gradualism" are heard from the same people who started this mess in the first place.

Despite the success of the Uncle Toms in the drawing rooms of "Mr. Charlie," the "brother" himself is more and more making the final decisions on who should represent him. And we are just as rapidly assigning the Uncle Toms to the role of bystander instead of leader.

"Free by '63" was the NAACP's slogan, adopted several years ago. It was taken up by all Negroes with united enthusiasm.

1963 is three and one-half months old and we are still submerged as a group of people in the white ocean of racial inhumanities. We are not "free by '63." But we are angrily determined to be free—completely free.

In this resolution, we are joined, heart and heart, hand and hand, by our African brothers, who have publicly vowed that it is no longer a question of "Will the racial explosion come to South Africa?" but "When and how?"

What makes 1963 different from previous years?

What separates it from 1960, the year of the "sit-ins," or 1961, the year of the "freedom riders," from other years?

Can 1963 be isolated as the big year in this era of the "Negro Revolt" or the "new Negro?"

It can, and several events, several people, several statements make it so.

1. 1963 is the year that Representative Adam Clayton Powell

issued his now famous statement of racial conscience on the role of the white participant in the struggle for racial equality. His attack on the NAACP, while decried by many and denounced by prominent leaders, nevertheless came closer to what colored people are thinking and feeling than Roy Wilkins's adolescent defense. "We will achieve only that which we fight for," declared Powell on that historic Thursday evening, March twenty-first, at Washington's Metropolitan Baptist Church, "and it can only be done by those organizations that are totally owned and controlled by Negroes."

This, of course, does not exclude white participation. It merely delimits and circumscribes its power.

2. 1963 is the year Dick Gregory, an entertainer, elected to involve himself physically in the battle for racial equality by going to Mississippi to help colored people register to vote. Another entertainer, Al Hibbler, went to Birmingham, Alabama, to be with the Reverend Martin Luther King, Jr. While other entertainers have given unstintingly of their talent and energy in this same manner, physical involvement represented a new dimension.

3. 1963 is the year a colored Congressman, Representative Charles C. Diggs, Jr. (Dem. Mich.), was invited by local residents in Greenwood, Mississippi, to come and make his personal assessment of the terrible situation in Greenwood—and Diggs went. The attempt on his life by a homemade bomb only heightened the seriousness of the Mississippi situation.

4. 1963 is the year the Howard University student body spotlighted the inconsistency of an all-white construction crew building a men's gymnasium at a predominantly colored university and demanded that the lilywhite pattern be changed.

The U.S. Government moved in and ordered the construction companies and subcontractors to comply with equal employment qualifications and an important battle was won.

5. 1963 is the year African leaders warned America that it must cease supplying Portugal with arms which can be used to put down revolts in Mozambique and Angola (Portuguese territories), that the African leaders of Northern Rhodesia, Southern Rhodesia,

Southwest Africa, and South Africa are prepared to spill blood without reservation to achieve complete independence.

All of these statements and events interact.

They all have a stimulating influence on each other.

In America, the two sections of the country are witnessing two separate methods of spotlighting the problem.

In the North, anger and frustration are expressed in a race riot, a gang attack on white people, an increase in crime.

In the South, the resentment is translated into the tactics and strategy of the voter registration program and the all-out assault on segregation, with colored leaders going to jail for this crusade.

This is the year of 1963, the year the colored community and its leaders bestirred themselves in one grand cathartic resistance against segregation.

It is the year that the Reverend Martin Luther King, Jr., Adam Clayton Powell, the Howard University students, Dick Gregory, Charles Diggs, and Al Hibbler, who together speak for colored people everywhere, served notice on the world:

"We will not yield to kiss the ground before the segregationists' feet. . . .

"Before our bodies, we throw our determination.

"Lay on, white folks . . . and 'later' for him that yells first, 'go slow.' "

December 1963

Who Commits All the Crime in the United States?

I DON'T KNOW WHO commits *all* the crime in America, but I know who most Americans believe commit most of the country's crime.

Negroes—who else?

Because of the daily newspaper accounts in Chicago, New York, Philadelphia, and Washington of muggings, burglaries, stabbings, murders, and auto thefts (most of which are committed by Negroes in those four cities), the collective impression exists that Negroes really are responsible for the pattern of criminal life in America.

Part of the fears of that mythological monster, *the white backlash,* are supposed to stem from the possibility of having Negroes —qua criminals—as next-door neighbors.

Let's examine a few facts about who commits most of the crimes in America, where the majority of crimes are committed, and who controls the entire criminal network and syndicate in this country.

According to the Federal Bureau of Investigation's report on crime in the United States for 1963, the following were the cities with the highest crime rates (number of serious crimes per 100,000 persons); the cities are ranked in the order of their crime saturation rate:

1. Las Vegas (Crime Syndicate, Inc.'s, hometown)
2. Los Angeles
3. Miami
4. Phoenix

5. Lexington
6. Chicago (Richard Daley's home-town)
7. Great Falls, Mont. (nobody's home-town)
8. Atlantic City (conventioneers' home-town)
9. Denver
10. Corpus Christi

New York City, which sometimes conveys the impression of rampant social disorder, ranked thirty-fifth, while Washington, D.C. (fifty-five per cent Negro, a fact so fondly emphasized by Southern Congressmen), ranked thirty-ninth, and Philadelphia (America's fourth largest city, almost thirty-three per cent Negro), ranked ninety-ninth.

Where do Negroes fit into this pattern of national crime?

1. Las Vegas, America's No. 1 crime city, is in Nevada, which ranks fortieth in the number of Negro residents (a paltry 13,000). Phoenix, No. 4 in crime and Goldwater's hometown, is in Arizona, which ranks thirty-second in Negro residents, and Great Falls, No. 7 in crime, is in Montana, which has a skimpy 1,500 Negroes in the entire state. (Why would a Negro want to live in Montana in the first place?)

2. Negroes control none of the organized crime in America. The Mafia is not integrated, the various crime syndicates in Chicago, New York, and Las Vegas are all white, and nationwide book-making, narcotics smuggling, gambling, and prostitution are totally controlled by whites. We have a hard time even trying to participate at the executive level.

3. Whereas Negroes, for example, in Chicago, are responsible for a majority of auto thefts, white-controlled rings are responsible for the disposal, sale, and fencing of these autos. (We haven't been able to break into the wholesale business yet.)

4. The biggest, most efficient, and most expensive prostitution rings in the major cities are not only operated by white madams controlled by a white syndicate, but they use only white women and cater only to prominent white visiting dignitaries and business men. Negroes haven't come up with any Bobby Baker yet.

5. The ten most wanted criminals on the FBI list rarely include more than two or three Negroes. For the most part, we do our best to try and keep the list integrated. For the last several months we had one Negro among the top ten until he got sloppy and careless and had the nerve to destroy the integrated pattern by getting himself caught. Sometimes we never do things right.

6. Even policy and the numbers, an illegal activity heavily supported by Negro communities all over America, is controlled by the white syndicate, which permits a few Negroes to operate their own wheels in Harlem, Chicago's South Side, Central Avenue in Los Angeles, and the West Side in Philadelphia.

Crime in America exists for one reason—the people want it to exist. When two cities as disparate in size, ethnic composition, distance, urban development, standard of living, and municipal philosophies as Chicago, Illinois, and Great Falls, Montana, rank sixth and seventh respectively as the cities with the highest crime rates, then crime is truly a national phenomenon—and a predominantly white phenomenon.

Negroes may be responsible for the high crime rates in the largest cities—and this bleakly unfortunate truth cannot be denied—but their crime is born out of a blanket denial of opportunity by a hostile white society. Crime is the Negro's desperate method of lashing back in unreasoned anger and, by necessity, earning a living, because of the closed job doors. Crime, to Negroes, is not some sort of professional accomplishment in which it is a badge of honor to deploy one's talents successfully.

When it comes to crime, Negroes enjoy the same status as they do in other activities in American life—strictly second class. And in this instance, we can thank God that our white brothers are so much more competent, efficient, and productive in this particular destructive activity.

None Can Kill You Like Your Own Kind

I HEARD TWO OF THE "brothers" in a barber shop on Thirty-Fifth Street near Indiana discussing the sad plight of the Negro, made even more gloomy by our "Negro leaders" and "spokesmen."

"Man, you know," said one, "our leaders are such a sack of (and he used a naughty four-letter word). They'll make you cry and gnash your teeth. Did you read all of that down-in-the-country this Rowan gave Negroes at that Urban League meeting? He must've forgot who started this whole mess."

The other discussant looked pensive for a moment, shook his head, and a woeful expression crossed his chiseled, ebony features. "It's so true, man—none can kill you like your own kind."

In the last few weeks, the Negro has been subjected to as much verbal abuse from "his own kind" as he has from "Mr. Charlie."

Rather than attack the debilitating pus of racial segregation that has almost destroyed the bodies and minds of many of today's Negro youngsters, a covey of our "Negro leaders" have now shifted to condemning Negroes for not reacting like well-behaved ladies and gentlemen to the hundred-years-long confrontation of this cancer.

Roy Wilkins, in a fit of intemperance and ill choice of language, assailed the Negro "foul-mouthed punks and hoodlums" responsible for violence who are setting back the civil rights movement (and implicitly undoing all of the noble work of Roy Wilkins). However, I don't recall ever hearing Wilkins talk about the poor white trash that has murdered and tortured Negroes in the South. Wilkins say anything nasty about those four Klansmen who are charged with killing Lieutenant Colonel Penn? Wilkins use any nasty words to describe the white men who tortured poor James Chaney in Philadelphia, Mississippi, beyond belief?

Even more recently, the brilliant and respected Carl T. Rowan, director of the United States Information Agency, succumbed to this current hysteria and jumped on the "I-hate-colored-crime-as-much-as-you-white-folks" bandwagon and called on "my fellow Negroes" to rid the civil rights movement "of the taint of street rioters, looters, and punks who terrorize subways." He went on at great length to question the continuing need for demonstrations and nowhere in his speech did he devote as much space and time to censuring the white murderers in the South who beat, torture, and kill Negroes as he did to denouncing the lawless Negroes in the North.

In their respective public statements and analyses, neither Wilkins nor Rowan demonstrated any understanding—which they both certainly have—of the sociological causes for these new outbursts of violence.

Nor did either man seek to explore the possible causal relationship between the rioting and violence and the understandable hatred that has mounted inside of these kids as a result of the Birmingham bombing, the use of police dogs and electric cattle prodders, the murder of Medgar Evers, and other barbaric acts against their people—all to be compounded by their own miserable lives as ghetto-sardined human beings.

Edward P. Morgan, a white newscaster, said in a broadcast on July twenty-third: "In 1936 there was rioting in New York City's Harlem. The root causes of the disturbances in the middle of the great depression were the frustrations and despair bred in a ghastly segregated ghetto which utterly lacked decent housing, adequate schools, sufficient jobs, and any satisfactory communication with the rest of the community. . . . And so now we come to the humid days of mid-July, 1964, and there are fresh riots in Harlem. The root causes are precisely the same. . . . How many more riots does Harlem need to spawn before the remedies it cries out for are instituted?"

In those few words by a white man are more compassion and understanding of the Negro's sorry condition in America than Wilkins and Rowan have uttered in weeks.

It's almost fashionable for a "Negro leader" to get up today and condemn "my people."

Sure, "my people" goof and mess up and just get downright uncouth about being mistreated so badly. And when they slide over the abyss into lawlessness, they should be arrested, convicted, and reminded that they gain nothing by taking the law into their own hands.

But if we're going to call "my people" "foul-mouthed punks and smart-alecks," I want these same phony Negro leaders to call white people who commit these very same crimes against Medgar Evers, four little Negro girls in Birmingham, Lt. Col. Penn, and three civil rights workers in Mississippi "dirty, filthy, rotten, red-necked poor white trash whose mothers and fathers and their mothers and fathers before them are some of the scummiest and slimiest mass of flesh that ever peopled God's beautiful earth."

If we're going to call on "my fellow Negroes" to rid the civil rights movement of the terrorists, let's call on "my fellow Americans" to gather ourselves in a new moral crusade to rid this country of the shotgun snipers, the southern law enforcement officers who will murder you as quickly as they'll book you, the southern law-defying perpetrators of hatred and their northern counterparts who seek refuge behind the hypocritical mask of a "backlash."

Let's—as Daddy-O Daylie says—"tell it like it t-i-s tis." And that's what our Negro leaders who condemn Negroes in order to save their jobs have not been doing.

I know we're plagued as a group of people with the irresponsibles, the lovers of violence, and the "unreachables." But I also know that we as a group of people have done so little ourselves to improve our own social, economic, and political conditions. One of the worst indictments of the Negro race in America is that instead of spawning bankers, financiers, industrialists, business men, statesmen, and distinguished physicists, we have birthed "Negro leaders" such as

Roy Wilkins, whose only *raison d'être* is mired in the social negativism of protest that has kept them in a job.

I don't have to sit down to my typewriter every time a riot erupts and condemn that violence, because I hate and despise violence, murder, lawlessness *ab initio*—from the beginning. Nor do I sit down and angrily castigate white people every time they murder or lynch another Negro. My entire emotional and intellectual posture is arrayed against primitive behavior.

But Wilkins and Rowan should be secure enough as Negroes, particularly among their white associates, to address themselves to the still basic problem in our society—the eradication of racial segregation and racial hate. If we can do this, the ancillary causation of reactive violence on the part of the Negro will disappear just as rapidly.

But it's so true, as my man said that day, "None can kill you like your own kind."

August 1964

No, Lori, There's No "Backlash"—It's Just Plain Ol' White Hatred

WHEN YOU WALK INTO the beautiful offices of the Chicago *Daily Defender*, the first person you see is a very lovely, brown-skinned beauty named Lori Clark.

Lori is our receptionist and switchboard operator.

Yesterday morning, I walked in and Lori greeted me with her usual pretty smile (She really is a doll.), then asked me, "Mr. Stone, what's a 'backlash'?"

I started to answer her and then it occurred to me that perhaps millions of other Negroes are wondering too: "What's a backlash?" I told Lori the answer would appear in today's *Defender.*

Lori, there's no such thing as the "backlash" which the white newspapers and the white leaders have been telling you exists.

You see, a "backlash" as defined by Webster means a "quick, sharp recoil." That means the recoil action of the backlash is a response to a previous action.

So, for example, if you were to snap a whip, the "backlash" or the recoil action of the whip could snap back and hit you.

White people would now have you believe that there is a "white backlash" to the Negro's aggressive push for racial equality.

White newspapers, white columnists, white editorials, white leaders, and even white liberals say that white people are now beginning to "recoil" in horror and fear at the sudden urgency in the Negro's fight for racial equality.

By hysterically screaming every day about this "backlash" (One local newspaper went out to various neighborhoods and took a poll and found evidence of this "backlash" among white people.), they really are saying to the Negro: "Look, we know this is a democracy and all people are supposed to be equal and we're all supposed to have been created by the same God and all that jazz, but do you niggers have to go around believing all that bull? You're pushing too hard for your equality and it's beginning to make us hate you—which we didn't before—so knock it off or we really will get rough with you."

Lori, there's just one fallacy in this whole sick way of thinking—a sickness which the white man has lived with ever since he discovered—or at least was led to believe—that his white skin made him superior to all of the colored people all over the world.

White people have always hated Negroes, that is, hated them for trying to get out of their place. White people only loved Negroes as long as they remained cooks, butlers, handymen, gardners, and servants.

In the South, we knew where the white man stood. And when we tried to get a little uppity (like maybe forgetting to say "sir" or owning a nice car), he simply went out and formed a group of white cowards who put sheets over their faces and killed a few of us.

In the North, they didn't lynch us or set up laws to keep us segregated, so we suffered from the delusion that the white man in the North didn't hate us quite as much as the white man in the South.

And don't you know, Lori, that these white psychopaths in the North believed the same thing? They really thought they were different from their barbaric brothers in the South.

But when the "Negro Revolt" exploded and we began to demonstrate and raise a little divine hell for our equal rights, white folks in the North suddenly realized that they didn't love us any more than their white brothers in the South.

However, they had to find a convenient rationalization for this newly discovered bigotry, so they waited until Governor Wallace came along and told it like it was to white folks in Milwaukee, Indianapolis, and other Northern cities: "Look, I'm a white man and you're white folks and if there's one thing we agree on, it's we don't like niggers. So let's us white folks get together and stop these black people before they take over our neighborhood and marry our daughters."

And a whole lot of white people in the North said to themselves: "Now, here's one white man who makes sense. Let's go with this stud. Maybe, he'll stop these black fools."

Then one day a white columnist living in the North who had never known he hated Negroes sat down to his typewriter and wanted to say Wallace was right, but he did not want to come out and admit he had been hating Negroes all along—just the same way all those thousands of white people had been hating them in the North—so he tried to think of a gimmick which would expiate his long-hidden guilt feelings. What could he call this? . . .

"Backlash!" That's it. Call it a "backlash!" That will say we really didn't hate Negroes all the time and that we are simply reacting—or "recoiling"—to their being so pushy. If they stop being so pushy, we'll stop reacting and go back to hating them quietly instead of coming right out and telling them so by voting for Governor Wallace—or Senator Goldwater.

No, Lori, there's no "white backlash" or any kind of "backlash" in America.

What has always existed is the white man's *frontlash.* He has never liked or respected Negroes. But now it's harder for him to be hypocritical about it and he's going around calling it a "backlash." White people are so phony.

Backlash, Lori? You're safer believing in Santa Claus. Yes, Lori, there *is* a Santa Claus.

August 1964

I Wonder If Charlayne Hunter's Daddy Wanted *His* Daughter to Marry One?

DO YOU KNOW WHY white folks are still on top?

Because they're so smart and we're so dumb.

For more years than most of us realize, American social progress has been paralyzed by a simple question: Would you want your daughter to marry one?

Whenever any decent, liberal, white person dared defend the God-conferred right of Negroes to enjoy the same economic, political, and educational privileges as whites, he would invariably be slapped in the face with that nastiest of all questions: "But would you want your daughter to marry one?"

Few white people had the courage to say, "Yes."

A fantastic red herring and sloppy non sequitur, the question never dealt with Christian obligations or democratic rights or Constitutional equality.

It simply put the whole problem of racial equality in the bedroom.

And all of us fell for it.

Every one of us went on a cultural binge, lightening our skins and straightening our hair in the desperate hope that "Mr. Charlie" might just one day approve our marrying his daughter because then, you see, we wouldn't be so black or our hair so kinky.

It's a wonder "nose-straightening" never caught on to make us look more Caucasoid and less Negroid.

However, "Charlie" still doesn't want us to marry his daughter, although we've produced Rhodes scholars, Nobel Prize winners, brilliant doctors like T. K. Lawless, peerless lawyers such as Thurgood Marshall, millionaire business men, and America's only indigenous cultural art form, jazz.

Despite these achievements, Negroes are not considered worthy enough to marry the daughter of the lowliest, most miserable, diseased, white man.

But, man, have they married ours!

Not only did the slave-masters have a ball with our women during and after slavery (Where do you think all of the Marinie colored folks came from?), but they've kept it up through the years.

No southern white man is considered a "man" until he's slept with a black woman.

Outside of all the illicit relations white men have pursued with Negro women (They keep our girls in business on the South Side.), there've been any number of legitimate, made-in-heaven interracial marriages between white men and Negro women.

Start with Lena Horne, Dorothy Dandridge, Eartha Kitt, Pearl Bailey, Nina Simone, Diahann Carroll, and Lurlean Hunter (two-time winner) and go for yourself.

Don't get me wrong. I dig this miscegenated action.

But I'm such a nut on racial equality, I believe in being allowed to do what others do. "He who would compel thee go with him one mile, go with him twain."

So, if you're going to marry my daughter, give me the right to marry your'n.

And I think Charlayne Hunter's daddy would buy that.

When Charlayne secretly married that brave young white boy, Walter Stovall, both she and he knocked into a cocked hat all of the myths which have been perpetuated *ad nauseum* by white supremicists.

And there's one thing white men and white women must never, never, never forget: That young white boy asked to marry her, she didn't ask him.

Still in all, though, I keep on wondering—do you really think Charlayne's father wanted *his* daughter to marry one?

September 1963

Riots Heap Bad for Negroes: Makum Act Like White Man

CHIEF STANDING BULL: Colored man, you walkum heavy like buffalo with many young. Face hangum down, lower lip draggum along ground like frightened brave on wedding day. What makum you sad?

NICODEMUS: Chief, I've had it! I mean like, man, I'm through, finished! I'm splitting.

CHIEF STANDING BULL: How you tearum self in half? Why you splittum self?

NICODEMUS: Oh, Chief, you square. I don't mean me. I mean I'm cutting out, taking out—I'm quitting the race. I'm putting my people down. I'm through with Negroes.

CHIEF STANDING BULL: Your talk soundum crazy, like Chief Yellow Hair's heap dumb battle at Little Big Horn when my brother Sitting Bull carvum him brand new scalp. You colored man—how you leavum Negro race?

NICODEMUS: Pay a quarter. Let me have a quarter, will you?

CHIEF STANDING BULL: Colored man, you standum in sun many days, makum no sense. Wampum no changum color. Why you no likum black brothers any more?

NICODEMUS: Chief, I'm so disgusted with my people, I don't know what to do. We're about to lose our natural minds! Really, we must be idiots. White man giving us hell already and what do we do? We join him in destroying ourselves, our neighborhoods, and our property, rioting, throwing rocks, bricks, homemade bombs. Give me that quarter, will you?

CHIEF STANDING BULL: Here, takum quarter. When colored man startum war against himself?

NICODEMUS: Just a few weeks ago. It started in Harlem. Then it was Rochester, then Jersey City, then Paterson and now Dixmoor. Dixmoor was the last straw. Oh, thanks for the quarter.

CHIEF STANDING BULL: Why you drawum line at Dixmoor?

NICODEMUS: Chief, I live in Chicago. The brother's messing with my pad now. This stuff could spread and engulf us all. Don't get me wrong, Chief, I'm not afraid of Whitey. But it's so senseless to destroy ourselves. Tear up Whitey's neighborhood, waste him. Don't ruin ourselves. We got enough troubles already from Whitey without us jumping into the act.

CHIEF STANDING BULL: You tellum me heap big battle all right as long as colored man no fightum himself, fightum only paleface?

NICODEMUS: No, no, no, Chief! All violence is wrong. That's what's disgusted me. It's a drag when you destroy property and act like a hoodlum and it's even more ridiculous when you direct all this action at yourself. My folks have got to go and I'm putting them down for good. That's why I'm paying my quarter and getting out of the Negro race.

CHIEF STANDING BULL: Colored man, how many Great White Fathers in White House killed by bad men?

NICODEMUS: Four, Chief: Abraham Lincoln on April 4, 1865; James A. Garfield on July 2, 1881; William McKinley on Sept. 6, 1901; and John F. Kennedy on Nov. 22, 1963.

CHIEF STANDING BULL: Colored man shootum any of fire-sticks?

NICODEMUS: No, Chief, but that doesn't. . . .

CHIEF STANDING BULL: Who startum heap big war between the states and killum many white braves, colored man or white man?

NICODEMUS: White men, but Chief, you're reaching back. . . .

CHIEF STANDING BULL: Who startum two world wars, try killum everybody, white man or colored man?

NICODEMUS: The white man and Chief, you're beginning to sound. . . .

CHIEF STANDING BULL: Who comum to the shores, stealum land, killum heap many braves, bringum black men in chains, beatum black man?

NICODEMUS: You're reaching me, Chiefy baby, you're reaching me —the white man, but still that doesn't excuse. . . .

CHIEF STANDING BULL: Colored man makum atom bomb and droppum on yellow man?

NICODEMUS: Like you know we didn't. But that was war and. . . .

CHIEF STANDING BULL: Who formum Ku Klux and lynchum many men at night?

NICODEMUS: Well, white folks did, but lynching's out of style and. . . .

CHIEF STANDING BULL: Who burnum fifteen churches in Mississippi, bombum church in Birmingham and killum four little black papooses, shootum many black and white braves who fightum for black man, beatum and killum three young braves in Philadelphia, Mississippi and. . . .

NICODEMUS: Knock it off, Chief, those are all in the South. What's that got to do with Negroes in the North acting up?

CHIEF STANDING BULL: Takum colored man's own teepee, Chicago. Who startum Trumbull Park riots, attackum people at 57th Street and Peoria, 56th and Morgan, Rainbow Beach, shootum little black papoose on State Street, fightum. . . .

NICODEMUS: All right, all right already! What are you trying to prove, anyway, Chief?

CHIEF STANDING BULL: Colored man livum in white man's society. White man's society builtum on violence, war, hatred. Colored man learnum white man's evil ways. Colored man no actum in vacuum. Him respondum to heap many years of white man's evil ways. Colored man, him late but him catch up now. If white man, him livum way white man's God tellum—lovum all men, treatum like brother—black man, him livum same way, and him no actum heap crazy and breakum up many brick teepees. What colored man is today, white man has madum. Dixmoor only mean colored man takum on white man's evil ways.

NICODEMUS: Chief, you're a gas! You're so right. But still that doesn't excuse us. We can't do this kind of thing. We've got to stop violence.

CHIEF STANDING BULL: Colored man, him stoppum when white man stoppum violence, no keepum colored man in many separate teepees and reservations, lettum work in many jobs. How you sayum—things equal to the same thing equal to each other.

NICODEMUS: Chief, you've brought me back to my senses—and to my people.

CHIEF STANDING BULL: What else you sayum?

NICODEMUS: Here's your quarter back.

August 1964

The Agony of Racial Conflict Between Negroes and Jews

WERE I TO CHOOSE a text for this tragically necessary sermon, I would offer the following three sources:

Oliver Cromwell Cox in *Caste, Class and Race* (Doubleday & Co., Inc., 1948):
"The question has been frequently raised as to the possibility of Negroes and Jews as 'minority groups' collaborating for the purpose of advancing their social position. . . . Yet it is doubtful whether Jews and Negroes have a common basis for continuing action against the dominant group. . . . Insofar as Jews are bourgeois-minded business men and manufacturers, they are likely to be, at least implicitly, race-prejudiced. . . . As Negroes become increasingly assimilated in the larger society, the likelihood is that they, too, will become intolerant."

Harry Golden in *Mr. Kennedy and the Negroes:*
"There is indeed considerable anti-Semitism among urban Negroes, an attempt, perhaps, to use another minority group as a substitute target for the hostilities they feel toward the more powerful white Gentiles. . . . It should be noted, on the other hand, and I base this on my own considerable communication with Negroes, that most realize that Jews are probably, on the average, less prejudiced against them

The first occurred several weeks ago near the all-Negro Bedford-Stuyvesant area of Brooklyn when a gang of Negro hoodlums attacked a group of orthodox Jews, beating them and yelling, "You don't belong in this country."

Just a few days ago, a Negro in New York City walked up to a white man in the subway and stabbed him in the chest. When taken into custody, he was reported to have said: "Jews, I hate them all. I must kill them."

Then, in this week's issue of a local Jewish magazine, *The Sentinel,* there is a stinging rebuke to a column which I recently wrote on the inefficacy of the civil rights movement in Chicago. In that column, I had deplored the absence of Jewish organizations in Coordinating Council of Community Organization. It was *not* a condemnation of Jewish groups. Rather it was a statement of fact in which I thought I had made it pretty obvious that I was unhappy because Jews have been of such tremendous help to us in our freedom struggle. If anything I was criticizing the Urban League's executive director, Bill Berry as the weakling in civil rights. I was suggesting the idea of getting the Urban League out of the civil rights movement and the Jewish organizations into the CCCO.

But *The Sentinel* columnist, J. I. Fishbein, who as a Jew is just as paranoid as I am as a Negro, saw it differently and proceeded to launch into one of the most dangerous and offensive diatribes I have read in a long time. He wrote:

> What has the Negro press or the leadership done to stem the rising tide of anti-Semitism among Negroes so obviously on every hand?
>
> Where were they when the American Jewish Congress—most active in the civil rights struggle—picketed the Jordanian anti-Israel exhibit at the World's Fair?
>
> Why didn't anyone protest the beatings of rabbis and Yeshiva students by Negro youth gangs that took place in Brooklyn a month ago? What has the "civil rights movement" done to prove to Jews that it is equally concerned

than are other whites; that Jews are more often willin
trade with Negroes, hire them, rent to them; and that J
in the North give a great deal of support in money
social-action experience to organizations dedicated to end
racial segregation."

The Bible:

"And the Lord said unto Moses, Thus thou shalt say un
the children of Israel, Ye have seen that I have talked wi
you from heaven. . . . And if any mischief follow, the
thou shalt give life for life, eye for eye, tooth for tootl
hand for hand, foot for foot, burning for burning, woun
for wound, stripe for stripe." (Exodus 20:20; 21:23–25)

"Ye have heard that it hath been said, An eye for an eye,
and a tooth for a tooth: But I say unto you, That ye resist
not evil: but whosoever shall smite thee on thy right cheek,
turn to him the other also. . . . And whosoever shall compel thee go with him one mile, go with him twain." (St. Matthew 5:38–39, 41)

The above three sets of quotations, at least for me, define the total dimensions of a tragic problem which appears to be worsening in America: the agony of racial conflict between Negroes and Jews.

While it has always been a fact and is an unchallengeable fact today: Most Negroes don't like Jews and most Jews dislike Negroes (for both their respective asinine and imbecilic reasons), both groups through their leaders, their organizations have never given operational credence to these hostilities. If anything, both Jewish and Negro leaders have knocked themselves out trying to communicate to their unresponsive communities the need to communicate with each other.

While neither of the leaderships have failed, they haven't succeeded as efficiently as would be desirable.

Recently, three events impelled a reconsideration of this relationship.

with their rights, too? Or is it more correct to state that they believe cooperation is a one-way street with no responsibility toward the other fellow?

Someone should tell Mr. Stone about the old saying that "one hand washes the other."

On the front cover of *The Sentinel* is the slogan, "Voice of Chicago Jewry for 53 Years." If that means that *The Sentinel* is the voice of Chicago's 285,000 Jews, then we're in serious trouble in Chicago as far as the maturation of a more beautiful relationship between Negroes and Jews is concerned.

The Chicago *Daily Defender* is not anywhere near as arrogant. We don't pretend to speak for any more than the 50,000 Negroes who read us daily. We're their voice—nobody else's.

To answer Mr. Fishbein directly:

1. His racist innuendoes notwithstanding, the entire Negro press has not been silent on this issue and he doesn't know because he's not reading the more than two hundred Negro papers in this country *each week.* And he's a liar if he says he does. The *Chicago Defender* has been quite vocal on this relationship. We wished our Jewish readers a "Happy Rosh Hashana" on page two at the top of the page last year. The *Defender* has given considerable up-front publicity to the problem of the Jews in Moscow, the celebration of the twentieth anniversary of the Warsaw Ghetto (during which I wrote a front-page column, comparing Morris Anielewicz, commander of the Jewish Fighting Forces in Warsaw, to the Rev. Bruce Klunder, who died in Cleveland, and William C. Moore, who was assassinated in Alabama), a story condemning a local service club for inviting a former Nazi to speak in Chicago, and, finally, we ran a four-column headline and a picture on the Jewish picketing for the World's Fair (a bigger play than any other daily in Chicago).

Do you know why Negroes weren't there picketing? Because we weren't invited, that's why.

Whereas Jews sit on the boards of every single civil rights organization in America, NAACP, CORE, SCLC, and SNCC, Negroes are barred from the boards of the Anti-Defamation League, the American Jewish Congress, and the American Jewish Committee.

Whereas Jews are welcomed into our civil rights activities, we are not welcomed into theirs.

Yes, Negro leadership has unfortunately been silent on the rising tide of anti-Semitism in the Negro community, but up until now, it has not been serious. In fact, we have tried to ignore it. But how has it expressed itself—until recently? Certainly not in violence. But the anti-Negro feeling of the Jew—many of their fantastic financial and magnificent volunteer contributions and their open-heartedness in many areas which Harry Golden delineates notwithstanding—has still expressed itself in a denial of jobs and housing, and in slumlordism, the worst form of economic exploitation of Negroes.

Secondly, it is psychologically impossible for either group to have a continuing and total involvement in the human-rights activities of the other. What a Negro considers important to him may not be felt by a Jew. What a Jew feels strongly about may have little meaning to a Negro.

Finally, Mr. Fishbein submits a dangerous thesis: "One hand washes the other." Up until now, I believed Jewish assistance in civil rights was being offered simply because Jews believed in the dignity of the human race; that as a minority group, they could appreciate the cultural and economic genocide being practiced against the Negro in America.

It never occurred to me—or to most Negroes—that if we didn't help Jews in their battle, they just might turn around and cut off financial assistance and volunteer efforts. Without Jewish help, the U. S. Supreme Court decision of 1954 would *never* have happened. Without Jewish help in the future, the civil rights struggle for total freedom for the Negro will slow down terribly.

But whether they stay in or not, *we are going to win this battle*—and you'd better believe it! The historical passion of human dignity and its inexorable climb to the surface of freedom is now on our side. We indeed shall overcome.

Implicit in Mr. Fishbein's dissertation is the "eye for an eye" philosophy. As Negroes, we've had to learn the hard way that violence only boomerangs. The redemptive beauty of the doctrine of Christian forgiveness guides our lives—even when we are not living up to the demands placed upon us by our Lord.

But we shall continue to try. We shall continue to love and we shall continue to hope our Jewish brothers can find a compassion in their hearts for our occasional silence on their problems and our seeming lack of involvement.

And I'll make Mr. Fishbein a bargain. Find me just one—that's all, just one—major Jewish organization that is willing to demand that Benjamin C. Willis be fired—and I'll personally walk every picket line that every Jewish organization in this city sets up.

Okay, Mr. Fishbein?

P.S. I wasn't invited to any of the activities sponsored by the Jewish groups for Israeli Prime Minister Eshkol, as all the *other* daily newspaper editors were, but I'm not crying in my beer about it. I still dig Levi Eshkol and still hope to visit Israel again as I did in 1957.

April 1964

Silly Billy Graham: Magnificent Phony

THE THUNDERING WRATH of his devoted partisans may come cascading down in torrents over my head after I write this, but I'm going to submit it anyhow: Billy Graham is one of the most magnificent phonies in America today.

In this papier mâché, assembly-line culture of instant coffee, instant tea, instant mashed potatoes, instant cake mix, and instant house construction, Billy Graham's "instant Christianity" is just about the most nauseating short-cut to heaven anybody's ever manufactured.

Machine-gunning his message in a Walter Winchell-like staccato, the golden-maned evangelist serves up a heaping dish of Southern fried, hominy grits Christianity that is more P. T. Barnum in presentation than it is Christ in inspiration.

Every time he walks to the podium and begins making like a combination of William Jennings Bryan and Willy Loman, thousands of confused, churchless Americans gobble up this wordy garbage and come away with the worst case of spiritual indigestion they have ever had.

They then spend the next few days trying to diagnose why they ever got excited in the first place.

Yes, Billy Graham "saves souls."

The trouble is a lot of these souls get lost the next day.

True product of a society almost totally conceived in the womb of an advertising account executive, Billy Graham merchandises Christianity with an impeccable eloquence that leaves corporation executives gasping in admiration. He is unchallengeably one of the most successful salesmen in America today. Rather than come to specific grips, however, with some of America's critical problems—race hatred, crime, unemployment, unequal education, inadequate housing, poverty, drop-outs—in terms of the precise demands Christ would have placed upon us for their remediation, Billy Graham skirts definitive answers by urging us to "take your burdens to the Lord and leave them there."

His attitude and pronouncement on the racial crisis in America attained their soiled apotheosis a few days ago when he pontificated that the racial problem would be solved at "the foot of the cross of Jesus Christ."

What the sinner is supposed to glean from this kind of vapid, silly declaration is that if he simply kneels down and prays to Jesus Christ, somehow his troubled, racist heart will be changed and he'll love his black brother.

Shucks, Billy Graham himself isn't even able to come out and unqualifiedly denounce racial segregation and those who practice it. Along with his segregated American church and white brothers of the clergy who every Sunday rise up in their lilywhite pulpits and preach to lilywhite congregations, he's too busy praying.

You don't see Billy Graham walking into the Southern temples of racial segregation and telling the racists to get out because they defile God's house with their denial of love and brotherhood: "And Jesus went into the temple and began to cast out them that sold and bought in the temple and overthrew the tables of the money changers and the seats of them that sold doves." (In short, Jesus gave 'em hell.)

You don't see Billy Graham walking any picket lines or even admitting they have a spiritual redemption for the sinner: "Moreover, if thy brother shall trespass against thee, go and tell him his fault between thee and him alone. . . . But if he does not hear thee, then take with thee one or two more that in the mouth of two or three witnesses every word may be established." (The Rev. John F. Cronin, assistant director of the social action department of the National Catholic Welfare Conference, agreed with Jesus about taking along "two or three witnesses" when he said this week that clergymen "should be in the forefront of demonstrations to show our support for the civil rights movement.")

You never see Billy Graham telling white people that Negroes are so unremittingly their brothers that they must live together next door to each other as neighbors and accept Negroes with love as neighbors: "And behold a certain lawyer stood up and tempted him saying, Master what shall I do to inherit eternal life? . . . And he answering said, Thou shalt love the Lord thy God with all thy soul and with all thy strength and with all thy mind and thy neighbor as thyself. . . . But he, willing to justify himself, said unto Jesus, And who is my neighbor?" Whereupon Jesus told the lawyer the parable of the good Samaritan, then asked: "Which now of these three thinkest thou was neighbor unto him that fell among the thieves?

And he said, He that sheweth mercy on him. Then said Jesus unto him, Go and do thou likewise." Negroes fell among thieves when their rights to live anywhere or be served as citizens in public places were stolen from them, but have you heard Billy Graham coming out for mercy-showing laws that would guarantee open occupancy and equal accommodations for Negroes?

And this is the tragedy of a Billy Graham—not his antiseptic evangelism that would keep us enslaved by simply "kneeling at the cross," waiting for a miracle to transform our souls, but his failure and refusal to invigorate the teachings of the Christ of Nazareth with the spiritual requisites of a jet-age society torn asunder by horse-and-buggy racial hatred.

"For God so loved the world that he gave His only begotten Son, that whosoever believeth in Him should not perish but have everlasting life." When the Reverend Bruce William Klunder placed his hand in God's in Cleveland last week and lay down before the terror of that life-crushing bulldozer, he understood in that quick moment of truth more about the soul-searing demands of Christianity than Billy Graham can ever hope to feel in the next twenty-five years with his phony summonses to merely "kneel at the cross" and be saved.

In an era which nurtures middle-class mediocrity and phony religious values, the Reverend Billy Graham is exactly what we Americans deserve in our present inability to find lasting salvation in the true meaning of brotherhood.

Why Negro Men Like Big Legs

A FEW YEARS AGO, my mother and I were walking downtown in Hartford (That shows you what a small town I came from—we have a "downtown."), and I chanced to appraise the legs of a passing maiden of Caucasian hue.

"How about the beautiful legs on that 'gray' girl!" I exclaimed, grabbing the arm of my mother, who, incidentally, turns a neatly sculptured calf herself. "Why is it," I moaned aloud, "white women have prettier legs than colored women?"

"Mr. Stone," indignantly retorted my very beautiful mother, "that just is not so." Naturally, a dialectic on the matter ensued. I ended the argument by telling my mother to be a good social scientist and make her own set of observations. Ever intellectually curious, she did. Two weeks later, she regretfully reported I was right.

I knew I was right, and thousands of Negro males would have heartily concurred. How many times has a group of males, in discussing the physical attributes of a female, laid that very highest of encomiums at her feet—". . . and, man, she's got 'big legs.'?"

"Big legs," of course, is descriptive vernacular, not analytical physiology. Translated, it simply means that the woman's legs are well-shaped, with a full calf and tapered ankles. The legs are not skinny. Because who likes skinny legs? Nobody.

This next statement will undoubtedly cast me in that most permanent of dog-houses, but it's a fact: The majority of Negro women have skinny legs. This is not a physical indictment of our women, but a social indictment of America.

A healthy pair of legs can be acquired by good diet, plenty of exercise, such as skiing in the winter and swimming all summer, and a well-rounded life. How many Negro families in America have access to the good life of economic abundance? Comparatively, very few.

Consequently, Negro families, who are denied the right to work at a good job and earn a decent salary, have been forced to subsist on a poor diet. Poor diets do not build sturdy bodies. A major part of a sturdy body is, of course, a sturdy leg.

The Negro man who admires "big legs" is only admiring the most favorable aspects of the majority culture, which in this instance is the white man's culture. "Big legs" are the physical trappings of what Thorstein Veblen would call conspicuous consumption. All those big words put together simply mean this: When a society develops a wealthy class of people, that class sets itself off by certain symbols—Cadillacs, yachts, penthouses, mink over slacks while noonday shopping, Riviera vacations, eggs Benedict, and *crème de caçao.* "Big legs" inevitably stem (Forgive the pun.) from such gracious living.

Do you want to make this test for yourself? Walk down 125th Street behind a young lady endowed with well-shaped legs. Watch the males glance at her briefly and then visually zero in on her legs. No matter how pretty she is, unless her legs are "stacked," she will lose attention. Pretty legs will always elicit the happiest sounds of approval.

So, Negro men like "big legs" for the same reasons that they like success and badges of distinction in our racially plural society. "Big legs" are such a badge. The Negro girl who spends her summers at camp swimming and hiking and her winters skiing and ice skating is bound to reflect this physical exercise in pretty legs *vis-à-vis* the Negro girl who is forced to stay within the dingy environs of the ghetto.

A statistical index of our rise up the economic ladder can be measured by the increasing number of "big legs" seen in the Negro community. (Oh, happy index!) But every Negro man worth his racial salt should be breaking his back to see to it that his women have the best of everything in this society—including the ultimate development of "big legs."

As for me? My wife has "big legs"—that's why I married her. I wasn't going to mess with my Oedipus complex.

Sure, Take Away Clay's Title, But Give Us Back Our Cockroach

YOU ALL KNOW that marvelous story, don't you?

A shabbily dressed Negro woman is standing on a crowded bus on her way to "bust some suds" in Miss Anne's kitchen.

A well-attired white lady (Note I use the proper cultural argot for both females.) is standing next to her when suddenly the white lady notices a small cockroach crawling along the collar of the Negro woman.

Not wishing to embarrass her traveling companion, the white lady quickly flicks the cockroach off the collar of the Negro woman who, in turn, recoils in anger. "What's wrong with you, woman!" she exclaims.

"Uh," whispers the white lady with a sick smile, "a-a cockroach."

"Oh, yeah!" roars the Negro woman. "Well, you just put it right back! You white folks have been stealing equal rights and everything else from us colored folks for the last hundred years, and now you want to steal our cockroaches. Well, you just put that cockroach right back, honey!"

I'm willing to make a trade with white America—and I'll wager Cassius—oops! I'm sorry, Muhammad Ali—would go along with this exchange: Give us our cockroach back, i.e., all of our unalienable rights conferred upon us by God and secured by the United

States Constitution, and we Negroes will go along with your taking the heavyweight title away from Cassius.

You see, what our good white brothers, including the phony white liberals fail to realize is that white America has been stealing our rights from us for over a century—even by their own historical admission.

Negroes didn't write the Declaration of Independence—white folks did. And back on July fourth, 1776, a group of white colonists wrote these immortal words: "We hold these truths to be self-evident, that all men are created equal, that they are endowed by their Creator with certain unalienable rights. . . ."

"Unalienable" means that which cannot be transferred or taken away. "Self-evident" means that it needs no proof or empirical evidence to sustain its submission for truth.

Yet white folks have been requiring Negroes to "prove they deserve equality" for the past 150 years. (Why don't *you* Negroes clean up your slums which we white folks created—Why don't *you* Negroes stop having illegitimate children and go out and find a job which we white folks won't let you have—Why don't *you* Negroes become better American citizens by voting when we white folks won't let you vote.)

In a democracy, citizens are not required to prove they deserve or merit full citizenship or full rights. They are born with those rights—they are (as it were) "unalienable."

Not accepting the truth of this moral truth, white Americans have proceeded to steal the American Negro's rights from him for the last 150 years. They freed him from the irons of slavery but kept him shackled to the legal and extra-legal chains of second-class citizenship by denying him access to the full blessings of this rich civilization.

And now they want to steal Clay's heavyweight title from him.

Did they steal Babe Ruth's home run title or Most Valuable Player title after he went out on some of his wild alcoholic toots with women?

Did they abrogate Hack Wilson's titles after some of his brawls?

And what about Max Schmeling? Here was an admitted Nazi, a member of the German party which committed itself to the destruction of six million Jews. Did they lift his heavyweight title? No sirree. Why? Because Max Schmeling, like Hack Wilson and Babe Ruth, was white.

Lassman, president of the World Boxing Association, has merely proved to nineteen million Negroes and an infinitely larger number of Asians and Africans that the white American is still capable of some of the most rotten, hypocritical, dishonest, and contemptible action, all in the name of his cherished white supremacy. And Lassman himself is the latest chapter in this historical denial of racial equality to American Negroes. He ought to be ashamed of himself.

Take away Clay's title? Sure, we'll go along with that, provided you give us back our cockroach and every single individual right to which we Negroes have been entitled for over 150 years.

It's funny, but if Negroes were to be given all of their rights, that would include the right to be as raunchy and rambunctious as the white man and Clay just might keep his title anyway.

August 1964

"America's Invisible Man": Merchandising Him into Society

"I am an invisible man. I am invisible, understand, simply because people refuse to see me. When they approach me, they see only my surroundings, themselves, or figments of their imagination—indeed, everything and anything except me. . . . Nor is my invisibility exactly a matter of a biochemical accident to my epidermis. That invisibility to which I refer occurs because of a peculiar disposition of the eyes of those with whom I come in contact. . . . You ache with the need to convince yourself that you do exist, that you're a part of all the sounds and anguish and you strike out with your fists, you curse and you swear to make them recognize you and alas! it's seldom successful."

Way back in 1947, long before any "Negro Revolt" or "Freedom Now" struggle, or "Marches on Washington" or "white backlash" talked harshly to the white man, Ralph Ellison told it like it really is for all of us.

In his book, *The Invisible Man* (from which the first paragraph above is extracted, Ellison peered down into the windows of the Negro's tortured soul and angrily shouted: "We are here, white people! Look at us! See us! Appreciate us! Be aware of us! And if your heart grants you permission, relate to us!"

Ellison discovered, or rather for the first time eloquently painted, the tapestry of a cardinal truth of American society: It has never seen American Negroes as human beings. Rather it has always seen us as a "race," as a "group," as "you people," from the vantage point of a "superior race."

Joe Louis was always a "credit to his race." While the open wounds of guilt feeling today prevent the verbalization of such a racist sentiment, it gently seeks expression in a more respectable and fashionable manner.

Ralph Bunche is revered by the white community because he is a Negro who has become a distinguished American, not simply because he is a distinguished American. This is true of many of the outstanding Negroes whom white people have clasped to their sociological breasts and have boasted to the world: "See? some of our little children have been permitted to become men!"

In America 19 million persons—all Negroes—are invisible to 160 million other people—all white.

The "invisible man" is rarely seen on television or in the newspapers unless he commits a crime or is picketing and demonstrating or is represented by a selected Negro to speak on a particular problem or development.

The "invisible man" is rarely seen in advertisements.

The "invisible man" is not employed generally in radio (except on Negro-oriented stations), nor is he employed in television.

The "invisible man" is not employed by the advertising agencies, the merchandisers of taste, of expectations, of desires.

The "invisible man" is never seen on television panel shows unless he is what we call the celebrity freak. He or she is only there because he is famous as a singer, dancer, comedian, civil rights leader, sports figure, actor, or entertainer. The "invisible man" is there because he is only visible as the most successful celebrity freak of his race at that given time. He or she is not there, nor is he ever there, as a fairly competent and outstanding doctor, lawyer, teacher, reporter, student leader, business man, civic leader, religious leader, or educator.

No matter in what capacity he is invited to appear on these panels, he's only there because he's a Negro and when he is not there, it is only because he is a Negro.

Can America anthropomorphize its "invisible man"?

Can America bring the Negro into focus in the eyes of the white community so that the white man's "generalized other" includes the Negro?

Can America "merchandise" the Negro into society?

It can. It can if the heads of all the top advertising agencies, the managers of all advertising agencies, the program managers of all the television stations and radio stations, the public relations agents, the editors of all the newspapers—in short, the people who control the communications media of this country, who determine the news presentation, what pictures appear in the billboards, in the ads, in the public's mind—if they all sit down together and start trying to "merchandise" the visibility of the Negro as successfully as they have manufactured the visibility of bad breath, body odor, living and curly hair.

This is part of the challenge of this great country.

Can we meet it? I think we can. At least, I hope we can. We don't really have much time because, as Ralph Ellison wrote way back in 1947, "You strike out with your fists, you curse and you swear. . . ." and you go to war with society only because society has arrayed itself against you ever since you discovered that the color of your skin carried a shameful denial of your right to be treated as a human being.

Yes, we may be "invisible," but in God's eyes we're not, and this gives us the courage to keep "pressin' on the upward way," because "the invisible things of him from the creation of the world are clearly seen, being understood by the things that are made, even his eternal power and Godhead; so that they are without excuse."

We are *here,* "Charlie." Deal with us as equals, as visible creations of God.

The Young Warrior

HE WAS STILL SO YOUNG and had so much yet to do.

To him, a skilled craftsman, life was a series of uncharted seas. He sailed each one he discovered with the same pressing determination. His energy and enthusiasm for accomplishing never slackened.

He had tremendous spirit. And it was joyfully contagious.

This was John Fitzgerald Kennedy, thirty-fifth President of the United States, cut down at the height of an extraordinarily brilliant career by a cowardly assassin's bullet.

Who can know in the dark aftermath of his death what greatness of achievement would have been his? Who can predict the infinite heights of glory he may have led this country to?

And this, by far, is the most enormous part of this tragedy—President Kennedy's career in public service was an unfinished symphony.

Still, in a short three years he transformed the entire country with his earnest dedication, unashamed patriotism, and rare sense of humor. He baptized all of us with his warmth whenever he grinned, lighting millions of hearts.

Many men are measured only by their deeds or solely by words. President Kennedy, himself singularly symbolic of the American spirit, can be judged magnificently by the total commitment of his crusade for the good life for all men.

This alone qualifies him for immortality.

Tears simply refused to be held back when my publisher, John H. Sengstacke, called me, and in a barely audible voice said: "Chuck, you'd better get ready to put out a special for tomorrow."

What a sorrowful task to undertake on this black Friday, November 22, because I loved this young warrior.

I loved him because of his youthful irrepressibility, his astonishing political savvy, but most of all for his tender concern for the family of man.

John F. Kennedy's election to the Presidency changed the entire course of my life. When the position of editor of the *Washington Afro-American* was offered to me in October, 1960, I accepted conditionally—only if Kennedy was elected President. The country desperately needed to get moving again and I knew Washington, D.C., could only be an exciting and meaningful place to live if Kennedy was President.

He was such a real person that many of us thought of him and his wife Jacqueline as our next-door neighbors "down at the bottom of Sixteenth Street."

And that was the added dividend of having John Fitzgerald Kennedy in The White House—Mrs. Jacqueline Kennedy was its First Lady. She became the charming molder of a reawakening cultural consciousness in America.

My thoughts go back to that icy cold day in January, 1961, when

I stood shivering in the press section listening to the pure beauty of his inaugural address.

"Ask not what your country can do for you. Ask what you can do for your country."

John F. Kennedy gave his life.

November 1963

"I-Ain't-Colored-No-More-Cuz-I've-Been-Elected" Club

1. "All I want is for people to listen to what I have to say and try to forget that I'm colored."

2. "I think it's progress. Hardly anyone mentions I'm colored anymore."

3. "I don't think my race had anything to do with my appointment. I think I was qualified."

4. "I do not want to and do not expect to run for the office of treasurer as a colored person any more than I do as a Waterburian, an Episcopalian, or dental technician."

The above four statements were made respectively by D.C. Commissioner John B. Duncan; newly elected Massachusetts Attorney General Edward Brooke; recently appointed Federal Trade Commissioner H. Leon Higgenbotham; and newly elected Connecticut Treasurer Gerald Lamb.

All four are charter members of the newest club of "brothers" in America: The "I-Ain't-Colored-No-More-Cuz-I've-Been-Elected" Club.

Requirements for membership are very simple. After appointment or election as a colored person, the latter rapidly issues a public statement denying his race as a factor in his selection and approval for the candidacy by the political party bosses and rejects any possible implication that the colored vote was a major factor in his selection.

Of all the minorities in America, we are the only ones who go around neurotically renouncing our race as a critical element of our success.

Instead of racial pride, many of our colored politicians are slowly developing a curious form of racial shame.

They seem to believe—at the advice and behest of many of their white supporters and advisers—that if they play down their race, they'll get more white support and enjoy the comfortable security of the white power structure's endorsement.

Nothing is farther from the truth.

When "Mr. Charlie" decides your usefulness has terminated, he'll go after you with a political hammer and tong and dump you before you can renew your NAACP membership.

Ask Hulan Jack and Frank Reeves.

As a group of people, we constitute a little better than ten per cent of the population in America.

We have a heritage which is more deeply rooted in the American way of life than the majority of hyphenated Americans.

Our ancestors' lives—and their toil and sweat as slaves—helped build this country.

We don't need to apologize for our color or our race.

But today's breed of colored politician is developing this new political syndrome in the belief that white people will really forget he's colored and spare him the stigma of political retirement.

Shucks, the day colored people forget they're colored—and the political party bosses know they have forgotten—that lil' ol' colored man is through.

John Duncan was selected to be District Commissioner for only one reason—he was colored.

And if he's not reappointed in 1964, it will be because the Democrats will have rejected him as any possible influence in the vote-getting process.

Of the Federal government's twenty-two regulatory agencies, there had never been a colored commissioner until Higgenbotham's appointment.

The fact of total racial exclusion was an important ingredient in finally breaking the barrier.

Unquestionably, Higgenbotham is one of the best qualified men for the post, but think of all the white men who are equally well qualified and those who possess superior talents.

As for Lamb in Connecticut, this guy is a real political noodnik.

The only reason Lamb was selected was because he is colored. The Republicans had already chosen Bill Graham (a terrific guy who should have won and who more than likely wouldn't have shot his big mouth off with this "so glad I made it because I'm like the rest of you boys" nonsense).

Had there been no colored candidate on the Republican ticket, Gerald Lamb would be right back there in Waterbury still nestling in political obscurity where he ought to be sent one day soon.

There's nothing wrong with being colored.

There's nothing wrong with running for a political office as a colored person.

There's nothing wrong with feeling unhappy about the slow pace of racial equality in America as a colored man.

And the good Lord knows there's nothing wrong with speaking out about it. You can do it intelligently, bravely, and factually. To speak as a colored politician does not mean you must climb to mountainous oratorical heights and trumpet your dissatisfaction with the status quo.

However, it does mean you ought to be able to incorporate the color of your epidermis as a biological fact of life into your psyche and translate it into a political advantage.

Irish Catholics did it with their religion in New York City and Boston.

The Jews have done it.

The Italians are pursuing the same course, and the Puerto Ricans have already begun to make this same maneuver pay off.

As different as Adam Powell, William Dawson, and Charlie Diggs are in their approach to politics, not one of them ever ran away from the fact of his race.

All three could teach these young political squirts a lesson or two about the dignity of being colored and the joy of being a successful politician.

There can be a relationship between the two, and this new breed of colored politician may have to suffer unnecessarily until he recognizes the equation and learns to live with it and preach this same political gospel to those who follow him.

November 1962

On Being Married Five Years

YOU GOOD FOLKS sit back and let an old married man give you some advice.

Tomorrow, October fourth, my lovely wife, Louise, and I celebrate our fifth wedding anniversary.

There's something special about a fifth: a fifth of whiskey, Beethoven's Fifth Symphony, and the Fifth Amendment.

But probably one unique value of the concept of the "fifth" is that it's the first fifth of twenty-five. And the twenty-fifth wedding anniversary is that incontrovertible recognition that the ship of matrimony has weathered all of the stormy connubial seas. (Go, Webster! On, Thesaurus!)

No five years of life have been more meaningful or more happy than these past five. Probably the only reason I've approached a reasonable degree of success in life is because of my wife.

Up until the point of my marriage to Louise, my mother had been the most meaningful influence in my life. A remarkably gracious, calm, and beautiful woman, my mother simply prepared me in life to learn to live intelligently with a wife.

And Louise has been the anchor, the inspiration, and a constant joy.

Just being with her has been a wonderful experience, and moods of depression and uncertainty quickly evaporate after a chat with her. (She looks good in shorts, too.)

Oh, it hasn't been all peaches and cream. Man, we hadn't been married one week when this chick served me a breakfast of strawberries and fresh orange juice. Now, the Stones were moderately impoverished folks. We were proud and well-educated, but we were poor. So I ain't nevah had no orange juice and strawberries at the same time, so I said to Louise, "Strawberries and orange juice at the same time?"

Well, this sassy little gal crawled all over me! She read me up and down and talked about me, my family, and their ancestors in the worst way! I was ready to give the marriage back to the Indians.

But we somehow managed to prevail and it has been one swinging gas of a marriage. We've had a whole lot of ups and downs (I was unemployed for two months during the second year of our marriage.), but we've had as much fun starving as we have had eating steak. (At the time, four straight days of beans and frankfurters didn't seem like an awful lot of fun, though.)

However, there has been that richest nourishment of all in our lives, Krishna and Allegra. Blessed with two beautiful daughters, we both can't help but thank God every day for bringing so much happiness into our lives together.

So, Sweet Hogbear Louise, happy fifth wedding anniversary. If the next five are as happy as these past five, I'm going to bottle you and put you on the market as "Instant Happiness."

October 1963

Toward a United States of Africa & a Common Market

WILL THERE EVER BE a United States of Africa?

As is true of all political questions, the answer depends on whether you're an optimist or a pessimist.

When it comes to Africa, I'm very much of a political optimist. (And I also suffer from a slight case of *la negritude* fever.)

However, as inexorably as the international economic facts of life are pushing both the United States and Great Britain toward a closer involvement with the European Common Market, the same dynamics are hastening more intimate ties between the thirty-five independent countries in Africa.

The facts speak for themselves. The six members of the European Common Market (France, West Germany, Italy, Belgium, the Netherlands, and Luxembourg) since 1958 have increased their collective gross national product by twenty-five per cent—and all with a lowering of trade barriers.

Britain's gross national product during this same period increased only seventeen per cent; America's increase was seventeen per cent.

That's why Britain wants to join the Common Market. That's why we can't afford to ignore it.

Two of the thorniest problems for the European Common Market have a direct relationship to African countries:

1. How many trade concessions are the Common Market members prepared to grant to the thirteen African members of the

French Community of States who will have a similar type of trade agreement with France?

2. If Britain is admitted to the Common Market, what happens to her low tariff arrangements with her Commonwealth members, particularly those in Africa?

Africa itself is going to help solve these perplexities both through a more mature attitude toward political federation and several fledgling economic unions.

While Europe has been a geographical expression for over five hundred years, it has torn itself apart through a series of the most destructive wars the world has ever known (including two near-global holocausts grandly styled World War I and World War II) and that continent is just now getting around to some form of economic cooperation. (White Americans are always worrying about us Negroes being split in our civil rights efforts. Shucks, it took their ancestral forebears in Europe over three hundred years to sit down and even begin to talk about unity. And they're not doing too well at it at that.)

On the other hand, Africa, which is at best today a mere racial concept, is working on several organizations for economic cooperation and development: an Inter-African Bank, French African Union, Ghana-Guinea-Mali Union, and the East African Common Services Organization (EACSO).

The political impetus for a United States of Africa will undoubtedly receive its greatest energies from East Africa.

Here, Tanganyika, Kenya, Uganda, and Zanzibar (a small island north of Dar-es-Salaam) stand on the threshold of some form of limited federation.

EACSO is its economic base and PAFMESCA (Pan-African Movement for Eastern, Central, and Southern Africa) is its political base.

So strongly is Tanganyika's Julius Nyerere committed to a political marriage of these countries, he actually tried to delay Tanganyika's independence last year until Uganda and Kenya could obtain their freedom.

He reasoned correctly that it would be easier to merge the four countries into a single nation-state before they became solidified into national entities with all the trappings of nationalistic egotisms.

Likewise, Tom Mboya, leader of the Kenya African National Union (KANU) and Minister of Justice and Constitutional Affairs in Prime Minister Jomo Kenyatta's cabinet is committed to such a federation.

In this drive toward African economic and political unity, naturally there are Balkanizing factors at work.

Africa is actually a continent of tribal and linguistic groups who live the way tribes of Indians lived on this continent before the French and English stole their lands.

Thus, virtually all of Africa's nation-state borders were artificially created by the European powers centuries ago.

To counteract the centrifugal tendencies of tribalization, most African powers favor a strong centralized form of government *vis-à-vis* a loose confederation of tribes or states. Expressed in American concepts, it's the old "states rights" controversy of the South versus the rest of the country. This is why you found Southerners like Senator Eastland supporting Uncle Tom Tshombe of Katanga during the Congo crisis.

In Ghana it's the Ashantis of the North who seek a loose confederation. In Kenya, it's the complex of smaller tribes who have formed the political base of Ronald Ngala's Kenya African Democratic Union (KADU) and who fear being overwhelmed by the stronger and more numerous Kikuyu and Luo tribes.

There has been another catalyst in this continent's political chemistry, cataclysmally affecting the African drive toward a twentieth century political unity.

This has been the white man.

Naturally, there are vestiges of bitterness toward white people for their colonial actions of the past, but Africans are notoriously free of racial prejudice. (When I was in Ghana, I saw so many interracial couples I thought Africanization was going out of style. Brainwashed by the folly of my own cultural prejudices, I was the only idiot staring.)

But the white settlers in the Federation of Rhodesias and Nyasaland occasioned great acrimony among the Africans. "Multiracialism" became a dirty word there and the Federation has already been interred.

Still, if the Rhodesian Federation's mineral wealth in copper (world's third largest producer), gold, chrome, asbestos, zinc, and lead, and their increasingly important agricultural export of tobacco are combined with Tanganyika's mineral resources and diamonds (eight per cent of world production) and her highly favorable balance of trade, there is already a base for economic growth in a political federation.

Africans can unite on their own terms and without the proscriptions and humiliating conditions imposed upon them by white men. Most friendly observers of Africa unhesitatingly believe that Nyasaland's mercural Hastings Banda, Northern Rhodesia's gentle Kenneth Kaunda and Southern Rhodesia's bundle of quiet fire, Joshua Nkomo, will merge their three countries into a new Central Federation, because politically and economically they must. However, they had to bury the present racist-founded Central Federation in order to win the respect of their countrymen. Once having achieved independence, those three countries' statesmen will sit down with Jomo Kenyatta, Julius Nyerere, and King Freddie of Uganda and evolve a new United States of East Africa.

To unite Kenya, Tanganyika, Uganda, Zanzibar, and the Federation of the Rhodesias (a black Federation, not the present racist apparatus of Sir Roy Welensky) is to evolve the second largest state in Africa (27 million people) and economically the richest and most powerful.

The United States of Africa is not just around the political corner. But neither is it way up the historical hill.

My two daughters will live to see a United States of Africa before they see a United States of Europe.

The black man's *la negritude* will flower this dream into reality.

Racial Yardsticks

ANYWHERE IN AMERICA twelve inches equal one foot.

For a baseball player, a .350 batting average qualifies him as a big-leaguer.

A bank account of $1,000,000 permits the reasonable presumption that its owner is a millionaire.

Passing the bar admits the student as a lawyer and the selling of a certain amount of insurance elevates the salesman into the lofty levels of the million-dollar round-table.

In each case, the measuring sticks are precise, universal, and impersonal.

They apply to all humans and success or failure is established by the unalterable coldness of these yardsticks.

We can be apostles of objectivity in America when it comes to measuring any kind of data, phenomenon, or kinetics.

But when it comes to Negroes, we throw away these objective yardsticks and lose all sense of impartiality.

If a Negro is president of a company, he's a "big business man." The fact that the business is grossing $756 a year is beside the point.

If a Negro is editor of a Negro weekly newspaper in a large city, he's an "outstanding newsman." The fact that the paper's circulation is 2,500 is ignored.

As Negroes, we exaggerate our accomplishments, and our white brothers compound the felony.

Many white people are so anxious to delude us into thinking we possess more power than honestly accrues to us they'll reach down into the center of our ghetto, lift up a mediocre business man, labor leader, minister, or lawyer and tell him: "You're a Negro leader."

And don't you know this idiot will believe them?

The mantle of the white man's approbation has been placed around his shoulders and he now believes this shroud protects him for a dubious or unbelieving Negro community.

It's such a melancholy truism, but in the field of sports and entertainment, the Negro's yardsticks are comparable to everybody else's.

But in the more important fields of economics, business and politics we simply disintegrate at the seams like an unraveled woolen sweater in our assessment of our worth.

It's impressive to claim that the sixty-five largest Negro insurance companies control almost two billion dollars worth of insurance in force and have over 250 million dollars in assets.

But both of those last two totals represent a paltry two per cent of the insurance companies' insurance in force and dollar assets in America, even though we as Negroes represent twelve per cent of the population.

This is true of virtually every business in America that is operated or owned by Negroes. We just do not begin to control the capital in America's economy in relation to our numerical strength.

Success, whether taken individually or collectively, must be related to something. That something is the universal standard by which everybody and everything is judged.

So many of our teachers, business men, lawyers, and politicians should meet the same professional and social requirements of this plural society, yet they don't.

They don't because Negroes are given a false image of their success by the majority group. We're so happy to be told we're running when in truth we are crawling.

If we do nothing else, let's not be afraid or ashamed to apply the identical standards for success and achievement to ourselves that whites do for themselves.

Let us not fear the exacting demands of *excellence* in our pursuit of the accomplished life.

Let us be realistic and recognize that our achievements, while seemingly impressive within the narrow confines of the Negro community, remain pitiful when measured against the yardsticks of the total society.

In the same way that twelve inches equal one foot, summa cum laude means intellectual excellence, a .350 batting average means physical excellence and a $50,000,000 business means economic excellence, let us use these same measuring rods for ourselves.

Let's wildly and enthusiastically pursue the golden standard of excellence.

Let's toss aside the racial yardsticks—even if it hurts.

Big Megilla Over a White Tennis Ball

LAST WEEK, we discovered we had racial prejudice at a place where they hit a white tennis ball back and forth.

And, what a big megilla* we made over it!

As soon as U. N. Undersecretary Dr. Ralph J. Bunche's feelings were made known publicly by himself (a sweet little scoop for Dr. Bunche's name-collecting columnist-friend Leonard Lyons), Americans, regardless of race, creed, or national origin, rushed into battle.

With them, they toted verbal fire-power that would have awed even the late Senator Bilbo.

How's this for big-name battlers:

Queens Borough President John T. Clancy

* Megilla—a Jewish word which means "hassle" or "tumult"—you know, like a big deal being made over the thing.

U. S. Representative Lester Holtzman
U. S. Senator Jacob K. Javits
Commission On Intergroup Relations Chairman Dr. Alfred J. Marrow
Newspaper columnist Jackie Robinson
New York City Council President Abe Stark
NAACP Executive Secretary Ray Wilkins
Mayor Robert W. Wagner

Pretty impressive, isn't it?

Not only that, but a whole host of organizations rose up like a mighty wave of oceanic thunder and sounded off on the West Side Tennis Club in Forest Hills. In short, everybody lost their philosophical perspective and racial sanity over the matter, including, we submit, Dr. Bunche.

Why? Because it happened to Dr. Ralph J. Bunche? Because he is a Negro?

No. Let us draw this distinction as sharply as possible.

The hassle was created because it happened to Dr. Ralph J. Bunche, who is a Negro who is Dr. Ralph J. Bunche. (My apologies to Gertrude Stein.)

About the only sane voice heard in the fray over the "case of the white tennis ball" was *The New York Times.* Making a careful dichotomy, *The Times* stated editorially:

> In its private capacity the club may choose, as it has done, to deny membership to the son of Ralph Bunche or in general to deny membership to any Negro or any person of the Jewish religion. In its public capacity, as an institution with some diplomatic functions, the club has no right to make these discriminations.

Apparently, nobody else exhibited this type of careful analysis. And it was such a wonderful opportunity to climb on a publicity-saturated bandwagon and go on record as being in favor of all the good there is in life. To have failed to have spoken out last week against the West Side Tennis Club's action would have meant that you were a bigot and that just isn't fashionable these days.

Consequently, nobody missed the pilgrimage to the land of verbal integration. And what a sorry mess of hypocrisy it made!

The Queens Borough President, who led the group of Glendale parents protesting the transfer of Negro pupils into Queens, in a conference with Mayor Wagner declared sanctimoniously: "In view of the rank prejudice and discrimination which the president of the club has avowed against our Negro and Jewish citizens, I will refuse any aid to the club."

Mayor Wagner, who only comes to Harlem when somebody dies or when they have "clean-up" campaigns, and whose record on civil rights is about as dismal as can be, warmed up with the hardhitting, aggressive comment, "It is certainly no credit to the tennis club to discriminate against anyone."

Doesn't that just tear you up inside? Kind of grabs you and brings tears to your eyes, doesn't it?

And Abe Stark! We never knew he felt so strongly about the disabilities we poor Negroes suffer! We just never knew because neither he nor Mayor Wagner had ever made any comments on Tax Commissioner Joseph Mafera's remarks that Negroes should be kept out of "one hundred per cent white communities."

Do you know what was infinitely more important in the total scheme of race relations, American foreign policy, and domestic affairs and which also occurred last week? The fact that a Chinese couple was barred from a Maryland beach. The Chinese was Dr. Chiao-min Hsieh, a brilliant former director of research projects for the Office of Naval Research at MIT. Declared Dr. Hsieh: "We now have to give serious thought to whether or not we want to become American citizens." Is what happened to this Chinese couple any less important than what happened to Dr. Bunche?

Is what happened to Dr. Bunche more important than the fact that:

Negroes in New York City still live in slums?

Negro children are daily bitten by rats?

rigid discrimination still exists in housing?
unemployment among Negroes is three times as high as among whites and is aided and abetted by employment agencies?

We don't think so, despite all the big-name noise made last week over the tennis club's refusal of membership to Dr. Bunche. We do think, however, that we are a short-sighted, head-in-the-sand, hypocritical bunch of troglodytes when it comes to honestly trying to solve the race problem in America.

The amazing fuss and megilla created last week over Dr. Bunche only serves to reaffirm that unfortunate truth even more.

July 1959

Colored Snow

THIS WEEK, Chicago was smitten with several inches of 1963 icy, cold snow. (And it's still cold!)

But, two kinds of snow fell: white snow and colored snow.

Chicago is one of the few cities in America that has colored snow. It's a special brand that falls only in Negro areas—the South Side and the West Side.

Colored snow is ornery. It doesn't melt. It doesn't go away and it takes a longer time to be shoveled by the city's Department of Streets and Sanitation. It just stays.

Meanwhile, the Department busies itself and its staff shoveling all the white snow in Chicago.

White snow falls primarily on Lake Shore Drive, the North Side and Southwest Side, particularly near Bridgeport, where Mayor Daley lives.

It's "disappearing snow." As fast as it falls, Chicago's Department of Streets and Sanitation dashes out there, scoops it up, and lo! It's gone.

Over on the South Side and West Side, that colored snow is just as happy lying on the ground, not bothered about a thing! The Department of Streets and Sanitation doesn't worry about it and you know those people on the North Side and Southwest Side aren't concerned.

Just as long as the colored snow and the white snow have enough sense to fall on their respective domains, there really is no problem.

But just let that colored snow—that ornery, adhesive, non-disappearing kind—fall on the North Side and Southwest Side, and there would be an avalanche of fury descending on City Hall which would make the storming of the Bastille look like a tea party given by Carson Pirie Scott for School Superintendent Ben Willis.

And City Hall knows this. That's why they keep Lake Shore Drive, the North Side and Southwest Side snow shoveled.

Every year, the Lord sends snow to cleanse the earth and make it wholesome again: "Come now and let us reason together saith the Lord: though your sins be as scarlet, they shall be as white as snow."

But the snow serves another purpose.

It is a yearly reminder of the political weakness of the Chicago Negro.

"So, we don't clean up the snow on the South Side and the West Side," politicians reason. "So what? It will just expose the dirt and the filthy slums. Negroes ought to be happy we allow that snow to lie there so people won't see the ugliness of their neighborhoods."

Politicians respect only one thing: power.

Whether power comes in the form of money, votes, political organization, or personal charisma, it's the only thing which will make politicians sit up and act in behalf of your interests.

Despite all of those votes we Negroes have given to Mayor Daley, their totality is an abysmal weakness compared to the money and charismatic power of the business men who live on the North Side and Lake Shore Drive.

We have so little money—comparatively—in the Negro community. Our political organization doesn't command the respect it merits. Our votes are being ignored by Mayor Daley right now. And nobody, but nobody, in the Chicago Negro community has charisma. (I can think of three nationally known Negroes who have charisma —the Reverend Martin Luther King, Jr., Malcolm X, and Adam Clayton Powell.)

Do you know who has charisma in Chicago? Ben Willis, Archbishop Meyer, Marshall Field, John T. Pirie, and the editor of *The Chicago Tribune.*

And those five men wield more power and influence with Mayor Daley than all of the Negro votes and six Negro aldermen put together.

There isn't a Negro area, house or apartment in Chicago that gets its snow shoveled before 5555 North Sheridan Road, where Ben Willis resides.

So every time it snows we are smothered with the reminder of just how ineffective we are as Negroes in Chicago.

The Lord only sends one kind of snow—His snow. But when it falls on Chicago, it becomes converted to white snow and colored snow—white snow for Ben Willis's neighborhood and colored snow for all Negro neighborhoods.

Until Negroes can make their voices truly heard in City Hall, they're going to keep on watching that colored snow fall.

And City Hall is going to keep on watching right along with them.

"Purge me with hyssop, and I shall be clean: wash me and I shall be whiter than snow."

White snow, children, white snow. Get up off the floor of racial inequality and make a loud noise unto City Hall to get rid of your colored snow.

On Representative Adam Clayton Powell

PERIODICALLY, when white folks have nothing to talk about, they talk about colored folks.

And that is just about ninety-nine per cent of the time.

Somehow we seem to fascinate our Caucasoid brothers, who spend a major part of their waking hours figuring out methods and devices to deny us equal rights in the land where we were all born.

But at least this keeps them busy and, undoubtedly, the tremendous technological advances of western civilization can be ascribed to this capacity for constructing a society solely on the basis that colored people were treated as inferiors.

Of the 18.9 million colored persons in America, nobody appears to have a more compellingly seductive influence on the behavior patterns of 158.8 million white people than Representative Adam Clayton Powell, Jr.

They sure do worry about Adam, don't they?

Last week, set off by that elderly gentleman, Drew Pearson, the white community screamed criticism and denunciations of one of few colored leaders in America today who can still draw a packed house of colored listeners when he speaks.

Perhaps Mr. Powell, as chairman of the House Committee on Education and Labor did not exercise the most prudent judgment in hopping off to Europe before Congress adjourned.

But we don't recall any of the critical legislation which President

Kennedy announced he wanted to see Congress pass before adjourning as coming before Mr. Powell's Committee.

As for the two young ladies who accompanied him, Mr. Powell is an adult, as are all the other 536 Congressmen.

What people like Drew Pearson, David Lawrence, and papers like *The New York Times* just can't seem to accept or realize is that colored people have been choosing Adam Powell to speak for them for eighteen years now.

"He may be a rogue," summed up one woman so eloquently several years ago as she announced her intention of voting for Adam, "but he's *my* rogue."

With all of his shortcomings—and let him without sin cast the first stone—Representative Adam Clayton Powell, Jr., has done more to advance the cause of the colored American than a thousand Drew Pearsons and all of his progeny to follow in the next hundred years.

Adam Powell has given colored Americans a thrilling pride in their identity as Americans of African descent and has whipped their ambitions into a keener understanding of the need to work together, vote together, and pray together.

His fiery speeches and crusades against the walls of bigotry which demean the dignity of the human spirit have inspired more colored Americans in his quarter of a century of public service than all of the editorials and news stories in the history of *The New York Times*.

Colored Americans hold jobs on Capitol Hill which were not held before Adam Powell appointed them as top-level staff members to the House Committee on Education and Labor.

Colored Americans in Harlem will benefit by a quarter-of-a-million-dollar juvenile delinquency project for that area created by white racism.

We hope and pray fervently the people of Harlem will return him to Congress with an even larger plurality than his 59,812 votes of 1960, which represented seventy-one per cent of the vote.

Yes, Adam Powell occasionally embarrasses us and even irritates us by some of his bewildering actions. But he's still *our* Adam Clayton Powell, who has built a foundation of militant achievements for colored folks which very, very few whites will ever match.

This newspaper predicts the people of Harlem will show their contempt for *The New York Times* and the other rocking-chair liberals by giving Representative Powell a resounding vote of confidence, and sending him back to Washington, D.C., where he belongs.

September 1962

President Lyndon B. Johnson: A New Political Symphony

THE ONE WORD which characterized the Kennedy administration was "style."

Starting from this uncommonly brilliant young President himself and filtering down to the stenographers and messengers in government buildings, style shaped the way people did and said things during an exhilarating three years in Washington.

Any leader can have a style, a *gestalt,* as it were.

President Kennedy was one of the very few who had style and it became his charisma, displaying itself in his speeches, poetical and eloquent; his handling of people, persuasive and determined; his confrontation with domestic and world tensions, cautious, but Machiavellian when necessary.

Style became almost a mystique of the New Frontier, the concept which shaped the kinetics and velocity of the Kennedy administration.

I've been searching for a word which will itself be the imprint of the thirty-sixth President's administration and the one word which keeps coming to the forefront is "orchestration."

We're in for a period of political orchestration such as this country has rarely witnessed in the Presidency.

Tormented and grief-stricken by the violence of a beloved President's death, the country will eagerly soak up the pacifying brand of 1963 normalcy which Johnson will peddle.

Lyndon Baines Johnson has that grand capacity for knowing precisely where lie all the political ingredients of any situation, then being able to orchestrate them into one harmonious symphony with a minimum of political cacophony to achieve not only what he wants, but most importantly of all, what he thinks the traffic will bear.

While the vigorous and sometimes brash mien of a youthful Kennedy made equally vigorous enemies (in the business community, for example), Johnson has rarely permitted an articulate opposition to materialize.

He honeys it into neutrality.

A good example is his invitations to the two mayors of the two biggest cities in America (both Roman Catholics, both staunch liberals, both northerners) to come to Washington to attend the joint session of Congress. It is in these areas where he could expect the most severe opposition to his Presidency and even his nomination. Lyndon Johnson is running for 1964 already.

Supremely confident, Johnson also has an honest humility about him and possesses that one quality few politicians ever know: the awareness of his limitations. In addition, he has enormous energy and sixteen-hour days are a way of life for him.

On civil rights, Johnson thinks and talks liberal. But between the poles of what he says and what he does in this critical area is the identical difference between the Democratic Party's campaign platform and its accomplishments in civil rights. Here, however, the determining factor will be what Johnson thinks he can get through Congress. And this man knows his Congress.

If you divide Johnson's political career by the four most important political dates in his life, you can gain some idea of what to expect not only in civil rights on the national level, but in the appointive process in government, where Kennedy excelled with a record superior to *all of the previous presidents combined.*

These are the four political periods of President Johnson's life:

1. April 10, 1937—elected as a Representative to the seventy-fifth Congress.

2. November 2, 1948—elected as a Senator to the United States Senate.

3. November 8, 1960—sworn in as Vice President of the United States.

4. November 22, 1963—sworn in as the thirty-sixth President of the United States.

As a Congressman, Johnson was known as a liberal, and many millionaires in Texas still refer to him in ungracious terms.

As a Senator, and more particularly as the Senate Minority Leader as of January 3, 1953, Johnson moved toward the conservative right.

He was the prime exponent of the art of compromise and political expediency which, in the final analysis, are the most successful politician's stock in trade. (I don't write that approvingly, I state that as political truth.) Compromise paid dividends and under Senate Minority Leader Johnson's gentle arm-twisting, back-slapping Senate cloakroom exchanges, and—by far the most productive—those strategy sessions in his office, reportedly laced with an occasional bourbon, Johnson steered legislation through the United States Senate as if he were the captain of a ship and the Senate were his personal vessel.

The first civil rights legislation in fifty years was passed in 1957 and in 1960 solely because Lyndon Baines Johnson, a knowledgeable politician, knew exactly how much political castor oil the Senate would gulp down. While both bills were far from the minimum safeguards desired by Negroes, Johnson could point with pride to one unassailable fact: Something was better than nothing.

As Vice President, Johnson talked an even more aggressive fight for civil rights. Sincere in his feelings, he spoke constantly about the need to make quality meaningful for all citizens.

However, when it came time to rule as President of the Senate on whether the Senate was a continuing body or had the right to make its own rules at the start of each session, Johnson ruled this year in favor of the latter, thus for all practical purposes killing civil rights legislation.

Liberals screamed on Johnson and accused him of a betrayal. I did the same thing in a front page story in Washington, and two of Johnson's assistants called me down and did an unnervingly brilliant job of showing me that whatever my historical predilections about the U. S. Senate were, the plain fact was the only thing that kept a filibuster going was the physical limitations of Southern Senators, and not the Vice President's ruling.

You know, they're right?

Besides, Johnson was really pulling Kennedy's political chestnuts out of the fire. At that time, the White House wasn't ready for any full civil rights imbroglio and Johnson went along with the program.

The pattern of Johnson's political career and his conduct during each of those periods would seem to indicate that whenever Johnson achieved supreme responsibility, he invariably became conservative.

I think he will be a conservative on civil rights. Not because he is a conservative on this issue—because he's not—but because this is the way he is going to orchestrate his domestic program: the most good for the most people with the least amount of political friction.

He has some close associates who may determine how fast and in what direction his civil rights program will go.

One is William S. White, a newspaper columnist who has absolutely no feeling or love for civil rights and is regarded in the capital as Johnson's editorial spokesman. Whenever White wrote about the Kennedy administration, he had talked with Johnson, and everybody knew it.

If he gets tapped for White House Press Secretary or any important post next to Johnson, look for a complete standstill on civil rights. Bill White is definitely no friend of Negroes.

On the other hand, there's ponderous, brilliant, bushy-haired George E. Reedy, a man who is well known by most of the Negro journalists and fondly respected by them. A key position for Reedy will mean there is a glimmer of hope for civil rights under Johnson.

Then there are people like Hobart Taylor, one of the keenest legal minds in Washington, a Texan, a good friend of the President's, and a man whom Johnson has pushed for top jobs, including the most recent post of executive vice chairman of the President's Committee on Equal Opportunity. Hobart now escalates to the position of one of the most influential Negroes in the country simply because Johnson knows him well, believes in him, and listens to him.

What can you expect from the Johnson administration?

A smooth operation, perhaps more constructive accomplishments than in the Kennedy administration, but at a very, very slow pace, particularly in civil rights.

That's the way this man orchestrates progress. The political symphony you hear emanating from Washington in the next few months will be branded "Made In Texas By LBJ."

He may make a good president but will never become a great one.

November 1963

"Ceremonial Negro Leaders"

THE PROBLEM OF Negro leadership is not one of divisiveness. That will soon pass.

Nor is it one between the "young Turks," "moderates," and "conservatives," a superficial analysis so lovingly caressed by naïve young white reporters who are discovering the Negro community for the first time as employees of white newspapers.

The essential problem is the quality of Negro leadership. It is essentially mediocre.

Despite the external differences in strategy and tactics, there is a melancholy sameness about the way Negro leaders operate.

They are not feared and certainly not respected for their power since they—both politicians and civil rights leaders—do not really have any.

Generally speaking, Negro leadership is most accurately characterized by what can be termed the "Ceremonial Negro Leader."

He is a Negro leader with limited power, chosen by the white community as a Negro leader and endowed with heavy support in the white community in its belief that his power is greater than accepted or wanted in the Negro community.

The "Ceremonial Negro Leader's" position in the white community is honorific.

In the Negro community, it is substantial, deriving additional power from his white support. Within the total power structure of a community, the "Ceremonial Negro Leader" only retains power so long as the white community permits it by appointing him to committees and allowing him to speak over radio and television when they need a Negro leader who conforms to their image of acceptability.

The "Ceremonial Negro Leader's" most important functions are two: committee-sitting and luncheon-attending in the white community.

The "Ceremonial Negro Leader" is *not* an Uncle Tom. Yet there are certain identifiable similarities:

1. Neither is really feared by the white power structure. They are invited to sit on committees because they willingly "go along with the program."

2. Both are totally predictable.

3. Neither is prepared to disturb the basic infrastructure of our

society, retaining their position as "Negro leader" at the white man's whim.

4. Both bargain and negotiate on the white man's terms, at his calling, on his home grounds, and on his timetable.

5. Neither is capable of energizing an entire community into a frontal assault on racial segregation in the community, nor are they prepared to utilize any latent possible power they may possess to do so.

6. Both prefer talk to action.

7. Both are the prime beneficiaries of the more militant posture of other civil rights groups.

But the differences between the Uncle Tom leader and the "Ceremonial Negro Leader," while not more in number than the similarities, are more significant in their substance.

The Uncle Tom operates from a position of naked fear.

The "Ceremonial Leader" maneuvers from a posture of hesitant caution.

The Uncle Tom openly and at all times accords white people superordinate status.

The "Ceremonial Leader" is at least prepared to challenge the periphery of the white power structure—but on a limited basis and with the previous approbation of white liberals.

While the "Ceremonial Negro Leader" is constantly checking in with the white power structure, he never fails to keep his political tracks covered in the Negro community. Whenever he is rebuffed in the white community on a particular issue, he will invariably turn to the Negro community for help, totally involving himself in maneuvers with the Negro community to achieve that particular goal.

Once having gained his point, he returns to his previous position of rebuilding his image in the white community as the "moderate" and "responsible" leader. He then repeats his frequent checking in process.

On the other hand, the Uncle Tom never involves himself with the total Negro community, but instead limits his contacts to just a few close associates.

The wonderful thing about the "Ceremonial Negro Leader" is that he can be a militant person when he's young and quietly ripen into a "Ceremonial Negro Leader."

Look around at our Negro leadership in any community.

How much honest-to-goodness power do they have?

Do they operate from a position of strength or do they pussyfoot from a posture of subservience?

You folks know who the "Ceremonial Negro Leaders" are. Though the white man picked them, they exist as "leaders" because we permit them.

I guess if most of us wait long enough, we can become "Ceremonial Negro Leaders."

And that's what has begun to worry me. Some day I'm going to grow old.

Can you imagine *me* as a "Ceremonial Negro Leader?"

Immoral Chicago, Vote Frauds, and This City's Cheap Negro Vote

THE NEGRO VOTE comes cheap in Chicago.

You can own it outright for a "Democratic Victory Basket Dinner" (as a circular from the Second Ward's Twenty-Sixth Precinct organization printed in last Thursday's *Defender* indicated).

Or you can buy it for $1.50, which was the going price for Negro Democratic voters in several West Side precincts last Tuesday.

Or you can enslave it with just a simple threat by a precinct captain standing on the sidewalk near the polling booth, greeting voters from the nearby public housing project: "Hi there, Mrs. Johnson.

Hope you do the right thing today now. We don't want to see you move, you know. How are those six children?"

But if a few Negroes have the gall to be too intelligent or too courageous to be cowed by such blandishments and tacit threats, you just get downright openly dishonest: You tape all the voting levers on the machine of your candidate's opponents or you walk into the voting booth with the voter, pulling down the levers of your candidate with a solicitous, "Here, let me help you, honey," or you just tell a bald-faced lie. As one hopeful Republican voter was informed in Alderman Metcalfe's third Ward: "We don't have no Republican ballots. They didn't print any this year."

Shocked? Please don't be. This is Chicago.

But such political immorality is not limited to Chicago's Negro wards.

It engulfs and impoverishes the entire city, because Chicago is the most successful apostle of municipal immorality and political corruption in America.

If anything, Negro political immorality derives from white political immorality. And the common voting frauds in the Negro wards last Tuesday were tiny icebergs of corruption above the waters of human complacency compared to the huge, unseen mass of white corruption below this same surface.

Last Thursday's front page of the *Sun-Times* was a typical report of a typical day's events in Chicago. Three headlines vociferated about corruption—and they all involved white people:

HOROWITZ'S
PAWNSHOP
ROLE TOLD

STRATTON
INDICTED
ON TAXES

U.S. JURY INDICTS DORFMANS
IN $100,000 EXTORTION PLOT

How's that for a front page to use for a Chicago school class civics lesson about ethics?

However, where Negro political immorality and white political immorality part company is the price.

Recently resigned Building Commissioner Horowitz is a millionaire.

Former Governor Stratton was indicted for allegedly evading $47,000 in taxes.

The Dorfmans were indicted for trying to extort $100,000.

And Negro voters meekly surrendered their votes for a paltry victory dinner basket and $1.50 per vote.

What a sorry contradiction to see so many of us Negroes out there screaming for "freedom now." Shucks, once we get it, we're only going to sell it back to the white political bosses and their groveling black connivers for thirty pieces of silver.

April 1964

Colored Employment in U.S. Government: Still One Sorry Mess

PERHAPS it's in the nature of man to be perpetually discontented. It sure is in my nature.

A depressing discontent swept over me after I had read the figures on colored employment in the U.S. government recently published by the President's Committee on Equal Opportunity.

What a sorry mess.

But then a happy thought struck me.

Think how safe the country is—white folks are still way up on top. And we aren't even close.

Of all the 2,260,000 employees in the Federal government, 290,000 or thirteen per cent, are colored. That's not bad, is it?

But look where we're concentrated.

Of the total 360,000 people in Grades GS–1 through 4, eighteen per cent are colored.

Of the 530,000 people in Grades GS–5 through 11, five per cent are colored.

Of the 168,562 people in Grades GS–12 through 18, only 0.8 per cent are colored—not even one per cent.

Obviously, we are still toting the barges and lifting the bales as far as the U.S. government is concerned.

However Vice President Johnson was most enthusiastic about the progress we've made under the Kennedy Administration (and I think there has been more progress for colored people under Mr. Kennedy than under any previous President).

But I never look to how far I've come.

I always look to how far I've got to go.

As a news story elsewhere in the paper points out, the greatest gain for colored employees in the Federal government during the last year has been in the middle grades, GS–5 to 11.

Of the 11,000 colored people hired during the period from June 1961 to June 1962 (seventeen per cent of the total hired in that same period), 5,000, or just about half, were in those middle grades.

But in the top grades, GS–12 to 18, there were only 363 more colored people hired, an increase of 0.1 per cent over the previous year.

Some index of where the most rampant racial discrimination lies can be seen in the racial breakdowns on a percentage basis of the better jobs in the various agencies and departments.

The unchallenged champion of bigotry in the United States government of those agencies and departments reporting is the Federal

Home Loan Bank Board, which doesn't have a single colored person above a GS–4!

The Railroad Retirement Board (and there are a lot of colored people working on the railroads, aren't there?) doesn't have any colored officials above a GS–11.

That's also true for the Interstate Commerce Commission, the Selective Service System, and one of the worst agencies for sheer racial hatred among its supervisors, the Government Printing Office.

Next in line with the "no-room-at-the-top-for-colored-people" policy are the Atomic Energy Commission (0.3 colored people in grades GS–12 to 18), the Department of Interior (0.2 colored people in those top grades) and surprisingly enough, the Department of Justice also, with only 0.3 colored persons in the top seven grades.

Bobby Kennedy ought to start worrying less about Mississippi and ascertain what's happening right under his nose on his own home grounds.

And of course, as one would expect, the State Department, the one agency in our government in charge of managing our overseas image, presented a bigoted front with only 0.7 colored persons in the top seven grades.

However, just how racially bigoted State is can be determined by looking at one fact: There are only two colored ambassadors out of ninety-seven.

But we have made progress and there is no gainsaying that central fact of the Kennedy Administration.

And when you want to excite yourself with this happy historico-philosophical concept of "Gee-look-how-far-we've-come," simply r'ar back and remember that Lincoln freed the slaves.

White Man, Him Heap Guilty, So Him Sayum Him Friend Now

CHIEF STANDING BULL: Colored man, you lookum heap sad. Bottom lip draggum lower than whale carcass that sleepum on ocean floor.

NICODEMUS: Oh, Chief, baby, I've had it with these ofays. I mean, like Mr. Charlie and I have split. When my wife called me this morning, I told her to call me "Nicodemus X."

CHIEF STANDING BULL: What makum you changum name to addum "X?"

NICODEMUS: Like, Chief, don't you read newspapers?

CHIEF STANDING BULL: No readum white man's lies. Stoppum reading white man newspaper after Battle of Little Big Horn when white man makum Chief Yellow Hair Custer heap big hero when him really heap big fool.

NICODEMUS: Well, Chief, pick up on the *Defender* then and dig because four Negro kids just had their guts blown to pieces this past Sunday while worshipping in church in Birmingham. I've been too sick to eat all week.

CHIEF STANDING BULL: Oh, yes, me hearum about white man's boom magic which takum lives of four little black papooses. Much talk in teepees about white man's evil.

NICODEMUS: Well, white man, him—I mean, these grays are on notice now, dad, and you'd better believe it. I've been stashing away a few "pieces" for the big show and when it comes, you can bet we'll be ready because. . . .

CHIEF STANDING BULL: Stoppum crazy talk, colored man. You

talkum like head heap full of fire water. Indians stashum away "pieces," too, fightum many battles. But white man, him many times in numbers like great buffalo and deer in forest. You no winnum battle, you only throwum lives away. War no solvum nothing. Battles end, smokum peace pipe, and everybody feelum stupid.

NICODEMUS: Well, what's the answer, Chief? Okay, I buy all this non-violence jazz you and my man the Rev. King are putting down. And look what it's getting me. A whole mouthful of bombs.

CHIEF STANDING BULL: White man in South, him like northern gangsters. Great White Father passum laws against crime, murders. Laws no stoppum murders, but laws good, stayum on books. Like small drops of rain fallum from sky, progress against gangsters in New York, Chicago, Las Vegas, Birmingham, slow. One day, Great White Father, him catchum Mafia in North and Mafia in South. Puttum both away forever.

NICODEMUS: Yeah, I'll betcha. White folks are not on our side. Look how all the white newspapers all over America fought the 1963 March on Washington. They went all over the place, tearing their editorial undershirts and wringing their lilywhite hands about the possibilities of violence. They ran editorial cartoons about public patience wearing thin because there were so many demonstrations in America. They kept telling us to ease up on this demonstration bit and knock it off. With the exception of the white folks who marched and gave money, a whole lot of white people—and all of the white newspapers—bitterly fought the idea of the March. Then, when it was a big success, they still knocked it. You dug that *Sun-Times* editorial, didn't you?

CHIEF STANDING BULL: No, me no diggum. Me spendum many moons lookum at small box with talking pictures, no gettum so much crazy white man's opinion that way. But, me thinkum you wrong about white man. Him beginning to feel heap guilty and ashamed now. Him speakum out that when him holdum tongue on Wallace or race hatred, him just as guilty of throwing big boom magic as evil white man does.

NICODEMUS: Ha, like, who sez, man?

CHIEF STANDING BULL: You really tryum red man's patience. You gottum lottum sass in big mouth.

NICODEMUS: Yeah, Chief, well, you don't frighten me and any time. . . .

CHIEF STANDING BULL: Colored man, that blade you feelum in back of head belongum to young brave's hatchet. Me would hate to handum you your head. Now, you listen. White man, southern Congressman, Weltner from Georgia, him sayum all white men must acceptum blame, big white lawyer in South, him makum big speech, him sayum same thing. Heap big editor of Chicago *Sun-Times,* Akers, him no heap friend of the Negro but him writum, "This slaughter of innocents in our own Southland . . . will cause many people heretofore moderate in their views to champion the cause of the Negro in his efforts to win all of the rights of citizenship guaranteed him by the Constitution." Now you believum?

NICODEMUS: Yes, Chief, now, I believum. I'm with you.

CHIEF STANDING BULL: Colored man, sometimes me thinkum you gottum sense. What you sayum we go and fixum big barbecue?

NICODEMUS: Crazy, Chief, who we going to barbecue at the stake, Gov. Wallace or Dr. Benjamin Willis?

CHIEF STANDING BULL: Colored man, what makum me love you?

The Negro Press & The Challenge of a Changing Social Order

IT WAS MY *privilege to give the keynote address at the National Newspaper Publishers Association's twenty-fourth annual convention in San Francisco in April of 1964. Theme of the convention was "The Negro Press and the Changing Social Order." The title of my address related the two to each other. An edited version of the speech follows.*

A simple statistic—sixty per cent—amply describes social change in America during the past fifty years, one lifetime.

In 1910, sixty per cent of all Negroes in this country lived in rural areas. By 1960, sixty per cent of all Negroes were living in urban areas, taking part in America's great transition from a rural to an urban society. The U. S. Supreme Court's recent decision destroying the "rotten boroughs" in rural areas, which have virtually disenfranchised urban voters, will bring added vitality and power to urban centers.

As this domestic change slowly shaped a new culture, a series of global changes left its mark on the American social order. This new dimension of international "we-ness" found eloquent expression in Leopold Senghor's *la negritude.*

Colonialism thrashed to an almost unnoticed death and Africans became aware of each other as black brothers and their black brothers all over the world. Americans began to develop a greater international awareness, after two world wars and the establishment of a United Nations.

In America, the sleepy giant, the Negro community, had begun to stir itself politically, and by 1944 the Negro vote was a power to reckon with. The NAACP continued to fashion legal success after legal success until it enjoyed its finest hour on May seventeenth, 1954, when the Supreme Court ruled separate but equal schools unconstitutional.

All of these social changes—domestic and international—interacted and funnelled their historical confluence into one cataclysmic upheaval known as the "Negro Revolution." The Negro Revolution was social change sui generis, telling the world, in Duke Ellington's words, "Things ain't what they used to be." It was simultaneously a loud fire bell clang-clang warning to the Negro press that it, too, must change.

As professional newspapermen, we in the Negro press became part of another social change—the decline of the American press. As the American press lost its sense of purpose and missionary zeal for moral indignation, it developed journalistic anemia. We slowly became a nation of one- and two-newspaper towns and cities, becoming brainwashed into a frightening intellectual conformity.

A good example of America's loss of confidence in its newspapers is a comparison of newspaper readers in London, England, and New York City, both cities of approximately eight million people.

In London, there are eleven daily newspapers with a circulation of 17 million, two of which sell a hefty four million each.

In New York City, seven daily newspapers can only offer a feeble 4.2 million circulation. Thus New York City, with only one-third less newspapers than London, has three-fourths less circulation than its English brother.

This decline of the American press has likewise impoverished the Negro press and the great giants of yesterday, the *Pittsburgh Courier* and the *Washington Afro-American,* are of lesser influence compared to the towering strength they once exerted.

What is the new social order, then, which confronts us today, as of Thursday, June twenty-five, 1964?

It is the social order of a thoroughly sensitive America to its racial diversities, resulting racial tensions and moral contradictions. It is a social order of the "involved generation," today's youngsters who aren't afraid to enmesh their talents, skills, and even their bodies in the freedom struggle. It is the social order of the "New Negro," a bitterly proud, almost over-sensitive Negro and his confused counterpart, the "integrated Negro," who seeks to flee from his racial identity, particularly as integration spreads its happy wings over many communities. And finally this is a social order of political swingmanship which has passed the Negro by completely. When white folks voted for Roosevelt in 1932 and 1936, we voted Republican, and when white folks voted for Eisenhower in 1952 and 1956, we voted Democratic. We've always been out of step politically.

In this new era of a changed social order, what is the responsibility of the Negro press?

1. Go daily! Seriously, as long as virtually all Negro newspapers are weeklies, we can never compete as equals in a society controlled by daily newspapers. There are 1,754 daily newspapers in America but only two Negro daily newspapers, the Chicago *Daily Defender* and the *Atlanta Daily World.*

2. Help inculcate in Negroes a reaffirmed pride in being Negro. Educate Negroes to an acceptance of institutions which are all-Negro or predominantly Negro—by choice. We must learn to distinguish between Negro institutions which are all-Negro because we choose to make them so and those institutions which are the result of enforced immoral and unconstitutional segregation. We must teach Negroes to pursue excellence instead of integration.

3. The Negro press must pursue power and make the totality of this power felt throughout American society. How? We must speak as one voice on the great issues of the day besides civil rights—foreign policy, religion in the schools, etc. The Negro press must undertake a total and unrelenting involvement in the Negro community to the extent that nothing—and I mean nothing—happens in the Negro community without its participation. The Negro press must not permit Negro leaders which it has singularly created to turn around and betray us. The Negro press must meet the challenge of Negro radio and *Ebony.* Too often the publisher of *Ebony* is equated as a substitute for all the Negro newspaper publishers in America and we can easily prove to politicians, particularly in this election year, just how dismally erroneous this notion is. Negroes follow us, they don't follow *Ebony,* and every one of you knows it. The Negro press must begin to show the power of unity by communicating with its members and by exchanging editorials and news stories.

4. We must develop a nation-wide program conceived and endorsed by the Negro publishers. A voter registration program in every city where a Negro newspaper is published must be initiated and that paper must offer free office space and other such facilities to assist the program.

5. We must improve our image, modernize our typography,

bring fresh ideas into our methods of reporting, brighten up our pages with more humor and sassy features. The Negro press is too dull and too angry. (I realize that last statement comes with ill grace from one who is known as the "angry young man of the Negro press," but I also like to swing!)

6. Finally, the Negro press must find the soul of the Negro community and reflect it in its news pages. Who are we? What are we becoming? Where are we going, not only as Negroes, but as Americans?

The new social order demands that the Negro press of today swim in the cultural, economic, and political mainstream. We can help American civilization realize an even greater tomorrow if we fully meet the challenge confronting us today.

Economics of Racial Equality: $$$ $$$ $$$ $$$ $$$ $$$

ALONG WITH MAX WEBER, Thorstein Veblen, and Ludwig Gumplowicz, one of my favorite philosopher-economists is S. B. Fuller, the wealthy cosmetics manufacturer.

Mr. Fuller, who built his economic empire by the door-to-door selling of his product, has always made a lot of sense to me. And because he is human like the rest of us, he's also made some absurd statements, bordering upon the incredible.

Despite the fact that he and I don't necessarily agree on the Negro's immediate priority in the freedom struggle as well as the immediate concentration of energies, I've always been nagged by the persistent thought that so much of what Mr. Fuller says makes sense —just plain ol' common, down to earth, tell-it-like-it-is sense.

The trouble is, this economic common sense is lost in an angry rejection by America's Negroes who bitterly resent any Negro who says they're solely to blame for their plight. Mr. Fuller has lost contact with his own people who helped him to make his fortune when he turns his back on the ethos of the "Negro Revolution" sweeping the country.

However, Mr. Fuller has one message that my "main man," Dick Gregory, cordially agrees with: Take your money and buy those stocks in those companies (like Toddle House in Atlanta, Ga.). Buy that stock, go sit-in, then dare them to throw your buns out.

Over and over, Mr. Fuller has urged Negroes to enter into the economic mainstream of American life and begin to build businesses, make money, invest capital, and tote the full economic weight of their numbers.

"Negroes have got a mouthful of 'gimme' and a handful of 'much obliged,'" the witty businessman has said many times.

And this pretty much describes our collective efforts as a race in the American economic system.

Not only do we not control anywhere near ten per cent of the gross national product, we have no seats on the stock exchanges, we don't control any major manufacturing, banking, transportation, distribution, or service industries—or companies for that matter.

There isn't a single major business or company that Negroes control, influence, or even remotely affect through finances or ownership.

True, we've been able to bring some companies to heel in the employment of Negroes by boycotts, but the number of instances when we have succeeded solely as a race of people without any help from our white friends is indeed few.

By no means do I abase the importance of the vote as a powerful lever in prying open the doors of racial equality. If anything, I lean toward this apparatus as the first and most important tool for Negroes to use in order to unlock the bastions separating the races.

But to eschew almost completely the importance of the dollar and the extent to which it can likewise open the same doors is to blind ourselves to the realities of the American economic system.

We're a capitalist country. Capitalism thrives primarily on two commodities: capital and credit. But whosoever would control the capital controls the credit.

Negroes have got all the credit and white folks have all the capital.

So we must begin to exercise control over capital. We must begin to comprehend the power significance of concepts like "risk capital," "stock portfolio," "appreciation of capital investment," and "holding companies." And we must start operating in the world of finance by pooling our resources.

It's a simple matter to get one thousand Negroes out to picket, sit-in, or demonstrate. Yet it's almost impossible to influence that same one thousand to invest a dollar each in a business which they could own and control.

In Chicago, 16,103 Negro families earn $10,000 or more (nine per cent of the city's Negro population).

Suppose we could get from that group alone just $50.00 apiece to invest in a Negro-owned bank. That would be $805,000—more than enough to start a bank.

I say more than enough because Houston Negroes chartered a bank last year with only $600,000. And they're doing right well now. Even more ironic is the fact that there are only 215,000 Negroes in Houston (about twenty-two per cent of the population). While Chicago has nearly a million Negroes now, we also only comprise twenty-six per cent of the population—but there are so many more of us in Chicago than there are in Houston!

Fortunately, in the U. S. Treasury, there is a Comptroller of the Currency, James J. Saxon, who, in addition to a belief in hearty competition in business, has decent social instincts. He happens to believe that Negroes ought to get a fair share of the American economy's capital.

Don't get me wrong. Don't stop the picket lines, the boycotts, or the sit-ins. Rather let's increase and extend them. We can use ten thousand more a day. "Moreover if thy brother shall trespass against thee, go and tell him his fault between thee and him alone. . . . But if he will not hear thee, then take with thee one or two more, that in the mouth of two or three witnesses every word shall be established." (In short, the Lord says let your pickets sound your grievances.)

At the same time, let's pour out the votes, bloc voting passionately whenever necessary to insure the election of more Negro representatives—and a better calibre of Negro politicians.

But let's also start aiming toward the control of at least one per cent of the gross national product of $553.9 billion. Let's begin developing more millionaires by becoming manufacturers instead of just consumers. "For unto every one that hath shall be given, and he shall have abundance; but from him that hath not shall be taken away even that which he hath." (The Lord doesn't want you to be poor.)

Let's try to be a race with a mouthful of "Gimme the latest stock quotation," and a handful of "Much obliged for the investment." (And I don't mean the numbers, daddy.)

Panama and Cuba: Failures in American Foreign Policy

"AGAIN, the devil taketh him up into an exceeding high mountain, and sheweth him all the kingdoms of the world and the glory of them.

"And saith unto him, all these things will I give thee if thou wilt fall down and worship me.

"Then saith Jesus unto him, Get thee hence, Satan: for it is written Thou shalt worship the Lord thy God, and him only shalt thou serve."

The makers of American foreign policy for the past century apparently never read the Book of Matthew.

Because Uncle Sam has been leading Chiquita Banana up that mountain for over 140 years, making Monroe Doctrine-Good Neighbor Policy love to her—and she still doesn't dig us.

Cuba proved that when she had the nerve to get uppity and go Communist.

And now Panama has become the latest South American sweetheart to jilt us.

Unlike the devil, the United States did more than just promise the Latin American countries "all the kingdoms of the world." We produced them—in the form of billions of dollars under the European Recovery program, Mutual Security Act, and most recently, the Alliance for Progress.

Our imperious assumption was that the munificence of all these Yankee dollars dumped into the sieves of the Latin American economies would impel them to "fall down and worship us."

History now conclusively proves how magnificently wrong we were.

About the best way to understand what is galling the Panamanians—outside of the historical contempt North Americans living in that country have displayed toward their southern brothers—is the fact of an "outside power" owning a piece of its country.

How do you think Texas—the home state of President Johnson—would like it today if there were a strip across Texas owned by a foreign power? Texas would never happily accommodate itself to this geographical affront and Panamanians never have.

When Panama came into existence as a state after a November third, 1903, revolt helped along by the Panama Canal's chief engineer, Philippe Jean Bunau-Varilla, the new republic gave the United States perpetual sovereignty (that means forever) over the

Canal Zone to the exclusion of all Panamanian rights. Panama merely retained "titular sovereignty," which meant she had no power over the Canal Zone, the area of the Panama Canal.

The United States, in effect, owns the Panama Canal.

Ever since 1936, the Republic of Panama has been whittling away our rights and privileges in the Canal Zone, hoping one day to completely control the area. There have been revised treaties, adjusted pay scaled to pay Panamanians the same wages as United States workers, and such small decrees as the one by President Eisenhower in 1959 ordering the Panamanian flag flown alongside that of the U.S. flag in the Canal Zone—our property, remember.

It would be easy to dismiss the Panamanian riots of last week as the fault of some overly jingoistic American kids, just as it would have been untroubling to blame all of the racial trouble at Little Rock, Jackson, and Birmingham on a few local white racists.

A fundamental distrust bordering upon hatred of the United States of America seems to be the identical ingredient in the political chemistry of Cuba and Panama's disaffection for us.

It goes back 140 years to 1823, the year of the Monroe Doctrine.

President Monroe, with arrogance typical of the ruler of a pipsqueak nation, which we were at that time, drew a line around the Western Hemisphere and told the European powers: This belongs to us, stay out.

His pronouncement wasn't the result of any bilateral agreement between the various Latin American countries at the time. It was a unilateral declaration that we were the boss of the Western Hemisphere.

Periodically, the Monroe Doctrine was reaffirmed in American politics, the most famous of all being President Theodore Roosevelt's "speak softly and carry a big stick" dictum in 1903. He was talking about retaining U.S. control over Latin America.

President Franklin Roosevelt next tried to alter our "Yankee imperialist" image with his "Good Neighbor" policy concept in 1933. And there has been a fantastic multiplicity of schemes, treaties, organizations, conferences, and alliances proclaiming that the United States and all of the other Latin American countries now agree *bilaterally* that the Monroe Doctrine was the sine qua non of mutual protection.

It is not, and the Monroe Doctrine has been violated many times whenever the United States felt it was in its best interest to permit abuse with impunity. (The most famous example was in 1864, when the government of Mexico was overthrown by French troops and the Archduke Maximilian of Austria was enthroned as the Emperor of Mexico.)

Latin Americans have long resented our self-appointed guardianship.

They have resented the economic colonialism which we have helped to maintain over that continent.

They have particularly chafed under our white supremacist policies and practices since, as is true in both Cuba and Panama, large numbers of the people are colored. Americans living in these countries have treated the people like dirt. Even CARE refused to send a Negro to Panama as mission chief because the Panamanian government informed CARE he was not welcome. And CARE went along.

Cuba and Panama and, to a lesser extent, Brazil, are the harvest of an outdated policy which is today as worthless as it was ridiculous when it was expounded.

There will be more Cubas, Panamas, and Brazils. The masses of the Latin American countries are slowly awakening, and what they see about them stinks. They relate this sociological stench to the foreign policy of the United States.

A new and imaginative foreign policy for Latin America is needed—one based upon co-partnership, not intellectual fiat. And that's all the Alliance for Progress was—a mess of intellectual hogwash conceived by an ivory-tower liberal, Arthur Schlesinger, Jr., who simply helped to re-line the pockets of the ruling cliques instead of aiding the impoverished masses.

There still persists in the State Department Policy Planning

Council the theory that we may "lose" Latin America, as if it were ours to begin with. We're still thinking "Big Brother," so color us stupid.

We've got to start all over again in Latin America. It's like Jesus said: We've got to be born again.

January 1964

Black Muslims, Colored Moderates, and Guilty Whites

JUST WHEN I HAVE CRAWLED into my own, nicely compartmentalized womb of ideological distinctions, along come some white folks to tear it all apart. (And I've got enough trouble, just trying to pay the "pusher.")

Until two weeks ago, I thought I had pretty successfully partitioned the radicals, the moderates, the Uncle Toms, and the listless in the intrastructure of colored leadership.

Having done so, it was then easy to declare oneself in this critical battle for racial equality and decide with which group or leader one's self-conception was most congenial.

But I'm right confused now—courtesy of the White Establishment.

Last Sunday, in *The New York Times,* a story indicated that the President's Committee on Equal Opportunity was seeking a "colored moderate" to coordinate both the enforcement-by-compulsion and voluntary "Plans for Progress" programs of the committee.

This means this "colored moderate" would have to get along with the folks who wish to move as rapidly as the law and President Kennedy's Executive Order 10925 will permit, and concomitantly drag his administrative feet at the same time with the Robert Troutman gang, who number among their closest friends the most neurotic, anti-colored southerners.

Already several colored leaders are apprehensive about this official designation because the person who takes the job will be labeled. He will be expected to be as cozy with Robert Troutman, Senator Richard Russell, and Herman Talmadge, as he is with John Feild, Herbert Hill, and Lester Granger.

I'm looking forward to the appointment of such a quintessentially perfect colored person. (All "moderates" believe they stand closest to the Lord and this helps to make them perfect, you see.)

But the use of the word "moderate" in that *Times* story didn't touch me off so much as a very sober and objective analysis by *Newsweek*'s Washington correspondent, Kenneth Crawford.

Speaking on a telecast, Mr. Crawford discussed two putatively antithetical approaches to the solution of racial inequality in America—the Black Muslims (who are still being blamed for the Lorton Reformatory riots) and the followers of the Reverend Martin Luther King, Jr., believers in non-violence, but physical involvement.

Mr. Crawford termed the Reverend King a "moderate."

And this is what confused me.

Is the Reverend King's American form of Gandhi's *satyagraha* "moderate?" Was Gandhi a "moderate?" Was Christ a "moderate?"

I don't think they were. I think they were radicals.

I think the admonishments to "love thy neighbor," "turn the other cheek," and "whosoever would compel thee to go with him one mile, go with him twain," are so radical the world still hasn't been able to follow them, much less believe in them.

A "radical" seeks to change the established order immediately. He works within the Constitutional fabric of the body politic, but he does seek immediate change—in men's hearts and actions, if not in their governments.

It's the "revolutionary" who wants to overthrow the government, use violence, and start a war. Remember those folks who threw all that tea in the Boston Harbor and then followed George Washington to stomp the British soldiers into the sea? They were revolutionaries.

Nobody can seriously accuse the Black Muslims of being revolutionaries. They're peaceful folks, and if their ideology or speeches upset some white people, it's primarily because white people have guilt feelings about their hundreds of years of persecution of the black men. The Black Muslims keep referring to that nasty ol' past. They don't want to forgive—as, frankly, most colored people are willing to do.

On the other hand, the Black Muslims' solution, I think, is radical, but not their method. They stand up, shout, exhort, and give the white man a ring-a-ding bad time and it sounds terrible. But their solution—a separate state for colored—I think is ridiculously radical.

The Reverend King's method—passive non-resistance—is indeed radical. His solution—equal rights for all Americans—is as conservative as apple pie and coffee.

"Moderate" is defined as "kept within due bounds; observing reasonable limits; not excessive; restrained; neither too much nor too little."

The Reverend King, whom I would follow bare-foot clear across America and back, doesn't quite fit that definition. He wants "much" racial equality. And not a "little" at a time either.

In the final analysis, the key to this problem lies with the white folks. We're only too happy to push them toward a solution. But they must demonstrate good will in moving with us if they want to see this problem resolved within the happy limits of our American tradition.

If they think the Black Muslims are bad—man, what would they say about the Mau Maus? Peace.

May 1964

Why Do White People Like Negro Babies?

AT FIRST BLUSH, that appears to be a ridiculous question, doesn't it? Because most human beings like babies.

It is such a God-like quality to love children. Jesus implored, "Suffer little children to come unto me." Pandit Nehru adored children and assiduously spoiled them while simultaneously being uncharitably unkind to adults. Many people who can't stand adults love children.

Like any proud father, I think my two lovely daughters, Krishna, five, and Allegra, two, are the sweetest things alive. Allegra particularly is a beautiful little doll, olive complexion, big walnut eyes, and an irrepressibly impish grin.

Sunday morning we went for a long walk. It's one of the few times in my demanding business that I can spend a couple of hours enjoying my favorite two girl friends.

During the walk, Allegra, of course, repeatedly attracted attention. People stopped to respond to her non-discriminatory "Hello" or to ask her name. It was interesting to watch several white people develop a fleeting involvement with this little tan child—the elderly, well-dressed, and distinguished white lady who ended up by hugging her and asking for some "sugar"—the middle-aged couple who strolled out of an exclusive apartment house whose white doorman bars Negro kids from standing in the doorway during snowstorms and who made brief conversation, patting her fondly on the head—the white man asked her to shake his hand and told "Honey" what a nice young lady she was.

After a few more comparable experiences, I suddenly asked myself: Why *do* white people like Negro babies?

Is this transitory outpouring of warm feeling the safe expression of brotherly love that can be offered without fear of reciprocity?

How much of this temporary public love is a catharsis generated by guilt feeling?

But the most curious sociological riddle of all is: At what point does the affection for Negro babies eventuate into disaffection for Negroes?

How old or how tall must the Negro baby grow before he or she begins to become a threat to the white society's values?

If you talk to most white southerners, Negroes are eternally children—"boy," "Mary Lou" (never "Mrs." or "Miss"). To a lesser extent, this attitude is controlling in the North and very much in evidence in Chicago. Once you assign a human being a permanent characterization of "child," he is never treated as an equal and can never assume his place in society as a contributing and productive member.

Krishna and Allegra are no exceptions. You take any two small, cute, well-scrubbed Negro kids on a tour of downtown stores and watch white sales clerks and white customers unleash a flood of tender sentiments toward the kids.

Of course, white people don't love Negro babies enough to adopt them, because one day they might grow up to become Negro adults. If we could keep Negro babies in a state of permanent infancy, the problem of foster children in Chicago, which emotionally cripples thousands of Negro kids, would exist no more.

In fact, if Negro babies would just stay Negro babies, we'd solve America's pernicious race problem tomorrow—now wouldn't we?

To Two White Americans and a Polish Jew, a Hymn of Love

THEY WERE THREE.

And all three loved their fellow man so passionately, so unreservedly, they surrendered their lives to make him free.

Each died in a different year, in a different part of the world, yet all three were fastened together by the golden thread of destiny in their common love of freedom.

For each, it was a time of spring when earth breathes new life. In the springtime of their own lives, Mordecai Anielewicz, William L. Moore and the Reverend Bruce Klunder closed their eyes forever to the winters of freedom's discontent.

All three left shrines of courage: at Warsaw, Poland, on the eve of Passover in 1943; at Attalla, Alabama, on April 23, 1963; and at Cleveland, Ohio, on April seventh, 1964.

Fighting his last battle in the Warsaw Ghetto during an extraordinary twenty-seven-day period in which 13,000 Jews died, Mordecai Anielewicz, commander of the Jewish Fighting Organization, wrote these immortal words: "Now it is clear for us—what has happened has far surpassed our expectations. . . . The last wish of my life has come true. Jewish self-defense has become reality. Jewish resistance and vengeance have become transformed into acts. I am happy to have found myself among the first fighting Jews in the Ghetto."

For William L. Moore, a thirty-five-year-old white mailman, belief in the right of his fellow Americans of black skin to be free meant the quiet probability of personal sacrifice. He donned a crudely lettered sandwich board with the message, "Equal Rights for

All—Mississippi Or Bust," and began the dangerous trek from Baltimore to Mississippi, believing in his heart that he would live long enough to deliver a message of hope to Governor Ross Barnett. They found him murdered along a deserted highway, bullet holes in his head and neck. His last written words described some stray dogs which had adopted him. In this land of racial hate, he himself was a stray human being.

For the Reverend Bruce William Klunder, Isaiah's command "to undo the heavy burdens and . . . let the oppressed go free and . . . break every yoke" was a personal summons to Calvary. Tragically, he had just promised a friend that if necessary he was prepared to give up his life in the civil rights struggle. Crushed to death by a monstrous symbol of segregation, he died on the unfilled site of a planned segregated school in Cleveland, loving his black brothers and finding a triumphant peace in the agonizing fulfillment of his love.

I keep thinking about men like Mordecai Anielewicz, William L. Moore, and the Reverend Bruce William Klunder because they possess a bravery I can hardly know.

Still I can cherish their memories. I can love their ideals. And with prayer, I may someday honor their sacrifices with the courage to become personally more involved in the freedom struggle.

Their souls no longer are troubled, and everywhere in this world where shackled man, lonely and despairing, cries out for his freedom, the names of Mordecai Anielewicz, William L. Moore, and the Reverend Bruce Klunder will be sung in hymns of love. We must never forget them.

And they, in turn, have already found that glorious meaning that still eludes us when we "survey the wondrous cross" where Christ was crucified:

See from His head, His hands, His feet,
Sorrow and love flow mingled down:
Did e'er such love and sorrow meet,
Or thorns compose so rich a crown?

Responsible Party Government: Senator Goldwater's Contribution

FOR THOSE OF US who view Senator Barry Goldwater's candidacy for President with mixed feelings of revulsion, dread, and just plain horror, there is still a minuscule bit of political virtue to be harvested from his nomination.

This is the political virtue of responsible party government, a sound and intelligent system of democratic rule completely alien to America.

Responsible party government means precisely what those three words put together say—that a political party is totally and inexcusably responsible for all of the political decisions and actions undertaken during the period it occupies a national elective office.

Thus a Democratic President would have a guaranteed Democratic majority in both the Senate and the House of Representatives to carry out a legislative program which he has outlined as most representative of the political philosophy of the Democratic Party. The President would be the actual ruling head, not the titular head, of the Democratic Party, and, as the elected leader, would exercise firm political control over the administrative decisions of government.

The same would hold true of a Republican President—a guaranteed Republican majority in both Senate and the House of Representatives.

The United States of America in the one hundred and seventy-one years of its governmental existence has never enjoyed responsible party government.

Where we have been fortunate enough to be governed by a President blessed with majorities from his political party in both houses of Congress, it has been an unanticipated accident stumbled upon by the irresponsible whims of an untutored electorate, and not by any purposive design.

More often than not in our history, Americans have been governed by a President of one political party (more recently, Truman and Eisenhower) with majorities in Congress of the opposition political party, resulting in a deliberate paralysis of the chief executive's legislative program. In both instances, the opposition party in Congress either deliberately emasculated the chief executive's program or watered it down through a series of bipartisan amendments and maneuvers to prevent the President from gaining any constructive political mileage.

This kind of political musical chairs is not responsible party government because a political party can never be held strictly accountable to the electorate if its President is hamstrung by the opposition party's control of the legislative branch of the government.

Concomitantly, a political party can never implement a sustained program of accomplishments reflecting with exactitude its philosophy if it must carry on a daily tug-of-war between the liberal urban northerners and the racist rural southerners in one party and the liberal eastern internationalist wing and the reactionary midwestern isolationist wing in the other party.

Further obscuring any real and fundamental party differences is the occasional union between the conservative or liberal elements of both parties in Congress to block or effect passage of bills.

But in Great Britain, democracy functions politically more efficiently and certainly more responsibly because the British have responsible party government.

When the British electorate places a political party in control, the party chooses its Prime Minister and he governs with a majority of the House of Commons until he can no longer continue to get a vote of confidence from the members in Parliament.

The secret lies in control. Political control of the British political parties rests in the national center, whereas in America, political control resides in the hands of state and city bosses. An American political party is really a loose confederation of state and city bosses to whom the President must knuckle under once every four years in order to get elected—a pattern stemming from what Harold Laski termed the "obsolescence of federalism."

Between elections, the President's control over patronage endows him with a certain amount of power and authority, and he is technically the head of the party. Even then, however, a state or city boss can challenge him for that title, and may succeed.

In order to achieve responsible party government in America, the election machinery would, of course, have to be overhauled, with increased power being delegated to the political parties at the national level. For example, the political parties would have the right to decide whether they want a particular person to run for senator or representative (not governor or mayor). Naturally, states-righters will scream bloody mayhem at this further centralization of power, but this is precisely what Barry Goldwater is doing now by using the Republican National Committee as the clearing house for all patronage jobs.

Barry Goldwater's candidacy doesn't necessarily start us on the road toward any major repairs in our political process. But his candidacy does serve to clarify and sharpen the distinction between the Republican and Democratic Parties. Goldwater's alternative is an inordinately crummy and destructive one, but it is nonetheless an alternative.

And, that, believe it or not, is the only honest definition of democracy—the existence of a political alternative.

As rotten and as dirty a campaign as we can expect from the Goldwater candidacy, we will also witness a political clearing of the air. America may be thrown back temporarily, but in the long run the country will crawl agonizingly forward one more inch toward responsible party government.

Joseph McCarthy rendered such a service; Barry Goldwater will, too.

July 1964

I Remember Panditji

HE WAS THE REASON millions of Indians believed in a tomorrow.

He was the lovely symbol of hope itself.

All at the same time, he was India's spiritual lighthouse, captain of her political ship, and ocean of her destiny.

No one man breathed more love for one's fellow man into the hearts of so many millions than Jawaharlal Nehru.

Freedom fighter, lawyer, scholar, father and husband, politician, prime minister, he was simply "Panditji" to all of India, the richest and the poorest. ("Pandit" means teacher; "ji" is a term of great respect or reverence in India, its closest approximation in English being "sir.")

I don't think Indians seriously believed Nehru would ever die. Panditji was indestructible, but more importantly Panditji was the charismatic sinew which bound together India's fratricidal, linguistic, religious, and caste differences.

From the Maharastrians and Gujeratis, whose tribal bitterness carved Bombay state in two; from the southern Tamil-speaking Madrassis, who wanted a separate state, Tamil Nad; from the gay northern Punjabis and Sikhs to the Urdu-speaking Moslems in the Gangetic plain and the Bengalis in eastern Calcutta, Panditji was the great father who alone—and this is the historical marvel of this man—could keep India from tearing herself apart at the political seams.

If Gandhi was India's Moses and her George Washington, Nehru was her Isaiah and her Jefferson and her Wilson and her Roosevelt and her Kennedy.

Seven years ago, I lived in India for a year while working for CARE, and saw more of that great country than most Indians. Whether standing on the southernmost tip of Cape Comorin looking out over the vast sea or riding on the back of a camel-pulled cart in the northernmost city of Amritsar, I was aware of Panditji.

No conversation in India ever sustained itself very long before "Panditji says" or "Panditji thinks" gave it broader meaning. I grew to love this incredibly complex, almost incomprehensible political expression known as India. And I simultaneously developed an even more passionate respect and bottomless love for Panditji. Several members of his family were very close to me and my oldest daughter is named for Nehru's youngest sister Krishna.

The tragedy of Panditji's death, like John F. Kennedy's, was the still uncompleted tasks before each. Both were so alike—brilliant, young in spirit, ever intellectually unsatiated, political pragmatists yet unshakable idealists. Both recognized that mankind must commit itself firmly to civilization's most critical goal—the universality of brotherhood—if mankind is to survive.

Nehru spent his entire life trying to bring beautiful illumination and meaning into the lives of his countrymen. He gave them a new sense of themselves and even a new dignity. Angrily impatient with ignorance, but immediately gentle in his understanding, he never lost his love for India's masses. As the daily rose he wore was a symbol of the beauty of a new day, so did his constant public displays of affection for little children teach grown-ups that the greatness of a nation lay with its young.

I remember a wonderful and gracious human being with twinkling eyes who enriched all our lives simply because we loved him.

I remember one of history's greatest men.
I remember Panditji.

May 1964

"In Choosing To Be Jews. . ."

WHEN I WAS A STUDENT at Wesleyan University, I attended a Student Christian Movement conference one summer in Maine.

The Rev. Herb King of New York City spoke to us one evening and told us what an elderly and distinguished minister had told him in divinity school: "All ministers have only one sermon.

"They may say it in different ways, with different titles, but it's only one sermon. I now have two sermons. Someday, you may have two sermons, but right now you only have one."

I've never forgotten those words—primarily, I guess, because I've always felt I only had "one sermon."

Were I to sum up my sermon, it would take only five words: racial achievement through racial unity.

No matter what I write, how I write, or what I feel about anything—be it nuclear testing, automation, unemployment, foreign police in Africa, or the political process—the intellectual and emotional substratum of my total psyche rests on those five words: racial achievement through racial unity.

A sermon needs a text.

I have chosen my text from a speech made two years ago this May by Dr. Joachim Prinz, president of the American Jewish Congress.

In a keynote address before the AJC national biennial convention, Dr. Prinz declared:

"No dictator, no anti-Jewish laws, not even surface anti-Semitism force us to accept our Jewish identity.

"But in choosing to be Jews, we must reject the idea of isolation, self-containment, and ghettoization."

Continuing, Dr. Prinz drove to the heart of an ethnic concept about which colored Americans still wallow in confusion:

"Obviously, we owe no political allegiance to the State of Israel. But we must emphasize the bond of kinship we feel with the people of Israel."

The most important five words in Dr. Prinz's entire speech, it seems to me, are: ". . . in choosing to be Jews."

At this historical juncture, the Jew in America has made a decision which cements him body and soul to his religious and ethnic heritage.

He "*chooses* to be a Jew."

He *chooses* to identify with his people in Israel as well as in America.

He chooses to be aware of himself as part of a larger ethnic whole, cleaving together for the politically pragmatic, but, as Dr. Prinz says, rejecting the "idea of isolation, self-containment, and ghettoization."

Maybe it is because there is a backlog of centuries of persecution that the Jew has been pushed to this sophisticated, but extremely practical and logical, "middle-of-the-racial-road" position.

But colored Americans have been unable to understand or define their twin roles as colored people and Americans. As a result, they suffer from a most pathetic case of racial schizophrenia.

Hell-bent in their compulsive quest for the happy hunting ground of integration, the colored American has summarily rejected all that is good and rich and beautiful in his heritage as a descendant of Africa, as a colored person.

While he has given marvelous lip-service to the doctrine of racial cohesion, he will turn around and sell out his brother for thirty pieces of political silver in the twinkling of an eye.

To preach today that colored people should stick together, fight for a larger share of political appointments, develop more colored businesses and educational institutions is to be labeled a "racist."

The New York Times, for example, never excoriates Jews or Italians or Irish for seeking more jobs based upon their numerical representation in the body politic, but it always condemns Adam Clayton Powell and colored people all over America for demanding that a percentage of certain jobs be allocated to colored people.

As colored people we must learn to make distinctions between enforced segregation and a voluntary banding together to build economic and political power.

We must learn to construct symbols of excellence so unchallengeable that white people will seek participation.

Whether it's a bank, a university, a savings and loan association, a restaurant, a beauty salon, an undertaker's, a law office, a hospital, a cosmetics company, a newspaper, an insurance company, or a construction company—our standards must be so high, so excellent that they will attract the best people, white or black.

But the power, the control, and the future guidance must seek its spiritual direction from the colored community.

We must build a cultural consciousness of such permanence it can be handed down to our children, who will look back with pride and say: "Our ancestors were colored Americans."

Most of us have some degree of racial pride, and it's been sparked by a comparatively recent combination of events.

Southern sit-ins have fired our imagination, arousing latent desires for racial togetherness. Africa's freedom drive has also finally given us a respectable crutch on which to lean for our ancestry.

But I'm not talking about racial pride.

I'm talking about racial achievement through racial unity.

We don't have to like each other to work together.

But we must understand that colored people in America will only advance as rapidly as they demonstrate both the concern and the capacity for equality through the use of the simple tools of political and economic cooperation.

And there is nothing wrong with an all-colored anything—as long as it's the best there is.

Integration *sui generis* has misguided and shamed more colored people into apathy than they realize.

Yet the Jew has not sought integration. He has sought freedom and he has done this by carefully "choosing to be a Jew." His integration has come as a Jew into the total society.

Some of us have got to start "choosing to be colored Americans."

Once we make this choice, we can distinguish between unity and ghettoization.

In 1947, the United Commission on Human Rights Proceedings contained a speech by the then delegate to the United Nations from Lebanon, Dr. Charles Malik.

Speaking on the importance of the individual in society, Dr. Malik said: "Man has other loyalties than his loyalty to the state.

"He has his loyalty to his family, to his religion, to his profession; he has his loyalty to science and to truth. These loyalties are *equally as exacting* as the loyalty to the state."

I would add—and I think Jews around the world would agree with me—he has his loyalty to his ethnic background.

What makes me unhappy is that many colored Americans would not agree and this is the heart of our problem today.

Should Negroes "Buy Black?"

SEVERAL DAYS AGO, the New York chapter of the NAACP led pickets in a knot-tightening effort to rope off the Harlem area for Negro whiskey salesmen.

After two days of "friendly" conferences and just a little bit of necessary picketing, seven liquor stores all agreed to demand that their wholesalers send Negro salesmen to service their stores.

For years the liquor stores in Harlem had been offering the excuse that they were in favor of Negro salesmen, but those recalcitrant wholesalers were to blame. Not wishing to depart from the lilywhite norm, the wholesalers were just as quick to turn around and blame it on the retailers. Nobody was prejudiced, but meanwhile no Negro salesmen were getting any of those dollar-laden accounts in Harlem. (Everybody knows how much whiskey Negroes drink in Harlem.)

It'll be interesting to assess the eventual success of this "buy black" rebirth for 1959. The movement has now taken on fairly respectable backing with the NAACP, a growing number of merchants, and innumerable citizens pledging enthusiastic cooperation.

But should Negroes "buy black?"

To answer this question, we ought first to decide what is meant by "buy black."

The concept "buy black" has different meanings to different people, running the emotional gamut from a kind of racist black nationalism to a mildly fervent reaffirmation of pride in one's colored ancestry. The intensity of its shading all depends on who's painting the picture.

Without wishing to offend some of the more zealous guardians of the Negro's economic ills, we offer three forms in which the "buy black" movement has sought expression in the past and still has significance for the present:

1. Negroes should only patronize businesses which are owned, operated, and run by Negroes.

2. Negroes should patronize businesses which, if they aren't owned by Negroes, at least hire Negro salespeople and other Negro employees.

3. Negroes should patronize businesses as a matter of preference where *ceterus paribus*—all other things being equal—the Negro business offers the same if not better quality of service and merchandise.

Call it racial pride, racial preference, ethnic coherence, economic common sense, or just plain ol' sticking together, it still comes out as "buy black."

And, it's probably one of the most intelligent things the Negro can do to pull himself up by his bootstraps, because, with all its racial overtones, any one of the three "buy black" forms are expressions of belief in one's race and a recognition of the need to survive.

In fact, it is a most logical manifestation of racial kinship.

What is wrong with an Irishman preferring to trade with Irishmen first?

What's negative about a Jew placing his business as a matter of principle with other Jews first?

What's bad about an Italian seeing to it that other Italians get the major share of his business?

"He that looketh not after his own, the same shall not be looked after." And that is the gospel truth. If Negroes don't take care of themselves, who's going to take care of them? (There's a whole bunch of colored fools around who'll say, "Welfare.") The trouble with us is that we have attached shame and the stigma of segregation to organized efforts of Negroes to corral Negroes into supporting each other's economic enterprises.

Yet all of us will jump like Jack over a candlestick to agree that Negroes should support Negro enterprises. By the same token, a few will even go further and declare that businesses in a Negro neighborhood should be boycotted if they refuse to hire Negroes.

This latter thought may be commendable for its effort to gain employment for Negroes, but it has usually started from a false premise. It is somehow assumed that the more Negroes who are hired—such as Negro salesmen—the more money will "stay in the community."

This is an economic myth.

When Negroes earn money, they spend it in the same places as white people—at Macy's, Lord & Taylor's, Gimbel's, S. Klein's, Town & Country, Stouffer's, Brass Rail, Hotel Statler, and the San Remo Cafe. Even if they do purchase their goods in Harlem the owners of the businesses—the vast majority of whom are white—aren't going to spend their earnings in Harlem.

No, the "buy black" concept today, if it is going to have validity

—and we think it should—must be based on something more rational than some mythical belief in "keeping money in the community." If anything, it must be based on the fact that Negroes, where they are prepared to muster sufficient power to make their demands met, must do so if only one more Negro gets a job.

The national office of the NAACP, we happen to know, does not make a practice of using the services of Negro companies or Negro businesses when these businesses offer the same standards of quality and service. So what we have is the anomalous and fantastic picture of an organization fighting for racial equality, yet denying it in certain areas.

We've said this repeatedly: don't buy black, buy competence. But if the standards and the services are the same, is there anything wrong with "buying black?"

The Lesson of Atlanta for Washington Voters

A COUPLE OF WEEKS AGO, Atlanta voters went to the polls and nominated a mayor in the Democratic primary.

Because the Democratic nomination is, tritely speaking, tantamount to election, the winner will be the next mayor of Atlanta.

His name is Ivan Allen, Jr., a business man who holds "moderate views" (This means he probably doesn't believe in intermarriage.) on the race question.

Allen defeated Lester Maddox, a staunch segregationist, 64,000 votes to 36,000 votes.

Many of us knew about the crucial role of the colored vote, but not until I picked up my last week's copy of the *Atlanta Inquirer* (a swinging little ol' newspaper) did I realize that colored people had de facto put Mr. Allen in office.

Segregationist Maddox actually won more white votes than did Allen. Maddox garnered 36,000 white votes to Allen's 33,000 white votes.

But enter the brother.

Colored people gave Allen 31,000 votes while only giving Maddox a paltry 179 votes.

You can add just as well as I can.

Those colored voters were clearly the balance of power.

Even if only two-thirds of the colored voters voted for Allen, he still would have won (assuming the white vote remained as it did).

I don't think there is any more pellucid demonstration of the colored vote as a "balance of power."

This concept simply means that in a close election in which the majority community is split, a colored community can determine the election's outcome. Why? Because we colored people are inordinately concerned about more things than just taxes, new schools, new streets, bus service, corporation taxes and an effective police department.

We want a candidate to assure us he will fight for equal employment opportunity so we can pay those taxes.

We want to be able to attend those new schools.

We want to see all streets paved, not just the streets in the white neighborhoods.

We want to be able to drive those buses and work for those corporations.

The candidate who comes closest to satisfying these demands gets our votes, hence this ethnic coalescence of attitude.

The colored vote rarely splits any more. It always gives a majority to one candidate or the other. Sometimes we can be as wrong as the *Literary Digest* in our choice and thus exercise absolutely no influence on the winning candidate (Eisenhower in 1952 and 1956, when colored people voted for Stevenson, and Rockefeller in 1958, when colored people voted for Harriman).

Naturally, a winning candidate will look with disfavor upon colored people when he doesn't owe a measure of his political success to this bloc. We call such a bloc "the unearned increment of politics." It ain't worth nothing.

Conversely, a winning candidate will be sympathetically inclined to colored people if he is cognizant they were the balance of power in his election.

Nobody appreciates this better than President Kennedy, who saw a country split its vote right down the middle, while colored people were giving him margins as high as eight to one in some cities.

There's a lesson in all of this for Washingtonians.

Right now, colored people comprise fifty-four per cent of the population in Washington, D.C., no small factor in Congress's refusal to give the nation's capital home rule.

Despite the power of this numerical majority, colored people can neither demand nor effect social changes unless this power is translated into votes.

Only a comparable percentage of voter registrations in the colored community as obtains in the white community will bestow the blessings of this power on the brother.

Now I am not suggesting that all the colored people get together and vote the opposite way white folks do. This suggestion is patently absurd. Were this to be done, whites would always out-vote colored people.

What I am proposing is that colored people understand and fully appreciate how much power they have when they register and vote. You don't get something for nothing, and colored people in Washington, D.C., aren't going to get anything until they give something —that something being their votes.

December 1961

Power in Our Society

"POWER CORRUPTS. Absolute power corrupts absolutely."

Ever since Lord Acton wrote those words, they have applied with amazing accuracy to individuals and groups who have tasted the heady wine of power.

Nobody uses power wisely. Few men use it intelligently.

A humble man when he gets a taste of power cannot help but feel a new status. Deference is paid to him, people listen to his mediocre ideas and obey his most ridiculous commands. Whether it's financial or political power, men are usually corrupted by its glowing promise of more power.

Hitler, McCarthy, Bilbo, Gould, Goldfine, and De Sapio are just a few examples of those who used their power unwisely. Ignoring the logic of compromise, they rammed their ideas down the throats of those who opposed them. The stronger they became, the more they abused their position.

During the last years of the nineteenth century, big business literally took over the economy of America. Combinations of capital were able to control the direction and pace of industrial development. Financial giants, manipulating stocks, and holding companies were able to restrain trade, competition, and new ideas.

Big business needed to be checked because big business placed the welfare of the public second to the welfare of big business.

As a result, the Sherman Act of 1890 was passed. Its purpose was to check big business.

Today we have a new source of power in America.

It can be called big labor, a term which has the same implication as big business.

Big labor, when it acts in concert, can paralyze all of us into inactivity.

A strike of the teamsters' union, steelworkers' union, railway union, airlines pilots' union, and a comparatively insignificant union such as that of the newspaper deliverers could bring this country's economy and communications system to the brink of economic anarchy.

The recent newspaper strike in New York City appalled even some of the pro-labor newspapers and writers. "We believe labor should continue to have the right to strike," they wailed in unison, "but something has to be done so that this won't happen again."

It is just possible that the pendulum has swung too far the other way. It is just possible that a corrective influence is needed in some form of legislation.

More and more, our society has become pluralistic. The individual has increasingly little meaning outside of the organization.

To get things done in America today, you form an organization. Then you lobby for your interests or you lobby against the interests of others, which automatically sustains your interests. This is as true of business and labor as it is true of the Negro, the Catholic church, the Protestant church, the Jew, the oil companies, or the outdoor billboard industry.

The difficulty arises when these interests cannot be reconciled.

And big labor has evolved to a point in our society where some of its interests are incapable of being reconciled with the general welfare.

No matter what freedoms are guaranteed by our Constitution, or by statutes, or by our courts, none of these must trespass on the freedom of the social whole. The general welfare remains paramount and all men must be protected if democracy is to have validity.

Big labor, when it stops the economy from functioning, when it dams up the streams of communication, trespasses on the good of the general welfare, and actually works against the Constitutional fabric of government.

At issue here, of course, is labor's freedom—its right to picket, its right to strike, its right to bargain for power in our economy.

But, as Justice Oliver Wendell Holmes once wrote, freedom of speech does not give a man the right to yell "Fire!" in a crowded theater, so the freedom to picket and strike does not give labor the right to endanger the whole society.

The right to strike is not more important than everybody's right to life, liberty, and the pursuit of happiness.

Big labor must learn that the use of power in our society implies a responsibility to use it wisely lest it, too, becomes subject to the law of historic necessity: "Power corrupts; absolute power corrupts absolutely."

Why Negro Men Wear Mustaches

GEORGE BERNARD SHAW once said that while a boy he was watching his father shave.

He asked him: "Father, why do you shave?"

His father looked at him and couldn't give him a good reason and from that day, he never shaved again.

Somebody should ask Negro men: Why do most of you wear mustaches?

Have you ever noticed how many Negro men cover their upper lips with mustaches? And have you also noticed how few white men wear them?

Perhaps such questions pose a condition which you don't think exists. But it's true. By far the vast majority of Negro males wears a mustache.

They're either convinced that they look like sepia editions of Caesar Romero or they've never gotten over the fact that the great benefactor who freed them wore a beard.

This symbol of ethnic designation extends itself even to our Negro leaders.

If, for example, one were to assume that the four top Negro leaders were A. Philip Randolph, the Rev. Martin Luther King, Lester Granger, and Roy Wilkins, only one—Mr. Randolph—has the security of a shaved upper lip.

We have four Negro Congressmen and two of them, our own A. Clayton Powell and William Dawson of Illinois, both wear mustaches. That's half the Negroes in Congress. Do half the white Congressmen wear a fuzz on their upper lips?

The only Negro on the U. S. Circuit Court of Appeals, Judge William A. Hastie, wears a mustache.

Out of six Negro aldermen in Chicago, William H. Harvey in the Second Ward, Ralph Metcalf in the Third Ward, Claude W. B. Holman in the Fourth Ward, Robert R. Miller in the Sixth Ward, Kenneth E. Campbell in the Twentieth Ward, and Benjamin Lewis in the Twenty-Fourth Ward, only one doesn't wear a mustache—Robert R. Miller.

That's eighty-four per cent of the Negro aldermen. That is indeed a whole lot of colored mustaches covering up the Chicago City Council.

The publisher, John H. Johnson, of America's largest and best-selling Negro magazine, *Ebony,* wears a mustache, but Henry R. Luce doesn't.

Other outstanding Negroes in the country who carry around this little ethnic badge of distinction are: topnotch architect Paul Williams, New York State Senator James L. Watson, cartoonist E. Simms Campbell, Hartford's only Negro councilman John Clark, the NAACP's brilliant legal strategist Thurgood Marshall, and like, man, three members of the Modern Jazz Quartet.

So why the mustache?

A mustache is probably the most immediately tangible proof of manhood.

Historically, the Negro (and we've written this before in these columns) has always been considered a boy. He was called "boy" even after he won his Ph.D. from Harvard. In the South they still call him "boy" and many a northern Negro has to ask a white man occasionally: "How big do boys grow where you come from?"

Nevertheless, some few years after the Negro began to feel his emancipated oats, he decided to prove to the white man that he, too, was a man. He didn't go out and build any huge factories or develop any new industry.

He didn't establish any big banks or corner the market on the manufacturing of goods. He didn't become a financier.

He sat down and grew a mustache.

And, he hasn't stopped growing those mustaches yet.

This is the kind of straight, solid, down-the-line thinking we do as Negroes. If we drive a Cadillac, we must be rich. If we wear a mustache, we must be men.

True, a mustache does impart the image of manhood to a person. But it's like a suit of clothes. If you don't have the money to back you up, people will find out what a phony you are.

And we don't have a thing as Negroes to back us up but the NAACP and the Urban League, and they are as valuable to the economic growth of America as the Young Ladies Bridge Club of Newport, R.I.

Anticipating the anguished cries which will well up when that last sentence is read, we hasten to add that within their particular areas of intent and accomplishment, both organizations have performed with outstanding competence.

But they haven't given us the economic and political power we need as Negroes to carry our weight fully in this society.

Like the cultivation of the mustache, we've been diverted from the main goals of life. We wouldn't have need of an NAACP if we had pooled our strength and our resources and begun to build up businesses, industries, and monopolized a few markets. With all the boycotting and blowing up of schools and churches, there's been no major effort directed at substantial Negro businesses.

Why? Because the dollar looks the same in the white man's hand as it does in the Negro's hand.

Yes, Negro men wear mustaches. And they're men.

White men don't wear mustaches and they've got all the money.

Violent Pupils in Our Schools and the Self-Fulfilling Prophecy

NEWSPAPERS—and that includes all of us—frequently fall prey to a most odious gimmick: the self-fulfilling prophecy.

Either through editorials or news stories, a newspaper will impart authoritative credence to the possibilities of a remote evil.

First, the newspaper will condemn a comparatively unknown or unlooked-for social iniquity in its editorial pages. At this point, only morality and the rule of reason are invoked.

Then a series of documentary stories will be published with interviews and supporting statistics that prove conclusively the existence of the malignancy.

If the newspaper is really blessed, the evil condition will suddenly explode into existence through several incidents, the newspaper will again spotlight these incidents, the community will indulge itself in an orgy of recriminations, meetings, and moral indignation to wipe out the evil—*et voilá!* A Pulitzer Prize is won!

The self-fulfilling prophecy is now enjoying an exquisite field day in several of the Chicago and New York City newspapers with stories on pupil violence in schools.

All of them have just rediscovered it. Nobody remembers *Blackboard Jungle.*

Here's how the self-fulfilling prophecy operates.

Most of the newspapers in Chicago and New York City opposed the two recent school boycotts—New York's first and Chicago's second. They mustered a number of logical arguments against them.

Anticipating the need for a public opinion counter-thrust to the boycotts, the Chicago and New York newspapers now appear to be deluging their readers with a spate of stories on acts of violence by pupils against teachers. Journalistic concern has attained such momentous proportions that the usually unruffled *New York Times* wrote a lead editorial Saturday on "Violence in the Schools" accompanied by a front-page story. The sassy New York *Daily News,* ever on the side of authoritarianism, gave New York teachers some good ideas with a three-column headline on page four:

SCHOOLS START HITTING BACK
AS STUDENT ASSAULTS GO ON

And the staid, in-search-of-a-new-identity *New York Herald Tribune* leaped in with this suggestive note:

THROW RASCALS OUT OF SCHOOLS,
GROSS ORDERS—VIOLENCE GOES ON

In Chicago, this new journalistic bandwagon has not been ignored. Last Wednesday, the *Chicago Daily News* front-paged a new series on "Violence In Public Schools." Refusing to acknowledge this kind of editorial one-upmanship by its afternoon competitor, Chicago's *American* screamed into print Friday with an eight-column banner head:

ACTION DUE ON SCHOOL VIOLENCE

Hoping it will be able to claim credit for subsequent remedial action, the *American* called a conference of civic leaders for Friday and, true to its lilywhite orientation, listed only white civic leaders and ignored Chicago's Negro community completely. The reason is obvious: Most of the violence in the schools stems from Negro kids. If Negro leaders were invited, some of them might want to start discussing *why* this violence exists instead of just sending them all to jail, which the *American* will probably support.

Violence in our public schools is a terrible indictment of us all. It exposes the inadequacies and sloppy administration of our school superintendent, whom we permit to stay among us, it exposes the callousness and indifference of parents, it exposes inefficient, weak principals, and it highlights the whole problem of the young "unreachables" in our society.

Violence in our schools is not due solely to pupils. While ninety-eight per cent of our teachers are outstanding in their professional commitment, there are a few rotten apples.

In the past week, the Chicago *Daily Defender* published two stories: one in which a teacher publicly threatened to beat up a boy for staying out because of the boycott (and the teacher admitted the threat to the boy's parents!) and the other in which a teacher beat a child about the face with a ruler.

How do you think children react when they see a teacher commit an act of violence? How do you think the children in a school respond when the story spreads from pupil to pupil? How do you think the parents of the pupils in that school react to just one act of violence by a teacher?

This is not to remotely suggest that stern discipline is not necessary or desirable, because it is. One of the mistakes our schools have been making is coddling some of these little incorrigibles when they should have a paddle applied to their rumps. I believe in spankings and I believe in administering a school system with a firm but understanding and sympathetic hand. But I think when teachers lose their tempers and begin assaulting pupils in fits of unrestraint, then the whole concept of legitimate corporal punishment has been violently abused. Spank 'em, but don't try to mutilate 'em.

Violence in our schools is a problem to which we must all dedicate ourselves. As far as the *Defender* is concerned, many of Chicago schools' most insidious difficulties will disappear overnight when Superintendent of Schools Willis is removed or is forced to resign.

Until that happy day occurs, our problems in the public schools will multiply and exfoliate in geometric progression to the racial segregation and racial antipathies with which Willis has administratively inoculated our school system.

And it is an unspeakable insult to the Negro communities of both Chicago and New York City for the newspapers to inferentially attempt to lay the blame for this suddenly rediscovered violence in our public schools at the feet of the boycotts—our last weapon in the battle for freedom from Willis-ism and second-class citizenship.

March 1964

What Welfare Does to Us As a Race of People

NEXT TO NEWBURGH, N.Y.'s, pre-Magna Carta attitude toward the dimensions of human frailties, no welfare program has ignited more controversy than Washington, D.C.'s.

Instead of an expected model operation in the nation's capital, a muddled, inefficient, highly racist pathogen has been injected into our social bloodstream.

Instead of solving human problems, the District welfare program has been creating them by the bucketload.

So, 764,000 of us have been forced to watch helplessly as four men—three white and one colored—busy themselves in a game of musical chairs with the stomachs of hungry children.

The first man, one of the Senate's least admired, Robert C. Byrd of West Virginia, has yet to publicly affirm his belief in the equal rights of colored Americans. Like many Senators who have a mystical propensity for riding to fame on the backs of political diseases, Byrd found himself one in welfare cheats and has been having a ball. (Have you heard him express comparable concern for welfare cheats in the state of West Virginia?)

A second man, District Board of Commissioners President Walter N. Tobriner, is now body and soul the political soulmate of Dixie Senators. He simply doesn't care any longer about the problems of colored citizens.

A third man is the District's prized Machiavellian politician par excellence, Welfare Director Gerard M. Shea, administrator of a department completely lilywhite in its hierarchy and totally inefficient in its conceptualization of human needs.

The fourth man, the only colored person of the group, Commissioner John B. Duncan, is also the only one who is good in heart and sincere in his efforts in the welfare program as it affects colored people.

But Commissioner Duncan has shown himself unable to deal with the hard facts of welfare in the District.

His position of penalizing hungry children for the transgressions of their parents is a heartless one, yet all of us who are colored know what he is attempting to accomplish.

While his goal is to weed out the cheats and grafters, one doesn't burn an entire house down to roast a pig.

Still, these other three men are going to impale Duncan on the sword of political shame—and with the help of the anti-John Duncan *Washington Post* already—unless he develops the courage to act decisively and forthrightly.

All four men appear to be searching for a solution to the welfare enigma of the District.

However, what worries many of us is what welfare is doing to us as a race of people.

Welfare is warping our initiative.

It's destroying our economic potential.

It's denigrating our political power.

The Eve Edstroms and the *Washington Post*'s don't really care whether colored people ever get off welfare. They are not concerned with the debilitating effects of welfare on us as a race of people.

Without realizing it, we have become, in many respects, a race of a "handful of 'gimme' and a 'mouthful' of much-obliged."

One set of correlating statistics cannot be denied.

As the number of racial barriers have tumbled in America, the percentage of colored people on welfare all over the country has increased.

Naturally, this twin social process has partial explanations. White people are abandoning welfare rolls because it takes a pretty dumb white man not to be able to find a job these days.

But the colored man hasn't been able to make his re-entry into the orbit of employment with the same despatch.

And so we continue to witness the queer relationship of more jobs available to colored people, yet more colored people going on welfare.

Another explanation for this phenomenon lies within ourselves—our indifference and lack of training.

Who's prepared to maintain that we as a race have done everything in our power to prepare ourselves for the doors which are opening faster than we are able to enter?

We haven't, and there has been little leadership in the colored community to give us direction.

A tragic instance inheres in the District, where this city's first colored Commissioner has sat by and allowed himself to be upstaged, out-maneuvered, and out-thought by three of the country's prime examples of political mediocrity.

Even if Commissioner Duncan is unwilling to take on the power structure of this city (and that *Washington Post* editorial which rapped his political fanny good this week just to convince him once and for all where his real problems are), at least he ought to take his case to the colored community.

It's up to him to come forth and lay his cards on the table and tell us he needs our help—that welfare can sap our political strength, that our enemies include those same people who publicly tut-tut over our impoverished condition, but are frightened at the prospect of any real upward change in economic status.

Maybe we can't out-maneuver the Byrds, the Tobriners, and the Sheas, but at least we can take the initiative ourselves as a group of people and begin a city-wide program of educational and mental rehabilitation which will bestir us to resist the compulsive clinging to welfare mentality.

Relief rolls will continue to sap our moral fiber.

And it's up to people with positions of responsibility such as Commissioner Duncan to play a crucial role in communicating this fact to the city's 418,693 colored people.

February 1963

Negroes in Foreign Service: Are We Making Any Progress?

ONE OF THE FIRST QUESTIONS I asked President Kennedy when I started attending his press conferences in 1962 was: "Do you think there should be more Negro ambassadors?"

The late President replied firmly that he did and not only should there be more Negro ambassadors, but Negroes all through the top echelons in the State Department and in AID (Agency for International Development), too.

Under his administration, the State Department was represented abroad by three Negro ambassadors (the largest number at any one time in the history of this country), three Negro Deputy Assistant Secretaries of State (including Carl Rowan in public affairs), a

Negro special assistant to the Deputy Undersecretary for Administration, and a raft of appointments to higher positions for several Negro foreign service officers abroad.

Despite this remarkable and historic breakthrough for the "brother" in the foreign service, the picture remains bleak and very bad indeed today.

And I think one of the principal reasons young Negroes have not exhibited a sudden major interest in the foreign service is due to the State Department's historical racist policies which, though no longer operative and controlling, are nevertheless exceedingly influential in appointments and promotions.

A couple of months ago, *Defender* publisher John H. Sengstacke was one of about thirty-five top-level Negro business men, presidents of colleges, civic leaders, club women and educators invited to the second State Department Conference on Equal Opportunity.

The person responsible for the immediate implementation of a fairer employment policy for State is William J. Crockett, Deputy Undersecretary of State for Administration.

One of the problems worrying State is the lack of Negro applicants to take the foreign service examination. In fact, they have actually diminished in numbers since last September. In September, 1963, 189 Negroes in the entire U.S. took the foreign service exam. In March, 1964, only sixty-five Negroes applied and even worse, only seventeen Negroes applied to take the United States Information Agency's exam.

In short, Negroes are going backwards when it comes to an increasing involvement in the foreign service.

Even though it's still a dismal commentary on our interest in foreign affairs, Chicago led the country with ten Negro candidates for the exam. We even strutted past Washington, D.C., which had eight. New York City had seven, Atlanta had six, and Boston, with Harvard, Tufts, Simmons, Radcliffe, Boston University, and Boston College, only had three.

Why aren't more Negroes interested in foreign affairs? Why don't more Negroes concern themselves with foreign policy?

Granted, we as Negroes have got much to worry about at home, what with white backlash, Barry Goldwater, sorry Negro politicians, Negro Uncle Tom civil rights leaders, escalating juvenile delinquency, welfare, crime, and unemployment rates, educational inequities, Governor Wallace, and Ben Willis.

But we're Americans first and what our country does and looks like abroad, the posture it submits to the world in an ideological confrontation, should seriously command our interests. We are to the world what the world sees overseas in our embassies, in our USIA offices, and in our AID missions.

That image is essentially lilywhite—and it worries the hell out of me because I may criticize my country at home, but I certainly don't want to see us looking like bigots overseas.

Of course, the State Department simply must essay an even more vigorous effort than it is even now making to convince young Negroes there is a place for them in the foreign service and that they, too, can advance as easily as their white counterparts.

However, in the appointive process State hasn't fared too well, because State has this disturbing habit of promoting Negroes and creating a vacancy in the previous position which is then not filled by a Negro.

Thus, Chester Carter, former Deputy Assistant Secretary of State for Congressional Liaison, was promoted to Deputy Chief of Protocol; Samuel Z. Westerfield went from Deputy Assistant Secretary of State for Economic Affairs to the Bureau of African Affairs; and Carl Rowan resigned as ambassador to Finland to become director of USIA.

What's the net gain for Negroes? Zero. Carl's appointment, of course, was unusually brilliant. But we now only have two Negro ambassadors and Clifton Wharton in Norway is about to resign because of ill health. (We don't really count Mr. Wharton as a Negro because he'll tell you proudly in a minute he didn't get that appointment because he was a Negro. We jes' ain't ready.)

President Johnson should be appointing three or four Negroes as ambassadors now to show greater progress in this area than President Kennedy, who pointed the way for him as far as a total liberal philosophy in race relations is concerned. But LBJ is dragging his hands and displays no interest in more Negroes in foreign service. In fact, he's not only said nothing—he's done nothing.

Out of our present ninety-seven ambassadorships and two ministerships, only two are held by Negroes—Wharton and the fluent French-speaking poet and author, Mercer Cook, who was just transferred from Nigeria to Senegal, a brilliant switch since he and Africa's poet laureate, Leopold Senghor, will get along famously.

But the United States still presents a ninety-eight per cent lily-white image to the world with its ambassadors.

That is the same image it presents at home.

And maybe this is one big reason why more Negroes are *not* lining up for that foreign service exam.

June 1964

The People Hollered

SEPTEMBER FIFTEENTH, 1959, to the majority of people in this country, was just another Tuesday following another Monday.

But to Carmine G. DeSapio it was a black Primary Day which saw the first nail pounded in the coffin of his political career. Despite his personal victory as district leader and a retained balance of power on the New York County Democratic Committee, DeSapio is clearly on his way out.

All during the campaign, the blue-bearded leader kept repeating that the "people will speak" and decide who will be the leaders.

This little bit of glib cockiness recalled to mind an incident in our hometown of Hartford, Connecticut, a few years ago when the Democrats swept into the City Council with a crushing 7–2 majority. The City Manager, who is regarded as not being overly sympathetic to the Democratic party, was met the next day by one of the victorious Democrats.

Beaming, he asked the City Manager what he thought of the election results, to which the municipal official replied: "Well, I guess the people spoke."

"Spoke?" blurted the politician incredulously. "They were screaming and hollering!"

In New York City on Primary Day, September fifteenth, 1959, the people hollered.

And, the biggest noise was heard in Harlem.

They almost screamed themselves into bad health.

In a way, this was the fulfilment of a promise made by Adam Clayton Powell on another Primary Day.

That day was August eleventh, 1959, when he massacred Earl Brown's political future and won the Democratic congressional nomination.

This reporter couldn't help but recall the story he wrote then at two in the morning sitting alongside one of the greatest reporters we know, Al Duckett. (We had the joy for twenty-four hours of seeing *The Age* come out like a daily newspaper.)

These were the words this reporter set down in the early hours of that post-primary day, August eleventh, 1959:

> In a flush of victory early Wednesday morning, three different men said three different things.
>
> Powell, inhaling the sweet smell of success, said: "I will drive the bosses and Uncle Toms out of Harlem. This is the beginning of a new leadership. This is the end of Jack."
>
> Brown tried to soften the kidney punch by saying: "This is a personal victory for my opponent, but not against the Democratic Party."
>
> DeSapio, who refused to comment on Powell's prediction of Jack's demise when questioned by *The Age,* confused

> things even more by saying: "The Democratic Party will now unite in Harlem as it is united throughout the state and work together with the people to an outstanding victory this fall."
>
> The question is obvious. Who's right?

Thirteen months later, the question can be asked again: "Who was right?"

DeSapio was right because the Democratic Party did unite in Harlem and stayed united . . . behind Adam Clayton Powell.

Brown was right because it was a personal victory for Powell.

Powell was right because he fulfilled his promise to drive "the bosses and the Uncle Toms out of Harlem." But Powell was also wrong on one count. It was not "the end of Jack." In fact, Jack is very much alive politically.

Besides making Powell the undisputed leader in Harlem, the primary results did another odd thing: They made Borough President Hulan E. Jack still more powerful. Jack is the only district leader in Harlem on whom Tammany Hall can rely on to go straight down the line as a party man and with whom they know they can do business. The fact that Jack successfully withstood the Powell onslaught also speaks well for his ability as a political leader.

But the one thing that everybody in New York City must recognize whether they like this fact or not is that Adam Clayton Powell is still the most important person to thousands of Negro voters.

With all of his shortcomings, he is still the man in whom Negroes have placed their political trust.

We think it is important to state this fact in just that manner because there seems to be growing in New York City among the self-styled liberals the belief that they and they alone have ultimate truth by the tail and unless one houses himself within their troglodytic cubicle of ideas, then, you ain't no liberal.

In short, we're getting just plain tired of Mrs. Roosevelt, the *New York Post* (both of whom are the Negro's friend, but on their terms), the respectable *New York Times,* and all the other New York City liberals who cluck-cluck like old hens every time Powell rises up and knocks off another political victory.

We're upset about Powell victories, too, because we'd like to see Negroes go to the polls and turn out the Democrats who have given Negro voters one of the rawest deals in political history. We'd like to see Negroes turn their backs completely on the Democratic Party and recognize the party for the undisguised phonies they are—and that includes the Democratic Party in New York City.

But Negroes haven't. They just continue to vote Democratic out of habit. If they're to pursue this tack, we'd much prefer that they at least turn over their confidence to a man who, if he does nothing else, is probably the biggest, most articulate, the most effective gadfly the Negroes have in the narrowing arena of civil rights.

Until the self-styled liberals can appreciate this fundamental fact about the suction of Adam Clayton Powell's attraction for Negroes, then they are not going to be able to convince Negroes that they are more of a friend of theirs than ol' jowl-hanging Eastland.

Furthermore, the liberals ought to be turning handsprings over Powell's victory in Harlem. He, more than any single person in New York City, helped to demolish DeSapio's aura of invincibility. Had Powell not won, those lil' ol' insignificant victories won by the insurgents would have looked like three cans of sardines in the A & P supermarket.

As far as DeSapio is concerned in his cocoon of disbelief, maybe the people did speak. But, up here in Harlem, they hollered, and come 1961, they're just liable to shout their way into a Negro being nominated for mayor.

September 1959

Foreign Policy by Pepsi-Cola

"WE THINK IT (the U. S. State Department) stinks.

"We have a hell of an influence abroad. If we want to disseminate information, we could do it faster than the State Department. And the Communists know it."

These sassy words of wisdom were uttered by Alfred N. Steele, board chairman of the Pepsi-Cola Company, last week at a meeting in Albany, New York.

No better criticism of our foreign policy has been stated than Mr. Steele's opinion.

He is, we submit, a hundred per cent correct.

Though we would not surround our criticism of the State Department with such colorful language, the plain fact is that our foreign policy is today, and has been for some time, an abominable failure.

The United States State Department pursues an ox-cart foreign policy governed by a stone-age mentality for a space-age situation.

New countries have come into existence, the balance of power has shifted from Europe to Asia and Africa, a world-wide menace continues to confront us, and the bleary-eyed diplomats in Foggy Bottom still look at the world with eighteenth-century rose-colored glasses.

Times have changed, but the State Department hasn't.

The twentieth century has suddenly become the century of the jet-age, the atomic bomb, the explorations into space.

With these new technological changes have come swift alterations in our ways of living and, above all, our ways of merchandising.

The only people who have managed to keep pace with these changes outside of the atomic scientists and the industrialists have been the advertising geniuses on Madison Avenue.

They have to stay in business and they have to keep the companies they represent in business. So, they experiment, try new ideas, new formats, new layouts, and new approaches.

Only one thing motivates their work.

Money.

Perhaps we ought to do one of two things to develop a successful foreign policy: turn it over to American business men; or pay diplomats on their ability to get results.

Take Pepsi-Cola or Coca-Cola for example.

Nowhere, but nowhere, are there two symbols more universally known and accepted in almost the entire world. (Just last Saturday one of *The Age* employees noticed an odd bottle in the Coca-Cola rack. It had "Coca-Cola" spelled out in Arabic.)

Mr. Steele is right. His company could get results. When he referred to the spread of information, he declared this meant American influence and the dissemination of its influence in specific market areas where his company operated.

Even on a limited basis, it would be a good idea to let Mr. Steele try. One thing we'll wager, Mr. Steele wouldn't lose any markets or countries to the Communists.

And this is the one thing our foreign policy has not been able to prevent.

Despite the fact that today we have a total of five multilateral treaties with forty-two countries and four bilateral treaties, all of which commit us to defend them against communism, we still haven't been able to check its spread.

We're actually committed to defending the whole world and the whole world doesn't really give a darn.

Our foreign policy, particularly post-World War II, has been solely negative.

Beginning with the Truman Doctrine, the Marshall Plan, "containment," NATO, SEATO, the Baghdad Pact, and Anzus on up to "brinkmanship" and "massive retaliation," we have conducted a foreign policy by reaction—reacting to what the Communists were doing around the world.

Our failure has been in not being positive.

If one can accept for a moment a tentative definition of foreign policy, we can test this statement. By foreign policy, we mean the things a country does in the world which enables its constitutional values to survive.

Our values are not surviving. In few places do people respect and follow the American way of life. Oh, they like our foreign aid (So, who's turning down food these days?), but they don't accept either the premise or logic of American economic philosophy, i.e., the capitalist way of life.

Perhaps if we had a foreign policy based solely on the ability to get results (If a country goes Communist, you don't get paid.), we might have more success than what we've been having.

Mr. Steele should be given a chance to spread a little much needed American influence abroad.

He'd probably do a darn sight better job than the so-called career foreign specialists who have used only feet and comparatively little brains so far.

June 1960

Funny Thing About Us Colored Folks—We're So Much Like White Folks

FOR SOME QUEER, unestablished reason, the white man in America expects his colored brother to be more noble, more honest, more virtuous and more moral than he is.

Every virtue the white man is incapable of possessing, every decent instinct which has deserted white people, and every benevolent attitude which is foreign to the white race is somehow expected to reside in the Negro race.

White people don't like us because we commit so many crimes—you know, muggings, purse-snatchings, robberies, stabbings, and murders.

But we learn it all from them.

In fact, white people ought to really dislike us for being so inefficient about our crime.

Negroes don't have any Cosa Nostra, which the whole United States government is fighting.

We don't control any billion-dollar vice ring in Chicago, which sucks the moral blood of this city and worries the hell out of the *Daily News.*

Negroes don't run around Chicago blowing up automobiles and stuffing dead bodies into car trunks.

We haven't handcuffed any white alderman and shot him in the back of the head.

And none of us colored folks ever assassinated a President of the United States.

Then there are those bad Negro gangs on the South Side and New York's Harlem and Brooklyn's Bedford-Stuyvesant and they have gang wars and do each other in. But we've never fought any Civil War which has torn this country in two.

White people say a lot of us are dirty and live in filthy buildings. That's true—and they own most of the buildings. Sure, some of us depreciate property values. You ever see the way that poor white trash from the Appalachian valleys lives in Chicago? Turn your stomach.

Unwed mothers? We're loaded with them. Negro women on the South Side are having illegitimate babies every day. They any worse than Elizabeth Taylor, who made an international public spectacle of her immorality? What about Christine Keeler, who almost toppled an entire government? Our colored gals are pikers compared to her. Then there are all those broads involved in the Bobby Baker scandal. Ain't no colored gals in that mess.

Finally, Negroes are accused of disunity in the civil rights struggle. White people just can't understand why all of our leaders aren't united and can't agree on tactics and strategy. The absence of a pachydermic monolith of opinion in the Negro community bewilders white people, particularly their newspapers.

Shucks, all of their leaders don't agree.

How much agreement are you going to find on race relations, religion, economic progress, and foreign policy among Senator Barry Goldwater, Walter Reuther, Cardinal Spellman, Norman Thomas, Governor George C. Wallace, Henry Ford, and Robert Welch?

The reason there are divisions, schisms, and factions in the Negro community is because there are divisions, schisms, and factions in the white community. They can't even get together to do in the "brother."

White folks have got their nuts and psychopaths and we've got ours.

White folks have got their brilliant statesmen and we have ours.

White folks have got their lazy, no-good, phony, do-nothing-until-we-get-scared politicians and we've got ours.

White folks have got their brown-nosers and we've got our Uncle Toms.

White folks have got their racists, and, because we want everything they've got, we have ours.

White folks have got their simple business men who go around making asinine statements just because they've made a million dollars and I'll be darned if we haven't got ours, too.

It's just about the healthiest fact of life for American democracy that there can flourish within the Negro community that happy diversity of opinion about how the race problem should be solved which is characterized by the respective philosophies of Representative Adam Clayton Powell (my man all the way), the National Urban League's Whitney Young (a truly fine human being), S. B. Fuller (puts his foot in his mouth, but I still love him), the Honorable Elijah Muhammad (He's given many thousands of Negroes new pride in themselves.), the Reverend J. H. Jackson (a preacher's preacher and true man of God), and Alderman Kenneth Campbell (who has launched his campaign to take over Congressman Dawson's political leadership in the Negro community by knocking civil rights groups).

None of them are all right and certainly none of them are all wrong. There is a truth in all of their positions—more truth in some than in others, but nevertheless truth.

Funny thing about us colored folks—we sure are just like white folks, aren't we?

A Thinking Man's Racial Prejudice

THERE'S A CLEVER LITTLE cigarette commercial that happens to appeal to our rational senses.

If we were to use it to interview a distinguished person on one of our most compelling obsessions, racial prejudice, it would go something like this:

"Hello, there! Say, those are some wonderful plaques and citations you have on your wall. What are they for?"

"Well, I got this one here from the National Conference of Christians and Jews for spreading interracial good will. This one here is from the Urban League. The one next to it is from the NAACP for outstanding contributions in the field of race relations. That large citation over there is from the National Negro College Fund, and. . . ."

"Say, you seem to be quite an expert on race relations, as shown by all of those awards and tributes. Are you dedicated to interracial good will?"

"No, I'm really the president of the White Citizens' Council. You see, I'm a man who thinks for himself."

And hundreds of prominent persons indulge in just this type of independent cogitation.

What could be described as a "thinking man's racial prejudice" is really unbridled hypocrisy. An emotional disease which afflicts large numbers of people in the field of race relations, it unfortunately incapacitates an equally large number of elected officials.

For one thing, they're all people who "think for themselves." Down deep inside, they don't believe in honest equality for the Negro any more than Arabs believe there should be an Israel. Because of this deep-seated hostility, they half-heartedly fight the battle of the bigots while masquerading as the Negro's friend.

Take, for example, the mayor of a large city which is continually exploding in racial tensions. The mayor can proclaim annually on Brotherhood Day, I Am An American Day, and all the other I-Dig-You-Dad-Because-You're-Different-From-Me days his concern for his fellow man. But, if he doesn't act in time of racial crises like he believes in human equality, all of the proclamations in the world will be as meaningless as "disestablishmentarianism" spelled backwards.

One thing cannot be denied. In the field of race relations, too many self-styled liberals are undermining the down-to-earth progress which is being made. By alleging their concern for the Negro's welfare, they're able to pass themselves off as friends. An enemy you can fight, but, pray tell, how do you fight a friend?

There's nothing worse than an award for "doing good." Once an elected official, business man, or labor leader gathers himself a whole roster of "human relations" citations, there isn't a thing you can do to convince him—or the public—that this man is essentially insincere when he drags his feet on the integration issue.

The "thinking man's racial prejudice" is the mask behind which our most successful white phonies and colored Uncle Toms hide. Too often the lover of his fellow man is busy preaching good will while his actions are accomplishing much more in the opposite direction. This they do simply by sitting on their hands in a racial crisis refusing to take sides, or when things really get hot—appointing a committee.

"Well, sir, seeing you sitting at your desk and listening to you talk about the Negro, you must be the mayor of a large northern city."

"Not quite. I'm the leader of the mob that took care of Mack Charles Parker. You see, I'm a man who thinks for himself."

Open Letter to Mother on Staying With *Afro*

EDITORIAL NOTE: *Mr. Stone and his sisters have long referred affectionately to their mother as "Hogbear." An extraordinarily beautiful woman, she nevertheless has always been unmercifully kidded by her offspring that she is so ugly she resembles the product of a union between a bear and a hog.*

Darling Hogbear:

You were so happy and proud of my impending appointment as public affairs officer for USIA to Tanganyika.

And now I'm not going.

After an intensified agonizing reappraisal, I turned this fine offer down and will remain as editor of the Washington *Afro.*

Why? I guess it's because I'm still an idealist and believe in people. And "the people" came through like champs last week.

A small group of wonderful folks went out into the community last week and within the incredibly short span of forty-eight hours raised over $12,000 in advertising contracts and subscriptions!

These were turned over to Dr. Carl Murphy (my boss and as great a human being as has ever been made—and if that's "brown-nosing," let folks make the most of it). The purpose of this move was to influence the *Afro-American* management to raise my salary and keep me here.

More money was of course important, mother. You've long known how we were struggling for the last year. But what overwhelmed me—as it did Dr. Carl—was this magnificent outpouring of solidly unified community support. And the people putting their money where their mouths were. It was just impossible to turn my back on this kind of love and respect within this community.

Two weeks ago, a committee under the chairmanship of Congressman Diggs had been formed to give Louise and me a testimonial. (A great idea, because I had planned to take all the food left over from the banquet and give it to Louise's family—you know how poor those Davises are!)

During the meeting, attended by some eighty people—business men, politicians, civic leaders, white folks, colored folks—it was decided to make an effort to keep me here.

Originally, I was scheduled to be sworn in on Monday, March fourth. But a few reports on my background (I did finally pass my security check.) were not in. USIA decided to postpone my swearing-in until March eleventh.

Had I been sworn in on March fourth as previously scheduled, I would be with the USIA right now.

But the week's delay gave this committee enough time to get out and work. And they swung!

By Thursday evening, they had reached their quota. Friday morning, Representative Diggs and Miss Flaxie Pinkett (I'm going to tell you more about this gal later.) met with Dr. Carl. He summoned me to Baltimore as soon as they left and made me an offer. I told him I would let him know in an hour.

Then I proceeded to go home and sit with Louise while the two of us wrestled with a decision. It was hell. I was so upset I couldn't eat. I talked on the phone to a couple of close friends who, like me, appreciated the dilemma and were of little help. After a long session with four very close friends at Flaxie's house, I made my decision and wobbled to a telephone to inform Dr. Carl. By then, I was just an emotional shell. As you can see, I'm in good shape now. (I've been out of my strait-jacket for two whole days now!)

You always taught us that whatever God wanted, would be. And that what happened always happened for the best. I can't help but feel that God intervened to delay my swearing-in so this would happen. Don't you agree?

As a newspaper reporter, I guess I make a good pinochle player (the same to you, Billy Simpson!) because I had no idea there was this kind of support in the community for the Washington *Afro* or the type of editorial and reporting approach to the news I had postured.

We've enjoyed a nice increase in circulation, but we're no threat to *The New York Times.* Most interesting and so gratifying to me personally was the widespread acceptance and endorsement of the militant, hard-hitting editorializing and exposé-type of reporting on which we have relied.

None of the successes we've enjoyed during the last year, however, could have ever been accomplished without the great reporting of Ed Peeks, Mary Stratford, Rose Marie Tyler, Charlie Tyler, Les Ledbetter, and that cute little assistant of mine, Jackie Taylor. I'll match all six of them with any group of six reporters on any newspaper in Washington, D.C., and they'll out-think, out-write, out-report, and out-edit them any day in the week. They're a bunch of real pros.

But, mother, let me tell you about colored unity. You know how deeply I feel about us as a group of people getting together to do something, to pool resources within our community to achieve an end. In this case, they did it. And they were joined by white people, many of whom are close friends.

Segregated effort is no goal to seek. But the spiritual genesis and inspiration for achievement must materialize in the colored community more often. And when it does, we should bring in as many white people as we can to join us. We can develop excellence, too.

While there were a host of wonderful people participating in this successful movement, there is a consensus among most that Miss Flaxie Pinkett, one of our town's truly outstanding business women, was the guiding genius. Flaxie was literally all over the place, talking, cajoling, organizing, synthesizing, and pulling together. What a woman! (Down, Louise!)

I don't want to leave you with the impression that your son is some kind of fair-haired boy and that everybody just loves him, because they don't.

One doesn't hit as hard and as often as I do without acquiring enemies. And I've got a private collection of them here. Combined, they're pretty powerful—the Board of Trade, the Washington *Post* (They hate me with a "perfect hatred," to quote David in the Psalms.), the U.S. Civil Rights Commission (that's right, they're not happy about me either), Commissioner John B. Duncan, and many of this city's "Uncle Toms" whom I think as dangerous as they do me.

For every action forward, there is a counter-action pushing that same force back. Resistance is an ecological fact of life.

But you know me, I have always enjoyed the confrontation of facts and issues. And these many, many wonderful people in this community have proved to me that we're pretty much on the right track—or at least headed in the right direction.

I hope you're happy about my staying.

A lot of people are. I could do some name-dropping from Vice President Johnson, three African ambassadors, and others right on down to a window washer who urged me to stay and then congratulated me on my decision. (Even my almost-to-be boss, Ed Murrow, in accepting my decision with deepest regrets, said he agreed with it.)

I'm proud of my people. This ol', lethargic Washington community went out, stirred itself, and did something.

How do I feel? Still weary, still a little awed by it all and thanking God every waking minute that He has blessed me with so many kind friends. Prayer meant much to me in these past few days.

So, back to the eternal crusade for human dignity, the denudement of hypocrisy, the exposé of dishonesty and Uncle Tomism.

Every day is Saturday night—and as one of the "brothers" once put it: "It's Saturday night, I'm colored, and I'm dangerous!"

March 1963

The Politics of *La Negritude*

DURING THE LAST FEW WEEKS, a virtually non-stop procession of important African leaders has visited the United States. Their purposes in coming here have been as divergent as their personalities, their countries, and their positions in government. But they have all clung tenaciously to a common goal: a determination to meet American Negroes.

No man has expressed the *raison d'être* of this desire more eloquently than the honorable Jaja Anucha Wachuku, Speaker of the Federal House of Representatives of Nigeria.

"We in Nigeria want to know you, your men, your women, your business people," he declared before a group of Negro civic leaders in Harlem less than three weeks ago. "We want you to help us build our country because we know if you benefit financially, we will benefit. Across the oceans, thousands of miles away, Negroes in America and Nigerians will join hands."

Jean Weregemere, assistant to the Belgian Congo Prime Minister Patrice Lumumba, expressed almost identical sentiments to a similar group two weeks ago. "I am truly comfortable for the first time during my visit to America," he declared, "now that I am here among you. We are all brothers."

However, to fulfill this international mission of "getting-to-know-you, getting-to-know-all-about-you" has not been easy for the Africans. Rather it has been comparable to running an army obstacle course with wet clothes on, heavy boots, and two bags of cement under each arm. Not only do most Africans have relatively—and unfortunately—few contacts among American Negroes, but there has been a shrewdly calculated official effort to prevent the two groups from developing close ties. The United States State Department has persistently refused to schedule visits of African leaders with American Negroes. As one high West African official declared recently in private: "I just became tired of seeing only white people and I went out of my way to seek Negroes and I found them. But it wasn't easy."

At the same time, there have been rumors, stories, and even newspaper articles (one just this past Sunday in *The New York Times*) to the effect that Africans and American Negroes have difficulty communicating. Some reporters have submitted that Africans consider it racial discrimination in reverse if American Negroes are sent to Africa in official positions.

"This is too fantastic even to comment on," said one East African official. "We must realize why the white man tries to do this."

One thing, however, is certain. Sweeping the black races throughout the world is a new, proud sociological sensitivity to the color black. African, West Indian, Afro-American, Latin-American Negro—all are aware of the black man's new balance of power in the world today. All are concerned about the black man's struggle for human decency in all countries.

Whenever two black people meet each other and establish rapport, despite the diversity of their cultures or the prohibitions of language barriers, there is a kind of racial mystique operating. This mystique has been labeled *la negritude.* Translated, *la negritude,* a concept first discussed and written about by French West African intellectuals, means the black man's reaffirmation of ties to each other because of color, because of common suffering. It defies particularizing as does any racial consciousness, but *la negritude* has at least two components: Politically, it is black brother helping black brother to be free everywhere in the world, even if it is nothing more than words of encouragement; psychologically, it is a feeling of kinship for Africans and those of African ancestry.

La negritude has long existed in one form or another in all nationalities, all races stung with the humiliation of minority treatment. While the differences are more of degree than kind, it is the same international empathy that gives world definition to Zionism or causes India to press for racial equality for Indians in South Africa. Only a citizen's first love of country keeps such racial feelings from getting out of hand.

La negritude continues to sharpen in intensity and spread its influence. Within a very few years, the international scales of power will tilt.

Africa and *la negritude* will decide the direction.

August 1960

What Makes White Right?

IS IT THE COLOR WHITE sui generis which makes it right?

Or is it the military and political power of the white race that defines rectitude for all peoples—regardless of race, creed, or color?

We live in a society which is structured on a most fundamental and universal premise: If it's white, it's right.

In this conceptual framework, "white" is more than just a color. It's a civilization, a frame of mind.

When we were kids, we used to chant a sassy ditty:

If you're white, you're all right.
If you're yellow, you're mellow.
If you're brown, you can stick around.
If you're black, step way back.

We thought this was cute.

But what a bunch of subconscious bigots we were, so full of self-hatred, so full of self-shame.

Without realizing it, we had incorporated into our thinking the two conceptual antipodes which placed the color white at one end of the scale of social acceptability and black at the other end, representing rejected untouchableness.

Rather than dare question the political doctrine and intellectual rationale of white supremacy, we simply adopted it.

We joined the majority group which had already colored us a "contrast conception."

Few people have expressed this sad truth more ably than Lewis C. Copeland, who wrote a marvelous article back in 1939 called "The Negro as Contrast Conception."

Read these truths:

> Relations between white and black people in the South have given rise to a distinctive conception of the Negro. As a natural outcome of the juxtaposition of two divergent ethnic groups, white people have sharply distinguished themselves from black people. It is not surprising then to find that there has been a marked tendency to conceive of the Negro in terms of contrast. In fact, one may speak of the Negro as a "contrast conception". . . .
>
> The popular conception of Negro character is dramatically portrayed in folk beliefs, fables, anecdotes, jokes, songs, and literature. To sound natural the anecdote must be told in the dialect which whites attribute to Negroes and which is believed to be peculiar to them. In striking contrast to the colored characters, the white characters speak in the most polished and stilted phrases. The things white people laugh at in Negro life are significant, for these are the traits that are considered distinctive.

It always disturbed me that ten per cent of America's population could grow up in a culture insulted and ridiculed nightly by two white men who were regarded as great comedians.

The stigma of "Amos 'n' Andy" gave American culture a blood transfusion of racism it will never completely throw off.

But if you place "Amos 'n' Andy" in the catalogues of history, it is almost of contemporary racist vintage.

America was a johnny-come-lately when it came to polarizing black and white.

For centuries, Europeans had been doing it with notorious success.

A white slave could escape his bondage and be absorbed into society's mainstream. A black slave was always the "heathen."

In order to justify enslaving the colored heathens, however, an ethical rationale had to be discovered.

Gaines De Sepulveda, a brilliant theologian, helped pave the way in 1550 when he debated Las Cases at Valladolid on the right of Spaniards to wage wars of conquest against the Indians.

Argued Sepulveda, it's all right to enslave the Indians "1.) because of the gravity of their sins. . . . 2.) because of the rudeness of their heathen and barbarous natures, which oblige them to serve those of more elevated natures, such as the Spaniards possess; 3.) for the spread of the faith."

The Portuguese in Mozambique and Angola readily accept this logic today in their tenacious perpetuation of these two countries as colonies.

However, white supremacy has even deeper historical roots than a debate in 1550. This all-embracing doctrine is timeless, extending back into mores, customs, and almost petty nuances of habit.

So much so that a mere thirty-five per cent of the world's population of 3.1 billion has been able to con the other sixty-five per cent or 2.0 billion colored people that the thirty-five per cent were, in fact, their superiors—and still are.

I've read few things which have spelled out so eloquently the doctrine of "white makes right" than the passage from Herman Melville's classic, *Moby Dick.*

In discussing the neurotic fascination Captain Ahab had for Moby

Dick, Melville does a delightful delineation on the white-right syndrome in Chapter Forty-Two, titled "The Whiteness of the Whale."

The historical greatness of what it is to be white is reflected in this passage:

> Aside from these more obvious considerations touching Moby Dick, which could not but occasionally awaken in any man's soul some alarm, there was another thought, or rather vague, nameless horror concerning him, which at times by its intensity completely overpowered all the rest. . . .
>
> It was the whiteness of the whale that above all things appalled me. . . .
>
> Though in many natural objects, whiteness refiningly enhances beauty, as if imparting some special virtue of its own, as in marbles, japonicas, and pearls; and though various nations have in some way recognised a certain royal pre-eminence in this hue! given the barbaric, grand old Kings of Pegu placing the title 'Lord of the White Elephants' above the modern kings of Siam unfurling the same snow-white quadruped in the royal standard; and the Hanoverian flag bearing the one figure of a snow-white charger! and the great Austrian Empire, Caesarian, heir to overlording Rome, having for the imperial color the same imperial hue; and though this pre-eminence in it applies to the human race itself, giving the white man ideal mastership over every dusky tribe; and though besides, all this, whiteness has been even made significant of gladness, for among the Romans a white stone marked a joyful day; and though in other mortal sympathies and symbolizings, this same hue is made the emblem of many touching, noble things—the innocence of brides, the benignity of age; though among the Red Men of America the giving of the white belt of wampum was the deepest pledge of honor; though in many climes, whiteness typifies the majesty of Justice in the

> ermine of the Judge, and contributes to the daily state of kings and queens drawn by milk-white steeds; though even in the higher mysteries of the most august religions it has been made the symbol of the divine spotlessness and power; by the Persian fire worshippers, the white forked flame being held the holiest on the altar; and in the Greek mythologies, Great Jove himself being made incarnate in a snow-white bull; and though to the noble Iroquois, the midwinter sacrifice of the sacred White Dog was by far the holiest festival of their theology, that spotless, faithful creature being held the purest envoy they could send to the Great Spirit with the annual tidings of their own fidelity; and though directly from the Latin word for white, all Christian priests derive the name of one part of their sacred vesture, the alb or tunic, worn beneath the cassock; and though among the holy pomps of the Romish faith, white is specially employed in the celebration of the Passion of our Lord; though in the Vision of St. John, white robes are given to the redeemed, and the four-and-twenty elders stand clothed in white before the great white throne and the Holy One that sitteth there white like wool; yet for all these accumulated associations, with whatever is sweet, and honorable, and sublime, there yet lurks an elusive something in the innermost idea of this hue, which strikes more of panic to the soul than that redness which affrights in blood.

Indeed, not only the country, but western civilization, is still quite safe. White folks are still on top.

And white is still right because history says so. But y'all just never did know why before, did you?

On Having a Second Daughter

FOR ONE HUNDRED AND EIGHTY MILLION Americans, the biggest news this week was astronaut John Glenn's spiralling around the earth faster than a paramour leaving a bedroom.

But for two other red, brown, and blue Americans (my pretty wife, Louise and me), the headlines in our hearts were being written by Allegra Esther Stone, who weighed in at a sassy seven pounds and eight ounces.

This is the second girl for me and the implications are frightening.

Percentage-wise, it lessens my chances, of course, of having a boy. I'm also helping women to take over the world. Run for your lives, men.

I like these conceited towers of masculinity who have already had nine boys in a row and who slap me on the back, and exclaim: "That's okay, Chuckie, boy. Try again in a couple of years."

At the rate I'm going, I'll have to borrow somebody's chromosomes to beef up these sagging genes so I can make a C. Sumner Stone, III.

You know, no matter how much pain women suffer or how groggy they are—man, they can always function like a general.

I was in my wife's room when she came out of "recovery" after having slept through the whole delivery process. She was still in a semi-opiated state when she began to remind me of certain things to do.

Weak and exhausted, she could hardly talk or move. Then, all of a sudden, she sat up—"Hand me a pencil!"—and proceeded to write down a list of instructions and orders that would have made General Patton envious. The annual budget? Nothing compared to the reams of paper this kid used to outline my life for the next forty-eight hours. And the baby wasn't even four hours old.

When I called Dr. Carl Murphy and told him the news ("It looks like I'm trying to follow in your footsteps."), he said to give Louise his best and she wouldn't be doing anything until she had five. (Dr. Carl has five daughters.) The way the Murphys are working me, I'll consider it a major scientific feat if I can just *live* as long as Dr. Carl, let alone have five daughters!

The one thing which has touched me deeply these last few days has been the love and concern of friends.

I'm convinced now that people walk around with a whole lot of love in their hearts waiting to be used. The moment a baby is born, or a dear one passes, this love just flows out toward you and kind of cradles you in a sea of tenderness. It's this love that tempers you and keeps you going.

I know—because there were times during these past few days when I didn't know which end was up. So many people were so wonderful, so kind, so helpful.

And poor little Krishna. This little gal ate out so much at various friends' houses she'd wake up in the morning, look at me, and ask, "Go bye bye?" But if we hadn't done that she would have developed a pizza-pie-tuna-fish-sandwich-soup-pork-and-beans complex because that's all we would have been eating. (I can cook—we just can't afford anything else.)

Allegra looks exactly like Kris when she was born and since Kris looks like me, here's another little girl who's got three strikes on her before she's even able to ask how long John Glenn was in orbit.

But I'm honestly thrilled about Allegra. Like other men, I've griped because I didn't have a boy. (It means I pay for the wedding —that I have to worry about whether the boy she's out with is as big a rogue as I was when I was his age.)

And I'll probably keep on trying, having more Krishnas, more Allegras, loving them all terribly, and never forgetting that the two greatest and sweetest influences in my life are my wife and my mother—and once upon a time, they were little girls, too.

Meanwhile, with my mother, my wife, my two daughters, and my wife's younger sister all living with me during the next few weeks, I've got my own built-in sorority house.

Democratic National Convention: Contrived Drama and One Big Bore

AFTER TWO DAYS of gaudy and politically tinseled existence, the Democratic National Convention is struggling desperately to escape its own manufactured boredom.

Despite the historical exuberance and almost built-in excitement that Democrats invariably bring to conventions, this particular orgy is already yawning to try and stay awake.

The guessing-game of "Pin the Tail on the Vice President" still goes on and delegates and reporters are manfully trying to make it appear as if somebody other than Senator Hubert Humphrey might get it.

But we all know how it's going to come out because we all know how Lyndon B. Johnson, politician and President, orchestrates. If the President had not wanted Humphrey as his running mate, the convention would have known it by Monday night. Johnson's political bluntness is legendary.

But he has permitted a kind of hourly momentum to build up for Humphrey and if he doesn't choose Humphrey, it's not only going to be the biggest political upset of the decade, it's going to dampen what little enthusiasm the delegates have been able to muster during the convention.

Even the fight over credentials for the two Mississippi delegations has an element of fatalism in it because, here again, everybody knows how it's all going to turn out. The President is determined not to have a floor fight and he has enough political resources at his command to prevent it.

In a strict political sense, everybody here who is involved in the Mississippi battle "has been reached." Pressure from the White House has touched and influenced all sides and parties and there is now only the necessity to go through the charade to salve everybody's pride.

This is not to cast aspersions on the honorable intentions of honorable men, because many of the Negroes who are taking part in the deliberations are agonizingly searching their souls, and I literally mean this to the point where one of the Negroes who probably had more to say on the final solution than any other Negro politician cornered me on the delegation floor Monday night just after the convention adjourned and said: "Chuck, you're about the most militant guy I know. What do you think ought to be done?"

When I replied that I thought the final solution should be whatever the Negro delegates from Mississippi would accept and that everybody then should go along with them because it was after all their battle, the politician smiled a wide grin of relief and said: "Good. And that just may happen." Obviously, somebody had given those folks from Mississippi a strong "talking to."

But the script for the convention was written well in advance and made, stamped, and published in Texas by Texans for America.

Nothing has been left to chance and the dominance of Texans at this convention in key roles is just a little disconcerting. Their drawls are not as honey-flavored as Georgia "y'alls," but they exhibit every bit of the Lone Star State's wide-openness and when one very important convention official walks into the room, one of his associates says, "You expect him to reach down on both sides of his pants and come up with two blazing .45's."

What a change from 1960 when the Kennedy forces, who ran the Democratic Convention then with the same ruthless efficiency and tight organization, still managed to inject that indefinable element we were to know as "style." The Kennedy people laid down the blueprint then on how to organize and run a convention. The difference now is that the leaders are not wearing button-down collars but ten-gallon hats.

Probably the most significant event of the convention to date has been the party given at the Jamaica Motel for the Negro delegates by the New Jersey delegation.

This was really a swinger—

Once again, everybody knew everybody else and those white people who attended (quite a few, but they had to sign "loyalty pledges" at the door that they were "brothers") watched in silent wonderment as all of the Negro delegates fraternized in the gayest of spirits around the attractively lighted swimming pool and "swapped lies."

It was another one of the "brothers'" combination NAACP-Urban League-Alpha Phi Alpha-Alpha Kappa Alpha-Omega Psi Phi-Links parties.

I crawled into bed at 5:00 A.M. and was up again at 8:00 to write this column and I promised myself as I dropped off to sleep that I must remember that I'm getting too old for this kind of nonsense. But what the hell, it's been such a dull convention, you had to do something to enliven it and, as usual, it was the "brother" who did.

August 1964

Mississippi Issue in Perspective—the Right Not to Compromise

When you've been on the inside and behind-the-scenes negotiations of a crucial issue for a straight forty-eight hours and then read a totally misrepresented account of the results by an uninformed, overweaned copy boy passing for a columnist, your editorial blood really percolates.

Joseph Alsop, who spent as much time on the convention floor as my five-year-old daughter, Krishna, leaped to some unjustified conclusions in a column last week concerning the Mississippi delegation seating compromise and was never farther off base.

Wrote Alsop, self-styled authority on everything from the next color of Pentagon uniforms to foreign policy decisions for Monaco: "There was only one hitch, caused by the Mississippi and Alabama delegations.

"Even that bit of bother looked ten times worse on television than it really was. The compromise concerning the Mississippi delegation was approved by voice vote, without any protest from the Southern delegations.

"Joseph Rauh and most of the Negro leaders also begged the Freedom Party delegates to accept the compromise. They were overruled only by the extremists in the group. The troubles on the floor were relatively insignificant compared to this central fact that the proposed compromise seemed reasonable to all but the extremists on both sides."

What an inaccurate crock of opinionated garbage that is. For Alsop's information and some of you who may have been misled by his account, here's what really happened:

By Monday night, the Credentials Subcommittee on the Mississippi delegation issue had failed to come up with any solution that would satisfy either side. Then, Representative Al Ullman, 50, from Oregon's Second District, came up with the compromise plan to seat all the traditional delegates if they sign a loyalty oath and allot two votes to Dr. Aaron Henry, chairman of the Freedom Democratic Party and the Reverend Edwin King, vice-chairman.

While this sounded reasonable, even the subcommittee members weren't sure if anybody would buy it and later that night two Credentials subcommittee members asked me if I would buy it. ("There are not many who are more militant than you, Stone," said one, "and I want to try this proposal out on you.")

My answer was to tell them I personally would support any decision the Freedom Democratic Party members would support and if they didn't go along, I would condemn neither them nor the initiators of the compromise. Incidentally, I felt the compromise was a sound one and regarded it as an important breakthrough even though it was far from achieving the political millenium.

Tuesday, members of the Credentials Subcommittee met with Walter Reuther in his hotel suite along with the Reverend Martin Luther King, Jr., Joseph Rauh (attorney for the Freedom Democratic Party) and a few others. Reuther, King, and Rauh all accepted the proposed compromise. Because Reuther's UAW-CIO has been a heavy contributor to the Freedom Democratic Party, because Rauh had worked aggressively on a no-holds-barred basis to get the Negroes seated, because the Reverend had spent considerable time and energy helping the Freedom Party and because all three had great influence and respect among the sixty Negroes and four whites in the Freedom Party, it was natural to assume that the Freedom Party would accept the suggestion from these three men of unchallengeable dedication and commitment in the freedom struggle.

Thus, when the Michigan delegation caucused at the President Hotel at 6:00 P.M. Tuesday to hear the report and recommendations from Representative Charles C. Diggs, Jr., the only Negro member of the Credentials subcommittee on Mississippi, there was every reason to believe that the Freedom Party would accept the Ullman compromise.

By 8:00 P.M., the word got out. The Freedom Party had caucused and voted unanimously to reject the compromise. Diggs and others were stunned when they heard it.

Any support for a minority report quickly evaporated in the whole Credentials Committee and of eighteen signatures which were ready to bring the issue to the floor for a floor fight (only eleven were needed), only three were left. The issue was dead. The Credentials Committee made its recommendation, the convention quickly voted to accept it and Mississippi became a closed issue to the delegates.

The rest of the events you watched on television, and if you looked hard enough Tuesday night while the Freedom Party delegates were busy sneaking in and seating themselves in the Mississippi section, you saw this sweating, harassed reporter along with ABC-TV's John Scali and Mike Wallace, *The New York Times* reporter Anthony Lewis, who did one of the neatest balancing acts on the back of the chair I've ever seen, *Time*'s Wallace H. Terry, III (that magazine's first Negro reporter and a damned able guy), Adam Clayton Powell, III, and Jimmy Booker of the *Amsterdam News.*

In light of these developments how accurate is Alsop's delineation that the "extremists" "overruled" the acceptance of the compromise?

The Mississippi Freedom Party's vote was unanimous. So there must be sixty-four Negro and white "extremists" who want freedom desperately in that group. One of these "extremists" was a 64-year-old gentle Negro minister who told me Tuesday night during the seating hassle, "I just think we all ought to be on this floor, son, and if they can give the votes to two, they can give them to sixty-four. I've waited too long for this."

He's an "extremist?"

Representative Edith Green, who fought unceasingly to get the entire delegation seated, didn't particularly dig the two-vote compromise either, and for a while, there were rumors that she was going to try for a floor fight.

Gentle, easy-going Mrs. Green an "extremist?"

After Congressman Diggs gave his report to his own delegation, there was an immediate hot discussion which split the delegation. A significant number of Michigan delegates, both Negro and white, did not want to go along with the two-vote compromise.

All of them "extremists?"

What ivory-towered lovers of the white status quo like Joseph Alsop have got to realize is that anybody who disagrees with their parochial and near-bigoted views on race relations is not an "extremist."

Alsop has written this sort of McCarthyism before in his column and witch-hunted for Communists in the Reverend King's SCLC. (Since Communists have invaded SCLC, according to Alsop, how does he explain the Reverend King's acceptance of this moderate compromise?)

Sure, I thought the compromise was a fair one because I also knew that virtually none of the traditional Mississippi Democratic delegates would have signed that loyalty oath and Wednesday Negroes from Mississippi would have cast that state's vote for President.

But who the hell am I and, even worse, who in the hell is Alsop to tell these people from Mississippi how hard they must work for their freedom?

What kind of mandate do cowards like me and Alsop who don't have the guts to go down to Mississippi and fight alongside these people have to tell them what is "moderate" and what isn't?

Every time I looked at the horrible red scars which have disfigured the white face of the Reverend Edwin King, given to him by white racists in his own state, I fought back tears. I'm going to call him an "extremist?"

This man so overpowered me, I wasn't even able to interview him and stood silently in admiration watching his dignity and self-restraint in the midst of the turmoil that night.

I also forgot my reportorial objectivity and leaned over and kissed Mrs. Fannie Lou Hamer on the cheek and she remembered our meeting at Etta Moten Barnett's house. Mrs. Hamer was beaten by white men until her skin turned to crust and then held down by Negro jail inmates and beaten by them on orders from the jail-keepers. She lost consciousness several times.

Is Mrs. Hamer an "extremist?"

I hope so much that they *all* are extremists and that their extremism will help emancipate this country from the chains of its racism and people like Alsop from the narrow-mindedness of their self-assured white supremacy.

In a democracy, political progress rests on compromise and only rarely do we attain consensus. This is as it should be.

But as fundamentally important as compromises are, there is an equally distinguished right, the right not to compromise.

And when this right is exercised, that person is every inch as good an American as a thousand Alsops put together. Let him and every other delegation including Illinois, which betrayed freedom in Mississippi, never forget this.

August 1964

You've Got to Pay Your Civic Rent

A COUPLE OF WEEKS AGO, I was chatting with a Negro business man who has one of the keenest minds in this city.

Both of us commented on the lack of civic consciousness among many colored people, and he said: "They're not paying their civic rent." I think that concept better hits the nail on the head than anything that ever has been said about community responsibility of the individual.

All of us, to some extent, are indebted to our families, our friends, our schools and colleges, our churches, and various civic organizations for the moderate success each of us enjoys today.

Nobody has ever made it alone. One of the biggest myths ever perpetuated in American folklore has been this nonsense about a "self-made man." Where did he live—on an island?

We are what we are and where we are because certain forces in society have collectively worked in our favor.

Some of us have been able to influence these forces more than others, but often we have succeeded merely because we happen to be on the scene at the proper time. Former Vice President Nixon humbly felt that many of the breaks he got were due to "fortuitous circumstances."

Yet his failure to court the colored vote, resulting in his defeat, demonstrates the extent to which he could have shaped his destiny.

It seems to me that if society has been good to you, you ought to be good to society.

If you've been fortunate enough to get a thorough education, obtain a good job, raise a family, buy a home, or just live a decent and comfortable life, you're 700 per cent ahead of two-thirds of the people in the world.

God has blessed you and you're already in debt both to Him and to society.

But some people think that going to work each day, doing their job well, coming home and playing with the kids, and making conversation with the family is enough.

It's not.

All of us have an obligation to something larger than our immediate selves or family. It can be our church, our fraternal organization, our civic organization, our political party, our neighborhood, our social club, or our school.

Whichever group it is, its success and effectiveness means another strong brick in the civic house we call Washington.

Do you think your city is as good a city as it can be?

Do you think colored people are doing everything they can to help make it so?

Do you believe that you as one individual can have no influence in helping to change things?

I say the answer to all three questions is *no.*

If your city is becoming strangled by crime, it's because you're sitting at home strangled by your television set instead of personally trying to do something about it.

If your neighborhood is going to pot, it's because you and your neighbors haven't organized yourselves to combat the rising blight.

If the school your kids attend is giving them an educational raw deal, it's because you're not active in the PTA and instead spend a lot of your time sitting around a table on Saturday nights asking somebody to "give me a whole card."

Instead of being a freeloader on society, you can make your city a great place in which to live if—and only if—you become active in some organized institution, be it a civic organization, political party, church, PTA, fraternal organization, or neighborhood club.

This is how you pay your civic rent.

And if you're colored, your rent is bigger because the white man has been cheating you all these years anyway. The only way you're going to surpass him is to pay more civic rent than he does.

So before you get ready to complain about something that has happened to you, your family, your neighborhood, or your school, ask yourself: If I had paid my civic rent, could I have prevented this?

You'll be amazed at the answer.

On Turning Forty

YOU'VE HEARD that wonderful story, haven't you, which is a take-off on one of the racial bromides of America?

A distinguished business man from the Bronx who happened to be Jewish was on a trip around the world and stopped off in Hong Kong on a Saturday.

He learned of a nearby synagogue and decided to go to temple that day. The house of worship, naturally, was filled with Chinese people. Leaving the temple, the Chinese rabbi was greeting the worshippers and as the American left, the rabbi welcomed him and hoped that he, as a tourist, enjoyed himself. The business man replied that he was Jewish.

"Odd," mused the Chinese rabbi, "you don't *look* Jewish."

Yesterday, July twenty-first, I turned forty.

Odd, I don't *feel* forty.

In fact, I still feel the same as I did the day before yesterday when I was only thirty-nine.

We live in a society of paradox and inconsistency when it comes to the chronicling of one's years.

On the one hand, nobody wants to get older, age is a feared monster that stalks among us ever threatening the tranquility of eternal youth. This rejection of added years is so universally accepted that women are permitted not to reveal their ages (even in court trials and on drivers licenses) and Jack Benny is a national hero because he discovered that Ponce de Leon lived forever by remaining thirty-nine years old.

On the other hand, age is synonymous with wisdom. Only the

elderly have sagacity, elder statesmen are ofttimes respected and revered only because they are older, and the one ace an older person can lay on your king in an argument is: "I've lived longer than you, son. I'm older and I know what I'm talking about."

At forty, I'm not quite sure what my cerebral capacities are. I somehow seem to feel that there's not much I really know when I realize I've had forty years in which to accumulate knowledge and there's not too much of that in me. Life becomes increasingly snarled with complicated problems for which there are no uncomplicated solutions. And you suddenly realize that you're old when you cluck-cluck disapprovingly about the scandalous conduct of "today's younger generation." Just the God-fearing determination of a magnificent mother and a brilliant father kept me from ending up playing checkers each day with Willie Sutton.

Life Begins at Forty was another parcel of Americana written to relieve the anxiety of an aging generation that saw itself being merchandised out of a productive future.

But life begins when you begin the pursuit of excellence and can translate this journey into happy and full days of productivity. That's true happiness—what the Greeks called the full utilization of one's intellectual faculties in the pursuit of excellence.

I haven't won my Pulitzer Prize yet (I will, I promise you.) and I haven't done or written many of the things that I want to. But the future never looked rosier, and life never never promised more exciting horizons to see than it does now—despite a Goldwater candidacy. With a very lovely and devoted wife and two swinging little daughters, I'm daily counting my blessings.

The one thing that saddens me in turning forty is that now I must turn in my membership card in the Society of Angry Young Men.

Are there any angry old men around?

Are We Capitalists or Integrationists?

ONE OF OUR SO-CALLED Negro leaders of whom this column has been particularly critical and who, we believe, has been thrust upon us poor Negroes without our permission, took issue with us recently on this matter of "Negro leadership."

In a moderately heated exchange, he defied us to come up with an alternative or better answer to what the present crop of Negro leaders were advocating.

Not being of the intellectual competence of this great leader, we took it upon ourselves to consult our favorite dialectician. Nicodemus graciously conducted the interview and we thought that its contents might provide just a little food for thought for this great Negro leader.

NICODEMUS: Oh, master, lately there has been a great hue and cry about Negro leadership. There is a feeling among many people that perhaps Negroes are not providing themselves with the best leaders. On the other hand, the leaders who are in power maintain that they are doing the best possible job under the circumstances and are continually battering down the doors of racial segregation in the United States. They offer the progress of the years as de facto proof.

SOCRATES: Certainly, incontrovertible evidence. Tell me, lowly one, where does this problem of Negro leadership assert itself as most serious?

NICODEMUS: It is the largest city in the United States, O master, known as New York. In this city resides the largest concentration of Negroes, 961,000.

SOCRATES: Who are their leaders?

NICODEMUS: This is indeed strange. They have sixty-eight leaders who were chosen by Mayor Wagner. Such stalwarts as Roy Wilkins, Tony Rasmus, Jackie Robinson, and Carson DeWitt Baker were included.

SOCRATES: Already, the problem of the Negro becomes obvious. Tell me, what do these leaders advocate?

NICODEMUS: Integration, master.

SOCRATES: A singularly worthwhile goal, but one which is worthless in itself as an end. Nicodemus, let us sit together and see if we can analyze this thing.

NICODEMUS: It is at your feet, master, that I am enlightened.

SOCRATES: Let us begin with America. It is a country whose economic system is known as capitalism. Under this system, the competitive price market, production, credit, and investment are the areas where the individual can acquire large sums of money. When these large sums of money are acquired and a man becomes a capitalist, he gains great respect from his fellow man, does he not?

NICODEMUS: Master, he is consulted by presidents.

SOCRATES: Every immigrant group which has come to America has pursued the goal of making money. As such, each of these groups, the Italians, the Irish, the Polish, have all developed capitalists, which enables them to wield immense political power, have they not?

NICODEMUS: It is as if you have been reading de Tocqueville lately, master. You are so right.

SOCRATES: Is there any other index to which you can point where a man is more equal than in the market place of dollars?

NICODEMUS: Ah, in the development of the mind, getting a college education.

SOCRATES: Nicodemus, you talk like a Negro now. How many capitalists have gone to college? What has a college education got to do with making money? Are you interested in making money or getting integrated?

NICODEMUS: Master, I am interested in making money. My motto is every man a capitalist.

SOCRATES: So, indeed, should have been the Negro's. Instead, the Negro finds it easier to follow behind his leaders, all of whom are great problem-solvers. Their race has produced nothing but a bunch of sociologists and social workers who continue to tell the Negro he must fight for equality. If the Negro should suddenly get hold of $500 million within his ranks, don't you believe he would be closer to equality?

NICODEMUS: Ah, but, Negroes have produced athletes who today are leaders and. . . .

SOCRATES: Nicodemus, can you show me how years of hitting a ball with a stick prepare a man to deal with the great economic and political issues of our times?

NICODEMUS: I cannot.

SOCRATES: You cannot, but Negroes can. In a country where the major emphasis has been on the acquisition of wealth, the Negro has placed his emphasis on the acquisition of welfare checks. In a country where the primary sources of income are manufacturing, mining, railroads, transportation, utilities, banking, and investment, the Negro has produced a group of entertainers and athletes. Nicodemus, the Negro does not have much in America, but if he built up that which he has and made it so good—in short, if he built a better mousetrap—that the white man would want to integrate himself with the Negro, would this not do more to solve this problem?

NICODEMUS: Indeed it would, master.

SOCRATES: If the Negro people could produce a few more capitalists, bankers, and business executives, would they not merit more respect? If they could even build their own housing projects, would this not gain equality? If their leaders would begin to tell Negroes that racial equality means also the responsibility of equality, would they not advance more quickly?

NICODEMUS: But, master, what about the schools, and voting rights?

SOCRATES: What is more important than earning a living? If the

Negro would build himself big businesses, manufacturing plants, and control some of the flow of dollars in this country, would not he be in a very strong position to secure educational and political rights as well?

NICODEMUS: True, O master, true. What about the NAACP? If Negroes start trying to become capitalists instead of integrationists, what would happen to the NAACP? What you propose means the Negro would have to begin concentrating on making money instead of giving it to the NAACP. That is heresy! Think of all the jobs the NAACP provides.

SOCRATES: I lie awake at night and the horrible thought overwhelms me. But the Negro must begin to ask himself—and soon—"Are we capitalists or integrationists?"

NICODEMUS: Alas, master, they may want to be capitalists, but their leaders are constantly telling them they are integrationists.

SOCRATES: A most deplorable situation.

The Unreachables

WHO ARE the unreachables?

An obvious answer is they're the people who can't be reached.

Not reached by whom?

By society—neighbors, social organizations, community groups, public institutions, community leaders.

In Washington, D.C., there are some 50,000 colored people who can be legitimately classified as "unreachables."

They're at the core of the District's crime and welfare problems. They make up the statistics on welfare cheats, crime increases, illegitimate children, and the myriad pathologies that a society structured on racial hate exfoliates.

Totaling up these statistics and their racial substratum, the Southerners and a few unreconstructed Northerners are able to impute a covering veil of immorality to colored people.

But no race, no religion, no ethnic group is inherently bad, nor does any race have a monopoly on fostering social disintegration.

A given set of conditions—urban society, immutable racial segregation, and cultural conflict—will develop a pattern of racial hostility that finds expression in the lack of incentive and a contempt for the established social order.

In turn, some people turn to crime, get on welfare, and even derive a secret joy in "getting back" at society by cheating.

These are the unreachables—the colored people who somehow just have not been able to cope with society's harsh denials of their essential dignity.

The NAACP in Washington hasn't been able to reach these people.

The Urban League hasn't.

CORE hasn't.

The churches have failed completely.

But here and there a few people, a few organizations, such as the Commissioners Youth Council, Northwest Settlement House, Hospitality House, and other agencies have been able to reach over the sociological dike of despair and lift one or two families up into the mainstream of society.

It's true these unreachables are going to flourish as long as the District of Columbia ruthlessly segregates them in housing and employment, and the police are permitted to beat them unmercifully whenever they wish.

But some of them can be reclaimed if all of us in the community can only reach them.

Who are they?

They're a significant percentage of the 32,575 persons (eighty-five per cent of whom are colored) who are on welfare.

They're the recidivists in the 21,802 who committed serious offenses last year, eighty per cent of whom are colored.

They're the ninety-three per cent colored who receive aid to dependent children and the ninety-eight per cent colored who receive surplus food in the District of Columbia.

They're the same people to whom the District real estate brokers close their doors, and who are confined to filthy, unlivable ghettos.

They're the same people who can't find jobs anywhere and when they do are forced to accept jobs as under-employables.

They are among the 11,691 colored families in the District who earn less than $2,000 a year.

In essence, they are the people who just don't give a damn.

These are the unreachables.

And unless some of us, or some of our organizations, including our churches, start reaching them soon, they are going to grow, and grow, and grow, and grow.

I agree we must not lose sight of the people and the companies in the District of Columbia who have produced the unreachables. Let's keep our collective feet in the white man's back until he surrenders his white supremacist ways. And I mean people like John Fischer of *Harper's* Magazine who is an apostle of this doctrine.

But let's save the unreachables at the same time.

Let's bring them back into the wholesome enjoyment of the total society.

Our ministers can lead this battle. It's nice for the Baptist ministers to honor Commissioner John Duncan and praise him for a job which everybody in the District knows he's not doing. And in a way, this is the kind of thing which avoids getting to the nitty-gritty of a social cancer. You give a man a plaque and honor him for the problems he hasn't helped solve.

But if our churches will just take the lead and prayerfully go out into the land of the unreachables, just as Christ did, every organization in the city will follow.

And the District of Columbia will be redeeming the greatest thing our society has—the dignity of the human spirit.

July 1962

From Protest to Production

I'VE BORROWED THE TITLE of this "sermon" from the Reverend J. H. Jackson, President of the National Baptist Convention who plans to speak on it when the NBA meets in Chicago next month.

According to the Reverend Mr. Jackson, in a pre-convention press release, the answer to the colored American's problem inheres not in Washington or the Supreme Court or Congress but within ourselves as a group of people.

The Reverend Mr. Jackson is wrong in his analysis, but is curiously right in his conclusions.

What has always distressed me about the Reverend Mr. Jackson —and I've long admired and liked this man, spending many a Sunday listening to him preach while a graduate student at the University of Chicago—is his rejection of all the magnificent work the protesters of our race have accomplished.

In fact, the Reverend Mr. Jackson is himself a member of a denomination whose inception lies in protest. Martin Luther protested, hence the term "Protestant."

To protest indignities and inhumanities is to register that divine discontent with social evils which Christ demands of us.

Unfortunately, the Reverend Mr. Jackson has failed to recognize the enormous value of protest.

He has scorned the Freedom Riders, the sit-ins, the picket lines, the boycotts, the protest marches, and the various movements (Montgomery, Albany, etc.), and sitteth at the seat of the Uncle Toms.

Instead of encouraging, praising, and stooping to help lift up, the

Reverend Mr. Jackson has criticized and even kept silent. Certainly, part of the current schism in the National Baptist Convention today is reflective of this division of philosophies.

For him to assume that the President, Congress, and the Supreme Court have not been massive tools in the drive toward racial equality for the colored American is to ignore the historical impact of the 1954 Supreme Court decision and the widespread accomplishments of political pressures of these protest movements.

However, the Reverend Mr. Jackson is as right as "the ways of the Lord" when he advocates the need for us as a group of people to produce.

There is a time to protest and there is a time to produce.

We haven't learned yet that we can do both simultaneously.

By all means, let us continue the insistent pressure of picket lines, sit-ins, boycotts, church rallies, and marches.

Let's keep hammering at those walls of bigotry until they crumble like rotted timbers.

But let us also become producers.

Let's begin to build captains of industry, industrial giants, and political generals.

Where we have held out our hand and begged for admittance to the white man's temple, let us pool our economic resources and buy it.

It is true, as the Reverend Mr. Jackson has declared, that much of our salvation lies within us.

A. A. Spaulding proved this.

S. B. Fuller did, too.

And our twenty-eight savings and loan associations, our banks, our businesses—even our "numbers bankers"—are eloquent testimonies to our collective ability to be our own salvation.

When we as a race of people begin to control stock in companies, to be able to affect the decisions and destinies of companies which discriminate against us by attending a board of directors meeting and kicking out the bigots, then we will emerge into the maturity of producers and cast off the enfeebling cloak of consumers.

I would amend the Reverend Mr. Jackson's title to read: "Protest *and* Produce."

We need both. One cannot achieve one without the complementary power of the other.

And you know something? What the Reverend Mr. Jackson is saying about "producing" and not "protesting" is exactly what the Black Muslims are preaching today. They likewise believe the sociological emphasis of the colored man's struggle should be on production.

Truth is a many-sectioned train. There's plenty good room, plenty good room for all of us to enjoy this ride to the happy hunting ground of racial equality.

July 1959

Great White Father's Chosen Negro Leaders

CHIEF STANDING BULL: Colored man, why you come talk to Chief Standing Bull?

NICODEMUS: Chief, like, I'm confused. And, man, so much is happening these days with us Negroes—well, like, chief, you've just got to give us some advice. I think some of us are being had.

CHIEF STANDING BULL: Why you no go to great Greek master of logic, Socrates? Him give you advice before.

NICODEMUS: Oh, Sock, he swings. And he comes on strong with his dialectics. But, man, he doth not understand the intricacies of our color problem. I figure since you were tangling with the white man long before we Negroes were a problem, perhaps you could shower enlightenment upon our predicament.

CHIEF STANDING BULL: You askum. Me answer.

NICODEMUS: How come the white man doesn't like Adam Clayton Powell?

CHIEF STANDING BULL: You askum easiest question in books. White man no like Adam Clayton Powell because him fight white man way white man fight him. White man, him lynch Negroes, blow up schools, build ghettos, no givum decent jobs, packum Negroes into rat houses. Adam Powell, him tell Negroes to fight back. White man no like it when you fight back. Adam Powell tell Negroes do war dance, get voting rights. White man think Powell drink fire water.

NICODEMUS: But, what about the charges that Powell is a racist?

CHIEF STANDING BULL: You gottum black skin, but askum white man's question. Adam Powell, him gottum white skin, but him fightum good, like black man should. Adam Powell, him no racist. Him only fightum way white man teach him. When white man think you rise too fast, him call you "racist" and say you makum "terrible" leader. White man, him shrewdest animal in forest. Him no like tough leadership.

NICODEMUS: But, the white man calls other Negro leaders good men. For example, the City Club in New York City said that Jackie Robinson and Roy Wilkins were "marvelous Negro leaders." How about that?

CHIEF STANDING BULL: You talk mouth full of corn meal. No wonder American Negroes no go nowhere fast. Great white father, him like Roy Wilkins and Jackie Robinson because they play game according to white man's rules for black men. They go not so fast, not so far, not so hard. They only talk tough in South. In North, both men heap big quiet.

White men pay their salaries. If Jackie Robinson talk big, white man fire him from his job in coffee company. White man on newspaper, him kick Jackie off too when him gettum up big talk. Jackie, him tellum white man what he wants to hear. Him talk "reasonable talk." Roy Wilkins, him no different. Him speak mad when Negro gettum lynched. Him puttum hand over eyes and foot in mouth when Negroes gettum big kick in the pants in New York wigwam.

NICODEMUS: But, don't you think we need different types of Negro leaders, even if they disagree with each other?

CHIEF STANDING BULL: White man, him think so. Him use policy all same over world—divide and conquer. Him take Negroes like Jackie Robinson, pat him on back, tellum get angry only sometime. Cuddle him next to—how you call him—Mister Charlie.

NICODEMUS: Well, you've got to admit that Adam Powell's statements are inflammatory and that they are stirring up Negroes.

CHIEF STANDING BULL: Adam Powell, him no stir up. Him only mix what already there. White man stir up. Great white father Kennedy who sittum in big chief sheriff chair, him say, "No putum Negroes in high jobs." Him use phony issue of race. Him makum Negroes mad. Police commissioner, him stir up, not Powell. Him play footsies with white man in South. White man in South, him say "regardless of race, creed, or color," and him lynch only Negroes. Kennedy, him say "regardless of race, creed or color," and appoint only paleface. Him also dangerous.

NICODEMUS: Well Chief, I've got to admit you've talked a lot of sense. Let me ask you just one more question. What should we do about George Meany?

CHIEF STANDING BULL: Easy. Burnum at stake.

We Stand Around While Others Work

BORROW A FEW MINUTES from your busy schedule the next time you're out driving or shopping and take a close look at Harlem. Start at 110th Street and Eighth Avenue and walk to 125th

Street. Cross over to 125th Street and Seventh Avenue and walk to 123rd Street, down 123rd Street to Lenox Avenue and up Lenox Avenue to 135th Street.

Of the myriad ordinary impressions which almost drown you, one claws its way to the surface like a swimmer gasping for breath and lies there in naked shame.

It is the bewildering sight of hundreds of Negroes standing around all day and doing nothing but standing.

A few are pensive as they gather for the morning round-table session on what's happening in Africa—others bend their elbows in a friendly game of checkers—some study the last numerical charts to find a desperate scientific reason why 734 should be played today (Haven't had a "hit," like, in eleven months.)—but no matter the activity, you'll find them all out there just standing—or as June Christy used to sing: "Just a-sittin and a-rockin all-l-l-l day."

These black legions of unemployed who draw unemployment compensation like it was an unalienable right provided for in the Declaration of Independence, who populate the welfare lists to make up sixty-seven per cent of the total number of welfare recipients—they are the unfortunate human slag from a society rigidly dedicated to the religious doctrine that "white is right." Because their skin is black, their next job is not just around the corner, and years of refusals, rejections, and denials have driven them into a shell of frustration.

Of the hundreds—almost thousands—of Negroes who stand around in Harlem all day and do nothing, are all of them unable to find a job? Is this lack of opportunity or lack of will power? How much of the unemployed black army can be blamed on racial discrimination and how much on sheer laziness?

Despite a nationally powerful number of eighteen million, we are indeed a poor people. Our median income is $3,740 while that of the whites if $5,685. Twenty per cent of the whites earn over $7,000 while only seven per cent of Negroes command that figure. More than thirteen per cent of the whites in America earn $10,000 or more. One per cent of the Negroes live on this plateau. In other words, there are more white people in America earning $10,000 a year than there are Negoes in all the fifty states of America.

With this sad state of economic affairs, wouldn't you think Negroes would be working harder to catch up to the white people? No, not us. We're standing on the corner, dad, looking sharp, talking trash, and making it with that welfare bit.

I believe in giving the white man inordinate hell when he assigns an inferior place in society to me because of my skin color. I believe in picketing, boycotting, "buying black," switching political parties, and employing every democratic measure to fight for total equality.

But I find it difficult to climb out on that flagpole of persecution and yell "racial prejudice" until I have exhausted every last ounce of energy to establish, build, or organize myself into an economic and political power. John H. Johnson, publisher of *Ebony,* S. B. Fuller of Fuller Products, Truman K. Gibson, Sr., of Supreme Liberty Life Insurance, Hope Stevens of United Mutual Life Insurance, and A. A. Austin didn't sit around and cry in their respective beers about the ignominies of segregation. They simply went out and did something about it by building comparatively large businesses.

Today, a lone Negro—Adam Clayton Powell—continues to try to awaken the Negro to his real power. This is why the white man labels Powell a "racist." I just hope he keeps on preaching to the year 2061 if necessary to shake several hundred thousands of Negroes loose from their political lethargy.

Returning to the economic front, we again demonstrate our lack of enlightened self-interest by our laziness. If we're so anxious to stand around and refuse to work, let's be consistent, particularly where our civil rights are concerned. A good example has been the Woolworth's boycott. We didn't fight this battle, white people did. For weeks after the boycott was announced, Negroes trundled themselves into Woolworth's on 125th Street as if they were going to be given free a year's supply of Thunderbird.

No, the awful truth is there for the world to see. Not only are we lazy, but we are disorganized. We who need to work harder than any race or nationality in America are still plagued by "stand-outs."

All over Eighth Avenue, Lenox Avenue, and Seventh Avenue, we have "stand-outs." But downtown on Fifth Avenue, Park Avenue, and Madison Avenue, others are working. It's a cruel and paradoxical world.

A Foreign Policy for Unpopularity

THE HYSTERICALLY IRRESPONSIBLE, Communist-led demonstrations in Japan during these past two weeks are, unfortunately, an eloquent indictment of American foreign policy.

The awful truth about America in the world today is that we have failed dismally to "win friends and influence people." We're one of the three major powers (Russia and Red China being the other two), we've got the highest standard of living, we're the richest and the most solvent, we're the most generous, and we're the most disliked and most misunderstood.

Why? The answer lies, perhaps, in the nature and intent of our international diplomacy.

Post-World-War-II American foreign policy has sat on a three-legged stool:

1. Anti-Communism
2. International piggy-backism
3. Bad horsemanship

By being inflexibly anti-Communist, we've attempted to divide the world into two polarities: the pro-Communist and the anti-Communist. In the words of the frontier, either you're for us or against us. To the struggling new nations, this ideological myopia has been for the birds. To them, self-determination and freedom from poverty have been the big issues.

International piggy-backism, a grandstand kind of payola, has been the primary apparatus for the conduct of our foreign policy ever since President Truman enunciated the Truman Doctrine in 1947.

Ignoring the morality of this economic serfdom, we've given bagsful of money to dictators and despots just as long as they said they were on our side. Some of this has admittedly paid off. Of the $40 billion in foreign aid spent since July first, 1945, $25 billion has gone to Western Europe. There's no question that this has helped stabilize the European economy.

But the $5 billion paid to Near East and African countries hasn't bought the desired equilibrium in that area, as recent events in Turkey, Iraq, and the present Israel-Arab stalemate will attest.

The $2.5 billion laid out to Asian and Pacific countries has not arrested the partitioning of three countries, Indo-China, Korea, and China, nor has it brought us Japanese cordiality.

Finally, we've displayed bad horsemanship by consistently backing the wrong horse—the French in Indo-China, Chiang Kai-shek in China, Syngman Rhee in Korea, Adnan Menderes in Turkey, and the present benevolent dictators of Thailand and Pakistan. Where it has been to our military advantage, we've lain in bed with Fascist Franco of Spain and Communist Tito of Yugoslavia.

If foreign policy can be defined as a series of actions enabling our Constitutional values to survive, we have been successful. If, on the other hand, it can be defined as a method of insuring that you get enough tough guys on your side to kick the hell out of the other guy, then we're not doing too well, because more and more nations seem to be neutral—neutral in favor of Russia.

As of June fifteenth, 1960, over half of the world's population, 1.6 billion people or fifty-seven per cent, are governed by sixty-four democracies. The rest, 1.2 billion people or forty-three per cent, are under the heels of twenty-eight dictatorships, the majority of which are Communist or Communist-dominated.

To preserve this present favorable balance, we must first shift our emphasis from Europe to Africa. Africa will hold the world's balance of power in a few years.

The second thing is to deal in terms of the fact that we, as a supporter of the colonial powers, France and Britain, are forced to bear much of the blame of their past imperialist iniquities. Furthermore, Asians and Africans, particularly the Japanese, will never forgive us for the fact that the first atomic bomb was dropped on a colored people.

Finally, our foreign policy must be positive, not negative. We must take the offensive and not wait for Russia to make a move and then hope we can checkmate her. If a democracy can posture an aggressive foreign policy, we had better find one quick. At the present time, we're on the short end of the stick.

CBS-TV Half-Bakes Harlem's Portrait

IF YOU WERE SITTING before your television set last Tuesday evening at 7:30 P.M., you may have seen what CBS-TV's public relations department touted as "Harlem—A Self-Portrait."

What this title was designed to communicate was a camera prowling around our community like a kind of sociological paint brush. Whatever the camera saw and the commentator bumped into, they recorded.

This, then, wasn't supposed to be CBS-TV's portrait of Harlem. It was Harlem's self-conception, or what George Herbert Mead would call the "generalized other." We were looking at ourselves.

And what a mess we turned out to be!

The alleged self-portrait was one of the most professionally concocted insults ever ladled out to Harlem. From our mail and telephone calls (at home immediately following the broadcast and again the next day at the office), Negroes resented the broadcast. Terms like "biased, inaccurate, incomplete, slanted, and untrue" were used.

Now, we realize that all Negroes who saw the broadcast or all those who liked the broadcast did not call us. There can be little doubt that a number of Negroes may have thought the show a competent one. Nevertheless, any intelligent dissection of the program's content will reveal its severe shortcomings.

Like most documentaries of Harlem, CBS-TV placed its emphasis on three areas: slums, shooting craps, and the plot to keep Negroes from buying businesses on 125th Street.

Is this Harlem?

What happened to the CBS-TV camera on Sunday, when thousands of Negroes faithfully went to church, as they do each and every Sunday?

What happened to the CBS-TV camera when the hundreds of small shopkeepers and business men opened their stores and offices every morning?

Where was the CBS-TV camera when the few hundreds of Negroes in Riverton, Lenox Terrace, 409 and 555 Edgecomb Avenues, Bowery Savings Building, and other middle-income residences gathered nightly to entertain on as smart a basis as some of those who work for CBS? Why didn't the camera go into any of these apartments?

Why didn't the CBS-TV camera explore the Negro businesses, the funeral homes, the insurance companies, the two Negro newspapers, the savings and loan association, the restaurants, the beauty shops, the political clubs, the real estate offices, the lawyers, the dentists, the doctors, the medical center, and the thousands of establishments all over Harlem where policy bets are placed. (The New York City police can't do a single thing about it?)

Why weren't these things shown?

Do you know why? Because the overwhelming majority of people who are serviced by a medium such as CBS like to believe still that today's Negro is a somewhat modernized version of *Porgy and Bess.* As far as they are concerned, the Negro is the kind of happy child who is solicitously described by Langston Hughes. We're still regarded as a depressed race living in slums, whose only outlet for happiness is in our dancing feet and our melodious voices.

CBS-TV's "self-portrait" didn't contribute to any understanding or appreciation of the Negro as a human being. All it did was to reaffirm existing biases and prejudices and to give the thousands of bigoted white New Yorkers another mental crutch to prove what they believed all along: "See? I knew they were a different kind of animal."

CBS-TV undoubtedly received all kinds of praise. (*The New York Times* critic just rolled his eloquent phrases and marveled at this sensitive documentary!) Governor Faubus has got a big following, too.

We'd like to issue a challenge to CBS-TV which we dare them to accept.

Why doesn't CBS do a show on what a successful place to live Harlem is becoming? Why doesn't CBS-TV recognize that despite the "near-riots," the craps-shooting, the depressing slums, the tensions, and the threadbare existence of thousands of Negroes, Harlem is struggling to become what Durkheim would call *"une autre chose,"* a new identity—that out of the seeming chaos and economic conflict a new, increasingly powerful Negro is trying to assert himself and gain a greater measure of respect and political power in our town—that the Negro is only trying to do (and one day he will succeed) what the Irishman did for a while, followed by the Italian, and now the Jew, i.e., to take over the running of this city—that the Negro enjoys the fullness and the benefits of this great country to an extent which has caused him to place a false emphasis on conspicuous consumption and pecuniary emulation?

Why doesn't CBS-TV, if they really want to be equally as ridiculous as they were in painting Harlem's "self-portrait," do a documentary on the number of Cadillacs Harlem Negroes own, the number of Lincoln Continentals, the number of yachts, the number of summer homes, the number of country homes, the number of Negroes who have charge accounts at Bonwit Teller's and Brooks Brothers, the number of families who send their children to ivy-league colleges, the number who go to Europe every summer, the number of fashionable clubs who give parties at the Waldorf-Astoria, and the number who attend interracial parties and who give interracial parties?

Why doesn't CBS-TV do a documentary on the policy racket in Harlem and try to prove that this is solely Harlem's responsibility and not the city's or the police force's?

Why not?

Because it was easier to do exactly what CBS-TV did—paint a half-baked portrait of Harlem that was as different from what Harlem sees of itself as Jackson Pollock is from Rembrandt. CBS-TV made a big thing of repeating all through the program, "This is the way Harlem sees itself."

Nuts.

The only reason CBS-TV did this is because the followers of Elijah Muhammad have got these people frightened. "Quick," probably exclaimed the CBS-TV wheel in charge of public relations, "let's get up there and find out what's going on. Give the public pathos and sordidness, really try to prove why there have been a couple of near-riots and preaching of hate."

It's obvious the "self-portrait" was a hurried job. If CBS-TV has the slightest good intention toward the Negro community, let's see another documentary which shows *all* of Harlem.

How about it, CBS-TV?

August 1959

"Stall-Ins" and "Mr. Charlie's" Colored Civil Rights Puppets

SEVERAL YEARS AGO, my youngest sister, Irene, and I were discussing a married couple in Hartford. It was my contention that the husband dominated the marriage. Irene disputed my opinion and proceeded to reel off a series of incidents to buttress her argument.

Finally convinced, I asked incredulously, "You mean to say she dominates him completely?"

Contemptuously dismissing me as only a younger sister can an older brother, Irene retorted: "Shucks, when she yells 'Jump!' he asks 'How high?' "

Last week in Washington, D.C., "Mr. Charlie" yelled "Jump!" to four of our "Negro leaders."

And to a man, they not only asked "How high?" they then leaped into the air, begging "Mr. Charlie's" approbation as they twirled and spun through several philosophical contradictions.

Scene of this emotional binge was the American Society of Newspaper Editors meeting in Washington. Participants were the National Urban League's Whitney Young, the NAACP's Roy Wilkins, CORE's James Farmer, and SNCC's John Lewis.

All four had come to kneel at the shrine of "Mr. Charlie" (great white father who pays their salaries and without whose permission they dare not speak) and pay homage to his fears and hysteria.

In a belly-crawling display of togetherness, all four condemned the proposed "stall-ins" at the New York World's Fair Wednesday opening day ceremonies, and made sure everybody would hear them by calling a press conference.

It's saddening to see our "Negro leaders" pushing the panic button on a technique which they have previously endorsed.

The sit-ins in the South were all illegal.

Those demonstrations in Birmingham last year were not only illegal, but were condemned by many people who thought it was reprehensible to use little children to fight a civil rights battle. Yet the Reverend Martin Luther King, Jr., led a glorious army of children, women, and men into the mouths of fire hoses and glistening fangs of police dogs.

And they won their battle.

You can't slice morality by degrees, nor can you tailor a civil rights technique to fit your convenience, your time schedule, and your leadership determination, as those four Negro leaders tried to do last week in Washington.

What is illegal today was illegal yesterday. And by the same token, what was morally right to do yesterday is morally right to do today. There are no degrees of immorality or morality.

If you accept the logic and discipline of the non-violent strategy of "wade-ins," "lie-ins" and other demonstrations with their attendant by-products of violence, you're stuck with the ultimate extension of this technique on a larger scale in the form of the "stall-ins."

Be against the "stall-ins" if you believe they are harmful to the public safety.

But don't look like a philosophical idiot, having endorsed the sit-ins and other "ins" which have all produced violence in the civil rights struggle in America.

What our illustrious "Negro leaders" were responding to in Washington last week was the white-press-created monster, "the white backlash."

I guess I should worry about the "white backlash" too, but I've been catching hell so long from the "white frontlash," I figure that the "backlash" can't be any worse. We might as well go on and waltz with that one for a while, too.

But perhaps this is what frightened Whitney Young, Roy Wilkins, James Farmer, and John Lewis into their hasty assurances to all of those big, powerful white editors that they as "responsible Negro leaders" were certainly on their (white editors') side and not with those rabble-rousing Negroes who've got the unmitigated gall to want their freedom now.

Negroes can spot a phony deal a mile away and it is this kind of nonsense that is causing the Negro community slowly to lose faith and confidence in its "Negro leaders."

Congressman Powell endorsed the "stall-ins."

He'll be around for a long, long time, enjoying the full confidence of American Negroes long after our "Negro leaders" have passed from the scene as "leaders."

And if, for one sacred moment, you had deluded yourself into thinking that maybe "Mr. Charlie" wasn't really on top and still in complete control, all you had to do was to listen to the obsequies of four civil rights puppets who to a man asked "How high?" when "Mr. Charlie" yelled "Jump!"

April 1964

"I'm Colored . . . and I'm Proud"

A FEW YEARS AGO, my youngest sister, Irene, was living in Washington and working at Howard University as a librarian.

On her way to her musky citadel of books one bright, pleasant morning, she squeezed herself into a crowded streetcar and was soon lost between lines of morning newspaper print.

Suddenly, a noisy confusion intruded into the sleepy quiet of the streetcar. There, near the front, was a man in work clothes, talking loudly about shoes and ships and sealing wax.

He was so drunk, he was weaving like an oriental belly dancer. Like, Irene says, he was swinging.

And, as the fates would have it, he was colored.

Watching and listening to this early morning cheerer-upper was a carload of predominantly colored—and thoroughly disgusted—passengers. Their faces wreathed in disdain, they confided in low tones to each other how the workman was throwing race relations back twenty years.

A kind of unanimously silent decision was made: Ignore him.

Human beings, however, have a curious way of feeling the emotions of others, even when they go uncommunicated. And so our workman friend began to feel the hostility from his colored brethren.

Eventually, it overwhelmed him and he struck back.

"Yeah, I know I'm drunk," he shouted, according to Irene. "And, I'm colored, too." He paused for a moment and apparently the immensity of that last statement hit him. He lashed out again.

"I'm colored—and I'm proud."

Of all the people on the streetcar that morning who shared his pigmentation, he probably was the only one who was proud to be colored.

But that situation is an eloquent indictment of the average colored man's predicament in America—his lack of pride in being colored. Oh, yes, many of us have proclaimed from the house-tops, the pulpits, the rostrums, and the leaves of pages our racial pride. We have extolled the virtues of color and praised its beauty.

But our daily actions have been a sorry mess of contradictions. Whether we accept this sociological fact or not, the plain truth is most of us are ashamed of our color. We have lived in a majority culture structured on the precept "white is right" so long that we unconsciously accept it.

A good example is the whole problem of integration. To the average colored man, integration is an end in itself. Once this golden end has been attained, he can sit back and relax. It rarely occurs to him that the battle is just beginning.

Equal rights means equality of opportunity and equality of achievement. After we become completely integrated, are we as a race going to be able to build equal big businesses, exercise equal political power, and continue equal educational institutions? I would feel a whole lot happier about the drive to be a first-class citizen if I felt I was leaving behind a legacy of first-class political and economic power for my kids.

As for integration, I want it so badly that my personal solution to the problem is one which would be better left unsaid, because my hostility toward the white southerner admits of no charity.

Yet I want to be proud of colored businesses, colored schools, colored politicians, colored barmaids, colored newspapers, colored doctors, colored scrub women, colored lawyers, colored seamstresses, and colored stenographers. May we never lose any of the warm feeling of togetherness whenever a group of us are in a happy state of communication. Let's always know we're colored—integration notwithstanding.

A good example of this happy medium is the Jew.

Who is better integrated in America, the Jew or the colored man?

At the same time, who has more, bigger, and better first-class schools, colleges, and businesses, the Jew or the colored man?

Who has been able to carefully define his role as a member of a minority race within a majority group and still take the best of two worlds, the Jew or the colored man?

It hasn't been easy for the Jew. In fact, it has taken him centuries to develop a set of rather precise racial definitions as to who he is. But the colored man in America has barely begun to struggle with this agonizing process.

For years, he was caught in the middle of a lopsided cultural bargain I call racial schizophrenia, trying to integrate himself and trying to be a colored man at the same time. What's the expression?—having our cake and eating it, too.

But this is the decade of the black man, and the pendulum of history is just now beginning to swing back. To be black today—to be colored—is no longer a smear of shame. Rather, it's a badge of greatest distinction. White is now only fifty per cent right.

For this new pride in ourselves, we can thank the African nations, because we certainly did nothing within ourselves as a group of people to bring it about. The African countries have given us this sense of belonging, of cultural identity, of historical legacy, and above all, racial distinction. No longer should we look into the mirror and ask ourselves: What are we?

We are colored. And for this, we should be grateful.

That man on the bus several years ago knew and felt this.

In a soggy, drunken state, on his way to work after a night of partying, he still realized one important fact about himself:

"I'm colored—and I'm proud."

Era of Managed Uncertainty: Washington, D.C., Revisited

IF YOU WALK INTO the office of Andy Hatcher, White House Associate Press Secretary, there is a huge picture—about five feet by four feet—of President Kennedy in a motorcade, looking up at the crowd and, with that sunny, infectious grin, waving.

Seated next to him is a smiling, proud Jackie Kennedy.

That picture has been in Andy's office since 1961.

It was still there last week. And I would submit it will probably remain as long as Pierre Salinger and Andy Hatcher run the news office in The White House.

And one suspects that a man named Lyndon B. Johnson sometimes begins to feel like the second Mrs. de Winter in *Rebecca.* It's really not quite his house yet.

I went back home to Washington, D.C., last week for a three-day visit. I can call our nation's capital home, having lived there for a delightful three years as an editor.

Even after two weeks, the grief in Washington over Kennedy's death is an overpowering reality. Washington was his home. Washingtonians were his family and there's been a death in the family.

Outwardly, the District of Columbia is its usual bureaucratic self, becalmed by its special brand of civil service lethargy. Those ponderous, gleaming white government buildings are concrete reminders that physically nothing has changed.

But among the people, everything has changed.

The top Kennedy aides honestly do not know what the new President will do and few expect to hang around after next year waiting to find out.

The Johnson people hope and expect him to succeed, but are daily made aware of the lingering vitality of the first Mrs. de Winter. Kennedy had style and the people loved him for it. Johnson is a political machine and the people fear him for it.

Government civil servants are not so much concerned about their jobs as they are about what it will now require to "get along" and succeed in government without really trying too hard.

The result? An atmosphere of managed uncertainty.

A heartbroken capital is carrying on with brave business-as-usual spirit, searching for a new identity to which to cling. Johnson was not an image you could cling to as Vice President. He may change that.

During my three days in Washington, D.C., last week, I talked with many old and dear friends—Senators, Congressmen, Democrats, Republicans, Negroes, Irishmen, Jews, White House aides (old and new), top government officials, ambassadors, and old pinochle cronies (lost three games and won two while there). Those three days saw the rekindling of an old love affair with some of the finest human beings in the world, and I was the happy butt of the innumerable jokes which only dear friends toss around: "C'mon, Stone, what are you really down here lobbying for?" "What's the matter, the syndicate run you out of Chicago?" "Don't tell us John Sengstacke is wise to you already?"

We were all still able to laugh, but when we weren't laughing we talked politics. And all any of us could do was wonder. . . . What's really going to happen? Nobody seemed to know.

There is an indisputable fact in Washington about the new President: With the exception of his aides and most Southerners, nobody is wildly enthusiastic about him.

"The President has personally asked me to stay on and told me he needed me more than Kennedy did." The speaker was one of those who had been closest to President Kennedy.

"I'm going to stay on." The speaker leaned back and began to reminisce. "I wouldn't give anything for those years I spent with that man. I loved Kennedy. . . . He was an extraordinary human being, a brilliant intellectual who was an astute politician. . . . It won't be too difficult to work with President Johnson and I intend to. (A long pause followed.) Of course, I could go back to——and run for office or go to work for——But I intend to remain with Johnson."

There was just a trace of melancholy doubt in his voice. Like everybody else in Washington, D.C., he has become a victim of the city's newest syndrome, managed uncertainty.

December 1963

On Choosing a "Negro Leader"

NEW YORK CITY'S Police Commissioner, Michael J. Murphy, two days ago attempted to decide for the Negro community of that city who its leaders should be.

In a speech denouncing Malcolm X, Jesse Gray, leader of the rent strike, and Herbert Callender, chairman of the Bronx chapter of CORE, Murphy accused all three of having a "lust for power," "sinister motives," and "and no real concern for the fight for equality. . . ."

Then he went on to praise the other nice lil', ol' docile Uncle Toms who fit his concept of what a Negro leader should be.

Murphy was attempting to do what so many white people in America have consistently done—choose leaders for the Negro community.

Pat this one on the head, condemn those over there, and hopefully the Negro community will submissively agree. Don't these folks know Negroes are getting tired of this charade?

One of these days, some bright young sociology or political science major is going to reel off a Ph.D. dissertation on the making of Negro leadership in America—who makes them and who keeps them in power. And he is going to make a fortune.

If we Negroes haven't given anything else to American culture, we've given our civilization "Negro leaders." No other ethnic group in America has "leaders"—only Negroes. Everybody else has distinguished business men, financiers, politicians, industrialists, atomic scientists, writers, publishers, bankers, and television network executives.

But us Negroes? We got "leaders."

The reason we have leaders is because we are mediocre as a group of people.

Who runs the white community? The business men, the politicians, the newspaper publishers, the television executives. They form the decision-making infrastructure of every American community. They are the apostles of excellence.

Who runs the Negro community? "Negro leaders"—usually social workers, ministers, and occasionally politicians.

Negro politicians get out the vote, elect candidates, and receive patronage to distribute—period.

"Negro leaders" do the social engineering, the orchestrating, the energizing, and the selling out.

And it's a darned shame, because so many of our "Negro leaders" —chosen by the white community—are parasites. They suck the sociological blood of us all by feeding on the social pathologies among us. If we are the rhinoceros, they are the tick bird.

Invariably, "Negro leaders" are made by the white press.

The white press made the Black Muslims important. Initially, they were of little consequence in the Negro community. After *Time, Life,* and the *Washington Post* exploded into print about their activities, they became a major fact of Negro American life—which up to that point, they were not.

Interestingly enough, one of the creations of the white press is Malcolm X (who is a good friend of mine, so let's clear up that nonsense before we go any further). Malcolm and I have been on many programs together. I feel he's wrong as hell on many issues and right on others, and I've debated with him publicly (and rarely won). To know him is to know a very charming, brilliant, and extraordinarily affable person.

But I didn't create Malcolm X—the white press did. This week in *Life* magazine, there's a two-page spread on "The Ominous Malcolm X Exits from the Muslims." Negroes reading this surely must say to themselves: "Man, this cat must be important. I'd better dig him."

Simultaneously, while it has created, or let's say enhanced, the reputations of the Malcolm X's, the white press has likewise given us our Uncle Toms, who have helped to keep the natives from getting too restless. Here, there's a difference, however. They play up the Malcolm X's because they're really frightened. They play up the Uncle Toms (particularly here in Chicago) because they want somebody with whom they can deal.

Beginning as of this column, you start taking cognizance of what "Negro leaders' " pictures appear the most often in:

The Chicago *Sun-Times*

The Chicago *Daily News*

The Chicago Tribune

Also, note what "Negro leaders" are invariably chosen to "speak" for the Negro community on social issues.

Then compare the incidence of these leaders' pictures in the white press and television with that in Negro publications. In Chicago, our "Negro leaders" rely heavily on the white media for their claim to fame.

This is what makes them "Ceremonial Negro Leaders." They have no actual power in the Negro community, they can organize no total community effort, they can command no vast reservoir of human resources, but they have prolific influence in the white community.

So many people have asked me why I continue to praise Representative Dawson and, of course, my ever-loving, dear friend, Representative Powell.

For only one reason—Negroes chose them both.

The white press didn't create Dawson or Powell. *Negroes* did. If anything, the white press is trying to destroy them. Powell and Dawson have fantastic power, both in Congress and among their political associates. As unhappy as I have been with Dawson's silence on Willis and the school crisis in Chicago, he's still a major counter-irritant to the white power structure. They still fear him.

Negroes will only grow in power and influence when we begin to accord to our business men and politicians the same kind of respect the white community accords to theirs.

And if our Negro politicians are not doing the job we should kick them out. Their inactivity and weakness is *our* fault, nobody else's.

But I would certainly urge our seven Negro aldermen in Chicago to really begin to exert a new influence and a new program of concrete accomplishments in this era of the "Negro Revolt."

It's time the Negro community buried its "Negro leaders" and developed some Negro power for a change.

March 1964

On Amos 'n' Andy—
Maybe I Was Wrong

YOU EVER GET THE FEELING that perhaps you are wrong, you're not quite sure because you're not in full possession of all the facts, yet if you are wrong, you hate to admit it?

That's precisely where I am right now.

On May twenty-sixth, I wrote a column decrying the television rerun of the "Amos 'n' Andy" series on Channel 26. I submitted that the series stereotyped the Negro, that Negroes would be offended by it, and that it just might heighten the social distance between the Negro and white races. I also indicated that the series presentation despite objections from many prominent Negro leaders represented another good example of the Chicago Negro's political impotence and inability to influence public opinion.

Last week, the Associated Press interviewed me the day the series started. I repeated my remarks and they were carried rather fully in the AP story—which went out all over the country. Virtually all of the newspapers which ran the AP story headlined it the same way—"Amos 'n' Andy" series touches off protests by Chicago Negro leaders, etc.

Within two days, my desk was flooded with mail—Yakima, Wash., Providence, R.I., Baton Rouge, La., Baltimore, Md., St. Louis, Mo., Los Angeles, Calif., Washington, D.C., Lexington, Ky., Chicago, Ill.—and even Birmingham, Ala.

All of the letters were from white people and all of them said the same thing—"Chuck Stone, you're off your rocker on this 'Amos 'n'

Andy' jag." Most of the letters were pleasantly written and I was impressed with the manner in which the writers went to great lengths to contradict my position. A few of course, did everything in the letter but call me "nigger."

The composite theme of these letters can be summed up in the following way: "Amos 'n' Andy" is an enjoyable piece of American humor and no more derogates the Negro than the "Beverly Hillbillies" denigrates all white people. It is possible to watch and enjoy "Amos 'n' Andy" without imputing their humorous shenanigans to all Negroes because, in this day and age of racial sensitivities, everbody knows all Negroes are not "Amos 'n' Andy." And besides you Negroes are getting paranoid as hell if you can't even enjoy good humor by Negroes without letting it offend you.

Are all of these white people from all over America right? Was I being over-sensitive? How do we Negroes who angrily denounced the television rerun of "Amos 'n' Andy" know we're right? Is it true that Chicago Negroes—or most Negroes in America, for that matter—really don't care whether the series runs or not?

The answer to that last question is all-determining. Negroes in Chicago or America aren't really concerned whether "Amos 'n' Andy" stays on the television screen all day long or for fifteen minutes. Furthermore, even if they did care, what could they do about it?—nothing.

But the strong probability also exists that Negroes are becoming so emotionally secure and politically sophisticated about this whole integration bit that "Amos 'n' Andy" is recognized for the truly ancillary issue it is. Whether "Amos 'n' Andy" runs in Chicago or not doesn't help us one way or the other to get rid of Benjamin C. Willis.

So, the issue has become at best moot. Neither Negroes nor whites for the most part have gotten exercised about "Amos 'n' Andy" in Chicago.

And I can't overlook that uncomfortable feeling way down in the pit of my stomach that I might have been wrong about the whole thing.

A Tribute to Dan Burley

DAN BURLEY is dead.

And so is a tender piece of colored communities everywhere in America.

If anybody knew his people, Dan Burley did.

He dug the "brother," and could talk about him like a dog while fighting for equal access to every closed bastion in America.

White people coined the phrases "cotton-pickin," "pea-pickin."

Well, Dan Burley was a pork-chop chewin', finger-poppin', box-anklin' swinger who could—as the late ofay swinger, Lord Buckley said—look right down into the window of the littlest cat's soul and make him understand all the sounds—the sounds of freedom riders, jazz, spirituals, political power, numbers racket, sit-ins, black nationalism, and the double-duty dollar.

It's so hard to pay tribute to a legend, and to a guy who, even as I write this, is probably looking down on me, laughing and calling me a square for getting so sentimental.

But I loved Dan Burley and although we only talked two or three times a year by telephone I'm going to miss him.

Most of us in this game called journalism begin where Dan Burley left off.

Man, he could write! He painted pictures with words and his message, biting, sarcastic, pleading, could sear your feelings.

But a lot of white people never read Dan Burley and I feel sorry for them. They are the poorer for it.

He had one column which he considered one of his best. I was the editor of a newspaper in New York City that ran it when we first hit the streets. It broke everybody up.

You read it—and remember this great human being who was such a wonderful guy, but, above all, a consummate artist with his typewriter.

WHAT HAPPENED ON THE 5:15 TO SUBURBIA

by Dan Burley

The magic word today is integration.

Watch colored faces light up when it's mentioned on the corner, in the drawing room or at a lunch counter.

Some take it to be integrated women—both races; some see it as political, still others as intellectual. Maybe this little anecdote will illustrate a more fundamental variety of integration.

It was the 5:15 to Suburbia and among the passengers hurrying home was a tall, blond, blue-eyed, crew-cut young man in Ivy League attire toting his alligator briefcase and with a light topcoat carried on one arm. At the same time, a fat, squat, jet-black, brown-eyed fuzzy-haired young man, also carrying a bag and with a light topcoat on one arm, got aboard.

They took seats on opposite sides of the aisle.

After a while, the blond young man reached into an inside pocket, extracted a gold-embossed cigar case, lit up a 3-for-a-dollar El Producto at the same time the squat, black young man across the aisle produced a diamond-studded case, extracted a $7.50 custom-made Upmann, lighted it with a $60 paper-thin butane lighter and slowly puffed in luxury.

The train droned ahead as passengers played poker or gin rummy while others peered out at the passing countryside. The young blond man picked up his alligator bag that doubtless cost $75, opened it on his lap and with a gold ballpoint pen began making notations on a pad.

At the same time without even looking up at the blond, the squat black man with the fuzzy locks picked up his bag, a $250 imported kangaroo hide job, opened it to reveal a complete portable secretary with a cigarette-pack-sized dictaphone, put the receiver to his ear and concentrated on dictating while fingering thick packs of blue ribbon stocks and other blue chip bonds.

Further along, the two men closed their briefcases and settled back to relax. Neither had noticed the other, apparently.

They acted as though what was happening was part of a well-rehearsed Broadway drama. Two Americans, one black, the other white, who a dozen years ago would be separated, the black one in the car behind the coal car, the other in the air-conditioned drawing room compartment section.

Now they rode opposite one another in the same car and the black man had no fear of being hauled off after a rednecked conductor had stopped the train to flag in the first Klan cohorts he saw on the wayside to drag the black off to a necktie party.

It was shortly after that the conductor came through, muttering "Suburbia, last stop. All out for Suburbia." Passengers began gathering belongings, breaking up card games, slapping one another farewells across the shoulders.

The blond blue-eyed young man with the crew-cut reached up and brought down his $350 camel hair topcoat from the rack.

But at the same time, the jet black, squat, frizzled-haired young man reached for his topcoat—an $850 vicuna—threw the tissue-thin garment carelessly across his shoulders and moved into the aisle as the train ground to a halt at the station.

Ahead of him, the white young man absent-mindedly bit at his unkept fingernails as the black young man gave a final glance at his well-manicured, immaculate hands.

They got off, one behind the other.

The white man walked with regal stride as though the world was his toward an elegant 1960 sleek, black Eldorado Broughham waiting at the curb.

The door was opened by his auburn-tressed youngish wife bedecked in a $10,000 black diamond mink. Happily hollering "Daddy" was his small son, trim in a $150 Buster Brown suit.

He kissed his wife and looked up in time to see the black, squat young man walking leisurely to a gleaming, gold-plated Rolls-Royce Silver Cloud with radio, telephone, built-in bar and hi-fi record-FM player.

The white young man, mouth opened, stared as a stoutish, black chauffeur in smart uniform with boots touched his cap visor, held open the door for his employer.

Inside, the white man, his wife and son gawked as the squat black young man kissed a coal black, handsome woman wearing a $30,-000 Russian Sable on the cheek, fondled his son attired in a $375 hand-stitched Brooks Brothers suit and prepared to lean back for the trip home. Meanwhile, a big black boxer barked joyously from the chauffeur's compartment.

Unable to stand it any longer, the young white man rushed from his Eldorado like a madman to the Rolls-Royce and losing complete control, began banging with his fist on the hood, screaming at the top of his voice, "Nigger, Nigger, Nigger!"

The black man, startled, looked apprehensively and excitedly turned around.

"*Where??*" he screamed.

November 1962

A Lynching Is a Lynching Is a Lynching

AND WHETHER IT FINDS physical expression in the snuffing out of Mack Charles Parker's life in Mississippi or reaps political hay in the destruction of Hulan Edwin Jack's leadership, a lynching still takes place—and the Negro people once again have been had, but good.

The fact that so many Negro leaders—and the Negro masses—have chosen to posture the political persecution of Borough President Jack on a racial basis is significant.

During the past few days, we have talked with a large number of honest-to-goodness, sincere, down-to-earth white people who just don't understand how Jack's present difficulty can be translated into a racial battle.

But it is that.

You destroy Jack and what have you done? Demobilized the Tammany machine? Rubbed more dirt on Mr. DeSapio's kingly crown? Proved Mayor Wagner's administration is one of the worst in the city's history?

Maybe.

But what has been accomplished is the massacre of what little Negro leadership exists in New York City today. "Yes," argues the white liberal, "but Jack is not good for the Negro or even for politics. He's just a Tammany hack. Surely the Negro people deserve something better than this."

Maybe we do, as we've been told repeatedly by articles and stories in the daily press, deserve something better than Jack, but he's the best we've got right now.

My minister in Hartford always told the story of a little boy who used to race the old trolley cars pulled by horses. The boy would run along for a while with the trolley car, sprint ahead, and then drop back to taunt the motorman. "What say, Mr. Motorman, can't you go any faster?" "Yes, son, I can," replied the motorman, "but I've got to stay with the car."

Jack is simply staying with the car. If he constitutes our present leadership, it's because we have continued to vote for him with confidence. Perhaps we're not politically sophisticated enough yet to believe in "reform," because with us, politics is bread and butter.

The *New York Post* can, if it wishes, sit astride moral Valhalla and tut-tut about us poor Negroes and all of our problems, but their handling of the Jack story was, in substance, an anti-Negro effort. Like George Meany, the *Post* has proclaimed itself a friend of the Negro. But it takes one—just one—boot in the backside with hobnailed boots like the *Post*'s series on Harlem two years ago or the so-called exposé on Jack to uncover the *Post*'s mask of racial hypocrisy.

Do you know which newspapers were the most objective in their handling of the Jack story this past week? Not the some-of-our-best-friends-are-Negroes *Post,* but *The New York Times* and *The World-Telegram.* Their editorials were restrained and objective. The *Herald Tribune,* on the other hand, rushed to the fray and sanctimoniously called for Jack's resignation, after sending a reporter to his apartment and "discovering" that Jack's neighbors rarely saw him and furthermore didn't like him. This, you realize, is most germane to the whole issue of Jack's fitness to hold office!

No lynching? Let's take the press conferences last week at City Hall and Ungar's office. They were something else. We went, we guess, as did Jimmy Hicks, because we felt this was certainly one time the Negro press should be represented.

It was during these press conferences we began to feel a creeping sense of racial persecution—the contempt, the hostility, the hand-rubbing glee of the reporters as they sat like spectators at the Roman Colosseum watching the lions tear the Christians apart.

It was open season on Negroes. One white-haired veteran of the reportorial wars punched his finger into the chest of another reporter just before the Ungar-Jack press conference started and boomed exultantly: "Boy, this is one time my newspaper is on the same side as yours!"

One other development of this whole unfortunate spectacle has been the surprising exercise in Negro unity. Negroes closed ranks like the Red Sea on Pharaoh's armies.

There is a unanimity of opinion on this issue which we would have never predicted. But it is also symptomatic of the strong feeling in Harlem that Jack is being persecuted for being too aggressive or too articulate—as a Negro.

It's ironic that had the *Post*'s article on Jack been published last year when he and Powell were feuding, there undoubtedly would have been little outcry in Harlem. Tempers were high, and in the heat of battle many such wishes were made.

But the din died. While Powell continued to peck away at Jack, the diminutive official went about his business reestablishing the communication between himself and the Negro community which Stanley Rose had helped to tear down.

While Jack's war on slums was believed to be largely political, in an effort to beat back the challenge to his district leadership, he nevertheless continued his fight for better conditions in Harlem. You might say he became quite serious about cleaning up the slums and you also might say that he began to step on a few big toes.

Aggressive, articulate Negroes have never felt the affection of our conservatively oriented society. If they talked too loud, they've been labeled Communists, or racists, or simply indicted for stepping out of their place.

Jack stepped out of "his place."

And he was indicted.

"What's in a name? That which we call a rose by any other name would smell as sweet."

And a lynching is a lynching is a lynching.

December 1954

When We Integrate, White Folks Migrate

THAT RHYMING COUPLET is funny, isn't it?

But, it's the truth and it's sad.

As fast as Negroes are walking all over God's heaven of integration, the white man is walking right behind them and de-integrating them.

As fast as Negroes stumble over themselves to luxuriate in the suburbs, whites bang up against each other moving back to the city.

If a Negro moves into a new neighborhood, "for sale" signs spring up around the countryside like daisies after a monsoon.

We're the ones who have got the anxiety neurosis for integration which is jet-propelling us down a one-way street of racial togetherness while the white man hasn't even started the motor.

In the year 1959, the world frowns on racial discrimination and few people except the most neanderthal are prepared to defend it. What's more, we have both the moral and legal rationale to propagandize against segregation.

Wouldn't you think that we would be winning the battle for men's hearts as well as for the right to live next door to them? Well, we're not. And, it's not too difficult to understand why.

What have we got to integrate with?

Our fight for integration is like telling a friend we're going to share a meal together. He shows up with all the food and we bring the napkins.

Instead of concentrating our efforts on raising the standards of what we have and making it so good that the white man will have to nibble just a little at our racial cake, we're busy trying to help him bake his cake.

If we made our schools, our businesses, our neighborhoods so successful, so attractive, and so desirable, don't you know that you couldn't keep the white man away from us? In fact, a few hundred years ago, he was so impressed with our ability to work, he picked up a whole bunch of us and hauled us over here from Africa, and we haven't gotten over it yet.

The difficulty today is that integration has become an end in itself. It's not. It's a means, and through this means, the Negro has got to develop his share of responsibilities and power. Otherwise he is only draining the resources of society.

There are very few people today who have the courage to stand up and say, "Let's not rush so fast toward integration. Let's try to build up those institutions within our cultural framework and make them equal to those of the majority group."

Do you know why nobody dares say this? Because it's so much easier to shout for integration instead of building an economic empire. In a democracy, where the chain of communications is open and free, people can organize for profit. People, it seems, except Negroes. Think of all the immigrants who have come to America during the last fifty years who couldn't speak a word of English and who today are industrial giants. They weren't concerned about integration. They just took up a small patch of ground, started cultivating their cabbages, and ended up replanting their dollar bills.

For every business, school, or service you can point to which is run by Negroes and enjoys the patronage of whites, there are a thousand others waiting to be discovered.

But we can only do this if we start being proud of who we are now and what we have today.

This means going back up on the mountain and retelling the world we're proud to be Negroes and that this same pride can do more for us than the clamor for integration.

It can build us a fortress of economic security, but more important, it can build us a tower of respect for ourselves and from other people.

Okay, Harlem, You're a Malted Milkshake

CHOCOLATE OR VANILLA, it doesn't matter, but it was this kind of thinking that oozed out of Mayor Wagner's mind last week.

The mayor appointed twenty-two people to a committee last week and as far as he is concerned, Harlem's problems are over. Just think, twenty-two people are now going to ease Harlem's racial tensions. Just like that.

Apparently, Mayor Wagner must think he's a Bronx genie.

Just in case you don't know who the Bronx genie is, we think you would appreciate a wonderful story about him. It seems that this Jewish merchant (Yes, Jewish—we love to tell ethnic jokes—next week, we're going to tell some about the Irish and the Italians.) was cleaning his store one day and happened to rub a dirty lamp.

There was a puff and an explosion and this big, black, burly genie (You see? We're being consistent.) appeared. He told the merchant he could have any wish he wanted, whereupon the merchant decided to go to Grossinger's for two weeks. Who would mind the store already? The genie said he would. "I can do anything," the genie promised him.

The next morning the genie opened the store and was busy using his magic to move chairs, clean up, and put things in order when a customer walked in. The genie asked what did he want. (The genie, being a magical kind of person, was prepared to grant any wish.)

Sleepily, the customer yawned and said: "Make me a malted milkshake."

"Okay," replied the genie, flashing his power on, "you're a malted milkshake."

Last week, somebody must have told Mayor Wagner he could be a genie. Appoint a committee and you'll solve Harlem's problems and its newspaper-discovered "racial tensions."

"Okay," replied Mayor Wagner, "twenty-two people, go thou and carry these programs forward and be an action group."

If it weren't for the fact that Mayor Wagner suffers from an odd administrative compulsion, "government by committee," we would wonder at his intentions.

But we don't question the mayor's motives in the least because this is the only methodology he knows. The best way to refuse to grapple with a problem is to appoint a committee. The British did it for years in their colonies and this former British colony, the United States, has been perpetuating this English tradition for years. Just look at Mayor Wagner.

In addition to this battered and withered approach to the problems of Harlem that the mayor has taken, two things disturb us about this committee: Where are the ministers and what determined the committee's composition?

Do you recall the first meeting in Mayor Wagner's office on Tuesday, July twenty-first, following that newspaper-manufactured "near riot?"

Sixty-eight Harlem leaders were invited.

Of that sixty-eight, thirteen were clergymen or the largest single group.

Now, Mayor Wagner appoints a twenty-two-member committee, seventeen of whom are Harlem representatives.

Not a single representative is a minister!

How could thirteen ministers lose so much power in just forty-nine days?

Not only that, what determined the composition of this committee? Are these seventeen people the most representative of Harlem? Can they get things done? Can they go to the people in Harlem and say, "Look, the mayor and his administration are not following any of our recommendations. The primary election is over and the politicians don't care about Harlem now."

Will the people of Harlem listen to such a committee?

They darned sure won't. We know it, you know it, and Mayor Wagner knows it, or he wouldn't have appointed this ineffectual group of good people.

We have no quarrel with the committee as it is presently constituted. Actually, it has some exceptional people on it, particularly Mrs. Evelyn Thomas, Glester Hinds, and Norman Saunders.

But we can't help but be puzzled as to why five other members are on the committee when they weren't invited to the first meeting in the mayor's office.

No, by any yardstick you wish to use, this committee is not going to be an effective committee. Committees don't solve problems. Votes, tough housing laws, court enforcement of these laws, and unbiased police protection solve problems.

And, in the final analysis, the real persons who are going to reduce Harlem's problems to their lowest common denominator are not Mayor Wagner or his genie-created, malted milkshake committee, but the Negroes themselves. The sooner Negroes realize this and start doing something about it, the sooner we'll stop acting like a race of cry-babies who have to rely on political genies like Mayor Wagner who go around making malted milkshakes out of situations.

September 1959

1964 Civil Rights Bill Places A Greater Responsibility On Us

By "us," I mean Negroes—particularly in the North.

If there's anything the Senate-passed civil rights bill does for Negroes in the North, it's cocooned in one simple word: Nothing.

No significant racial barriers in the North are demolished by the bill's eleven titles and a scrupulous analysis of its contents merely reaffirms this legislative Emancipation Proclamation's total applicability to the South.

Title I, forbidding use of discriminatory tests for voting registration, has no relevance for Northern cities. In fact, cities like Chicago and Boston are so American many people even vote twice in one election.

Title II, outlawing racial discrimination by hotels, motels, restaurants, lunch rooms, theaters, sports arenas, and other places of entertainment, has been law in Illinois, New York State, and other northern states for over fifty years. During the Illinois' law's operative existence, hotels in Springfield (capital and home of Lincoln) refused to accept Negro guests, and racial discrimination by Chicago hotels, restaurants, and theaters was savagely rampant.

Title III, barring discrimination in public facilities such as parks, playgrounds, pools, etc., again was covered by law many years ago in the largest Northern states and urban centers.

Title IV, authorizing the Attorney General to bring suit to end school segregation, applies only to de jure Jim Crow in the South and not its fraternal counterpart, de facto segregation in the North. Thus, Ben Willis remains secure from Federal inquiry into his administrative practices.

Title V, extending the life of the Civil Rights Commission through January 1968, makes no meaningful impact upon the North. The Commission is only the heuristic arm of civil rights.

Title VI, barring racial discrimination in programs receiving Federal assistance, is already operative under President Kennedy's Executive Orders, but still has not been able to prevent racial discrimination in employment on federally assisted construction projects.

Title VII, outlawing discrimination by employers and unions in membership policies and hiring halls, has been covered by FEPC's in New York, Illinois, Connecticut, New Jersey, and Philadelphia, and very little headway has been made over the years while these laws were on the books.

Title VIII, directing the U. S. Bureau of the Census to collect voting and registration data in areas pinpointed by the Civil Rights Commission and then to report to Congress, unquestionably excluded the North.

Title IX, granting the Attorney General broad power to intervene in court cases brought under the Fourteenth Amendment's guarantee of equal protection of the laws, is virtually meaningless because a.) the Attorney General's office has already been doing this and b.) very few cases are initiated by Negroes in this area.

Title X, establishing a Community Relations Service to work with local agencies to settle racial problems through conciliation, is rendered superfluous by such northern local and state agencies as Chicago's Commission on Human Relations and the Illinois Commission on Human Relations.

Title XI, granting individuals charged with criminal contempt of court arising under the bill the right to a jury trial, is specifically directed to Southern communities since this title's sponsorship was Southern-conceived and was one of the few compromises in the bill with the South.

There they all are and it's fair to submit that the passage of the 1964 Civil Rights Bill by the U. S. Senate actually accomplished just two things:

1. It re-admitted the Confederate South into the Union by subjugating that region's centrifugal states rights independence to his government's centripedal Federal sovereignty on the most crucial issue governing their political relationship—the right of the Negro to unqualified equal rights and his enjoyment thereof.

2. It has placed an even greater responsibility on Negroes themselves to utilize available legal tools to destroy racial segregation and now forces us to begin almost immediately a revived exercise of the rights we already enjoy.

In those states where we Negroes have been privileged to vote, we haven't bothered to get out of bed on election day and our registration figures are eloquent testimonials to our civil apathy.

In those cities where schools are open to all pupils, we Negroes sat passively and watched in silent acquiescence as school officials deliberately gerrymandered school systems to contain Negro students in third class educational ghettoes. Even worse, we have failed to become active in PTA's and other directly related educational activities.

For those of us who have attained a measure of economic success, racial equality and human dignity have been concepts reserved only for the extension of these previous successes. We have felt no responsibility or compassion for our more deprived Negro brothers and sisters—"the unreachables." As a result, Negro crime, Negro welfare recipiency, Negro family disorganization, and juvenile delinquency have escalated while most of us did nothing to reverse their ascent.

So many Negroes have not involved themselves in the struggle for human dignity and there is now a dangerous bi-polarization taking place in the Negro community between the "unreachables" and the middle-to-upper income Negroes who don't want to relate to the former's problems.

Rights by definition imply obligations and responsibilities. In a democracy, the educational process of becoming a citizen is fulfilled only through a full participation in the political process or community activities. There is no other path to productive citizenship.

With the passage of the Senate Civil Rights Bill, there is no guarantee of equality for the Negro. All that law will do is legalize the climate for the growth of racial equality. Unless the law is used, unless the deprived citizen fully takes advantage of every legal, political, and economic apparatus available to him, unless the disinherited Negro organizes into an intelligent and powerful political phalanx and relentlessly worries city, state, and Federal officials to implement full racial equality—it will all remain a dream.

This, then, is the renewed responsibility placed upon Negroes, particularly in the North, by the Civil Rights bill.

This is an obligation Negroes must accept if we are ever to compete as equals in American society.

July 1964

Schuyler Speaks for White Fascists and Colored Morons

MY GOOD FRIEND in New York City, Jackie Robinson, has occasionally commented on something that newspaper columnist George Schuyler has either said or written.

I, too, used to gnash my teeth at Schuyler's editorial rantings, but recognized several years ago that this unreconstructed reactionary was virtually alone as a colored man in his opinions.

Like a growing number of colored Americans through the years, I have just ignored him.

But I have recently been informed by one of Africa's most distinguished leaders that this man cannot be dismissed that easily.

Because he writes and says what so many backward white people want to hear—particularly some in the opinion-making infrastructure—Schuyler receives a wider distribution of his paleolithic ideas than is healthy.

Some of these white people actually believe he speaks for colored people.

Well, he doesn't. And the dwindling readership of his column proves it.

However, if there's one black man in America whose prickly intellect still manages to anger most colored Americans, it's George Schuyler.

And if there's any one colored writer to whom colored Americans pay little or no attention—most of the time—it's George Schuyler.

For years, this sullen and acerbic curmudgeon has tilted at every philosophical windmill in the field of race and international relations as if he had ultimate truth by the tail.

Called the "black Westbrook Pegler," Schuyler has been as fanatically reactionary, politically stupid, sociologically naive, and hysterically anti-Communist as the former Hearstling.

Like Pegler, Schuyler should have been retired ten years ago. But it is one of the indictments of us as a race that we permit the Schuylers to mildew among us long after they should have been put out to the soggy pastures of contentment.

Schuyler—whom one must admit is a fine writer and possessor of an agile mind—continues to spew forth a type of logic and opinion that placates two types of people: white fascists and colored morons.

Whenever a movement or idea or group displeases Schuyler, he consigns it to his pet irreducible minimum: Communists or Communist sympathizers.

If a discussion revolves around the feasibility of mass movements in race relations (sit-ins, etc.), Schuyler contemptuously dismisses their Marxist natality.

Schuyler is indeed sui generis.

He is one of two colored Americans—the other being the politically disillusioned and intellectually shattered Max Yergan—who will publicly line up with an incorrigible racist, Mississippi Senator James Eastland, to lustily tout the stature of Africa's most distinguished Uncle Tom, Moise Tshombe.

Schuyler is a man who enthusiastically endorsed the ideas and program of the Dominican Republic's wretched tyrant, the late Trujillo.

Schuyler is a man who even now defends Portuguese policy in Africa, thus making him the most regal of rare species: a black man who supports colonialism in Africa in 1962.

This, then, is George Schuyler, a weary old man waving his tattered escutcheon of super-perfect anti-Communism for a generation who never reads him and who simply wonders why his therapist can't resolve his levophobia.

Who listens to Schuyler today?

Who quotes him?

Who believes in him?

White bwanas who want to preserve the status quo in Africa and set Moise Tshombe up as Most Elegant and Superior Grand Pontiff of all Africa.

White segregationists and Citizens' Council members who wax happy at the idea of a colored man knocking the freedom riders, sit-ins, and other mechanisms of the colored man's freedom struggle.

Colored people who have not yet grasped the full meaning of their potential strength and are content to idle in the wilderness of a segregated mentality.

History will be kind to George Schuyler because he did write great thoughts once upon a time.

But every writer eventually suffers the ravages of editorial dotage.

Just sittin', rockin', and sippin' is a much nicer way to walk off the editorial stage than to sit there dashing off typewriter ribbons of vapidity to a stilled theater of colored patrons who stopped applauding years and years ago.

Christmas Boycott Could Hurt the Innocent With the Guilty

SEVERAL WEEKS AGO, *Newsweek* magazine, in an article on the Negro press of America, referred to me as "the angry young man of the Negro press."

That's a fairly honest delineation.

I am angry.

I'm angry about the daily horror of racial persecution in America, which we somehow seem unable to eradicate. I'm angry about the white liberal's hypocrisy in race relations. I'm angry about the Negro's embarrassing impotence in the civil rights struggle and our continuing inability to really muster the political and economic power of 20 million American Negroes for an all-out assault on the racial iron curtain.

But anger is a lousy substitute for progress.

It's one thing to be angry. It's another to resolve the reasons for the anger. As Congressman Dawson once said in that historic remark: "Don't get mad, get smart."

American Negroes today are indeed mad—and don't we have every justification—but we're not smart!

This collective anger now sweeping the Negro masses of America has sometimes produced more than frustration. It has produced a confusion of techniques, preventing us from being smart. I don't think any one technique can be submitted as the over-all best technique. During World War II, the Negro press raised so much hell about racial discrimination in the armed forces, steps were taken to remove this blot on America's forces for democracy.

Nine years ago, the NAACP's technique of litigation produced the magnificent May seventeenth, 1954, Supreme Court decision outlawing segregation in public education.

Three years ago, sit-ins became an integral part of the civil rights struggle.

Today massive disobedience and mass marches are now necessary to convince America we mean business.

In between the successful applications of these various techniques, the economic boycott has been tried with varying success in different parts of the country.

The most recently successful economic boycott—ooops! I'm sorry—selective patronage campaign—I know was conducted by the Negro ministers of Philadelphia against specific companies and products.

And they won every battle they entered. Negroes were hired in higher positions in all of the companies.

But there was a specificity about the selective buying campaign in Philadelphia.

What bothers me about a nation-wide Christmas boycott is its undifferentiation.

"Don't buy presents. Don't buy clothes. Don't buy toys."

From whom?

In Chicago, are you Negroes prepared to tell me that you make no distinction between South Center Department Store, Goldblatt's, Sears & Roebuck, A & P, and Walgreen's on the one hand, and Kroger's, Rexall's, and Marshall Field's, on the other?

All these years Marshall Field's has consistently and persistently refused to hire Negroes in any white collar or sales capacity. In fact, they barely hire Negroes—period.

Yet you Chicago Negroes trot yourself down there in numbers just as proudly and buy everything from mink stoles to basement kitchen sinks. And what's more, you brag about it! "I bought this in Marshall Field's!"

What would happen in a generalized boycott of Christmas? A fairly large number of businesses which have made some determinable progress in hiring Negroes and which have gone out to woo the Negro dollar would get hurt economically.

Sure, let's go after specific businesses which bar Negroes in anything but the most menial jobs and specific products which are manufactured by lilywhite hands.

But let's not injure the already committed.

Let's not hurt our friends, too.

We'll do this if we boycott Christmas.

We can boycott the bigots in Chicago businesses.

We can boycott the stores and products which will take a black dollar but do nothing to inform you it is welcomed.

We can boycott the over-commercialization of Christmas. For example, everybody—particularly every Negro in this country—should hang a picture of Jesus Christ in their front room during the holidays to remind ourselves of our love for Him and His way of life.

And if you want to do something truly Christlike at Christmas, buy all the presents you want—from those businesses and companies which really want your dollar—and at the same time, send a Christmas card to four parents in Birmingham, the parents of little Carole Robertson, Addie Mae Collins, Cynthia Wesley, and Denise McNair.

Negroes and Convertibles:
The American Dream

If spring comes, can summer be far behind—with Bermuda shorts, tanned legs, picnic lunches, sheer dresses, and open convertibles?

Of these hedonistic components of summer, open convertibles are the most indigenously American.

Why do Americans buy convertibles?

1. They're sporty (and Americans consider themselves the biggest sports in the world).

2. They symbolize the spirit of freedom (with their tops down, there is a fast, constant, and breezy communion with the unchained elements).

3. They provide a healthy exposure to the health-building rays of the sun (and it's an easy, economical way to get a sun-tan).

Those three reasons are exactly the identical reasons why Negroes buy convertibles.

Negroes are Americans and whatever Americans do, Negroes are going to do—for all the same, silly, inane, unexplainable reasons (except vote for Goldwater).

Years ago, the "brother" had a terrible inferiority complex about his color. He wanted to be white in the worst way and skin-lighteners did a boom business with their ads in the Negro press. If the "brother" in his compulsion to be American bought a convertible during those days, both he and his chick covered up something fierce. Neither permitted the sun to radiate its blackening rays upon their already burnt epidermis. With the convertible's top down, it wasn't a question of "the wind and the rain in your hair," but "don't let anythings mess up the process" and the newly relaxed kinks.

Then came the emancipating "Negro Revolt."

To be black became fashionable. A new pride among Negroes welled up, endowing them with a new serenity about their dark skins, their nappy hair, and their thick lips.

Negroes even started lying out in the sun on the beaches just like "Mr. Charlie." If his skin got darker—well, that's the way the epidermis wrinkles.

With this new-found security, the "brother" has begun to realize an irreducible minimum of the American dream—to buy that convertible and ride around all day with the top down just like "Miss Anne."

So you'll see the "brother" in a lot more convertibles this summer. That's because he's not ashamed to get darker.

General Motors, Chrysler, and Ford ought to be thankful for the "Negro Revolt." They'll sell more convertibles to Negroes who, strangely enough, want to be nothing more than good ol' red, white, and blue Americans.

And none of this involves marrying Governor Wallace's daughter —now, does it?

The Negro Revolution Comes of Age: After the March, Where Do We Go?

I STOOD ON THE gleaming white steps of the Lincoln Memorial Wednesday, August twenty-eighth, 1963, and saw an American Revolution come of age.

High above the famed reflecting pool which solemnly ripples from the Lincoln Memorial to the Washington Monument, I stood transfixed, watching a vast ocean of black and white humanity slowly flood these historic grounds.

Quiet, good-humored, but deadly serious, wave upon wave of 300,000 marchers filed to the base of the shrine of the Great Emancipator to make the Negro Revolution a dynamic reality.

For Rosa Parks, who six years ago decided her aching feet and her dignity were more important to her than the threat of bodily harm, for those two young students who decided in South Carolina in February, 1960, that they were going to sit-in until they could eat where they could buy merchandise, for the thousands and thousands of Negro women, children, and men who braved fire hoses and vicious police dogs, bombs, and death by rifle snipers at night in Birmingham, Jackson, Danville, and Cambridge—this day of glory, this triumphant vindication was worth it all.

God's hand had to be working.

I think He reached down and gently picked up the beloved Dr. W. E. B. Du Bois and told him, "Come, it is time. Your people have finally begun to finish what you started seventy years ago. You may have wanted to watch the whole thing at your television set by Telstar, but you'll have a much clearer view from up here. Come now and be with us and sit beside Medgar Evers and William L. Moore."

It was such a wonderful time to be Negro.

Black Americans could finally proclaim to the world: "Yes, we *are* in charge of our revolution and because it has happened, American democracy breathes a fiercer red, white, and blue."

Some of you who read this were not there.

Your reasons for not marching are your own—perhaps lack of money, laziness, or just plain indifference.

You would have hung your head in shame, or wept, as I did, when I saw a lovely middle-aged, brown-skinned woman with an iron cast on her leg, dragging its near-lifeless uselessness for freedom.

Every step was painful, and as she walked nobody reached out, because she didn't want help, nor did she beg for pity. But she marched and dragged that leg and there wasn't a dry eye within yards of her.

She became my symbol of the Negro Revolution. She understood why she was there. Those of you who stayed home should fall down on your knees and thank God for letting her fight your freedom battle.

But the "March on Washington for Jobs and Freedom" is now tucked away in the catalogues of history.

It has made its point.

The cultural catharsis has spent itself.

Where do we go from here now?

Do we let the fires of freedom flicker into embers of lethargy?

Do we ignore the new spiritual thrust lovingly created by so many or do we place our hands in theirs and ask them to show us how to move faster, more forcefully, and—with Mr. Kennedy's kind permission—more vigorously?

I know where we must go.

We must have some more marches.

We must march every day—right down to City Hall and register to become voters. If you marched and you're not a registered voter, don't you know you're a phony?

We must march every day for more jobs, hammering away at the iron curtain of racial exclusion which so many companies and industries in our cities have lowered between us and complete equality.

We must march every day to protest and protest and protest until our cities and our mayors decide they no longer can afford to have bigots anywhere in their midst.

We must march every day to protest the black ghetto of houses which stunt the healthy flowering of our children.

And we must raise every kind of legitimate and Constitutional hell we can until America recognizes that all of America's 20 million black men, women, and children, created in the eyes of God, are equal to their white brothers and sisters.

Finally, we must march to a new consciousness of ourselves as black people. We must march with a new pride that congratulates the fact of colored togetherness.

Togetherness—togetherness: This is where our power lies. And we must seek this power in the highest councils of this land, at the same time cremating forever the "Uncle Toms," the "Ceremonial Negro Leaders" and the dishonest compromisers.

That new day has arrived. It's here right now.

Walk together, children! Don'tcha get weary.

September 1963

THE HISTORY OF NATIONS

England

Other books in the History of Nations series:

China

Germany

THE HISTORY OF NATIONS

England

Clarice Swisher, *Book Editor*

Daniel Leone, *President*
Bonnie Szumski, *Publisher*
Scott Barbour, *Managing Editor*

San Diego • Detroit • New York • San Francisco • Cleveland
New Haven, Conn. • Waterville, Maine • London • Munich

For more information, contact
Greenhaven Press
27500 Drake Rd.
Farmington Hills, MI 48331-3535
Or you can visit our Internet site at http://www.gale.com

Cover credit: © Tate Gallery, London/Art Resource, NY
Library of Congress, 75, 80
National Archives, 163, 176, 183
North Wind Picture Archives, 139
Prints Old and Rare, 148

LIBRARY OF CONGRESS CATALOGING-IN-PUBLICATION DATA

England / Clarice Swisher, book editor.
p. cm. — (History of nations)
Includes bibliographical references and index.
ISBN 0-7377-1129-9 (pbk. : alk. paper) — ISBN 0-7377-1130-2 (lib. : alk. paper)
1. Great Britain—History. 2. England—Civilization. I. Swisher, Clarice, 1933– .
II. History of nations (Greenhaven Press)
DA28 .E54 2003
942—dc21 2002023171

Printed in the United States of America

CONTENTS

Chapter 2: The Tudor Monarchy, 1485–1603

Chapter 5: Modernism and War, 1900–1990

Chapter 6: Recent Challenges

FOREWORD

In 1841, the journalist Charles MacKay remarked, "In reading the history of nations, we find that, like individuals, they have their whims and peculiarities, their seasons of excitement and recklessness." At the time of MacKay's observation, many of the nations explored in the Greenhaven Press History of Nations series did not yet exist in their current form. Nonetheless, whether it is old or young, every nation is similar to an individual, with its own distinct characteristics and unique story.

The History of Nations series is dedicated to exploring these stories. Each anthology traces the development of one of the world's nations from its earliest days, when it was perhaps no more than a promise on a piece of paper or an idea in the mind of some revolutionary, through to its status in the world today. Topics discussed include the pivotal political events and power struggles that shaped the country as well as important social and cultural movements. Often, certain dramatic themes and events recur, such as the rise and fall of empires, the flowering and decay of cultures, or the heroism and treachery of leaders. As well, in the history of most countries war, oppression, revolution, and deep social change feature prominently. Nonetheless, the details of such events vary greatly, as does their impact on the nation concerned. For example, England's "Glorious Revolution" of 1688 was a peaceful transfer of power that set the stage for the emergence of democratic institutions in that nation. On the other hand, in China, the overthrow of dynastic rule in 1912 led to years of chaos, civil war, and the eventual emergence of a Communist regime that used violence as a tool to root out opposition and quell popular protest. Readers of the Greenhaven Press History of Nations series will learn about the common challenges nations face and the different paths they take in response to such crises. However a nation's story may have developed, the series strives to present a clear and unbiased view of the country at hand.

The structure of each volume in the series is designed to help students deepen their understanding of the events, movements, and persons that define nations. First, a thematic introduction provides critical background material and helps orient the reader. The chapters themselves are designed to provide an accessible and engaging approach to the study of the history of that nation involved and are arranged either thematically or chronologically, as appropriate. The selections include both primary documents, which convey something of the flavor of the time and place concerned, and secondary material, which includes the wisdom of hindsight and scholarship. Finally, each book closes with a detailed chronology, a comprehensive bibliography of suggestions for further research, and a thorough index.

The countries explored within the series are as old as China and as young as Canada, as distinct in character as Spain and India, as large as Russia, and as compact as Japan. Some are based on ethnic nationalism, the belief in an ethnic group as a distinct people sharing a common destiny, whereas others emphasize civic nationalism, in which what defines citizenship is not ethnicity but commitment to a shared constitution and its values. As human societies become increasingly globalized, knowledge of other nations and of the diversity of their cultures, characteristics, and histories becomes ever more important. This series responds to the challenge by furnishing students with a solid and engaging introduction to the history of the world's nations.

INTRODUCTION

England: The Island Nation

Geography has affected England's history more than any other single factor. England is an island surrounded by the English Channel, the North Sea, and the Atlantic Ocean. Rivers interrupt England's coastline all around the island, providing inland transportation and access to the sea from all points. Being isolated and surrounded by seas has influenced the history of England in several ways. England's remoteness has shaped the character of the people, who in turn have shaped the nation's institutions and actions to suit that character. In addition, its easy access to the sea has influenced the development of the nation as a center of trade and industry.

Finally, the sea has played a crucial role in determining England's status as a world power. During its early years, England's proximity to the oceans made it vulnerable to invasion. In later years, its closeness to the sea gave the country an increased capacity to wage wars, conduct trade, and acquire colonies. As historian George Macaulay Trevelyan writes, "In early times, the relationship of Britain to the sea was passive and receptive; in modern times active and acquisitive. In both it is the key to her story."[1]

The English National Character

England's geography has contributed to the national character of the people, and the people's characteristics have affected the history of the nation. As a result of its location and climate, its early inhabitants developed strength and endurance. Its colonizers tamed a wet, windswept island of dense forests, swampy lowlands, and heavy clay. Though the climate was harsh, it was tempered by a current from the southwest Atlantic. The elements, according to historian Arthur Bryant in *Spirit of England*, "steeled, but did not ossify, stamina and character . . . [and] bred vigorous, hardy, adaptable plants, beasts, and men."[2] These qualities of strength, endurance, and adaptability affected historical events. Bryant sums up the effect of England's geography on the people:

> Our history is the history of the people of a northern island. . . . Seafaring, adventure, resilience, and dogged endurance in the face of difficulties was in their mixed—very mixed—blood; characteristics strengthened over the centuries by the vicissitudes of an island climate.[3]

Gradually the early qualities of the settlers developed into a spirit of independence and resistance to domination. Trevelyan attributes the independent national character to the blending of invaders:

> By a significant paradox it was under this foreign [Norman] leadership that the English began to develop their intense national feeling and their peculiar institutions, so different in spirit from those of Italy and France. Already among the fellow-countrymen of [poet Geoffrey] Chaucer, . . . we see the beginnings of a distinct nationality, far richer than the old Saxon, composed of many different elements of race, character and culture which the tides of ages had brought to our coasts and the island climate had tempered and mellowed into harmony.[4]

In *History of England*, historian W.E. Lunt, however, attributes the independent spirit to isolation. Isolated on the fringe of the civilized world, Lunt suggests, England received moral, social, and political ideas more slowly than continental countries did and, consequently, had more time to reflect on them and accept only the ones it wanted. Lunt suggests that an Englishman's conservatism, his adherence to tradition, "what in short is often termed his insularity of mind—may be attributed in large degree to his insular environment."[5]

Tolerance also developed as a trait in the national character. As Bryant states "All [England's] original inhabitants came here by sea and were, therefore, seafarers; all of them learnt, as a result of bitter struggle and difficulty, to live with, intermingle with, and tolerate, one another."[6] Moreover, England has been free from military invasion by land since the eleventh century; peace at home has provided a sense of security that in turn has allowed for tolerance and the continuity of cultural development. Finally, Trevelyan suggests that the English language, whose chief merits are "grace, suppleness, and adaptability," is a manifestation of the English character and was destined "to be spoken in every quarter of the globe, and to produce a literature with which only that of ancient Hellas [Greece] is comparable. It is symbolic of the fate of the English race itself."[7] In short, the national spirit that evolved from the location and climate of England charted the course of England's institutions and undertakings—its democratic government, its Protestant religion, its sea power, its commerce and industry, its imperial ambitions, and its wars.

From Fringe to Center of the Western World

England's geography alone determined its earliest history. England was populated by primitive Celts, who were powerless to withstand three sets of invaders. In A.D. 43 Romans came by sea and conquered England, occupying it until 410, when the soldiers were called back to Rome. During their occupation they built roads and towns and left London an established city, but they had little effect on the culture or language of the Celts. Beginning in A.D. 300 the second wave of invaders came—the Angles, Saxons, Jutes, Danes, and Norsemen, all of whom were various tribes of Nordic people. They came by sea and went inland on the rivers; these warriors subsequently brought their families, settled down, farmed, and intermarried among the various tribes. Trevelyan states, "The mingling of the armed races poured into Britain," forming a new world, "not Latin, not Saxon, not Scandinavian, but a blend."[8] Then, in 1066, the Normans from northern France, led by William the Conqueror, invaded southeast England, where they met little resistance. Under William, the Normans centralized government, established feudalism, strengthened the church, and began opening communication with the continent.

England remained an outpost of feudalism until the Tudor monarchs, Henry VII, Henry VIII, and Elizabeth I, began England's transformation from a geographically isolated island to a central power in the world. Their leadership and foresight brought new respect and power to England. The sea was certainly a major factor in their success, but equally important were the people's endurance and independence acquired in the early history.

First, the Tudor monarchs, all strong leaders, acknowledged their subjects' desire for freedom and led the nation by giving the people what they wanted, which was peace and order. Second, the Tudors, who brought the Renaissance to England by promoting learning and the arts, were educated themselves and were widely respected among other world leaders. Trevelyan remarks, "It was said that Henry's [VIII] Court had better store of learned men than any University."[9] Of Elizabeth, he says,

> "Mere English" as she was, her education had been the broadest that modern and ancient Europe could afford. She discoursed in Greek and Latin to the Universities of Oxford and Cambridge, and in fluent Italian to the natives of the land of [Italian Prince] Machiavelli. . . . She was a child of the Renaissance.[10]

England's move to the center of power, however, had most to

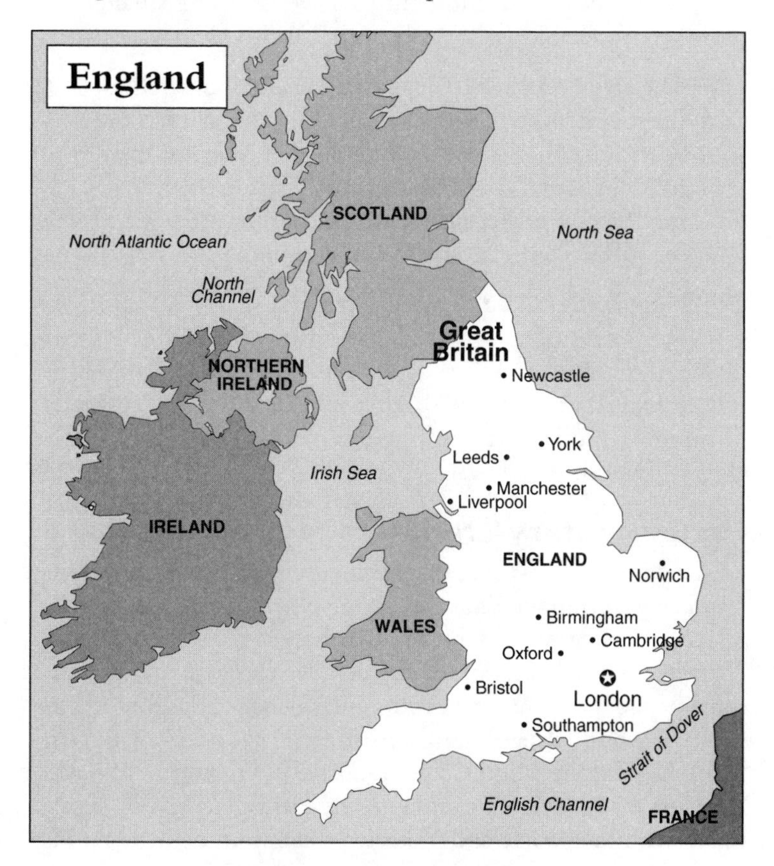

do with the sea. Geography forced English seamen out onto the water reaching farther and farther from their island shores. The sixteenth century was a turning point. Before that century, the English passively took what came to them by sea; afterward, they took an active role on the global waters.

By the sixteenth century of the Tudors, explorers had discovered ocean routes to the east, to Africa, and to North America. These voyages "did something to fire the imagination of contemporary Englishmen and helped to create the spirit which later sent Englishmen forth into all parts of the newly discovered world."[11] Moreover, when these routes opened, Henry VIII had already created the Royal Navy, equipped with newly designed ships for war and commerce. The turning point came when King Philip of Spain challenged English sea power in the Battle of the Spanish Armada in the English Channel in 1588. The English had fewer sailors and ships, but their vessels were smaller and more maneuverable. Lunt explains the British victory:

> The crews numbered only seven to eight thousand, but they were better sailors and better gunners than the Spaniards. Their spirit was indomitable. Many of them had fought and conquered Spanish ships. In their opinion, "twelve of her majesty's ships were a match for all the galleys in the king of Spain's dominions."[12]

The victory over the Spanish Armada made England the supreme power of the seas. The English people gained confidence in themselves, and the Western world gained respect for this evolving nation. By 1600, at what historians consider the beginning of modern times, England was in the center of the Western world.

Parliamentary Democracy

England became a world power through its culture of peace and its stable government. England's geography indirectly contributed to its form of government because the geography affected the character and deliberation of the people who formed it. With a spirit of independence, reflection, and tolerance, England led the Western world in developing a parliamentary system of government. During the Middle Ages England was fortunate to have a long line of Anglo-Norman kings, the Plantagenets, who kept in touch with the people and protected them from oppression. The first Plantagenet king, Henry II (1154–1189) established juries to hear the people's complaints, ending a system of "trial-by-battle and private war."[13] His judges decided cases in all parts of the country, made decisions that set precedent, and thus established national, or common, law. Today, England's constitution is not a written document; rather, it is the accumulation of judicial decisions, statutes, and tradition passed down through the centuries.

Another major step toward democracy was the signing of the Magna Carta, or the Great Charter of 1215, during the reign of King John (1199–1216). Angered by the king's losses of land during the war with France and his taxation abuses at home, English barons, who were low-ranking noblemen, presented him with a list of demands. When the people sided with the barons, King John was forced to agree to their demands. The list was rewritten into an official charter, which says that no person shall "be deprived of life, liberty, or property, without judgment by his social equals" in a trial, words that the framers of the U.S. Constitution borrowed. In essence, the Magna Carta established that in England no one is above the law, not even a king.

Another step toward democracy was the establishment of Parliament, also a product of the Middle Ages. Plantagenet King Edward I (1272–1307) established a means to gather the Great Council (later renamed Parliament) at regular intervals to obtain the people's consent on issues that departed from Common Law. On the Great Council sat the representatives of small landowners, knights, and local officials from trading towns. The power of Parliament grew over time in two ways: People supported Parliament under strong monarchs who sought their opinions, and they rallied around Parliament under insecure monarchs who tried to deprive Parliament of power. Thus, by the end of the Middle Ages England had the major elements of parliamentary democracy: juries, a constitution, and a parliament.

At the beginning of the modern era, the Tudor monarchs continued the established practices and used them to their own and the country's advantage. They listened to the people and worked closely with Parliament, promoted strong local governments, and provided courts that enacted justice for ordinary crimes.

The Stuart monarchs, James I (1603–1625), Charles I (1625–1649), Charles II (1660–1685), and James II (1685–1688), on the other hand, flaunted Parliament and disregarded public opinion in their belief that they had a divine right to rule. Moreover, Stuart kings favored Catholicism and tried to strengthen it after Elizabeth I had established Protestantism as the state religion. These practices flew in the face of British independence and fostered resistance. The resistance led to civil war, the execution of a king, and an interim without a monarch. Finally, Parliament and the people had had enough of the Stuarts, and parliamentary leaders invited Protestant prince William of Orange to invade, oust the last, most extreme Stuart, and become king. It was a risky action that resulted in the Glorious Revolution of 1688. The outcome was a permanent agreement that gave equal power to Parliament and the Crown, moving England closer to a democracy. The spirit of the English people tolerated a strong monarch as long as the people were represented in their local institutions, but they did not tolerate absolute authority that deprived them of freedom.

Though Parliament and the people had secured the major elements of democracy by 1700, four additional elements developed later. After the Revolution of 1688, the two political parties, the Whigs and the Tories, became stronger and played a more active role in governing. Another change occurred in the cabinet. Robert Walpole, head of the cabinet (1721–1742), reorganized the ministers, or advisers, requiring that they come from Parliament and agree on policies with their leader, the prime minister. The third change occurred during the nineteenth century, when reform bills extended voting rights to all classes of people. Prior to these reforms, only property holders—the aristocracy and the gentry—could vote. The reform bills gave suffrage first to the middle class and, by the late 1800s, to males of the working classes. The fourth change occurred during the twentieth century, when women gained the right to vote.

Commerce and the Navy

Besides allowing for the peace and stability that enabled a transition to democracy, England's geography contributed to the development of commerce and trade. Since England is an island surrounded by navigable seas and blessed with numerous rivers and inlets, it would seem logical that seafaring would have been the first important way for the country to gain wealth and power, but history did not develop that way. Until the time of the Tudors, the English people had few ships. Even though all of England's invaders arrived by sea, none built a fleet of ships after they settled. Saxon king Alfred (871–899), who wanted to build ships, had to hire outside craftsmen. Later, Viking king Canute (1017–1035) built a small navy of forty ships, and during the Middle Ages Henry V (1413–1422) began to build a royal fleet. During the Middle Ages British merchants had to depend on foreign ships for trade. Merchants, many of them wool traders, developed trading companies and bought and sold goods to countries along the Atlantic and the Mediterranean, but most were at a disadvantage because foreign ships carrying the cargo charged large fees. Only a few English merchants did business on such a large scale that they could afford to build their own ships, and they ran the risk of encountering pirates, who infested the seas around England. In spite of these disadvantages, commerce did continue to grow.

The Tudors built ships and made England an active trader on the seas. Henry VII (1485–1509) favored merchants and established new trading companies. He trained sailors by sending them on fishing voyages, and he built a large merchant fleet, but the ships needed protection from pirates and from Spain, the dominant military power at sea. Henry VIII (1509–1547) created the Royal Navy with newly designed fighting ships that had cannons jutting from portholes. Trevelyan describes them: "It was Henry VIII himself who had insisted that his naval architects should mount heavy cannon in the body of the ship; they had devised the expedient of piercing apertures in the very hold itself through which the great shot could be discharged."[14] With a merchant fleet for commercial trading and the Royal Navy equipped with warships, England was ready to exert its economic and military power throughout the world.

The English knew that superiority on the seas required both well-equipped ships and skillful and brave leaders to command them. England was fortunate over the years to have outstanding fleet commanders. Queen Elizabeth had Sir Francis Drake, to whom she granted a privateer's license, which gave him governmental approval to use his private ship to attack enemy vessels. Drake attacked Spanish vessels near the West Indies, was the first to circumnavigate the globe, and fought in the Battle of the Spanish Armada. English sea power waned during the reign of the first two Stuart kings, but Commander Robert Blake restored it during the mid-1600s. Trevelyan says, "When called, a few days after the execution of the King [Charles I], to take command of the fleet and recover for the English marine the lost freedom of the sea, he obeyed marvelling. Doubtless he had been chosen because his knowledge of ships and seamen was at least greater than that of other soldiers."[15] He led the English fleet against the Dutch and the Spanish, helped create a professional navy, and developed naval tactics to use in war. The most successful commander, however, was Horatio Nelson. Between 1794 and 1805 he led the British navy in eight successful battles against Danish, French, and Spanish fleets. His greatest victory occurred during the Napoleonic Wars in the Battle of Trafalgar, where he defeated the French and the Spanish fleets at the southern tip of Spain.

England maintained its dominance at sea into the twentieth century. During World War I, when the German navy used submarines against British ships, new methods were developed to fight them, and the navy succeeded. After World War II, however, British naval dominance declined; in a cost-cutting measure in 1981, the Royal Navy was reduced to about a hundred vessels, down from three hundred in 1957. Today, the American navy dominates the seas, but the British Royal Navy still plays an important part in supporting American ventures and its merchant ships in transporting England's commerce.

The British Empire

The vast empire that England built over centuries was both a cause and an effect of its geography. As a small island nation, England needed trade to supplement its resources, but the English could not transport goods by land. Consequently, they built a strong fleet of merchant ships with a navy to protect them from pirates and invaders. As a result of their success in shipping and trade, they built an empire. The Tudors developed the navy and trade; the Stuarts began building the empire, a development that spanned four hundred years.

Acquiring colonies followed trade. Trading companies, such as the East India Company and Levants, brought raw materials and marketable imports into England and found markets for British goods abroad. First, merchants traded in local bazaars and then built their own trading posts. As foreign trading posts grew, they required more territory for transacting business and protecting merchandise. These posts required workers, who left England for permanent or temporary assignments. As the trading posts grew and prospered, they attracted settlers looking for opportunities not necessarily related to trade, such as farming, construction, administration, or missionary work. These settlements, in turn, became colonies.

At its height, the British Empire included a fourth of the world's land and a fourth of the world's population. England founded its first colonies in the West Indies and on the Atlantic coast in America. Though England lost the American colonies in the Revolutionary War of 1776, others had already been acquired. England had control of India by 1757, after struggles with French trading companies, and it won control of Canada from the French in 1763 after defeating them in the Seven Years' War. The 1769 voyage of the famous explorer Captain James Cook paved the way to make Australia a colony, which was settled in 1788 by English convicts from crowded English prisons. New Zealand became a colony when convicts escaped from Australia and settled there. England acquired the Union of South Africa in 1806 and then gained control in Burma (now Myanmar), Ceylon (now Sri Lanka), Malaya (now Malaysia), Singapore, and Hong Kong. When Victoria became queen in 1837, the British Empire stretched across the entire globe, and it continued to grow in Africa until World War I.

While the empire was still growing, some of the early colonies wanted the freedom to establish their own governments. Rather than using military force to control them, Parliament helped them set up governments. By 1900 Canada and Australia had federal governments modeled on the English system, and in 1909 India established a similar government. After World War I the British Commonwealth of Nations was created to "strengthen their [the colonies'] loyalty to the empire, . . . to sharpen their consciousness of nationhood, [and] to give them [their governments] a voice in foreign policy."[16] Though the members of the commonwealth varied in culture and governments, they were held together by annual imperial conferences. The 1926 conference formulated a statement of the constitutional status of the community composed of Great Britain and the Dominions, as the colonies were now called. It says: "They are equal in status, in no way subordinate one to another in any aspect of their domestic or external affairs, though united by a common allegiance to the Crown, and freely associated as members of the British Commonwealth of Nations."[17]

The decline of the empire was in part a result of economic

necessity. Maintaining a vast empire was growing too expensive for a small nation. When colonies wanted independence, the British realized that they could not fight multiple wars to resist independence. Consequently, Britain moved rapidly during the 1930s and 1940s to grant self-government in the Crown colonies; the goal was to achieve complete independence for all colonies, which would be held together in the commonwealth. Colonies were able to achieve dominion status as soon as the native people were sufficiently educated to conduct their own government and manage their own institutions. As a result of World War II, England's economy was severely depressed, and the loyalty of commonwealth countries offered the best hope for a semblance of the old empire.

The Industrial Revolution

The rise of the British Empire coincided with the Industrial Revolution. The Industrial Revolution, according to historian Robert Edwin Herzstein, was "a revolution caused by the substitution of machinery for hand labor in many manufacturing processes. These new machines changed conditions in the handicraft trades so radically and multiplied output so enormously that the accelerating consequences of the Industrial Revolution still dominate modern civilization."[18] The invention of machines and new processes revolutionized the textile industry first. The spinning jenny increased the output of thread, and the flying shuttle and power looms increased the output of cloth. Improvements in iron refining and later in the steel-making process allowed the invention of durable machines, but this process needed coal. New hoisting apparatuses meant that coal pits could be mined deeper to produce enough coal to keep the blast furnaces burning in iron foundries. Small railcars moved the coal within mines and on the surface to the loading docks at the canals. The most important invention, however, was James Watt's steam engine, which was used first in coal mining, then in iron foundries, and finally in factories. Within a few decades, the textile industry had increased production enormously.

The Industrial Revolution evolved most directly from the empire, which supplied raw materials and demanded manufactured goods faster than the handwork system in England could accommodate. The vast trade throughout the world also increased the demand for new products at home. Fortunately, wealth created by successful trade and revenue generated by the merchant fleet gave British industrialists the capital to invest in new methods that could supply the demand.

England's geography contributed to the Industrial Revolution. First, as a small island, England lacked the fields and climate to grow cotton for the textile factories, and its grazing hills produced too few sheep to keep up with the demand for wool; consequently, importing raw materials was a necessity. Second, England had an abundance of two natural resources—coal and iron—in close proximity, and both were necessary for the new industries. Third, industrialists connected England's numerous rivers by canals to facilitate transportation of materials within the island and to the seaports. Fourth, the numerous seaports allowed ships to load and unload at the point near the place where materials were needed or produced. All of these factors contributed to efficiency and rapid growth.

The Industrial Revolution had profound effects both at home and abroad. In England huge numbers of workers left the rural areas and moved to factory towns, where they worked under terrible conditions and lived in squalid, hastily constructed housing. The middle-class industrialists, who subscribed to the laissez-faire philosophy (of limited government intervention in the economy), ignored these conditions for several decades until after 1830, when reformers were able to pass bills in Parliament to improve the plight of workers. Historian Arnold J. Toynbee says that the Industrial Revolution also had a worldwide effect:

> Industrialism set to work, a hundred and fifty years ago, to re-shape the economic structure of the World in two ways, both leading in the direction of world unity. It sought to make the economic units fewer and bigger, and also to lower the barriers between them. . . . If we consider the size of the economic units, we find that at the end of the eighteenth century, Great Britain was the largest free-trade area in the Western World, a fact which goes far to explain why it was in Great Britain and not elsewhere that the Industrial Revolution began.[19]

The Industrial Revolution was a phenomenon that grew out of a complex set of circumstances related indirectly to England's geography: the worldwide empire, British domination of the seas, and the independent spirit that produced democracy and capitalism.

England and War

England's involvement in wars also resulted from a complex set of circumstances relating both directly and indirectly to its geography. As a small island nation with a powerful navy, England could prevent land invasions and fight its wars at sea. Indirectly, its national character and institutions directed the course of its wars and times of peace. Since 1066, no hostile army has ever invaded England by land. Trevelyan explains:

> To invade Britain was singularly easy before the Norman Conquest, singularly difficult afterwards. The reason is clear. A well-organized State, with a united people on land and a naval force at sea, could make itself safe behind the Channel even against such military odds as Philip of Spain, Louis XIV, or Napoleon could assemble on the opposite shore. In recent centuries these conditions have been fulfilled, and although an invading force has sometimes been welcomed, as when Henry Tudor or William of Orange came over, no invasion hostile to the community as a whole has met with even partial success owing to the barrier of the sea.[20]

Before the modern era, however, fighting on land was commonplace. Without a navy, early settlers were defenseless against invaders who took their ships up the rivers and conquered the inhabitants. After William the Conqueror unified and strengthened the country, England fought foreign wars over disputes regarding trade, landownership, and the throne in France. In 1453, after expending large amounts of money and the lives of many soldiers on foreign soil, the British accepted their losses and sought peace. Peace only lasted two years, however, before the War of the Roses, an English squabble between the House of Lancaster, associated with a red rose, and the House of York, associated with a white rose, began; each house was ruled by one of Edward III's sons. This war was a savage feud involving nobles who confiscated land and killed each other. The chaos paved the way for Henry Tudor to take control and restore order.

At the beginning of the modern period of the Tudors, new attitudes about war evolved. Henry VII claimed that the power of the throne rested on the popular will of the people, who were tired of feuding and disorder and wanted peace. Unlike despots on the continent, Henry VII had no standing army or paid officers to govern the countryside; he depended on Parliament and Common Law to instill order. This tradition prevailed through all of the Tudor reigns and, except for the civil wars during the mid-1600s, has succeeded in keeping England free of internal wars ever since. When James II threatened to raise a standing army in the 1680s, parliamentarians were frightened that he might bring to England the kind of fighting prevalent in continental countries. The British were keen to watch the balance of power among those countries, especially France and Spain. Any country gaining too much power might invade the island or threaten England's world trade. Though members of Parliament were willing to fight wars with other countries to maintain balance of power, they carefully avoided entangling soldiers in land wars. Until World War I, England fought its wars primarily at sea.

England has participated in several wars in modern times against France and Spain, Catholic countries with strong navies; against Holland, a Protestant country but England's major trading rival; and against America. Disputes with Spain over trade in South America brewed in 1737 and broke into war in 1739 when British captain Robert Jenkins's ear was supposedly torn off by a Spanish custom-house official. The incident caused such a storm that Prime Minister Walpole declared war against Spain, a war that escalated into a European war lasting until 1748. Then, after eight years of peace, disputes with France broke out in India and Canada, which began the Seven Years' War. England's victory secured the colonies of both India and Canada. England fought two wars with America. English armies lost the Revolutionary War when the French entered to help the Americans. They fought over territory and shipping intrusions during the War of 1812, in which the Americans won some battles and the British others. Concluded by the Treaty of Ghent in 1814, this war produced little except "The Star-Spangled Banner," the American national anthem. Napoléon became the commander of the French armies in 1796, the beginning of a European war that lasted until 1814. The British navy, protecting territories and shipping lanes in the Mediterranean, successfully defeated both the Spanish and the French navies during the Battle of Trafalgar.

Finally, during the twentieth century, England committed large land armies on the continent to stop the Germans. England fought Germany in World War I to stop German advances toward Belgium and France and to protect its navy against German U-boats. The war ended in November 1918, one year after the United States had entered the conflict. England sent troops to the continent again in 1939, when England and France declared war against Adolf Hitler's Germany. The two armies were unable to stop the Germans, and France fell, leaving England alone to stop Hitler from invading the homeland. The British fought a successful air war against the Germans, but the German bombers destroyed many British cities. The Americans entered the war in 1941, turning the tide against the Axis powers—Germany, Japan, and Italy—in 1942. After the war ended in 1945, the British spent ten years rebuilding cities and recovering from war debt.

England at the Beginning of the Twenty-First Century

At the beginning of the twenty-first century, geography still affects the history of this island nation on the edge of the European continent. The national character and institutions that England developed in its early history and modified over the centuries still prevail. Yet many things have changed.

After World War II England was transformed from a major power at the center of the world stage to a minor power. English industry, once the world leader, has been overtaken by industries in the United States, Germany, France, and Japan. England rapidly lost its empire and turned over its last Crown colony, Hong Kong, to China in June 1997. At the same time that England lost its empire, its economy declined when it had to repay huge war debts and rebuild cities. Hoping to maintain the Royal Navy, Parliament overreached and rebuilt more than the country could afford. As a result of all of these factors, England's power in the world declined.

Yet England's long-standing institutions remain in place. England has the same parliamentary government, still has an unwritten constitution, and still has two major parties, though they are now called the Conservative Party and the Labor Party instead of the Tories and Whigs. Parliament still shares power with the Crown, though the role of the monarchy has diminished to ceremonial functions. Free trade is still vital to England's economy. Though trade has declined, England, with one-one-hundredth of the world's population, does one-twentieth of the world's trade. The island still has not been invaded and is unlikely to be. In *Britain and the World in the Twentieth Century*, John W. Young, speaking of England in 1997, says that "violence in other regions, even as close as Bosnia, was unlikely to reach British shores. . . . The main challenge that faced Britain was not how to deal with likely enemies, but how to manage relations best with its partners."[21] Internally, aside from the crime and social ills characteristic of most Western developed nations, England is still relatively free of political and social unrest. Exceptions include the conflict between Catholics and Protestants over Northern Ireland and riots among ethnic groups and unemployed immigrants in industrial cities.

Moreover, British national character, forged early in history, still prevails. The independent spirit was nowhere more evident than in England's relationship with the European Union (EU). England joined the EU on January 1, 1973, as a defensive measure, its leaders reasoning that not joining might leave England in a worse position. Young says, "Britain's constitutional and economic background fitted badly with the EC [European Community] from the outset."[22] The English, committed to their unwritten constitution, are uncomfortable with a written EU constitution and also fear their free trade might be hampered. England refused to adopt the currency of the European Union, the euro, on January 1, 2002, when thirteen of the sixteen nations adopted it. But England is, nonetheless, an active player with Europe. In the spirit of harmony that Trevelyan identifies and tolerance that Bryant notes, England is working to foster free trade and to persuade EU countries that protective tariffs are unwise. Those same qualities of harmony and tolerance have also made England a partner in the North Atlantic Treaty Organization, a strong ally with America, and the leader of the British Commonwealth of Nations.

Although England's power and wealth have declined, its ideas have not. The parliamentary democracy that England forged is now the model for developing nations throughout the world. The system of free trade that England developed in the age of the Tudor monarchs is now the model for globalization. And the language that reached its form in the age of William Shakespeare is becoming the lingua franca throughout the world.

England's relation to the sea, as Trevelyan says, sometimes "passive and receptive" and at other times "active and acquisitive," still describes England's history.[23] Its geography affected its people, and they affected the events that brought the country to the height of world power and maintained it when its power declined. Today this small island nation is still a major player on the world's stage.

Notes

1. George Macaulay Trevelyan, *History of England*. New York: Longmans, Green, 1926, p. xx.
2. Arthur Bryant, *Spirit of England*. London: Collins, 1982, p. 40.
3. Bryant, *Spirit of England*, p. 219.
4. Trevelyan, *History of England*, p. xix.
5. W.E. Lunt, *History of England*, 4th ed. New York: Harper Brothers, 1956, p. 2.
6. Bryant, *Spirit of England*, p. 219.
7. Trevelyan, *History of England*, p. 134.
8. Trevelyan, *History of England*, p. xix.
9. Trevelyan, *History of England*, p. 292.
10. Trevelyan, *History of England*, p. 327.
11. Lunt, *History of England*, pp. 299–300.
12. Lunt, *History of England*, p. 347.
13. Bryant, *Spirit of England*, p. 225.
14. Trevelyan, *History of England*, p. 296.
15. Trevelyan, *History of England*, p. 426.
16. Lunt, *History of England*, p. 813.
17. Quoted in Lunt, *History of England*, pp. 813–14.
18. Robert Edwin Herzstein, *Western Civilization*. Boston: Houghton Mifflin, 1963, p. 490.
19. Arnold J. Toynbee, *A Study of History*, abridgement of vol. 1–4 by D.C. Somervell. New York: Oxford University Press, 1956, pp. 287–88.
20. Trevelyan, *History of England*, p. 1.
21. John W. Young, *Britain and the World in the Twentieth Century*. London: Arnold, 1997, p. 222.
22. Young, *Britain and the World in the Twentieth Century*, p. 195.
23. Trevelyan, *History of England*, p. xx.

Chapter 1

From Tribes to Feudalism: England Prior to 1485

The First Invaders and Settlers

BY HAZELTON SPENCER AND BEVERLY J. LAYMAN

Hazelton Spencer and Beverly J. Layman, who sketch England's earliest history, explain that Britons, a Celtic people, first occupied the island. In A.D. 43 Roman emperor Claudius established a province that lasted until Roman troops were withdrawn in 410. In their absence, Germanic tribes of Angles, Saxons, and Jutes invaded and inhabited the land, driving Britons to the fringes. In 597 the pope sent priests Augustine and Patrick, who, with their monks, converted the British Isles to Christianity. Hazelton Spencer, who taught at Johns Hopkins University, is the author of The Art and Life of William Shakespeare. *Beverly J. Layman, who taught at Wellesley College, is the author of numerous scholarly articles.*

The curtain goes up on Britain's history when the Romans first turn a calculating eye toward Gaul's[1] northern neighbor. Though in 55 B.C. Julius Caesar threw a couple of legions across the English Channel, neither that brief landing nor the campaign of the following summer led to occupation. Julius, however, wielded pen as well as sword; his description helped maintain a lively interest in the island and its inhabitants, the Britons (a Celtic people), until the next invasion, under the emperor Claudius in 43 A.D. This time the success was complete, and the troops stayed. They made Britain, as far north as the Scottish Highlands, a Roman province; and it remained part of the empire until the year 410, when a hard-pressed emperor recalled the garrison. Until that fateful event, the speech of Britannia—as the province was called—was Latin and Celtic.

1. Gaul was a region covering Belgium and France.

The English Conquest

Though the Picts of Caledonia (Scotland) and the Scots of Hibernia (Ireland) immediately renewed their pressure from the north and west, the real conquerors were Angles, Saxons, and Jutes from the southern and southeastern shores of the North Sea. They were raiding tribesmen, bold sailors and savage fighters speaking dialects (highly inflected, in comparison with modern English) of the Germanic tongue's western branch, to which modern German as well as modern English belongs. For many decades they had found easy pickings along the fringes of the mighty but decaying empire. Combat and rapine came naturally to these tough spearmen. In 449, according to tradition, the Jutes established the first bridgehead on British soil, in Kent.

Widespread settlement followed the marauding forays, and by 600 the newcomers held about half the island. Such of the Britons as had not been killed, enslaved, or assimilated either were living in the mountains of the west and north, rolled back from the areas of attack and infiltration, or had crossed salt water to Brittany. That is why varieties of the Celtic language survive to this day not only in Ireland but also in the Scottish Highlands, Wales, and northwestern France.

Of the fight put up by the island's defenders, history affords the scantiest of glimpses. Here and there local forces were rallied and a stand was made; but it was a lost cause they fought for. One attempt at resistance was perhaps headed by a leader named Artorius; in any event, later legend credited a leader so named with an heroic role in the British defense. Worked up long afterwards by poets and storytellers in the age of chivalry, this tradition flowered in the romances about King Arthur and his knights.

Out of the welter of hostile settlements, each with its own local king, there rose a number of states, small or large, with boundaries that shifted with the fortunes of war. Their number also varied; it was never stabilized until, in the ninth century, the royal house of Wessex made good its claim to the overlordship of all England. By that time Angles, Saxons, and Jutes alike were known as English. This was originally the name of the principal settlers in the north and northeast, where three kingdoms of Angles (or English) waxed and waned: Northumbria, which ran straight up the coast from the River Humber to the Firth of Forth beyond Edinburgh; Mercia, extending southward from the Humber to the Wash and thence nearly halfway to the English

Channel; and, less important than the other two, East Anglia, which occupied the island's eastern hump. Britain's extreme southeastern tip, between the Thames estuary and the Strait of Dover, was settled by the Jutes, who also held the Isle of Wight and a strip of adjacent coast. The inhabitants of the main Jutish territory were called Kentishmen. The other principal kingdoms were Saxon. The East Saxons lived between the Thames and the lands of the East Angles. Along the southern coast between the two Jutish regions were the South Saxons. Most powerful and politically advanced of all, the West Saxons controlled a large area bounded on the west and north by Bristol Channel and the valley of the Severn, and on the south by the English Channel from the border of Cornwall to the Isle of Wight.

Teutonic Customs

The invaders, originally sea-wolves, harriers, and plunderers, grew tamer, as settlers always do when they turn for subsistence from dependence on booty snatched with spear and sword to an economy based on agriculture. Yet the old rugged ideals lived on; and, in the ordinary course of events, there was still plenty of fighting: private feuds; struggles of the local chiefs and petty kings when a kingdom's throne, semihereditary yet elective, fell vacant; quarrels among the kingdoms; and, in the end, a desperate defense of Saxon England against the next wave of invasion, the terrible onslaught of the Danes. Christianity, which had been introduced during the Roman occupation, had been obliterated when the withdrawal of Rome's disciplined troops pulled the props from under the provincial government and left the island a prey to pagan attack. To the reign of Roman law and order there succeeded, while Britain was being conquered, shared, and reorganized by the English, a dreadful era of fire and sword.

The code of the Teutonic settlers was fierce and bloody; but it was better than no code at all, and it had its lofty side. Centuries earlier the Roman historian Tacitus had written of their German forebears—of their bravery, of their ideal of Personal honor, of the devotion of the *comitatus* or warrior band whose duty was to die if need be to the last man in battle at their chieftain's side, of the lord's obligation to shield and reward his fighting men, of the special closeness (it appears, for example, in *Beowulf*) of the bond between uncle and nephew. The invaders who brought to Britain their customs, their language, their religion of Woden and his fellow divinities of Germanic mythology, swept from the east and south nearly every trace of the Celto-Roman civilization.

The way of life that took its place rested on the warrior's loyalty to his kingly chief. The fighting men or "earls" formed a rude but proud military aristocracy. There were a few freedmen and even landholding yeomen who were not reckoned nobles; but the largest social class was the lowest, the bondmen. These serfs tilled the soil, tended the herds, caught the fish—menial tasks, beneath the dignity of the earls or "athelings." Justice was originally less a public concern than a matter of private revenge, on the principle of an eye for an eye or a tooth for a tooth. If someone killed a member of your family, you killed, if you could, the slayer or, as the next best thing, a member of his family. Yet, except when a man had committed the unpardonable offense of crime against an actual kinsman, the violent exaction of vengeance, even for murder, could be averted by payment of blood money, "wergild" (="man-payment"). That institution—it was a system of fines graduated according to the extent of the injury—was a long step toward civilization. It meant the triumph of law. To be an outlaw, exiled from home and beyond the pale of the code—that was a fearful fate.

Christianity and the Northumbrian Revival

If by the end of the sixth century the Teutonic occupation was assured, it was not till late in the seventh that the first literary epoch arrived. Then, for close to a hundred years, education and the arts flourished. [Historian] Christopher Dawson, in *The Making of Europe* (1932), asserts that "there has never been an age in which England had a greater influence on continental culture. In art and religion, in scholarship and literature, the Anglo-Saxons of the eighth century were the leaders of their age." Since this cultural renascence occurred in the north, the home of the Angles, Britain's new language came to be known as English—Old English, we call it, because we speak its lineal descendant, enriched, of course, by subsequent large infusions from other tongues, especially Latin and French.

The Northumbrian revival was possible only because Christianity—at this stage of European history the Western world's only hope of a better day—had meanwhile been brought back to England, with education in its train. Its return meant another collision between two antagonistic cultures. But this time the result was not, as in the fifth century, the extermination of one; it was a compromise—and in every way a remarkable one—accounting for much that is most distinctive in Anglo-Saxon poetry and art.

Britain was reconverted from both the south and the north. In 597 a mission sent by Pope Gregory the Great and headed by an Italian priest named Augustine (not the famous theologian) landed in Kent, soon converted its king, and established in Canterbury a center of religious instruction from which the chief prelate of the Church of England still takes his title. Not long after, the marriage of a Kentish princess to a Northumbrian king gave the new religion a northern foothold, and York became England's second ecclesiastical capital. The heathen raged with considerable success when pagan Mercia overwhelmed Christian Northumbria, but this setback was temporary. In the west, Christianity had persevered among the Celts; about the time the Romans abandoned Britain, Saint Patrick had converted Ireland. Thence missionaries carried their faith to western Scotland, and

Anglo-Saxon Records
The Germanic Invasions

In 892 the Saxon king Alfred began keeping records of major events, using available documents and stories to fill in the history to that date. The following excerpt from The Anglo-Saxon Chronicle, *as his history was called, records the Germanic invasions.*

A. 449. This year Martianus and Valentinus succeeded to the empire, and reigned seven years. And in their days Hengist and Horsa, invited by Vortigern king of the Britons, landed in Britain on the shore which is called Wippidsfleet; at first in aid of the Britons, but afterwards they fought against them. King Vortigern gave them land in the south-east of this country, on condition that they should fight against the Picts. Then they fought against the Picts, and had the victory wheresoever they came. They then sent to the Angles; de-

thence again it was brought southward into Northumbria. By 650 most of England was nominally Christian.

At first the Church in Britain was loosely organized; and, besides, there was dissension between adherents of the Celtic and advocates of the more directly Roman forms. At the Synod of Whitby in 664 both sides were heard by the Northumbrian king; he decided in favor of the southern or Roman practices. After that, organization proceeded rapidly, with the building of churches, the establishment of bishoprics under the archbishoprics of Canterbury and York, and the foundation of monasteries where, vowing themselves to poverty, chastity, and obedience, men or women, ruled by an abbot or an abbess, withdrew from the turmoil and anxieties of secular life. Long before the Wessex kings succeeded in replacing the separate and rival kingdoms with something like a national state, the Church had achieved a unity that fostered, at any rate on its own ever-increasing lands, an environment favorable to the arts of civilization and peace.

sired a larger force to be sent, and caused them to be told the worthlessness of the Britons, and the excellencies of the land. Then they soon sent thither a larger force in aid of the others. At that time there came men from three tribes in Germany; from the Old-Saxons, from the Angles, from the Jutes. From the Jutes came the Kentish-men and the Wightwarians, that is, the tribe which now dwells in Wight, and that race among the West-Saxons which is still called the race of Jutes. From the Old-Saxons came the men of Essex and Sussex and Wessex. From Anglia, which has ever since remained waste betwixt the Jutes and Saxons, came the men of East Anglia, Middle Anglia, Mercia, and all North-humbria. Their leaders were two brothers, Hengist and Horsa: they were the sons of Wihtgils; Wihtgils son of Witta, Witta of Wecta, Wecta of Woden: from this Woden sprang all our royal families, and those of the South-humbrians also.

J.A. Giles, ed. and trans., *The Anglo-Saxon Chronicle.* London: G. Bell and Sons, 1914.

It was the Church that took the lead in education, literature, agriculture, and even industry. There were important schools at Canterbury and York; and, though Latin was long to remain the language of British scholarship, English as well as Latin was taught in the monasteries. Among the most valuable of the monkish contributions to enlightenment was the systematic reduplication of Latin and eventually of English manuscripts by the copyists who labored in the monastery's scriptorium. It was the incessant toil of these scribes that provided Anglo-Saxon Britain with its books, both the writings of the Church Fathers and some of the secular classics of Latin literature; and it preserved for us that fragment which has survived of what must once have been the considerable body of Old English literature.

The conversion of the English was an event of major importance to our literature. The marauders from over the North Sea undoubtedly had an oral literature—of ballads, songs, and snatches, of riddles (many of which got written down and have survived), of charms (against all and sundry of the aches and pains that flesh is heir to), of "gnomic verses"—these last embody pithy saws and maxims. There was also an important genre of more or less extemporized poetry composed and sung by the scop or bard in early times. At the feast he raised his voice in praise of the deeds of heroes, thus honoring, either directly or by the subtler flattery of implied comparison, the chieftain whom he served. He combined the functions of poet laureate, entertainer, and historian. Sometimes he was also the wandering minstrel, a welcome sojourner at many a court. Thus wide currency was given to an international body of Germanic history and legend. Few of the early English could write; though in the runes they had an alphabet, it was used chiefly for inscriptions.[2] A literary epoch like the Northumbrian revival could not begin until Christianity had brought education.

Bede

Many of the historical facts already cited are recorded by the Venerable Bede (673–735) in his *Ecclesiastical History of the English People*. The honorary epithet that a succeeding generation tacked onto the name of the first English historian is a tribute to Bede's

2. Germanic tribes were using runes as early as the second century B.C. Certain letters of the runic alphabet resemble their Roman phonetic equivalents.

devotion to religion and scholarship; its continued employment acknowledges his permanent value as a major source for Anglo-Saxon history. Bede was a monk in the monastery at Jarrow on the Northumbrian coast; his writings are among the monuments of the cultural revival in that kingdom in the seventh and eighth centuries. He wrote on many subjects and won international fame as a scholar of encyclopaedic learning; Dante in Canto X of the *Paradiso* assigns him an honored place beside the great Isidore of Seville. For us, however, he lives as the author of the *Ecclesiastical History.*

Like all medieval scholars he wrote in Latin; hence a selection would be inappropriate here, even though an English translation was made as early as King Alfred's time. "One of the most valuable and one of the most beautiful of historical works," declared Charles Plummer, his brilliant nineteenth-century editor. "His earnest yet sober piety, his humility, his gentleness, appear in almost every line."

Augustine Brings Christianity to England

BY VENERABLE BEDE

Writing in the early eighth century, Venerable Bede reports on the Italian priest Augustine's travels to England to convert the English to Christianity. After a brief hesitation, Augustine continues at the pope's urging to lead his party of monks to southern England. He lands in Kent near Canterbury, where he succeeds at converting the king and the citizens. Venerable Bede, a monk, was the most important scholar in his time and the first great scholar in England. He is the author of A Book of Hymns *and* On Orthography, *both written in Latin.*

How the holy Pope Gregory sent Augustine, with other monks, to preach to the English nation, and encouraged them by a letter of exhortation, not to desist from their labour. [596 A.D.]

In the year of our Lord 582, Maurice, the fifty-fourth from Augustus, ascended the throne, and reigned twenty-one years. In the tenth year of his reign, Gregory,[1] a man eminent in learning and the conduct of affairs, was promoted to the Apostolic see of Rome, and presided over it thirteen years, six months and ten days. He, being moved by Divine inspiration, in the fourteenth year of the same emperor, and about the one hundred and fiftieth after the coming of the English into Britain, sent the servant of God, Augustine,[2] and with him diverse other monks, who

1. Gregory the Great. Bede places the date of his accession a year too late as well as that of his death (but in the same chapter he rightly places his death in the second year of Phocas, *i.e.*, 604). 2. Augustine was prior of St. Gregory's Monastery dedicated to St. Andrew in Rome.

Excerpted from *Ecclesiastical History of England*, by Venerable Bede, edited and translated by A.M. Sellar (London: G. Bell and Sons, 1912).

feared the Lord, to preach the Word of God to the English nation. They having, in obedience to the pope's commands, undertaken that work, when they had gone but a little way on their journey, were seized with craven terror, and began to think of returning home, rather than proceed to a barbarous, fierce, and unbelieving nation, to whose very language they were strangers; and by common consent they decided that this was the safer course. At once Augustine, who had been appointed to be consecrated bishop, if they should be received by the English, was sent back, that he might, by humble entreaty, obtain of the blessed Gregory; that they should not be compelled to undertake so dangerous, toilsome, and uncertain a journey. The pope, in reply, sent them a letter of exhortation, persuading them to set forth to the work of the Divine Word, and rely on the help of God. The purport of which letter was as follows:

The Pope Urges the Missionaries on to England

"*Gregory, the servant of the servants of God, to the servants of our Lord.* Forasmuch as it had been better not to begin a good work, than to think of desisting from one which has been begun, it behoves you, my beloved sons, to fulfil with all diligence the good work, which, by the help of the Lord, you have undertaken. Let not, therefore, the toil of the journey, nor the tongues of evil-speaking men, discourage you; but with all earnestness and zeal perform, by God's guidance, that which you have set about; being assured, that great labour is followed by the greater glory of an eternal reward. When Augustine, your Superior, returns, whom we also constitute your abbot, humbly obey him in all things; knowing, that whatsoever you shall do by his direction, will, in all respects, be profitable to your souls. Almighty God protect you with His grace, and grant that I may, in the heavenly country, see the fruits of your labour, inasmuch as, though I cannot labour with you, I shall partake in the joy of the reward, because I am willing to labour. God keep you in safety, my most beloved sons. Given the 23rd of July, in the fourteenth year of the reign of our most religious lord, Mauritius Tiberius Augustus, the thirteenth year after the consulship of our lord aforesaid, and the fourteenth indiction."

How he wrote to the bishop of Arles to entertain them. [596 A.D.]

The same venerable pope also sent at the same time a letter to

Aetherius, archbishop of Arles,[3] exhorting him to give favourable entertainment to Augustine on his way to Britain; which letter was in these words:

"*To his most reverend and holy brother and fellow bishop Aetherius, Gregory, the servant of the servants of God.* Although religious men stand in need of no recommendation with priests who have the charity which is pleasing to God; yet because an opportunity of writing has occurred, we have thought fit to send this letter to you, Brother, to inform you, that with the help of God we have directed thither, for the good of souls, the bearer of these presents, Augustine, the servant of God, of whose zeal we are assured, with other servants of God, whom it is requisite that your Holiness readily assist with priestly zeal, affording him all the comfort in your power. And to [this] and that you may be the more ready in your help, we have enjoined him to inform you particularly of the occasion of his coming; knowing, that when you are acquainted with it, you will, as the matter requires, for the sake of God, dutifully dispose yourself to give him comfort. We also in all things recommend to your charity, Candidus,[4] the priest, our common son, whom we have transferred to the administration of a small patrimony in our Church. God keep you in safety, most reverend brother. Given the 23rd day of July, in the fourteenth year of the reign of our most religious lord, Mauritius Tiberius Augustus, the thirteenth year after the consulship of our lord aforesaid, and the fourteenth indiction."

Augustine and the Monks Arrive in Kent

How Augustine, coming into Britain, first preached in the Isle of Thanet to the King of Kent, and having obtained licence from him, went into Kent, in order to preach therein. [597 A.D.]

Augustine, thus strengthened by the encouragement of the blessed Father Gregory, returned to the work of the Word of God, with the servants of Christ who were with him, and arrived in Britain. The powerful Ethelbert was at that time king of Kent[5];

3. This is a mistake. Aetherius was archbishop of Lyons. Vergilius was archbishop of Arles. The letter given here, however, is the letter sent to Aetherius. Similar letters were despatched to other bishops at this time; among them one to Vergilius of Arles. 4. A presbyter sent into Gaul by Gregory in 595 A.D. to administer the little patrimony of St. Peter in Gaul, to collect its revenues and to invest them in raiment for the poor, or in English slave lads to serve in the monasteries and receive a Christian education. 5. Ethelbert was the third Bretwalda or dominant king. He had established a practical hegemony over the East Anglians, the Mercians of the Trent Valley, the South Saxons, East Saxons, and even the West Saxons.

he had extended his dominions as far as the boundary formed by the great river Humber, by which the Southern Saxons are divided from the Northern. On the east of Kent is the large Isle of Thanet, containing, according to the English way of reckoning, 600 families,[6] divided from the mainland by the river Wantsum,[7] which is about three furlongs in breadth, and which can be crossed only in two places; for at both ends it runs into the sea. On this island landed the servant of the Lord, Augustine, and his companions, being, as is reported, nearly forty men. They had obtained, by order of the blessed Pope Gregory, interpreters of the nation of the Franks, and sending to Ethelbert, signified that they were come from Rome, and brought a joyful message, which most undoubtedly assured to those that hearkened to it everlasting joys in heaven, and a kingdom that would never end, with the living and true God. The king hearing this, gave orders that they should stay in the island where they had landed, and be furnished with necessaries, till he should consider what to do with them. For he had before heard of the Christian religion, having a Christian wife of the royal family of the Franks, called Bertha;[8] whom he had received from her parents, upon condition that she should be permitted to preserve inviolate the rites of her religion with the Bishop Liudhard,[9] who was sent with her to support her in the faith. Some days after, the king came into the island, and sitting in the open air, ordered Augustine and his companions to come and hold a conference with him. For he had taken precaution that they should not come to him in any house, lest, by so coming, according to an ancient superstition, if they practised any magical arts, they might impose upon him, and so get the better of him. But they came endued with Divine, not with magic power, bearing a silver cross for their banner, and the image of our Lord and Saviour painted on a board; and chanting litanies, they offered up their prayers to the Lord for the eternal salvation both of themselves and of those to whom and for whom they had come. When they had sat down, in obedience to

6. families, *i.e., hides* The hide, probably, was as much land as would support a family, hence the extent must have varied with the different conditions in different parts of the country. 7. In Bede's time Thanet was divided from the rest of Kent by a broad channel called the Wantsum, now partly represented by the River Stour. 8. daughter of Charibert, king of Paris 9. Said (on doubtful authority) to have been bishop of Senlis. He acted as the queen's private chaplain. There is nothing to show that either he or Bertha attempted to spread their religion in England, though probably their influence may not have been without effect on Ethelbert.

the king's commands, and preached to him and his attendants there present the Word of life, the king answered thus: "Your words and promises are fair, but because they are new to us, and of uncertain import, I cannot consent to them so far as to forsake that which I have so long observed with the whole English nation. But because you are come from far as strangers into my kingdom, and, as I conceive, are desirous to impart to us those things which you believe to be true, and most beneficial, we desire not to harm you, but will give you favourable entertainment, and take care to supply you with all things necessary to your sustenance; nor do we forbid you to preach and gain as many as you can to your religion." Accordingly he gave them an abode in the city of Canterbury,[10] which was the metropolis of all his dominions, and, as he had promised, besides supplying them with sustenance, did not refuse them liberty to preach. It is told that, as they drew near to the city, after their manner, with the holy cross, and the image of our sovereign Lord and King, Jesus Christ, they sang in concert this litany: "We beseech thee, O Lord, for Thy great mercy, that Thy wrath and anger be turned away from this city, and from Thy holy house, for we have sinned. Hallelujah."

The Missionaries Succeed

How St. Augustine in Kent followed the doctrine and manner of life of the primitive Church, and settled his episcopal see in the royal city. [597 A.D.]

As soon as they entered the dwelling-place assigned to them, they began to imitate the Apostolic manner of life in the primitive Church; applying themselves to constant prayer, watchings, and fastings; preaching the Word of life to as many as they could; despising all worldly things, as in nowise concerning them; receiving only their necessary food from those they taught; living themselves in all respects conformably to what they taught, and being always ready to suffer any adversity, and even to die for that truth which they preached. In brief, some believed and were baptized, admiring the simplicity of their blameless life, and the sweetness of their heavenly doctrine. There was on the east side of the city, a church dedicated of old to the honour of St. Martin,[11] built whilst the Romans were still in the island, wherein the

10. the old Roman town of Doruvernis, which is the name Bede gives to it throughout the History 11. St. Martin was regarded with special reverence in Britain and Ireland.

queen, who, as has been said before, was a Christian, was wont to pray. In this they also first began to come together, to chant the Psalms, to pray, to celebrate Mass, to preach, and to baptize, till when the king had been converted to the faith, they obtained greater liberty to preach everywhere and build or repair churches.

When he, among the rest, believed and was baptized, attracted by the pure life of these holy men and their gracious promises, the truth of which they established by many miracles, greater numbers began daily to flock together to hear the Word, and, forsaking their heathen rites, to have fellowship, through faith, in the unity of Christ's Holy Church. It is told that the king, while he rejoiced at their conversion and their faith, yet compelled none to embrace Christianity, but only showed more affection to the believers, as to his fellow citizens in the kingdom of Heaven. For he had learned from those who had instructed him and guided him to salvation, that the service of Christ ought to be voluntary, not by compulsion. Nor was it long before he gave his teachers a settled residence suited to their degree in his metropolis of Canterbury, with such possessions of divers sorts as were necessary for them.

How St. Augustine, being made a bishop, sent to acquaint Pope Gregory with what had been done in Britain, and asked and received replies, of which he stood in need. [597–601 A.D.]

In the meantime, Augustine, the man of God, went to Arles, and, according to the orders received from the holy Father Gregory, was ordained archbishop of the English nation, by Aetherius, archbishop of that city. Then returning into Britain, he sent Laurentius the priest[12] and Peter the monk to Rome, to acquaint Pope Gregory, that the English nation had received the faith of Christ, and that he was himself made their bishop.

12. He succeeded Augustine as archbishop.

Medieval England

BY ROBERT C. POOLEY, GEORGE K. ANDERSON, PAUL FARMER, AND HELEN THORNTON

The authors of the following selection explain the great changes that occurred in 1066 when William the Conqueror, a Norman earl, invaded England and became king. During the next four hundred years, two forces controlled England: the feudal system and the Church. Under the feudal system, a relatively few lords and knights lived in luxury while the masses of serfs toiled in poverty. According to the authors, near the end of the Medieval period, the declining power of the feudal lords and the Church opened opportunities for peasants to gain more freedom. Robert C. Pooley taught English at the University of Wisconsin. George K. Anderson, who taught English at Brown University, is author of The Literature of the Anglo-Saxons *and* Middle English Literature. *Paul Farmer was teaching consultant at the Georgia Institute of Technology. Helen Thornton was English department chair at Arsenal Technical High School. Both Farmer and Thornton contributed numerous articles to* The English Journal.

To many readers the words "medieval England" and "feudalism" suggest all the romance of the past. Into mind flash images of King Arthur and his peerless knights, of minstrels singing in castle halls, of Sir Walter Scott's Norman villains and Saxon heroes battling before a besieged castle, and of Chaucer's pilgrims wending their slow way toward Canterbury Cathedral. These literary images of the Middle Ages are true but woefully incomplete. They omit the serfs, living with their livestock in dirt-floored huts. They overlook the fact that terrible plagues kept the cathedral bells tolling night and day as funeral followed funeral. They fail to recognize the dominant part the Church played in the life of king and serf, knight and freeman. . . .

In 1066 the purely Anglo-Saxon history of England came to an end. In that year William the Conqueror and his Norman

Excerpted from *England in Literature*, edited by Robert C. Pooley, George K. Anderson, Paul Farmer, and Helen Thornton (Glenview, IL: Scott, Foresman, 1968).

warriors invaded England and overcame the Anglo-Saxons at the Battle of Hastings. Originally the Normans, like the Danes who had overrun eastern England in the ninth century, had been Vikings. A hundred years earlier they had invaded that part of France which has since been called Normandy and gradually adopted the culture, customs, and language of the French. At the time they conquered England, their civilization was more highly organized and more elaborate than Anglo-Saxon culture. Its foundation was the feudal system, a system based upon the holding of land. Immediately upon conquering England, William laid claim to all the land in the realm. Dispossessing its Anglo-Saxon owners, he granted large areas to his lords, who, in return, promised William their services and those of their retainers. The lords, in turn, might grant portions of their lands to knights pledged to assist them in battle. At the bottom of the social scale were the serfs, who belonged to the land. They eked out a scanty and often desolate existence, paying goods and services to the lord in return for the land they farmed.

This system of organizing men into specific classes was accepted even by the feudal serf because medieval man believed that full equality could not exist on earth. In this mortal life each man assumed the place in society for which God had destined him. The earthly hierarchy was a reflection of the divine order in which God held the highest position, followed by angels, men, animate and inanimate objects, and finally, in the lowest position, Satan.

Feudal society was essentially a society geared to war. Disputes arose not only between one country and another but between rival barons in the same land. A king possessed only a little more power than the strongest lords. National unity as we know it today did not exist. A man thought of himself as first the subject of the lord from whom he held his lands and then as a subject of the king.

Chivalry

The feudal system revolved about the knight—the mounted warrior who became the symbol of chivalry. In fact, it was from *chevalier*, the French word for "mounted soldier," that the word *chivalry* evolved.

The training of a knight began in early childhood. At about the age of seven the well-born boy left his own home for service first as page, then as squire at some lord's castle. The lady of the castle taught him the elaborate code of courtesy and manners that a knight must follow. With other pages he was trained in horsemanship and the use of the shield, sword, and lance. When he became a squire, he waited upon his lord and, if need arose, followed him into battle. Finally he was dubbed knight and swore to uphold the code of chivalry—loyalty toward Church and King, reverence toward women.

The institution of chivalry softened the harshness of medieval life. It bound the often lawless warrior by a code, violating which meant loss of honor. In combination with a wave of devotion to the Virgin Mary which swept across Europe late in the eleventh century, it raised the status of woman and gained her a larger rôle both in life and in literature.

The Medieval Church

The pageantry of chivalry with its flashing tournaments, its banquets at which minstrels sang of valorous deeds, its elaborate ritual of courtly love, brightened the lives of only a relatively small number of upper-class Englishmen. The mass of people—the serfs, and the artisans in the growing towns—lived a life different in every respect. Only in the Church were Englishmen of all classes united.

The magnificent cathedrals which throughout the Middle Ages raised their towers above the towns of England testified to the fact that these ages were centuries of faith. In a world of war, plague, and violent death, medieval man clung to the Church's teaching that the world in which he lived was relatively unimportant while the world to come was of vast importance. Membership in the Church also secured him his place in society. If, for a serious transgression, he was excommunicated, prohibited from participating in any of the rites of the Church, he lost his status. Excommunication was equivalent to being condemned to a life of total isolation.

In Norman England as in Saxon England, education was the province of the Church. In the long centuries before the printing press was invented, manuscripts were painstakingly copied by hand in the monasteries. Monks and priests passed the culture of Greek and Roman scholars as well as the teachings of the Church on to young students who flocked to the monasteries to learn. From such beginnings in the twelfth and thirteenth centuries came the formal organization of Oxford and Cambridge as universities.

The Church was also intimately bound up with political affairs. In medieval thought Church and King were necessary instruments of the divine scheme for maintaining order in society: They were, in medieval terms, the "two swords of God." The question of which sword was indeed the greater on this earth was a major source of dispute. The most famous quarrel between Church and King in Medieval England was that of Thomas à Becket, Archbishop of Canterbury, and Henry II. It was Henry's belief that certain rights exercised by the Church belonged to the King. Confident that he could bring about the changes he desired if a man sympathetic to his views were Archbishop of Canterbury, Henry had Becket, his chancellor and close friend, appointed to this position. But once he had become Archbishop, Becket staunchly upheld the rights of the Church. By 1170 matters had reached a climax. According to an often told story, one day Henry in exasperation exclaimed to a group of his followers, "Will not one of you avenge me of this turbulent priest?" Four knights straightway dashed off to Canterbury, found the Archbishop at his prayers in the cathedral, and struck him down with their daggers. The Christian world was shocked; Henry II himself deplored the killing and did penance; and the tomb of Thomas à Becket at Canterbury became the favorite place of pilgrimage for Englishmen of all classes.

The Crusades

The widespread religious zeal of the Middle Ages inspired the great religious movement known as the Crusades, whose object was to retake the Holy Land from the Mohammedans. Kings, knights, and commoners flocked to take up their swords in this Holy War. Leader of one of the Crusades was Richard the Lion-Hearted, King of England, son of Henry II, and one of the most dazzling figures produced by the Age of Chivalry.

The First Crusade was launched in 1095; and for almost the next two hundred years wave after wave of men from every Christian country battered against the Moslems. While the Crusades were ultimately unsuccessful in their efforts to liberate the Holy Land from the Turks, they had a profound effect on all of Europe. For the first time since the fall of the Roman Empire, great numbers of men traveled widely. Knights from the bleak fortress castles of England saw the palaces of Venice, the opulent cities of Asia Minor. Scholars rediscovered the literature of ancient Greece and Rome. The horizons of men were widened and civilization took a great step toward the modern world. . . .

Warfare

For centuries it had been the dream of English kings to bring the entire island of Britain under one dominion. Edward I spent most of his reign (1272–1307) trying to achieve this goal. He successfully subdued the Welsh; but the struggle against the Scots, a freedom-loving Celtic people toughened by centuries of bor-

THE ANGLO-SAXONS LOSE THE BATTLE WITH WILLIAM

The Anglo-Saxon Chronicle, *which was begun by the Saxon king Alfred in the ninth century, records the battles fought by Anglo-Saxon leaders to repel William when he invaded at Hastings. Much English blood was shed in the efforts. Ultimately Archbishop Alfred of York crowned William the king and made him pledge to govern England well.*

A. 1066. . . . Then came William earl of Normandy into Pevensey on the eve of St. Michael's-mass: and soon after they were on their way, they constructed a castle at Hasting's-port. This was then made known to king Harold, and he then gathered a great force, and came to meet him at the estuary of Appledore; and William came against him unawares, before his people were set in order. But the king nevertheless strenuously fought against him with those men who would follow him; and there was great slaughter made on either hand. There was slain king Harold, and Leofwin the earl, his brother, and Girth the earl, his brother, and many good men; and the Frenchmen had possession of the place of carnage, all as God granted them for the people's sins. Archbishop Aldred and the townsmen of London would

der warfare with Romans, Saxons, and English, dragged on and on. Edward I died with Scotland still unconquered.

During the fifty-year reign of Edward III (1327–1377), the grandson of Edward I, commerce developed and England prospered. Particularly important was the wool trade. Wool from English sheep was shipped to Flanders to be woven into cloth for English markets. So important was this trade that the export duty on raw wool was the chief financial mainstay of the English government. This prosperous trade irked the King of France to such a degree that he began to seize English wool ships. In retaliation, Edward III revived an old claim to the crown of France. The war

then have child Edgar for king, all as was his true natural right: and Edwin and Morcar vowed to him that they would fight together with him. . . . And William the earl went afterwards again to Hastings, and there awaited to see whether the people would submit to him. But when he understood that they would not come to him, he went upwards with all his army which was left to him, and that which afterwards had come from over sea to him; and he plundered all that part which he over-ran, until he came to Berkhampstead. And there came to meet him archbishop Aldred, [of York] and child Edgar, and Edwin the earl, and Morcar the earl, and all the chief men of London; and then submitted, for need, when the most harm had been done: and it was very unwise that they had not done so before; since God would not better it, for our sins: and they delivered hostages, and swore oaths to him; and he vowed to them that he would be a loving lord to them: and nevertheless, during this, they plundered all that they over-ran. Then, on mid-winter's day, archbishop Aldred consecrated him king at Westminster; and he gave him a pledge upon Christ's book, and also swore, before he would set the crown upon his head, that he would govern this nation as well as any king before him had at the best done, if they would be faithful to him.

J.A. Giles, ed. and trans., *The Anglo-Saxon Chronicle.* London: G. Bell and Sons, 1914.

thus begun in 1337 was waged intermittently for a hundred years and is known as the Hundred Years' War.

Eight years after war was declared, the Battle of Crécy [a town in northern France] (1346) marked the beginning of the end of the Age of Chivalry and the emergence of the common man. For at Crécy the English longbowmen dramatically routed the French cavalry and proved that the unarmored foot soldier was the equal of the horseman in armor. Ultimately England lost the war and relinquished her claims to French territory. But the war had one beneficial effect. No longer was there friction between Normans and Anglo-Saxons; henceforth all were Englishmen.

Instead of the needed period of peace to recover from the war with France, the second half of the fifteenth century was marked by warfare between the descendants of the Duke of York and the Duke of Lancaster, who were both sons of Edward III. Because the House of Lancaster had a red rose as its emblem and the House of York a white rose, this civil war is called the War of the Roses. After a period of bitter warfare during which the crown changed hands several times, the Earl of Richmond of the House of Lancaster married Elizabeth, heiress of the House of York, and ascended the throne in 1485 as Henry VII, the first of the Tudors.

The Rise of the Common Man

During the declining years of the Middle Ages the pageantry of chivalry with its armored knights jousting in tournaments still dazzled the people but no longer blinded them. The great lords of the castles and the powerful religious leaders could no longer hold the poor villagers in complete subservience. The common man began his slow rise. In the mid–fourteenth century the terrible Black Death killed an estimated forty percent of the population, and serfs, left without masters, escaped to a freer life in the growing towns. Other serfs were driven from the manors when the lords turned to sheep raising, which required fewer workers. In towns and villages families deprived of home and work became vagabonds and robbers. Out of the desperation of the laborers emerged the Peasants' Revolt of 1381, which was savagely crushed by the nobles.

During this same century a middle class of merchants and craftsmen began its rise to power and stability. Craftsmen were prospering and were establishing guilds—the forerunners of unions or trade organizations—to protect their rights. Many of these guilds—such as the weavers, the carpenters, the haberdashers—had fine halls, and their members dressed in gay, distinctive liveries.

Along with the social upheaval came a change in the attitude toward the Church. The way was being paved for a new phase in English history. The country was moving toward nationalism, a more modern economy, a more questioning attitude toward the powers of the Church, and above all toward the idea that a man's place in society was not necessarily a fixed thing nor was his earthly life so unimportant. The first whisper of the Renaissance was in the air.

The First Stages of the English Language

BY OWEN BARFIELD

Owen Barfield traces the development of English language from its earliest roots. Only a few words remain from the language of the first Britons, or Celts, as well as the earliest Roman invasion. Subsequent invasions of Romans, Jutes, Angles, Saxons, and Danes had the most significant impact on the emergence of a distinctive English language. According to Barfield, the Norman invasion added a rich variety of French and Latin words that changed forms when they blended with Anglo-Saxon. Owen Barfield taught literature at Drew and Brandeis universities. He is the author of Poetic Diction: A Study in Meaning *and* History, Guilt, and Habit.

Looking back down the corridors of time from the particular perspective to which we have attained in the twentieth century, far away in the past—it may be in the Stone Age—we seem to be able to perceive a remarkable phenomenon. At some particular spot in the vast plains stretching from Eastern Europe to Central Asia it was as though a fresh spring bubbled up into the pool of humanity. Whether it represented the advent of a new "race-type", what a race-type exactly is, and how it begins are questions which we must leave to others to settle. That spring was the Aryan [also called Indo-European] culture.

Throughout much of Europe and Asia there were already in existence different civilizations in different stages of development; such were the Egyptian, the Chaldean, and farther west the great Minoan civilization, which in its Bronze Age was to ray out an influence from Crete all over the Aegean world. It may be that

Excerpted from *History in English Words*, by Owen Barfield (New York: George H. Doran, 1926).

there was something static in the very nature of these pre-Aryan cultures, or it may be that they were ageing and passing in the natural course of events; what is certain is that there was something dynamic, some organic, out-pushing quality in the waters of this Aryan spring. For these waters spread. They have been spreading over the world ever since that time, now quickly, now slowly, down into India and Persia, north to the Baltic, west over all Europe and the New World. . . .

Aryan Migration into the British Isles

There could hardly be a better example of the uneasy movement of Aryan migrations than the history of the settlement of the British Isles. We find them, first of all, as far back as we can look, inhabited by an unknown population who left their barrows and tumuli dotted about the country, whose society seems to have been matriarchally organized, and who, if the name *Pict* may be taken as any indication, probably had the habit of painting or tattooing their bodies. At length, several centuries before our era, the first Aryan wave reaches these shores in the persons of the Celts, who spread over England, Wales, Scotland, and Ireland, where they have been pointed out and variously described by historians as *Britons, Ancient Britons, Welsh, Gaels, Celts,* . . . They settle down and live for some centuries the primitive life of savages, till half-way through the first century B.C. they are disturbed by a little Aryan tongue reaching out from the wellnigh spent Italian wave. Pagan Rome establishes a brief dominion over a small portion of Britain, drives roads, builds camps and cities, and after some four hundred years is sucked back again to the Continent. Another century, and the Angles and Saxons, borne forward on the crest of the Teutonic wave, overrun the main island, driving the Celts into its extremities, whence they regurgitate, before finally settling down, upon various military and missionary enterprises which have played an important part in our history. But already another ripple of the Teutonic wave is upon us, rocking over the seas in the long boats of the Scandinavian Vikings, and almost before they have left their impress on the eastern quarter of the land, a third—the Normans this time—is breaking on Britain once again at Pevensey. The liquid metaphor is unavoidable, for no other image seems adequate to express what actually happened. To watch through the glasses of history the gradual arrival and settlement of the Aryans in this country is to be reminded irresistibly of the rhythmic wash and backwash, the little accidental interplays of splash and ripple, which accompany the tide as it fills an irregularly shaped pool.

Every one of these motions has left its mark on our language, though the traces of the earliest immigration of all—that of the Celts—are rather scarce. The clearest vestiges of it are to be found in the proper names of our rivers, for a surprising number of these contain one or other of the various Celtic terms for 'water' or 'river', e.g. *avon, dwr (ter* or *der), uisge (wye, usk, is, ax),* while the other parts of the name are often composed of words for 'water' taken from another Aryan language, as in *Derwentwater, Windermere, Easeburn, Ashbourne,* . . .

The Romans, Angles, and Saxons Enter Britain

The four hundred years of Roman colonization, following Julius Caesar's landing in 55 B.C.—years which left such permanent and conspicuous vestiges on the face of England—have made little enough impression on her language. Fresh as the memory of that civilization must have been when the Angles and Saxons arrived, they seem to have learnt nothing from it. A few towns, such as *York* (Eboracum), retain in a more or less corrupted form the particular titles given to them by their Roman founders, but outside these almost the only Latin words which our ancestors can be proved to have taken from the Britons are *port* and 'castra' (a camp), surviving to-day in *Chester* and in the ending of many other town names such as *Winchester, Lancaster, Gloucester,* . . .

Then, during the fifth and sixth centuries of our era the Angles and Saxons began to flow in from the Continent, bringing with them old Aryan words like *dew, night, star,* and *wind,* which they had never forgotten, new words which they had coined or developed in their wanderings, and Latin words which they had learnt as provincial subjects of the Roman Empire, bringing, in fact, that peculiar Teutonic variant of the Aryan tongue which forms the rich nucleus of our English vocabulary. Their arrival here was followed almost immediately by their conversion to Christianity; and this moment in our history was a pregnant one for the future of Europe. For now the two great streams of humanity—Teutonic blood from the one side, and from the other the old classical civilization, bearing in its dark womb the strange, new Christian impulse—met. The Latin and Greek words which entered our language at this period are concerned for the most part with the dogma and ritual of the Church; such are *altar, candle, clerk, creed, deacon, hymn, martyr, mass, nun, priest, psalm, shrine, stole, temple*, and many others. Far more important was the alteration which now gradually took place in the *meanings* of many old Teutonic words—words like *heaven*, which had hitherto denoted a 'canopy', or *bless*, which had meant to 'consecrate with blood'. . . .

Although Christianity did not come officially from Rome to England until Augustine landed in A.D. 597, it had already found its way here indirectly during the Roman occupation. Obliterated by the pagan Anglo-Saxons, it had continued to flourish in

The Old English of Beowulf

Beowulf, *a long poem celebrating the deeds of the hero Beowulf, was the first important poem written in English. It was told orally until it was written down around 1000. The lines that follow are a translation into modern English.*

List to an old-time lay of the Spear-Danes,
Full of the prowess of famous kings,
Deeds of renown that were done by the heroes;
Scyld the Sheaf-Child[1] from scourging foemen,
From raiders a-many their mead-halls[2] wrested.
He lived to be feared, though first as a waif,
Puny and frail he was found on the shore.
He grew to be great, and was girt with power
Till the border-tribes all obeyed his rule,
And sea-folk hardy that sit by the whale-path[3]
Gave him tribute, a good king was he.

1. Scyld ("Shield") had been found as an outcast babe adrift in an open boat lying upon a sheaf of wheat. This story closely resembles that of the infant Moses. 2. homes or palaces where they drank mead [honey wine] 3. Such metaphors as this one for the sea are very common in Old English poetry. They are known as "kennings."

Bernard D. Grebanier et al., *English Literature and Its Background*. Vol. 1. Rev. ed. New York: Dryden, 1949.

Ireland, and the actual conversion of most of the English is believed to have been the work of Celtic Christians, who arrived from Ireland and established missionary bases in Scotland and Northumbria. Their influence was so extensive that 'Scotia', the old name for Ireland, came to be applied to the country which we still know as *Scotland*. *Pat* and *Taffy*, the popular nicknames for an Irishman and a Welshman, are descended from the Celtic saints, Patrick and David, and it is interesting to reflect that the Celtic missionaries were starting their work in Northumbria at almost exactly the same moment as St. Augustine landed in Kent. Thus Christianity enfiladed England, as it were, from both ends; and while the southern Anglo-Saxons were learning the Greek and Latin words to which we have referred, the Irish Christians in the north had been making the language a present of a few Celtic words, two of which—*druid* and *lough*—have survived. Again, although the name for the instrument of the Passion comes to us ultimately from the Latin 'crux', yet the actual form which the word *cross* has taken in our language is very largely due to these Irish Christians. But for them it would probably have been something like *cruke*, or *cruce*, or *crose*. This word has an interesting history. It was adopted from the old Irish 'cros' by the Northmen, and it is due to them that the final "s" took on that hissing sound which is represented in modern spelling by "ss". We may suppose, therefore, that but for the Irish Christians the word would have been something like *cruce*, and but for the Northmen it might have been *croz* or *croy*.

The Danes Invade

In the ninth and tenth centuries these Northmen, the Scandinavian Teutons, whom our ancestors called Danes, established an ascendancy over a large part of England. They seem to have mingled easily with the English, and we can trace back to their dialect some of the very commonest features of our language. Thus, the Scandinavian pronouns, *they, them, their, she*, gradually replaced less convenient Anglo-Saxon forms, and it is to the Northmen that we owe that extremely useful grammatical achievement which has enabled us to form both the genitive and the plural of nearly *all* nouns by merely adding the letter "s". Other Scandinavian words are *call, get, hit, husband, knife, leg, odd, same, skin, take, want, wrong*; and there are many more hardly less common. The mighty word *law*, together with *outlaw, hustings, wapentake, moot,* and *riding* (division of Yorkshire) serve to remind us that the Danish ascendancy was no hugger-mugger affair, but a firm political organization. The old Anglo-Saxon words which these Northern intruders replaced, such as *niman*, 'to take', and *Rood* (the Cross) have mostly fallen out of use; but in some cases the two words survive side by side. Thus, our useful distinction between *law* and *right* was once geographical rather than semantic, the two words covering roughly the eastern and the western halves of England.

The Norman Influence on the Language

And now there followed an event which has had more influence on the character of the English language than any other before or since. The conquest of England by the Norman[1] invaders brought about an influx of French words which went on increasing in volume for more than three centuries. At first it was little more than a trickle. For a long time the Norman conquerors did not mix much with their Saxon subjects. There are plenty of indications of this; for the languages, too, moved side by side in parallel channels. The custom of having one name for a live beast grazing in the field and another for the same beast, when it is killed and cooked, is often supposed to be due to our English squeamishness and hypocrisy. Whether or not the survival of this custom through ten centuries is due to the national characteristics in question it would be hard to say, but they have certainly nothing to do with its origin. That is a much more blameless affair. For the Saxon neatherd who had spent a hard day tending his *oxen, sheep, calves*, and *swine*, probably saw little enough of the *beef, mutton, veal, pork*, and *bacon*, which were gobbled at night by his Norman masters. There is something a little pathetic, too, in the thought that the homely old word, *stool*, could be used to express any kind of seat, however magnificent, until it was, so to speak, hustled into the kitchen by the smart French *chair.* Even the polite, however, continued to use the old word in the idiom "to fall between two stools." *Master, servant, butler, buttery, parlour, dinner, supper*, and *banquet* all came over with William, besides the names of our titular ranks, such as *duke, marquis, viscount, baron*, and *countess*. . . .

1. These Normans, or *North-men*, were the descendants of a Teutonic Danish tribe, which had taken possession of Normandy about a hundred and fifty years before.

Not the least interesting of the words that must have come over from France about this time are such courtly flower-names as *dandelion* and *pansy*, from 'dent-de-lion' (describing the ragged leaves) and the sentimental 'pensée'—remembrance. Many of these early Norman words seem to have a distinctive character of their own, and even now, after nearly a thousand years, they will sometimes stand out from the printed page with peculiar appeal. . . .

The Influence of Latin and Literary Words

It will be noticed that nearly all these words are directly descended from the Latin, *beef* going back through 'boeuf' to 'bovem', *master* to 'magister', *duke* to 'dux', . . . Thus already, by the thirteenth century, we can trace in our vocabulary four distinct layers of Latin words. There are the Latin words learnt by our ancestors while they were still on the Continent, such as *camp, mile,* and *street*; there are the Latin words brought over by the Roman invaders, of which *port* and *Chester* were given as surviving examples; and thirdly there are those words—*altar, candle, nun*, . . . brought over by the Christian missionaries as described earlier. These three classes are reckoned to account for about four hundred Latin words altogether; and lastly there is this great deposit of Norman-French words, of which the number must have been running into thousands. For it was not only terms of general utility which were transferred from one language to another. A second and entirely different kind of borrowing now sprang up—the literary kind. For two or three centuries Poetry and Romance had been making rapid strides in Italy and France. The medieval habit of writing only in Latin was dying out. Dante and, long after him, the Frenchman, [Joachim] Du Bellay, had written treatises extolling the beauties of their native tongues. French lyric poetry burst into its early spring blossom among the troubadours, with their curious "Rose" tradition, and for two hundred years the English poets imitated and translated them as fast as ever they could. It was just at the end of this long period of receptiveness that an event occurred which fixed the ingredients of our language in a way they had never been fixed before. The printing press was invented.

A modern poet, looking back on that time, can scarcely help envying a writer like [Geoffrey] Chaucer with this enormous store of fresh, unspoilt English words ready to his hand and an unlimited treasury across the channel from which he could pick a brand-new one whenever he wanted it.

> Thou hast *deserved* sorer for to smart,
> But *pitee* renneth soone in *gentil* heart.

Here are three Norman French borrowings, three fine English words with the dew still on them, in two lines. It was the May morning of English poesy.

The Blend of Anglo-Saxon and French

For these were not "French" words. Right at the beginning of the thirteenth century the English kings had abandoned Normandy, and the English Normans, separated from their brethren, began to blend more and more completely with their neighbours. In England French remained at first the exclusive language of the Court and the law, but, as the blood of the two peoples mingled, the Norman words which were not dropped gradually altered their shapes, developing various English characteristics, which not only differentiated from their original French forms the words already in the language, but served as permanent moulds into which new borrowings could be poured as they were made. *Gentil* changed to *gentle, pitee* to *pitie* or *pity*; and it was the same with innumerable others. Familiar French-English terminations like *-tion, -ty, -ance, -age, -able, -on*, were already nearly as common in Chaucer as they are in the pages of an average modern writer. Begotten on Latin words by generations of happy-go-lucky French and English lips, they were fixed forever by the printing press, and to-day, if we want to borrow a word directly from Latin, we still give it a shape which tacitly assumes that it came to us through the French language at about that time. . . .

We have borrowed so many that it has lately been calculated that as many as one-fourth of the words which we can find in a full-sized Latin dictionary have found their way directly or indirectly into the English vocabulary. A large number of these are Greek words which the Romans had taken from them. Thus, taking into account those Greek words which have come to us by other channels, Greek and Latin form a very large and a very important part of the English language.

The Plantagenet Dynasty: Wars and the Beginnings of Democratic Institutions

BY JOSEPH WARD SWAIN

Joseph Ward Swain enumerates major events occurring during the dynasty of the Plantagenet kings, a period lasting from 1154 to 1485, when Henry VII became the first Tudor king. During this period some of the kings fought wars in France, one went on a crusade, and others engaged in power struggles with barons, resulting in the Wars of the Roses. According to Swain, three major institutions had their origin during this period: trial by jury, the Magna Carta, and Parliament. Joseph Ward Swain taught history at the University of Illinois; he is the author of The Ancient World *and* Beginning the Twentieth Century.

While the Hohenstaufen rulers of Germany were building and losing an empire in Italy, the English kings of the Plantagenet dynasty were following much the same course in France. Almost a hundred years had passed since William the Conqueror had won the battle of Hastings and become king of England. The founder of the Plantagenet dynasty, Henry II, then inherited the English throne in 1154. He was young, energetic, and ambitious, with a large empire and high ideas regarding kingship. . . .

Henry was succeeded by his eldest son, Richard I (1189–1199), who is commonly known as Coeur de Lion, or Lion-

Excerpted from *The Harper History of Civilization*, by Joseph Ward Swain (New York: Harper, 1958).

Heart. Legend pictures Richard as the most chivalrous and romantic of the English kings, partly because of his participation in the ill-starred Third Crusade (1189–1192). Returning overland through Europe, Richard was captured at Vienna and held prisoner until the English paid the Emperor Henry VI an enormous ransom that amounted to almost two years' revenue of the crown (1194). The remaining five years of his life Richard passed largely on the Continent, waging war against the king of France, Philip Augustus. He was succeeded by his younger brother, John (1199–1216), who had been regent during the king's absence on the crusade. . . .

Conflicts Between Kings and Barons

Ever since the coming of William the Conqueror in 1066, the government of England and the high offices in church and state had fallen to the Norman barons, either to men who themselves had fought under William at Hastings, to their descendants, or else to newcomers from Normandy. A sharp distinction was therefore drawn between Norman and Anglo-Saxon, between the governing class and the governed. The Normans and the court spoke French, but the common people continued to speak Anglo-Saxon. The Norman aristocrats therefore developed a strong class feeling that enabled the king to set up the strongest central government in western Europe.

Though the Normans introduced feudalism into England, William the Conqueror took great precautions to prevent the disruptive tendencies usually encouraged by that system. He maintained royal, nonfeudal, officials in all parts of the country; he made sure that no baron held estates in any one region that were large enough to provide formidable armies; he forbade building fortified castles without his express permission; he compelled all sub-vassals to take a special oath declaring that their first loyalty was to him. William thus created so strong a government that his son, William II, easily crushed the barons who rose against him. . . .

Nevertheless the Norman kings did not have everything their own way. Like all European sovereigns at this time, they were in constant controversy with the church over investiture [conferring the authority of high office] and countless other matters. They also had trouble with their Norman barons. This trouble was not due solely to the feudal pride and arrogance of the nobility or to their desire for extreme personal liberty. All the nobles holding fiefs directly from the king were automatically members of the *Magnum Concilium* (Great Council), which William consulted regularly, but when it became apparent that this body could not govern efficiently, the kings turned for advice to a small group of trained administrators and trusted barons known as the *Curia Regis* (King's Court). The barons deeply resented the activities of this court, whose members' exalted position and power were due to ability rather than to ancestry. Moreover, the system was expensive, and the barons knew that in the end they paid the bill. They therefore set themselves to limiting the powers of the king and his agents. The ensuing struggle was less disastrous than the parallel struggles on the Continent, and out of it sprang the institutions that have since caused England to be hailed as "the mother of parliaments." Three of these institutions—trial by jury, Magna Carta, and parliament—deserve our close attention, even though the first of them had no connection with the controversy between the kings and their barons.

Trial by Jury

Toward the end of his reign William the Conqueror ordered a thorough survey of the resources of his realm. The findings were assembled in the famous *Domesday Book* (1086), which is still extant and which is of the greatest value to the economic historian of the Middle Ages, nothing comparable having been attempted elsewhere in Europe. We mention it in this paragraph, however, because of the method by which it was compiled. William sent agents into every shire and hundred (a subdivision of the shire, or county) to collect information. Upon arrival in a community the agents summoned several local inhabitants whom they forced to answer under oath various questions regarding the population, the acres of plowed land, pasture, and forest, and the revenue of each manor, what they then were and what they had been twenty years before in the days of Edward the Confessor (d. 1066). William thus established the practice of using juries to provide information required by the government. Later Norman kings had frequent recourse to such juries—so-called from the French verb *jurer,* "to swear."

Almost a century later Henry II began using juries in the administration of justice. The *Curia Regis* had long been the principal court of law in the kingdom, but as its members followed the king in his constant travels, litigants never knew where their cases would be heard. Henry therefore appointed a number of special judges to hold court regularly in each shire. As these judges traveled from place to place, following a regular annual circuit, they were called "itinerant justices." They looked after all the king's business in the shire, inspecting local administration, levying taxes, and dispensing justice. They formed an important link between the local and central governments. Upon arriving in a shire the justice would summon a jury and inquire what crimes had been committed there since his last visit. The jury replied under oath, giving him the names of the persons suspected of committing the crimes. Such juries were called "presentment juries" and resembled the grand juries of today, which may "indict" a person—that is, order that he be brought to trial—but do not actually try him or convict him. . . .

Magna Carta

Though Magna Carta dates only from the reign of John, it was the outcome of more than a century of controversy between the kings and their barons. When Henry I (1100–1135) came to the throne his royal title was none too good, and he sought popularity by promising to refrain from various practices of his predecessor, William II. This Coronation Charter marks an important step in the progress of limited monarchy, for though Henry quickly broke his promises, the charter was remembered and became the precedent for stronger limitations of royal authority. Henry II likewise had his troubles with his nobles, but controversy did not become acute until the days of John.

John was determined to be an absolute monarch like his father, Henry II, but unfortunately for him he lacked his father's genius and good fortune. He quarreled with everybody—the pope, the king of France, his barons, his loyal supporters—and eventually he was defeated. His loss of Normandy was a terrific blow to Norman pride. His great quarrel with the pope (during which Innocent kept England under an interdict for five years and John retaliated by outlawing all the clergy) caused great consternation and distress, alienating many of the common people. Apparently John's surrender to Innocent (1213) was not greatly resented, but a year later his defeat by the French king at Bouvines (where he was aiding his uncle, Otto of Germany) was a much more serious reverse. The burghers of London and other towns had been inclined to favor John at first, but his merciless taxation turned them to his enemies. The year after Bouvines the barons, now supported by the clergy and burghers, met the king at Runnymede, on the Thames above London, where, on June 15, 1215, they compelled him to accept Magna Carta, the Great Charter.

This Magna Carta is the most famous document in English history, often extravagantly praised and often misunderstood. Its sixty-three clauses enumerate abuses of power from which John promised to abstain thereafter. Many clauses deal with matters of taxation, but others reaffirm various ancient rights of the barons, the church, and the burghers. The document was thoroughly feudal in spirit, setting forth rights and liberties that had long been implied in the feudal contract. It is quite incorrect to say that Magna Carta guaranteed trial by jury, or habeas corpus, or no taxation without representation. . . .

Nevertheless, Magna Carta is a fundamental document in the history of liberty in the Western world. It clearly implies, though it nowhere states explicity, that there are things which even a king must not do, for above him stands the law. Magna Carta thus checked those who preached the all-powerful state. In later times its clauses were misunderstood and misinterpreted until they were made to guarantee, not the feudal rights of a few thousand barons, but the fundamental rights and liberties of all men. Most of these rights and liberties were not conceived until much later, yet without Magna Carta the world today would be a much worse place than it is.

Cruel necessity forced John to sign Magna Carta at Runnymede, but he had no intention of giving up the fight with his barons. . . . Shortly thereafter John died and was succeeded by his nine-year-old son, Henry III (1216–1272). . . .

Even when a grown man Henry III showed no great strength of character, and he did little that is worth remembering, yet his long reign was a period of important developments in the English constitution. These developments culminated in the rise of parliament.

Parliament

A famous clause in Magna Carta promised that the king would not collect more than the traditional feudal dues except after receiving express permission from his barons assembled in the *Magnum Concilium.* As the traditional feudal dues were never enough to meet the constantly rising costs of government, Henry had to call rather frequent sessions of the council (now coming to be called "parliament," from the French verb *parler,* "to speak") in order to beg new subsidies from his barons. The king's financial difficulties were increased by his bad management, by his unlucky wars in France, and by his subservience to various popes whose demands for money became utterly insatiable. At the same time his personal unpopularity was being intensified by the favors he showered upon foreigners, either Italian prelates or relatives of his French wife. . . .

The parliaments which Henry III summoned in the early years of his reign were composed only of the barons who held fiefs directly from the crown, but presently it became customary to summon a certain number of knights from each shire as well. These knights were members of the lowest class in the feudal aristocracy, and for them attendance at parliament was a duty rather than a privilege. Their sole task was to grant the king money, and the king's officers in the shire selected the particular individuals who were to be summoned. Sometimes, however, the knights were able to make their influence felt enough to obtain redress of minor grievances before authorizing the grants to the king. Simon de Montfort, a man of broad views who wished his government to be popular with all classes of English society, summoned a parliament in 1265 which included not only the barons, the higher clergy, and two knights from each shire but also two burghers from each town and representatives of the lower clergy.

After Simon's death, parliament was summoned by the king as before, but the plan of having various social classes represented was continued. Thirty years later Edward I (1272–1307) summoned what came to be called (or rather, miscalled) the "Model Parliament" (1295). In this parliament, as in Simon's, the five social classes were represented. Each group then met as a separate body, but in later times the barons and high clergy united to form the House of Lords, the knights and burghers made up the House of Commons, and the lower clergy dropped out. . . .

Several English kings tried to rule without parliament, but they never succeeded. By insisting upon the right to approve taxation, English parliamentary leaders made government without their coöperation impossible. On the other hand, they allowed England to keep her monarchy. By gradually limiting the powers of the king, the English prevented royal absolutism, and in the end they reduced the royal power virtually to zero. Today the English monarch still has a throne, but functions primarily as a symbol of English national unity. . . .

The Wars of the Roses

The course of political development in England and Spain in the fifteenth century resembled that in France. In each of these countries the kings strove to create strong central governments, and in each they were opposed by great lords who used the word "liberty" as a euphemism for "feudal anarchy." At first the barons were rather successful in England. They deposed and murdered Edward II (1307–1327), and, as parliament alone had the right to levy new taxes, they profited greatly from the financial difficulties of Edward III (1327–1377). During a lull in the war [the Hundred Years' War, 1337–1453], Edward's grandson and heir, Richard II (1377–1399), attempted to strengthen royal power in England. The barons opposed this move strenuously, and at last parliament dethroned Richard and replaced him with his cousin, Henry IV. Parliament thereby won its greatest victory to date.

The next three English kings (Henry IV [1399–1413], Henry V [1413–1422], and Henry VI [1422–1461]) owe their present reputation largely to Shakespeare's plays about them. Being descended from John of Gaunt, duke of Lancaster (1340–1399), an extremely able man who was a younger son of Edward III, they are known as the Lancastrian line. No one of these kings was a strong ruler (though Henry V's armies won famous victories in France); and Henry VI verged on feeble-mindedness, perhaps an inheritance from his maternal grandfather, the insane French king, Charles VI. The lords and parliament therefore continued to govern England. They fell to quarreling among themselves, however, with some ambitious leaders hoping to seize the throne while others merely hoped to control it. As soon as hostilities in France were concluded (1453), these baronial conflicts assumed the grandeur of a civil war, known to historians as the Wars of the Roses (1455–1485) because rival factions supposedly took the red and the white rose as their symbols. The two principal contestants were the families of Lancaster and York—the latter being descended from Edmund, duke of York (1341–1402), another son of Edward III—but the wars were more than a mere family feud.

Many sweeping changes had come over England during the long war with France. At the beginning of that conflict, England had been largely an agricultural and wool-producing country, with the wool being sent to Flanders to be made into cloth. During the war many Flemish weavers fled to England, where they set up their looms and began to weave. Other men launched other industries, trade grew, cities sprang up, and a powerful capitalist class arose. The capitalists were highly discontented with the Lancastrians, for the prevailing feudal anarchy interfered with trade, and royal taxation annoyed them greatly. They therefore gave their support to the Yorkists, and after the death of Henry VI (1461) three Yorkist kings ruled in succession: Edward IV (1461–1483), Edward V (1483), and Richard III (1483–1485). Edward IV restored peace, curtailed the powers of parliament, and financed his government largely by confiscating the estates of Lancastrians—whom he called rebels. The nobility had by this time been decimated by the wars, and the confiscations completed their ruin. In the long run, however, the Yorkists were no more successful than the Lancastrians. Richard III was scarcely the monster pictured by Shakespeare, but he was a usurper whose critics accused him of tyranny, and he could not preserve peace in England. The rich burghers therefore transferred their favor to Henry Tudor—he was a descendant of the Lancastrian John of Gaunt but had married a daughter of the Yorkist Edward IV—and after defeating Richard at Bosworth Field he became King Henry VII (1485–1509). He successfully united the two factions, and under his skillful leadership the "tyranny" of the Yorkists was gradually transformed into the "absolutism" of the Tudors.

THE HISTORY OF NATIONS

Chapter 2

The Tudor Monarchy, 1485–1603

Tudor Kings Bring Order and Stability

By Mortimer Chambers, Raymond Grew, David Herlihy, Theodore K. Rabb, and Isser Woloch

In the following selection, the authors describe the Tudor dynasty from its founding by Henry VII to the arrival of Elizabeth I. Henry VII used his fiscal responsibility and his effective domestic and foreign policy to bring order and strength to the monarchy. The next Tudor king, Henry VIII, further strengthened the position of the crown, using his divorce from Catherine and his break with the Church of Rome to his advantage. His administrative reforms made the monarchy strong enough to survive the brief but weak reigns of his son Edward VI and his daughter Mary I until his daughter Elizabeth became queen. All of the authors taught history at universities: Mortimer Chambers at the University of California at Los Angeles, Raymond Grew at the University of Michigan, David Herlihy at Harvard University, Theodore K. Rabb at Princeton University, and Isser Woloch at Columbia University. All have scholarly publications on historical topics.

During the last quarter of the fifteenth century, England, France, and Spain were governed by remarkable rulers, whose accomplishments have led historians to call them "new monarchs": Henry VII, Louis XI, and Ferdinand and Isabella. Their reigns are generally regarded as marking the end of a long trend toward fragmentation and anarchy and the beginning of a revival of royal power that would ultimately create the vast bureaucratic apparatus characteristic of the modern state. Moreover the successors to their thrones not only inaugurated more active and aggressive policies in international affairs but also—and this was of momentous significance—gradually gained ground over traditional competitors for power such as the Church.

Excerpted from *The Western Experience: The Early Modern Period*, by Mortimer Chambers, Raymond Grew, David Herlihy, Theodore K. Rabb, and Isser Woloch (New York: Alfred A. Knopf, 1974).

Governing with Help from the Gentry, Parliament, and Common Law

The English monarchs had relied for centuries on local cooperation to run their kingdom. Unlike other European countries, England contained only fifty or sixty families out of a population of perhaps 2.5 million who were legally nobles. But many other families, though not technically members of the nobility, had large estates and were dominant figures at the parish, county, and even national level. They were known as gentry, and it was from their ranks that the crown appointed the local officers who administered the realm—notably the justices of the peace (usually referred to as J.P.s). Each of these voluntary, unpaid officials served as the principal public servant in one of the more than forty counties of the land.

For reasons of status as well as out of a feeling of responsibility, the gentry had always sought such appointments. From the crown's point of view, the great advantage of the system was its efficiency: enforcement was in the hands of those who could enforce, for as a "great man" in his neighborhood, the justice of the peace rarely had trouble exerting his authority. By the Late Middle Ages, the king had had at his disposal an administrative structure without rival in Europe. This cooperative approach to the task of governing had created a strong sense of duty among the members of the ruling class, and the king had come to consult them more frequently over the years.

In the sixteenth century an institution that had developed from this relationship, Parliament, began to take on a general importance as the chief representative of the country's wishes; it was increasingly considered to be the only body that could give a ruler's actions a wider sanction than he could draw from his prerogatives alone. Although for a long time to come it would remain firmly subordinated to the crown, England's kings already realized that they could not take such measures as raising extraordinary taxes without Parliament's assent.

Another of the monarch's assets was England's common law, the country-wide system of justice based on precedent and tradition. Like Parliament, the common law would eventually be regarded by opponents of royal power as an independent source of authority with which the crown could not interfere. But under the conditions facing the "new monarch" in the 1480s, it proved an effective tool in his work of restoring the authority of the throne after two centuries of weakness.

Henry VII's Fiscal Responsibility

Henry VII (1485–1509), who founded the Tudor dynasty, came to the throne as a usurper in the aftermath of thirty years of civil conflict, the Wars of the Roses. England's nobles had been running amuck for decades, and the situation hardly looked promising for a reassertion of royal power. Yet Henry both extended the authority of the crown and restored order with extraordinary speed.

His first concern as he set about establishing a stable rule was finances. The crown's income was about £52,000 a year, but Henry's immediate expenses were considerably higher.[1] He knew that unless he could balance his budget, his position would remain insecure. Yet extra taxes were the surest way of alienating subjects who expected a king to "live of his own," that is, from the income his lands provided, customs payments, and the traditional contributions made to him at special times such as the marriage of his daughter. It is a testimony to the care with which he nurtured his revenues that by the end of his reign he had paid off all his debts and accumulated between one and two million pounds as a reserve.

Part of his success was due to his beginning his reign with more property than any of his predecessors, a consequence of forfeitures and inheritances that had devolved to his benefit during the civil wars. But Henry also sharply increased the profits from the workings of justice—fees and fines—which had the added advantage of cowing unruly subjects. Moreover he radically improved his financial administration by taking the tasks of collection and supervision out of the cumbersome office of the Exchequer and placing them in his own more efficient household. By careful management of this kind, he was able to "live of his own."

Henry VII's Effective Domestic and Foreign Policy

Where domestic order was concerned, the main impetus behind the revival of royal authority was clearly the energy of the king

1. To give a sense of scale, a man who made £100 a year was considered very rich.

and his chief servants. Henry increased the powers of the justices of the peace, thus striking severely at the independence attained by leading nobles during the previous two centuries. Under his leadership, too, the council became a far more active and influential body. The ministers not only exercised executive powers but also resumed hearing legal appeals, primarily because the government was determined to exert all its force to quell disorder. Plaintiffs could be sure that at such a hearing, where there was no jury and where deliberations would not be influenced by the power of a local lord, decisions would be quick and fair, and the popularity and business of the councillors' court grew rapidly.[2]

The dual objective of government stability and fiscal responsibility guided Henry's foreign policy. He never became involved in costly adventures, and he allowed no challenge to the Tudor dynasty's claim to the crown. In 1492 for example, after Henry halfheartedly invaded France as a protest against the French annexation of Brittany, Charles VIII signed a treaty promising to pay him £160,000 and guaranteeing not to support any claimants to the English throne. A succession of agreements with other rulers from Denmark to Florence bolstered the position of England's merchants, whose international trade was essential to the crown's customs revenues. Henry encouraged the manufacture and export of the country's great staple product, cloth, and protected shipping with a navigation act. Turning to more distant possibilities, he granted an Italian sailor, John Cabot, a patent to search for a westward route to China. The result of this undertaking was the discovery of enormous fishing banks off Newfoundland whose exploitation was to be the basis of the growing prosperity of many English ports in the sixteenth century.

Henry VIII Achieves Early Victories

The first Tudor was a conservative, building up his authority and finances through traditional methods and institutions that had long been at the disposal of England's kings but that the founder of the new dynasty applied with exceptional determination and vigor. The young man who followed him on the throne, Henry VIII (1509–1547), was an expansive, dazzling figure, a strong con-

2. The room where the royal council met had stars painted on its ceiling; the council sitting as a court eventually came to be known by the name of the room, the Star Chamber.

trast to his cold and careful father. Early in his reign he removed a longstanding threat from England's north by inflicting a shattering defeat on an invading Scots army at Flodden in 1513, and the following year he brought a sporadic war with France to a favorable conclusion. With his prestige thus enhanced, he spent the next fifteen years taking only a minor part in European affairs while he consolidated royal power at home with the capable assistance of his chief minister, Cardinal Thomas Wolsey, whom he appointed lord chancellor in 1515.

Henry VIII

Wolsey was not an innovator but a tireless and effective administrator who continued the consolidation of royal power begun under Henry VII. To meet the rising demand for royal justice, he expanded the jurisdiction and activities of the Star Chamber and the Chancery and guided another offshoot of the king's council to independent status: the Court of Requests, or Court of Poor Men's Causes.

Henry VIII Seeks a Divorce

Wolsey fell from power in 1529, ruined by the king's wish to obtain a divorce from his wife, who had failed to produce a surviving male heir. Henry had married his brother's widow, Catherine of Aragon, under a special papal dispensation from the biblical law that normally prohibited a union between such close relatives. Obsessed with continuing his dynasty, for which a male heir seemed essential—and infatuated with a young lady at court, Anne Boleyn—Henry had urged Wolsey to ask the pope to declare the previous dispensation invalid. Under ordinary circumstances there would have been no trouble, but at this moment the pope was in the power of Charles V, king of Spain and emperor of the Holy Roman Empire, who not only had a high sense of rectitude but also was Catherine's nephew. When all Wolsey's efforts ended in failure, Henry dismissed him.

For three years thereafter the king attempted fruitlessly to gain his objective. He called Parliament and gave it free rein to express bitter anticlerical sentiments; he sought opinions in European universities in favor of the divorce; he attacked his own clergy for having bowed to Wolsey's authority as papal legate; he even extracted a vague recognition from the clergy of his position as "supreme lord" of the Church. Finally he placed his confidence in Thomas Cromwell, a former servant of Wolsey, who suggested a radical but simple solution: that Henry break with the pope, declare himself supreme head of the Church, and divorce Catherine on his own authority. The king agreed, thus unleashing a revolution that dramatically increased the powers of the royal government.

The Influence and Stature of Parliament

The instrument chosen to accomplish the break with Rome was Parliament, the only body capable of giving the move legal sanction and an aura of national approval. Henry called the assembly in 1529 and did not dissolve it until 1536. During its sessions it acted on more matters of greater importance than a Parliament had ever considered before. It forbade litigants from making ecclesiastical appeals to Rome, thus allowing Henry to obtain his divorce and remarry, and finally declared him supreme head of the Church in England in 1534. Royal power gained enormously from these acts, but so too did the stature of Parliament, thanks to its unprecedented responsibilities and length of meeting.

Previously membership in Parliament had been considered a chore, particularly by the townsmen and landed gentry in the House of Commons, who found the expense of unpaid attendance and its encroachments on their time more irksome than did the nobles in the House of Lords (so named during Henry VIII's reign). But this attitude began to change in the 1530s as members of the Commons, returning to successive sessions, came to know one another and in time developed a remarkable esprit de corps as jealous guardians of Parliament's traditions and privileges.

Administrative Reorganization

Following his successful suggestion for solving Henry's conflict with Rome, Thomas Cromwell rose rapidly in his monarch's service. He was an indefatigable bureaucrat: he reorganized the administration of the country into six carefully distinguished departments with specific functions and gave himself the chief executive position, the secretaryship. A Privy Council, consisting of the king's principal advisers, was also established to coordinate and direct the administration.

Unquestionably the principal beneficiary of the events of the 1530s was the crown. Royal income rose markedly when Henry became head of the English Church and took over the ecclesiastical fees that previously had gone to the pope. He gained an even larger windfall when he dissolved all English monasteries and confiscated their immensely valuable lands, which were sold over the next few decades. Fortunes were made by speculators, and new families rose to prominence as major landowners.

For all the stimulus he gave to parliamentary power, Henry now had a much larger, wealthier, and more sophisticated administration at his disposal, and he left no doubt where ultimate authority lay. He did not establish a standing army, as some of the Continental kings did, but he had no need for one. He was fully capable of awing ambitious nobles or crushing an uprising.

Competition from Religious Movements

Royal power was put to the test very soon. Where doctrine and the structure of the Church were concerned, Henry was a conservative; he allowed few changes in dogma or liturgy. As the Protestant reform movement on the Continent created a serious schism, Henry tried to restrain the spread of Reformation ideas and persecuted heresy, but he could not avoid compromises. Perhaps realizing the shape of things to come, he had his son, Edward, tutored by a committed reformer. Moreover in the 1540s a leading Continental dissenter, Martin Bucer, spent a few years in Cambridge, deeply influencing a number of future leaders of the English Church.

During the reign of Edward VI (1547–1553), who died while still a minor, the nobility attempted to resume some of their old powers in government, and the Reformation advanced rapidly in England. Edward's half-sister Mary I by contrast attempted to reestablish Roman Catholicism when she ascended the throne in 1553, forcing many Englishmen into exile and others into two major revolts during her five-year reign. Royal power, however, was strong enough to withstand these strains. The revival of the nobles was short-lived, and Mary's death, in 1558, brought an end to the reversal of religions. She was succeeded by Henry VIII's last surviving child, Elizabeth, a woman of determination who demonstrated that the growth of the monarchy's authority had been but briefly interrupted under Edward and Mary.

Queen Elizabeth I Enhances England's Power

BY JOSEPH R. STRAYER, HANS W. GATZKE, AND E. HARRIS HARBISON

In the following selection, Joseph R. Strayer, Hans W. Gatzke, and E. Harris Harbison explain Queen Elizabeth I's strategy for making England a stronger nation. As she deflected threats on her life and throne, she kept England out of war long enough to expand English industry, commerce, and shipping. When conflict with Spain eventually came, England went into battle prepared to defeat the Spanish Armada in 1588; the victory lifted the spirits of the English people. Joseph R. Strayer and E. Harris Harbison both taught history at Princeton University. Strayer is the editor of Dictionary of the Middle Ages. *Harbison is the author of* Christianity and History: Essays. *Hans W. Gatzke, who taught history at Johns Hopkins University, is the author of* The Present in Perspective: A Look at the World Since 1945.

Queen Elizabeth I (1558–1603) is generally accounted the greatest of the Tudors and one of England's ablest rulers, though to some of her critics she was simply a woman of petty emotions and limited vision who did her best to cramp the expanding energies of her people. Whatever the judgment, she left England immeasurably stronger at her death than she had found it at her accession, and she died beloved of the great majority of her people. At twenty-five when she came to the throne she had already lived through a great deal: disgrace, humiliation, and even danger of execution during her sister Mary's reign. She had seen how Mary had lost the love of her people by marrying a foreigner and burning heretics. She came

Excerpted from *The Course of Civilization*, by Joseph R. Strayer, Hans W. Gatzke, and E. Harris Harbison (New York: Harcourt, Brace and World, Inc., 1960).

through these early experiences a strong-willed and shrewd young woman, aware of how precarious both her own situation and that of her nation were, determined to put politics before religion and follow a purely national policy.

Elizabeth Rules by Temporizing and Compromising

Her instinct was always to temporize and compromise. As the daughter of Henry VIII and Anne Boleyn, she could never allow England to submit to papal authority. But she wanted a religious settlement which would not alienate patriotic Catholics, and she hoped she could deceive the Catholic powers of Europe for a time into thinking that she could be won back to Rome. On the other hand, she resented the attempt of the Puritan minority to dictate a radical religious settlement to her, and she rejected the schemes of some of her Protestant councilors to support Protestant parties and Protestant revolts all over Europe. But she never completely broke with her patriotic Puritan subjects and never lost their loyalty, even when she clapped some of them in jail for speaking too boldly in Parliament. Elizabeth's policy was nationalist first and Protestant second, but the long-term result was to encourage that fusion of patriotism and Protestantism which became a permanent characteristic of English public opinion after her death.

In the same way she compromised and temporized in her foreign policy. Her instinct was to avoid clear-cut decisions, to keep a dozen intrigues afoot so that there were always avenues of escape from any policy, and to avoid war at almost any cost. The chief danger at her accession was from French intrigue in Scotland. The Frenchwoman Mary of Guise was regent for her daughter Mary Stuart, who was married in 1558 to the heir to the French crown. When in 1559 the fiery reformer John Knox returned to his native Scotland from Geneva, where he had imbibed the purest Reformed doctrine from Calvin, his preaching had an immediate and striking success. A religious revolution led by Knox was soon under way, and the whole French position in Scotland was undermined. The French connection with Scotland went back several centuries, and since Mary Stuart's husband was now king of France, it was clear that France would make every effort to restore Catholicism and French dominance. For once Elizabeth made a rapid decision to ally with the Calvinist party in Scotland and keep the French out. By 1560 Knox, the Kirk (Church), and the pro-English party were in control, and Scotland was never again to become a dangerous foothold for French intrigue. The way was paved for the ultimate union of the English and Scottish crowns in 1603.

The Threat Posed by Mary Queen of Scots

Mary Stuart—or Mary Queen of Scots, as she is known to history—returned to Scotland in 1561 after her husband's death. She was a far more charming and romantic figure than her cousin Elizabeth, but she was no stateswoman. A convinced Catholic, she soon ran head-on into the granitelike opposition of Knox and the

During her reign, Elizabeth enjoyed political power while maintaining the devotion of the English people.

Kirk. Her marriage to her cousin Lord Darnley turned out badly and she became involved in a plot resulting in his murder. In 1567 she was forced to abdicate, and in the following year she fled from Scotland and sought protection in England from Elizabeth. No visitor could have been more unwelcome. Mary, as Henry VII's great-granddaughter, had the best hereditary claim to be Elizabeth's heir, but she was a Catholic and a foreigner. Elizabeth would never formally recognize her as her successor, nor would she marry in order to produce another heir, nor would she do anything to harm her fellow sovereign, except keep a close watch on her through her agents. This policy exasperated Elizabeth's Puritan advisers and left Mary free to become the center of almost every French or Spanish plot against Elizabeth's life during the next twenty years. In 1569, for instance, the Catholic nobility in the north of England rose in revolt in an effort to oust Elizabeth and put Mary on the throne with foreign aid.

The Anglo-Spanish Conflict

Philip of Spain had made cautious offers of marriage to Elizabeth at her accession, but she had rejected them. For over twenty-five years the governments of Philip and Elizabeth remained on good terms, determined to preserve the peace in the face of increasing friction. But conflict was almost inevitable. England was a small country with perhaps half the population of Spain, but during the quarter century of peace which Elizabeth's cautious temporizing gave her people, English industry, commerce, and shipping expanded considerably. . . .

It was the revolt of the Netherlands, however, which finally brought England and Spain to blows. For years the economic ties between England and the Low Countries had been close. The English people sympathized with the victims of Alva's tyranny,[1] and English Sea Dogs cooperated informally with Dutch Sea Beggars and Huguenot [French Protestants] privateers to prey on Spanish shipping and to cut Spanish communications by sea with the Netherlands. Philip's ambassadors in England became deeply involved in one plot after another against Elizabeth's life, usually with the object of setting Mary Stuart on the throne. In 1587

1. Spanish Philip II had sent the duke of Alva to the Netherlands to punish Calvinist mobs that were vandalizing Catholic churches. Alva acted severely and executed thousands of people.

Elizabeth reluctantly consented to Mary's execution when confronted with unmistakable evidence of her complicity in these plots. Now the way was cleared for Philip to attack England in his own interest (to put Mary on the throne of England might have benefited France even more than Spain), and in 1588 he sent his "Invincible Armada" north to hold the Channel while Parma[2] ferried his Spanish veterans across to conquer England for Spain.

The Defeat of the Spanish Armada

The story of the defeat of the Armada has become an allegory of the triumph of the young, vigorous nation over the old and senile. The Spanish ships were large and slow, equipped with inferior cannon, and commanded by a landlubber [a person unfamiliar with seamanship]. The fleet was conceived as a means of transporting troops, not of fighting battles at sea. The English ships that put out from Plymouth to harry the Spanish up the Channel were smaller and more maneuverable, trained to fire their cannon at longer range. Parma was not ready when the Spanish reached Calais and anchored there. The English sent in fire ships among the Spanish ships as they lay at anchor, drove them northward in panic, and attacked them fiercely off Gravelines. Stormy weather completed what the English had begun. Hardly half the galleons which left Spain made their way back northward and westward around Scotland and Ireland. The victory gave a lift to the morale of Englishmen and of Protestants everywhere. It ended all further thought of Spanish conquest of England—or reconquest of the Netherlands, for that matter. It did not mean the end of Spanish sea power. During the Anglo-Spanish war that began in 1585, English troops were heavily involved in suppressing a rebellion in Ireland, which was backed by some Spanish help, and in supporting Dutch Protestants and French Huguenots. England had neither the resources nor the ships to crush Spain at sea, and Spanish land armies were still the best in Europe. War lasted till 1604, when a peace treaty was signed by the successors of Philip and Elizabeth. The only thing that was clear by then was that the English and the Dutch had taken their places beside the Portuguese and the Spanish as major powers on the sea.

2. Philip's representative in the Netherlands, a military commander

The Success of Queen Elizabeth I

BY JOHN E. NEALE

In a speech delivered at the Folger Shakespeare Library on the fourth centenary of the accession of Elizabeth I, John E. Neale describes the traits that enabled Elizabeth to rule successfully from 1558 to 1603. He praises her leadership and instincts, which allowed her to make policies that alleviated problems successfully, and he cites her charm, which won the hearts of the people who became her devoted admirers. John E. Neale, who taught history at the University of London and Oxford University, is the author of a biography entitled Queen Elizabeth.

This is November 17, 1958. Four hundred years ago today, Queen Elizabeth "of glorious memory"—Good Queen Bess, as she was affectionately known to generations of Englishmen—ascended the throne of England. . . . Here are we met to commemorate the day. In the words of the simple ballad writer, composed in 1600:

> Now let us pray
> and keep holy-daye
> The seaventeenth day of November;
> For joy of her Grace
> in every place,
> Let us great prayses render.

But why should we? you may ask. It is my business to supply the answer.

First af all, we are associating ourselves with an old English tradition that lasted for two centuries. It was about ten years after Elizabeth's accession that villagers and townsmen in England took to ringing their church bells and rejoicing on November 17. The

Excerpted from "England's Elizabeth," by John E. Neale, *Life and Letters in Tudor and Stuart England*, edited by Louis B. Wright and Virginia A. LaMar (Ithaca, NY: Cornell University Press, 1962).

custom began spontaneously. So far as I know, there were no precedents, though in Catholic England there had been saints' days galore. After a few years, the Anglican Church adopted this popular innovation, making a Protestant holyday of November 17; and as the cult of the Queen intensified, the day was celebrated throughout the land in a pleasing variety of ways, ranging from elaborate tilts [jousting tournaments] at Westminster, where the royal Court assembled, to the simple service, bell ringing, and bonfires of the rural village. . . .

Escape from Mary I; Anticipation of Elizabeth I

Posterity has never wavered in regarding the Elizabethan period as one of the golden times of history. How indeed could it, when the age gave birth to such immortal names and achievements as those of [Philip] Sidney, [Edmund] Spenser, [Francis] Bacon, and [William] Shakespeare; [John] Hawkins, [Francis] Drake, and [Walter] Raleigh? What a people's instinct did was to associate this astounding flowering of an age with a single event—the accession of Elizabeth Tudor to the throne of England.

The people were right. Consider the alternative: imagine that Queen Mary Tudor,[1] Elizabeth's sister, had lived the normal span of life and produced an heir to the throne. Tied to Spain and Catholicism, England's story—Europe's and America's as well—would have been very different. The enterprising minds and personalities of high Elizabethan days were associated with the fresh ideology of that age—Protestantism. In the circumstances we have envisaged, it seems certain that the energies of such men would have found an outlet and been absorbed in civil dissension. As it was, Mary's brief reign hovered on the brink of civil war, and the gloom cast on the nation by subordination to a foreign king, along with the priestly cruelty of burning heretics at the stake—it would have been less offensive to call heresy treason and use the gallows—all this was tolerable only because Mary was childless and ailing, and a bright future seemed at hand in the person of Elizabeth. . . .

We should not be misled by the peaceful and uneventful accession of Queen Elizabeth into thinking of November 17,

1. Mary I, daughter of Henry VIII and Catherine of Aragon, a Catholic married to Philip of Spain, also Catholic

1558, as an ordinary transfer of the throne from one dead monarch to her natural successor. The exiles returning to England after their flight abroad from the Catholic regime of Mary Tudor, the citizens of London in their welcome to the new Queen, and the majority in the House of Commons when the first Parliament of the reign assembled—all these, and many more, saw the occasion as the overthrow of one ideology and the victory of its rival: we might almost say, a revolutionary *coup d'état* [sudden overthrow of a government]. And, in fact, there is evidence to suggest that Elizabeth was organized to fight for her throne, if the need had arisen.

To ardent Protestants, the miraculous preservation of their Queen from all the perils of her sister's reign was the admirable work of God's own hand. In an oration, written for the accession, [Chaplain] John Hales imagined God saying to Englishmen: "Ye see, my people, what I have done for you. . . . I have not only discovered mine, yours, and my land of England's enemies . . . but I have also taken away their head and captain. . . ."

The Need for Ability, Leadership, and Good Fortune

To harness this [inspiration] to the broader emotion of patriotism; to nurse the ardor of men like Hales and yet restrain their harmful fanaticism; to cultivate the Puritan sense of a divine purpose guarding and promoting the welfare of England, as God in the Old Testament had watched over Israel—to do this and at the same time qualify that exclusive spirit by tolerance, here was the problem of statecraft.

It called for exceptional ability and a genius for leadership; and since that leadership, in a period of personal monarchy, had to come from the sovereign, and the sovereign was a woman, ruling men who believed the regiment of women to be monstrous, it also called for extraordinary will-power. Happy fortune too was needed: a combination and succession of accidents, not least of which was the long life of the Queen. Elizabeth's reign might be interpreted as a gamble, a gamble of hers with time. She preferred to run the gravest risks rather than act against her deeper promptings. "Safety first" was not her motto. Her ministers—all of them, including the ablest and most trusted—wrung their hands in despair over her. "To behold miseries coming and to be denied remedies!" moaned Lord Burghley. . . .

The harnessing of the revolutionary spirit began almost at once with the religious settlement made at Elizabeth's first Parliament. It was a Protestant settlement,[2] but with comeliness and tradition preserved and fanaticism excluded. We know too little about its story, but all that little shows that it was the personal policy of the young Queen, stubbornly forced through a reluctant, radical House of Commons. The Anglican Church, now four hundred years old and venerable, was uniquely the creation of this woman. Though not so conservative as she wished, it has certainly proved, what she wanted it to be, amazingly comprehensive. At all times it has harbored high, low, and also moderate churchmen. It might be regarded as the symbol of her rule. . . . Rather than be a party leader, she chose to lead the nation. In so doing she created a left wing of discontent.

Affection Between the Queen and Her People

The paradox of the Elizabethan age is that its flavor and dynamic came from this left or Puritan wing, and came through a romantic attachment between them and their Queen. It was an attachment for which I think the closest parallel in our history is that between Englishmen and [World War II prime minister] Winston Churchill in our own time.

What is the explanation? As in the case of Winston Churchill, undoubtedly the supreme art and deliberate policy of the Queen. But there were more specific reasons—reasons of an accidental character. The first was the Queen's failure to marry, the consequent lack of an heir, and the uncertainty about the succession to the throne. If no religious problem had existed, Mary Queen of Scots [niece of Elizabeth] would have been the obvious heir apparent; but she was a Catholic, the spearhead of the opposing ideology, and English Protestants would on no account tolerate the prospect of her succession. . . .

The second reason for the romantic attachment of Queen and people was the mounting concentration of the Catholic Counter Reformation against Elizabeth and her England—the cold war of the two rival ideologies of that age, with its hot spots. The crucial event was the flight of Mary Queen of Scots to England

2. The Elizabethan settlement of 1559 restored the monarch as supreme governor of the Church of England and restored the Prayer Book.

in 1568, after her lurid tale of misadventure in her own country.[3] Thenceforward, until her execution in 1587 put an end to this frightful danger, the alternative, Catholic Deborah was in England, a focus—though captive—for every plot and scheme of the counter revolution. Granted a similar revolutionary climate and a similar life-or-death struggle, who could be confident that, even in our modern civilized days, a bloody end would not be put to such an intolerable situation in less than twenty hazardous years? Elizabeth's statesmen, Parliament, and people exerted their utmost pressure to exact that solution, and exact it rapidly, from their Queen. Her obstinate refusal was an even more personal policy than her religious settlement. She pursued the *via media* [middle way] in politics as well as religion, gambling with her own life and the country's apparent welfare for the sake of rooted principles and instincts. We may doubt whether any masculine ruler would have shown such compunction. . . .

Increasing danger imparted a new and peculiar intensity to the bond of affection between Elizabeth and her people. She herself cultivated the relationship with consummate art, playing her part, on set occasions, with the skill of a born actress. She was as sensitive to public relations as any modern publicity agent. She wrote her own speeches for Parliament, fining and refining her phrases like the most finicky stylist. When, for example, at the final crisis over Mary Queen of Scots, two of these speeches were needed for propaganda purposes at home and abroad, she secretly worked over the printer's text herself rather than permit a mere report to be printed. Her courtly progresses [entourages] through the countryside—her summer holidays—were episodes in publicity, marked by most elaborate and artificial entertainments and relieved by innumerable touches of the unconventional. . . . Her court was a community in itself, thronged with visitors, especially on Sundays, come to see the Queen, perhaps to catch her eye and be spoken to. . . .

The cult of the Queen was expressed in the literature of the age, in courtly pageantry, and by artists in her portraits. Much, of course, was highly artificial, though that does not mean that it was necessarily false, and the ballads were usually simple enough.

3. After the murder of Mary's husband, Lord Darnley, Mary married the earl of Bothwell, after which opinion turned against her. She was imprisoned by Protestants, escaped to England, and was imprisoned there until her execution.

The parliamentary debates of the high Elizabethan period—from the arrival of Mary Queen of Scots to the post-Armada[4] years—throb with the pride of Englishmen in their sovereign. Even the most obstreperous Puritans—indeed, they above all—rejoiced in her. "It makes my heart leap for joy to think we have such a jewel," declared one of them in the House of Commons. "It makes all my joints to tremble for fear when I consider the loss of such a jewel." . . .

The Queen's Steady Course of Moderation

Thus, there was this cult of the Queen as the symbol of patriotism and the Protestant ideology. The other aspect of England's reaction to its perils was the desire to promote political security by penal laws, increasingly drastic as the danger became more acute. The State in those days was inevitably ideological. How far it went along the totalitarian road depended on policy. Quite early, Elizabeth's Councillors and Parliament wanted to enforce attendance at Communion in church by statute, in order, as one Puritan Member said, that "the very secrets of the heart in God's cause . . . must come to a reckoning, and the good seed [be] so sifted from the cockle that the one may be known from the other." The Queen vetoed that bill, and when in a later Parliament an attempt was made to revive the measure, she interfered to stay its course. Though requiring outward conformity to the law, she abhorred all inquisitional practices and would open no windows into men's souls.

By 1580 the cold war was hotting up, and the infiltration of Catholic missionaries was reinforced by the beginning of Jesuit missions. The menace had to be dealt with, and when Parliament met statesmen and both Houses drafted what they regarded as the necessary legislation. They wanted to stop the missionaries by making their work treasonable and their converts traitors, to prohibit saying or attending Mass under the severest penalties, and to bar Catholics from entry into the professions. With these and other proposals they would have imposed (or tried to impose) orthodoxy in their ideological State as ruthlessly as the totalitarian regimes of our contemporary world. The Queen intervened to prohibit many of their proposals, scale down the penalties of oth-

4. The British Royal Navy defeated the Spanish Armada in 1588.

ers radically, and insert a secular instead of a doctrinaire principle into the Act. . . .

This legislation was mild—astonishingly mild—compared with the penalties that Privy Councillors, Lords, and Commons did their utmost to secure. Their obstacle was always the Queen.

It was the same at the other extreme. In the passionate atmosphere of the time, doctrinaires of the left—the Puritans—acquired an authority and following out of proportion to their number or their gospel. In the name of Truth and Patriotism they wanted to reform the Anglican Church root and branch, to obtain what had been denied them in the Settlement of 1559, and even to go the whole hog in Protestant ideology. It is the perennial story of revolutions, except in the sequel. In the name of patriotism, if not of truth, they generally found a majority of fellow travelers in the House of Commons ready to back them, and substantial sympathy for many items of their program in the House of Lords and among Privy Councillors. After all, what surer defense was there against the enemy than a nation legislated into Protestant godliness? The saints seemed to have the right answer to the country's grave political problem.

Elizabeth would not budge an inch. Always at hand, always vigilant, she argued, threatened, sent prohibitory messages, imprisoned offenders in the Tower, and wielded her legislative veto. Then, when the doctrinaires, having secretly built up a subversive Presbyterian movement within the Church itself, tried to legislate the revolution into existence, she disciplined them with rigor and put up her best orators in the House of Commons to expose their conspiracy. It was deliberate, consistent, and personal action, and undoubtedly saved the Church of England. . . .

The Queen's Dependence on Experience, Instinct, and Principle

Doubtless there were those near Elizabeth who whispered advice against the majority opinion of Council and Parliament; but we know enough about some of the most striking instances to be sure that the overwhelming weight of authority was against her. In this sense she may often be said to have gambled with the fate of the kingdom. It is worth asking how this could be.

In the first place, the constitution of the country was personal monarchy. The sovereign received counsel or advice, but all decisions were hers. One of the remarkable features of Elizabeth's rule is the extent to which she kept both major and minor decisions in her own hands. Again, she chose her own Councillors. Their superlative quality is equally remarkable. Even her "favorites" were men of parts [talent] and were made to work hard. . . .

It is an interesting reflection that masters who have the faculty of choosing servants of outstanding ability usually remain nonetheless masters. To diagnose why this was the case with Elizabeth is easy. A person of exceptional intelligence and studious, inquisitive temperament, she was educated in the rigorous manner of the Renaissance by the finest scholars of the time. She was a cultured woman, the intellectual peer or superior of her advisers, and had the requisite linguistic and historical knowledge to keep even foreign policy in her hands. Moreover, in her youth she had passed through a school of experience where everything—even her life—depended on her wit and intelligence. Her political instinct was already mature when she came to the throne at the age of twenty-five, and over the years, judging solely by results, she made so few blunders that time could only confirm and justify her trust in it. Her greatest statesman, Lord Burghley, who was inclined at first to share contemporary prejudice against a woman ruler, was brought at length to acknowledge her surpassing wisdom. The divergences of policy between him and his mistress seem often to have been divergences between logic and instinct. Perhaps her greater trust in instinct was a feminine trait, though experience, as so often can be said of instinct, was a predominant ingredient. She worked hard and conscientiously at her job and lived for it, with mind and emotion. She had every reason for self-confidence except that of sex, and her masterful nature and birth compensated here. Tradition has portrayed her as unprincipled. It is a superficial judgment, bred of ignorance. In fact, no sovereign or statesman has clung more obstinately and daringly to certain fundamental principles, though in small things few women have tantalized men more frequently by their mutability.

It was principle, deep-rooted in instinct, that led Elizabeth to restrain the passion of an angry nation against Catholics and stand adamant against the dreams of doctrinaires. For this, surely all who in any degree owe something to English civilization still remain indebted to her. Our tradition is one of tolerance. In England the fanatic has never got his way. We have had a Civil War: it did not go to the extremes normally experienced in such strife.

We have had our revolutions: that in 1688 is always known as "Glorious," it was so bloodless and respectable. . . .

The Devotion of Her People

That the Queen, at this critical time in our history, remained sensitive to civilized feelings and resisted her advisers is surely cause for us to salute her memory on this, her day. Politically it was folly. She was much too intelligent not to grasp the force of the advice she was given and success alone could justify the responsibility she assumed. By the mercy of God and the devotion of her people success was granted her.

The devotion of her people! Inevitably I return to that theme. It was as Gloriana, Belphoebe, and other conceits of the Elizabethan imagination; it was as an orator who in her great Armada speech spoke these words, "I know I have the body of a weak and feeble woman, but I have the heart and stomach of a King, and of a King of England too"; who, later, in her Golden Speech told her Commons, "Though God hath raised me high, yet this I count the glory of my crown, that I have reigned with your loves"; it was also as one whose impromptu dressing-down of an insolent Polish ambassador, spoken in Latin, thrilled that generation and remained a memory in early Stuart Parliaments; and finally it was as one who, in her last State address to the Realm, rendering a final account of her stewardship, could phrase her peroration in words magical and moving in their simplicity, "This testimony I would have you carry hence for the world to know: that your Sovereign is more careful of your conservation than of herself, and will daily crave of God that they that wish you best may never wish in vain"—it was as such a person, a great woman in a great office, with an unsurpassed gift for romantic, intrepid leadership, that she won the adoration of her subjects and conjured from individuals and the nation as a whole their utmost genius. She was, wrote Francis Osborne some fifty years later, "the choicest artist in kingcraft that ever handled the sceptre in this northern climate."

English Colonists Settle in America

By Allen Nevins and Henry Steele Commager with Jeffrey Morris

Allen Nevins and Henry Steele Commager recount the history of English settlements along the Atlantic coast in America. After a slow beginning with Virginia in 1607 and Massachusetts in 1620, other colonies emerged in rapid order as far south as Georgia. Chartered trading companies and grants to individual proprietors provided the means for the English to leave their homeland and settle in America. Allen Nevins, a journalist and a teacher at Columbia University, is the author of A Brief History of the United States *and* American Social History as Seen by British Travelers. *Henry Steele Commager, who taught at New York University, is the author of* The Growth of the American Republic *and* The American Mind. *Jeffrey Morris, a lawyer who also taught political science at the University of Pennsylvania, is the author of* Federal Justice in the Second Circuit: A History of the United States Courts in New York, Connecticut, and Vermont, 1787–1987.

To the raw new continent the first British settlers came in bold groups. The ships that under Christopher Newport sailed into Hampton Roads on the 13th of May, 1607, carried men alone. They laid out Jamestown, with a fort, a church, a storehouse, and a row of little huts. When calamity fell upon them, Captain John Smith showed a nerve, resourcefulness, and energy that in the second year made him president and practical dictator of the colony. Agriculture was slowly developed; in 1612 John Rolfe began to grow tobacco, and as it brought high prices in the London market everyone took it up, till even the market place was planted with it.

Yet growth was slow. By 1619 Virginia had no more than two

Excerpted from *A Pocket History of the United States*, by Allen Nevins and Henry Steele Commager with Jeffrey Morris (New York: Pocket Books, 1992).

thousand people. That year was notable for three events. One was the arrival of a ship from England with ninety "young maidens" who were to be given as wives to those settlers who would pay a hundred and twenty pounds of tobacco for their transportation. This cargo was so joyously welcomed that others like it were soon sent over. Equally important was the initiation of representative government in America. On July 30, in that Jamestown church where John Rolfe several years earlier had cemented a temporary peace with the Indians by marrying Pocahontas, met the first legislative assembly on the continent: a governor, six councilors, and two burgesses each from ten plantations. The third significant event of the year was the arrival in August of a Dutch ship with Negro slaves, twenty of whom were sold to the settlers.

Pilgrims Arrive in Massachusetts

While Virginia was thus painfully managing to survive and grow, a congregation of English Calvinists who had settled in Holland were making plans to remove to the New World. These "Pilgrims," who had been persecuted because they denied the ecclesiastical supremacy of the king and wished to set up a separate Church of their own, had originally come from the village of Scrooby, in Nottinghamshire. In every way they were a remarkable body. They had three leaders of conspicuous ability: the teacher John Robinson, a learned, broad-minded, generous-hearted graduate of Cambridge University; their sage elder, William Brewster, also a Cambridge man; and William Bradford, shrewd, forcible, and idealistic. The rank and file possessed integrity, industry, and sobriety, as well as courage and fortitude. They had endured popular hostility in England; they had withstood loneliness and harsh toil in Holland. Now, securing a patent to settle in America, a ship called the *Mayflower*, and a store of provisions, they prepared to face the rigors of the wilderness. Sailing from Plymouth one hundred and two in number, the Pilgrims on December 11 (Old Style), 1620, landed on the Massachusetts coasts. That winter more than half of them died of cold and scurvy. Well might William Bradford write:

> But here I cannot but stay and make a pause and stand half amazed at this poor people's present condition. . . . Being thus past the vast ocean and a sea of troubles before in the preparation . . . they had now no friends to welcome them, nor inns to entertain or refresh their

> weatherbeaten bodies, no houses or much less towns to repair to, to seek for succor. . . . And for the season, it was winter, and those that know the winters of that country know them to be sharp and violent and subject to cruel and fierce storms, dangerous to travel to known places, much more to search an unknown coast. Besides what could they see but a hideous and desolate wilderness full of wild beasts and wild men? . . . What could now sustain them but the spirit of God and His grace?

But the next summer they raised good crops, and in the fall a ship brought new settlers. Their resolution never faltered. When the Narraganset chief, Canonicus, sent them a bundle of arrows in a snakeskin as a challenge to war, Bradford stuffed the skin with bullets and returned it with a defiant message.

London Sends Settlers to Colonies Along the Atlantic Coast

Then in rapid succession emerged other English colonies. The parent hive was ready to send forth its swarms. A May day in 1629 saw the London wharves a scene of bustle and cheery excitement; five ships carrying 400 passengers, 140 head of cattle, and 40 goats, the largest body thus far sent across the North Atlantic at one time, were sailing for Massachusetts Bay. Before the end of June they arrived at Salem, where John Endicott and a small group of associates had planted a town the previous autumn. These people were Puritans—that is, members of the Church of England who at first wished to reform or purify its doctrines and who finally withdrew from it—and they opened a great Puritan exodus. In the spring of 1630 John Winthrop reached Salem with eleven ships carrying nine hundred settlers, enough to found eight new towns, including Boston. The Massachusetts Bay colony grew so rapidly that it was soon throwing off branches to the south and west. Roger Williams, a minister of Salem who courageously taught the separation of Church and state, with other radical views, was driven into the Rhode Island wilderness. Here in 1636 he founded Providence as a place of perfect religious toleration. In that year, too, the first migration to Connecticut began under the resolute Reverend Thomas Hooker, who moved a great part of his congregation from Cambridge westward in a body. Another notable colony sprang into existence in 1634, when the first settlement was made in Maryland under the guidance of the liberal-minded Cecilius Calvert, second Baron Baltimore. Most of the gentlemen who first went thither were, like the founder, English Catholics, while most of the common folk were Protestants. Toleration was therefore essential, and Maryland was a home of religious freedom, attracting people of varied faiths. Settlers from Virginia drifted into the Albemarle Sound region of what is now North Carolina as early as the 1650's, but it was not until 1663 that Charles II granted a charter to eight of his favorites for the vast area now embraced by both the Carolinas and Georgia. The proprietors named both the colony and the first city after their royal benefactor, and induced John Locke to draw up for them a Fundamental Constitution which, happily, never went into effect. Settlers drifted down from Virginia and others, including many French Huguenots, came directly to the coast from England and the West Indies. Charleston, established in 1670, speedily became the cultural as well as the political capital of the colony.

New York Begins as a Dutch Settlement

The seat of one rich colony was gained by conquest. The Dutch had sent Henry Hudson, an English mariner, to explore the river which bears his name—a task executed in 1609. Dutch fur traders had followed him, and in 1624 a small settlement was effected on Manhattan Island. The province of New Netherland grew but slowly and failed to develop institutions of self-government, but did leave a permanent mark in the patroon system of plantations along the Hudson, in architecture, and in "Knickerbocker" families who were to play a leading role in the history of New York and of the nation. Meanwhile, the English never gave up their claim to the entire coast, and the Connecticut settlements were anxious for the seizure of their troublesome neighbor. Why permit this alien element in the very center of British America? Charles II granted the area to his brother, the Duke of York, who took vigorous action. In the summer of 1664 three warships arrived before New Amsterdam. They carried a body of soldiers who were reinforced by Connecticut troops, while forces were promised from Massachusetts and Long Island. Most of the Dutch settlers, sick of despotic rule, made no objection to a change of sovereignty. Although old Peter Stuyvesant declared he would rather be "carried out dead" than surrender, he had no choice. The British flag went up over the town renamed New York and, save for a brief intermission during a subsequent Anglo-Dutch war (1672–1674), it stayed there. Indeed, the British flag now waved from the Kennebec to Florida.

Quakers Settle Pennsylvania and Delaware

Yet one of the most interesting colonies did not take on firm outlines till late in the century. A number of settlers, British, Dutch, and Swedish, had found their way into the area which later became Pennsylvania and Delaware. When the pious and farsighted William Penn came into control of the region in 1681, he prepared to erect a model commonwealth on the principles of the Quakers—that sect which Voltaire later called the most truly Christian of peoples. In his benevolent fashion, he quieted the Indian title by friendly treaties of purchase. To attract colonists he offered liberal terms, assuring all that they could obtain land, establish thrifty homes, and live in justice and equality with their neighbors. No Christian would suffer from religious discrimination. In civil affairs the laws would rule, and the people would be a party to the laws. He directed the establishment of Philadelphia, his "city of brotherly love," with gardens surrounding each house, so that it would be "a green country town . . . and always be wholesome." In 1682 he came over himself, bringing about a hundred colonists. Pennsylvania throve wonderfully, attracting a great variety of settlers from Britain and the Continent, but keeping its Quaker lineaments.

The Role of Chartered Trading Companies

Roughly speaking, two main instruments were used in this work of transferring Britons and others across the seas and founding new states. It was the chartered trading company, organized primarily for profit, which planted Virginia and Massachusetts. The London Company, so-called because organized by stockholders resident in London, had been granted its charter in 1606 to plant a colony between the thirty-fourth and forty-first degrees of latitude. The Plymouth Company, whose stockholders lived in Plymouth, Bristol, and other towns, was chartered that same year to establish a colony between the thirty-eighth and forty-fifth degrees. These companies could distribute lands, operate mines, coin money, and organize the defense of their colonies. The king, who granted the charters, kept ultimate jurisdiction over the colonial governments. After heavy financial losses, the London Company in 1624 saw its charter revoked, the king making Virginia a royal colony. The Plymouth Company promoted various small Northern settlements and fishing stations, but made no money, and after reorganization asked in 1635 for annulment of its charter, calling itself "only a breathless carcass."

Yet if neither the London nor the Plymouth Company was profitable financially, both did an effective work in colonization. The London Company was in a very real sense the parent of Virginia; the Plymouth Company and its successor, the Council for New England, founded town after town in Maine, New Hampshire, and Massachusetts. And a third corporation, the Massachusetts Bay Company, had a peculiar character and a special destiny. It originated as a body of stockholders, most of them Puritans, who had commercial and patriotic motives. Undaunted by the failure of the earlier companies to pay dividends, they believed that better management would yield profits. Charles I granted a charter early in 1629. Then a strange development took place. When the king and High Church party under Archbishop Laud became masters of the Church of England, many Puritan leaders wished to emigrate. They had property, social position, and an independent spirit. They did not wish to go out to Massachusetts Bay as mere vassals of a company in London. Moreover, they hoped to secure liberty to set up the kind of Church government they liked. Therefore, the principal Puritans of the company simply bought up all its stock, took the charter, and sailed with it to America. A commercial company was thus converted into a self-governing colony—the colony of Massachusetts Bay.

The Role of Proprietors

The other principal instrument of colonization was the proprietary grant. The proprietor was a man belonging to the British gentry or nobility, with money at his command, to whom the Crown gave a tract in America as it might have given him an estate at home. The old rule of English law was that all land not otherwise held belonged to the king, and America fell under this rule. Lord Baltimore received Maryland; William Penn, the son of an admiral to whom the king owed money, received Pennsylvania; and a group of royal favorites under Charles II received the Carolinas. All these proprietors were given large powers to devise a government. Lord Baltimore, who had some of the absolutist ideas of the Stuarts, was averse to giving his colonists any lawmaking power, but finally yielded to a popularly created assembly. Penn was wiser. In 1682 he called together an assembly, all of whom were elected by the settlers, and allowed them to enact a constitution, or "Great Charter." This vested many of the powers of government in representatives of the people—and Penn accepted the scheme.

As soon as it was proved that life in America might be prosperous and hopeful, a great spontaneous migration from Europe began. It came by uneven spurts and drew its strength from a variety of impulses. The first two great waves went to Massachusetts and Virginia. From 1628 to 1640 the Puritans in England were in a state of depression and apprehension, suffering much actual persecution. The royal authorities were committed to a revival of old forms in the Church and determined to make it completely dependent on the Crown and the archbishops. Political as well as ecclesiastical turmoil racked the land. The king dissolved Parliament and for ten years got on without it. He imprisoned his chief opponents. As his party seemed bent on subverting English liberty, many Puritans believed that the best course was to quit the island and build in America a new state. In the great emigration of 1628–1640, some twenty thousand of the sturdiest people of England left home. No fewer than twelve hundred ship voyages were made across the Atlantic with settlers, livestock, and furniture. Boston became one of the important seaports of the world, ministering to an area full of bustle and vitality. Harvard College was founded. Among the settlers were the ancestors of Franklin, the Adamses, Emerson, Hawthorne, and Abraham Lincoln. One striking characteristic of this movement was the migration of many Puritans not as individuals or families but in whole communities. Certain English towns were half depopulated. The new settlements consisted not of traders and farmers alone, but of doctors, lawyers, schoolteachers, businessmen, craftsmen, and ministers. New England became a microcosm of old England, carrying in extraordinary degree the seeds of future growth.

THE HISTORY OF NATIONS

Chapter 3

Major Changes in City and State, 1603–1760

English Civil Wars Led to Representative Government

By T. Walter Wallbank and Alastair M. Taylor

The Tudor era (1485–1603) was characterized by a strong monarchy that enjoyed popular support. Following this period of stability, conflict ensued between monarchists and those who favored a stronger parliamentary system as well as between Puritans and pro-Catholics. In the following selection, T. Walter Wallbank and Alastair M. Taylor explain how these conflicts led to civil wars between 1642 and 1660. While the religious issues were important in the conflict, the authors emphasize that the movement toward representative government was a more important outcome of the wars. T. Walter Wallbank taught at the University of Southern California in Los Angeles, and Alastair M. Taylor taught geography and political studies at the University of Edinburgh, Scotland, and Queen's University, Kingston, Ontario. They are co-authors of The World in Turmoil, Promise and Perils, *and* Western Perspectives: A Concise History of Civilization.

The English civil wars (1642–1660) were in many respects quite different from the other religious wars. Like most of the wars on the continent, the English conflict was a complex blend of politics and religion. But unlike the Thirty Years' War, which saw the Germanies as a battleground for conflicting ambitions of various nations, the English political struggle was a domestic duel. And unlike the other wars, the English conflict carried with it a traditional English movement, the growth of representative government. Indeed, although the reli-

Excerpted from *Civilization Past and Present*, by T. Walter Wallbank and Alastair M. Taylor (Chicago: Scott, Foresman and Company, 1949).

gious implications of the English civil wars were important, they were overshadowed by the constitutional results.

King Henry VII, gaining the throne after the Wars of the Roses, had established what might be called a popular despotism and restored law and order. In order to secure speedy results, Henry VII had made his Parliaments subservient to his wishes and created a machinery of despotism which hunted down and imprisoned any malefactor who opposed the king's will. In breaking with the Church of Rome, Henry VIII had acted in the main with the approval of the English people. For hundreds of years there had been strong feeling manifested in England against what was felt to be unwarranted interference in domestic affairs by the Pope. The fact that the religious revolt in England had popular support, although its prime mover was a despotic king, reflected the essential nature of Tudor rule. The strong Tudor government, whether in the hands of Henry VII or his granddaughter Elizabeth, was accepted by the English people.

From 1485 to 1603, therefore, the forward march of English constitutional progress was halted. After the defeat of the Armada in 1588, however, a new spirit began to manifest itself in England. After more than a century of benevolent despotism, the English people were ready to resume the development of representative government.

James I, Parliament, and the Religious Issue

Elizabeth's successor in 1603 was James Stuart, king of Scotland, who was imported from Edinburgh to reside in London. Scotland and England, though not united, now had a common king. It was of supreme importance that James I appreciate the temper of his new subjects, but this the new monarch did not do. From the outset of his reign he made it plain that he meant to be an absolute monarch. Dubbed "the wisest fool in Christendom" because of his immense book-learning and his lack of political tact, James believed in the divine right of kings.

As the constitutional issue of king against Parliament crystallized, it became complicated by religious issues. The religious changes brought about by Henry VIII were not basically a doctrinal revolt. Henry became head of the English Church, and independence from Rome was declared, but much of the old theology and ceremony was retained. During the reigns of Edward

VI and Queen Elizabeth there was a decided trend toward Protestant changes in doctrine and ceremony. When James came to the throne, some Englishmen were content with the English church as it then stood; some, while not actually wishing to return to papal control, did wish to reintroduce much of the old ritual and some of the tenets of the Catholic Church; and some took an extreme Protestant position.

The extreme Protestants were called Puritans, because they wished to purify the Anglican Church still further, simplify the ritual, and lessen the authority of the bishops chosen by the king. The ranks of the Puritans were made up largely of men engaged in trade and commerce—the middle class living in the cities. These businessmen resented very much the growing tendency of James to resort to illegal and arbitrary taxation. The middle class was interested in influencing government in order to avoid useless and expensive wars and to secure laws to protect and expand the commercial interests of the nation. Also in the Puritan ranks were the lawyers, who supplied the middle class

The Crowning of Charles II

Samuel Pepys, who described important London events in a diary he kept for many years, attended the coronation of Charles II in Westminster Abbey, where English monarchs are always crowned. He recorded the following description of the event:

At last comes in the Dean and Prebends of Westminster, with the Bishops (many of them in cloth of gold copes), and after them the Nobility, all in their Parliament robes, which was a most magnificent sight. Then the Duke, and the King with a scepter (carried by my Lord Sandwich) and sword and mond before him, and the crown too. The King in his robes, bareheaded, which was very fine. And after all had placed themselves, there was a sermon and the service; and then in the Quire at the high altar, the King passed through all the ceremonies of the Coronation, which to my great grief I and most in the Abbey could not see. The crown being put

with historical precedents as ammunition against the growing absolutism of the Stuarts.

James I Quarrels with Parliament and the Puritans

James's arbitrary taxation, his evident sympathy with the pro-Catholic, or High Church, movement, and his insistence upon the royal prerogatives were the first steps leading to civil war. James quarreled with Parliament over taxation and bluntly told its members to mind their own business and not discuss church matters. This led the House of Commons to draw up and pass what it called an *Apology,* in reality a statement of its parliamentary rights. The Commons especially claimed the right "that in Parliament they may speak freely their consciences without check and controlment." In retaliation, James ruled the country practically without Parliament from 1611 to 1621.

In the latter part of King James's reign England was confronted by the Thirty Years' War. The Puritans sided with the

upon his head, a great shout begun, and he came forth to the throne, and there passed more ceremonies: as taking the oath, and having things read to him by the Bishop; and his lords (who put on their caps as soon as the King put on his crown) and bishops come, and kneeled before him. And three times the King at Arms went to the three open places on the scaffold, and proclaimed, that if anyone could show any reason why Charles Stuart should not be King of England, that now he should come and speak. And a General Pardon also was read by the Lord Chancellor, and medals flung up and down by my Lord Cornwallis, of silver, but I could not come by any. And the King came in with his crown on, and his scepter in his hand, under a canopy borne up by six silver staves, carried by Barons of the Cinque Ports [five English ports], and little bells at every end. at every end. After a long time, he got up to the farther end.

Bernard D. Grebanier et al., *English Literature and Its Backgrounds.* Vol. 1. Rev. ed. New York: Dryden, 1949.

German Protestants and were quite willing to enter the struggle. James, however, was not only pacifistic but pro-Spanish as well. Because of James's ambition to marry his son Charles to one of the daughters of the king of Spain, the Spanish ambassador at London was able to twist him in any direction he wished. James's foreign policy infuriated the Puritans, to whom Catholic Spain was anathema.

The Mistakes of Charles I Lead to War

At the death of James I in 1625 his son Charles I inherited the English throne. The mistakes of the father were repeated by the son, to an even greater degree. Charles was well-meaning and his private life was irreproachable, but he too insisted on absolute royal power. The new reign began with stormy debate between king and Parliament. Three years later, in order to obtain revenue from Parliament, the king agreed to the famous Petition of Rights—a parliamentary declaration that ranks with *Magna Charta* as one of the great documents in the development of representative government. The most important provisions of the petition denied the right of the king to tax without parliamentary consent or to imprison a freeman without cause.

Little immediate good came of this petition, however, for Charles soon broke its provisions and ruled England from 1629 to 1640 without calling Parliament. During this period the king resorted to methods of taxation which the supporters of Parliament considered illegal. He supported the High Church party and punished those, mainly Puritans, who refused to fall in line with his religious beliefs. Several outstanding Puritan leaders of the House of Commons were imprisoned for their political and religious views. The king's taxes fell heavily upon the shoulders of the wealthy—often Puritan merchants and shopkeepers.

Charles's personal rule was terminated in 1640. When he attempted to force his brand of High Church Anglican religion on the Presbyterian Scots, they promptly took up arms against the king. Faced by a hostile army and without sufficient funds to put forces of his own into the field, Charles was forced to convene Parliament. When Parliament refused to vote any money until Charles had redressed certain grievances, Charles promptly dissolved it. But riots in England and a Scottish invasion compelled him to recall Parliament. This session became known as the "Long Parliament" because it lasted nearly twenty years. Sensing the weakness in the king's position, Parliament immediately set to work to make its powers at least co-equal with those of the king. Its reforms represented a great victory for Parliament.

Trouble also arose over the question of religion. Few wanted a High Church system, but there was no unanimity as to what form of Protestantism should take its place. Out of this stalemate there quickly developed two bitterly antagonistic parties. The parliamentary, or "Roundhead," faction, was composed largely of the middle class, and won the support of the Puritans. The Puritans were divided between Independents and Presbyterians, who differed over questions of church government but agreed in holding generally to a Calvinistic system of religion and demanding even further reduction in the politico-religious prerogatives of the king. The Royalist party was called the "Cavaliers." It was supported by a great many of the landowning nobles, who opposed extreme Protestantism and, although one with the Puritans in opposing royal despotism, were unwilling to see the monarchy stripped of all its powers.

The Civil Wars Result in Rule by Cromwell

Civil war broke out in 1642. In the end, control of the sea, possession of greater economic resources, superior generalship, and alliance with the Scots enabled the Roundheads to defeat the king's armies, the fighting coming to an end in 1646. For two years there was an interlude in which Charles tried to play his enemies—the Scots, the Presbyterians dominant in Parliament, and the Independents dominant in the army—against each other. He actually succeeded in splitting Parliament and making a secret alliance with the Scots. The upshot was the rise of fierce resentment against the king in the ranks of the Independent army, and in 1648 a second civil war broke out. The allies of the king were defeated, and in December 1648, all Presbyterian members of the House of Commons were excluded from that body by the victorious Independent army. Following a brief trial, King Charles was executed in January 1649.

The next month the House of Commons abolished the House of Lords and declared the office of king unnecessary. In May 1649, England was proclaimed a Commonwealth. The main figure in the new republican government was the Independent leader Oliver Cromwell, whose military genius had been largely responsible for defeating the king's cavalier armies. Cromwell, adopting the tactics of Gustavus Adolphus, had drilled the parliamentary forces into crack regiments of God-fearing soldiers who fought as well as they prayed.

In 1653 the Puritan army, still distrusting Parliament, overthrew the Commonwealth and set up a new form of government based on a written constitution called *The Instrument of Government.* This document, one of the earliest written constitutions of modern times, was to become influential in the later European constitutional movement. Cromwell was given supreme power as Lord Protector for life, assisted by a council and Parliament.

Now virtual dictator of England, Cromwell endeavored to achieve a religious settlement for the nation, favoring a rather tolerant religious system. But it was impossible to reconcile the Independents, the Presbyterians, the High Church party, and other religious factions, and the last three years of Cromwell's life were filled with disappointment and trouble. Although he did not favor it, his more extreme Puritan colleagues foisted on a pleasure-loving folk a series of hateful prohibitions which closed the theaters, muzzled the press, and stamped out many wholesome as well as unwholesome amusements of the people.

The Monarchy Restored with Charles II

Cromwell died in 1658 and was succeeded by Richard Cromwell, his son. A man of blameless character and high ideals but without any qualities of leadership, Richard found it difficult to carry on his father's work and resigned in less than a year (1659). The restoration of the monarchy seemed the only solution to most men. Arrangements were made for Charles, the son of the late king, to return to England to become Charles II. In 1660, amid wild excitement and enthusiasm, the exiled Stuart returned to London as the legal king. But civil war and revolution had not been for nought. When Charles II became king of England it was with the explicit understanding that he should not emulate his father and grandfather but should rule through Parliament. Thus the monarchy of England was made responsible to a representative body, in contrast to the continental pattern of absolutism.

The Great Fire of London

BY SAMUEL PEPYS

When the great fire burned four-fifths of London in 1666, the tragedy followed two decades of difficulties—the execution of a king, civil wars, a failed interim government, the restoration of the monarchy, and the plague of 1665. In his diary Samuel Pepys recorded his personal account of the fire. Each day he wrote about what he had seen after walking about central London, watching ordinary people trying to save their possessions and government leaders coping with the disaster. When the fire subsided after five days, it had destroyed eighty-seven churches and over thirteen thousand houses, but only twenty people had died. Samuel Pepys held numerous government positions during a long public career. He began The Diary *on January 1, 1660, and recorded his observations of London life until May 31, 1669. He also wrote* Memoirs of the Navy, 1690.

September 2 (Lord's Day), 1666

Some of our maids sitting up late last night to get things ready against our feast today, Jane called us up about three in the morning, to tell us of a great fire they saw in the City. So I rose and slipped on my nightgown,[1] and went to her window, and thought it to be on the back-side of Marke-lane at the farthest; but, being unused to such fires as followed, I thought it far enough off; and so went to bed again and to sleep. About seven rose again to dress myself, and there looked out at the window, and saw the fire not so much as it was and further off. By and by Jane comes and tells me that she hears that above 300 houses have been burned down tonight by the fire we saw, and that it is now burning down all Fish-street, by London Bridge.

1. dressing gown

Excerpted from "The Great Fire of London," by Samuel Pepys, *English Literature and Its Backgrounds*, edited by Bernard D. Grebanier, Samuel Middlebrook, Stith Thompson, and William Watt (New York: Dryden Press, Inc., 1949).

So I made myself ready presently, and walked to the Tower,[2] and there got up upon one of the high places, Sir J. Robinson's little son going up with me; and there I did see the houses at that end of the bridge all on fire, and an infinite great fire on this and the other side the end of the bridge; which, among other people, did trouble me for poor little Michell and our Sarah on the bridge. So down, with my heart full of trouble, to the Lieutenant of the Tower, who tells me that it begun [*sic*] this morning in the King's baker's house in Pudding-lane, and that it hath burned St. Magnus's Church and most part of Fish-street already. So I down to the water-side, and there got a boat and through bridge, and there saw a lamentable fire. Poor Michell's house, as far as the Old Swan, already burned that way, and the fire running further, that in a very little time it got as far as the Steele-yard, while I was there. Everybody endeavoring to remove their goods, and flinging into the river or bringing them into lighters[3] that lay off; poor people staying in their houses as long as till the very fire touched them, and then running into boats, or clambering from one pair of stairs by the water-side to another. And among other things, the poor pigeons, I perceive, were loth to leave their houses, but hovered about the windows and balconys till they were, some of them burned, their wings, and fell down. Having stayed, and in an hour's time seen the fire rage every way, and nobody, to my sight, endeavoring to quench it, but to remove their goods, and leave all to the fire, and having seen it get as far as the Steele-yard, and the wind mighty high and driving it into the City; and every thing, after so long a drought, proving combustible, even the very stones of churches, and among other things the poor steeple by which pretty Mrs.— lives, and whereof my old schoolfellow Elborough is parson, taken fire in the very top, and there burned till it fell down: I to White Hall[4] (with a gentleman with me who desired to go off from the Tower, to see the fire, in my boat); to White Hall, and there up to the King's closet in the Chapel, where people come about me, and I did give them an account dismayed them all, and word was carried in to the King. So I was called for, and did tell the King and Duke of York what I saw, and that unless his Majesty did command houses to be pulled down nothing could stop the fire. They seemed much troubled, and the King commanded me to go to my Lord Mayor from

2. London Tower 3. flat-bottomed barges 4. a palace in central London

him, and command him to spare no houses, but to pull down before the fire every way. At last met my Lord Mayor in Canning-street, like a man spent, with a handkerchief about his neck. To the King's message he cried, like a fainting woman, "Lord, what can I do? I am spent: people will not obey me. I have been pulling down houses; but the fire overtakes us faster than we can do it." People all almost distracted, and no manner of means used to quench the fire. The houses, too, so very thick thereabouts, and full of matter of burning, as pitch and tar, in Thames-street; and warehouses of oil, and wines, and brandy, and other things. And to see the churches all filling with goods by people who themselves should have been quietly there at this time. Met with the King and Duke of York in their barge, and with them to Queenhithe, and there called Sir Richard Browne to them. Their order was only to pull down houses apace, and so below bridge at the water-side; but little was or could be done, the fire coming upon them so fast. River full of lighters and boats taking in goods, and good goods swimming in the water, and only I observed that hardly one lighter or boat in three that had the goods of a house in, but there was a pair of Virginals[5] in it. So near the fire as we could for smoke; and all over the Thames, with one's face in the wind, you were almost burned with a shower of fire-drops. This is very true; so as houses were burned by these drops and flakes of fire, three or four, nay, five or six houses, one from another. When we could endure no more upon the water, we to a little ale-house on the Bankside, over against the Three Cranes, and there stayed till it was dark almost, and saw the fire grow; and, as it grew darker, appeared more and more, and in corners and upon steeples, and between churches and houses, as far as we could see up the hill of the City, in a most horrid malicious bloody flame, not like the fine flame of an ordinary fire. Barbary and her husband away before us. We stayed till, it being darkish, we saw the fire as only one entire arch of fire from this to the other side the bridge, and in a bow up the hill for an arch of above a mile long: it made me weep to see it. The churches, houses, and all on fire and flaming at once; and a horrid noise the flames made, and the cracking of houses at their ruin. So home with a sad heart, and there find every body discoursing and

5. a small, rectangular spinet without legs, usually spoken of in the plural as a pair of virginals

lamenting the fire; and Poor Tom Hater come with some few of his goods saved out of his house, which is burned upon Fish-street Hill. I invited him to lie at my house, and did receive his goods, but was deceived in his lying there, the news coming every moment of the growth of the fire; so as we were forced to begin to pack up our own goods, and prepare for their removal; and did by moonshine (it being brave dry, and moonshine, and warm weather) carry much of my goods into the garden, and Mr. Hater and I did remove my money and iron chests into my cellar, as thinking that the safest place. And got my bags of gold into my office, ready to carry away, and my chief papers of accounts also there, and my tallies into a box by themselves.

September 3, 1666

About four o'clock in the morning, my Lady Batten sent me a cart to carry away all my money, and plate, and best things, to Sir W. Rider's at Bednall-Greene. Which I did, riding myself in my nightgown in the cart; and, Lord! to see how the streets and the highways are crowded with people running and riding, and getting of carts at any rate to fetch away things. The Duke of York come this day by the office, and spoke to us, and did ride with his guard up and down the City to keep all quiet (he being now General, and having the care of all). At night lay down a little upon a quilt of W. Hewer's in the office, all my own things being packed up or gone; and after me my poor wife did the like, we having fed upon the remains of yesterday's dinner, having no fire nor dishes, nor any opportunity of dressing anything.

September 4, 1666

Up by break of day to get away the remainder of my things. Sir W. Batten not knowing how to remove his wine, did dig a pit in the garden, and laid it in there; and I took the opportunity of laying all the papers of my office that I could not otherwise dispose of. And in the evening Sir W. Pen and I did dig another, and put our wine in it; and I my Parmazan cheese, as well as my wine and some other things. Only now and then walking into the garden, and saw how horridly the sky looks, all on a fire in the night, was enough to put us out of our wits; and, indeed, it was extremely dreadful, for it looks just as if it was at us, and the whole heaven on fire. I after supper walked in the dark down to Tower-street, and there saw it all on fire, at the Trinity House on that side, and the Dolphin Tavern on this side, which was very near us; and the fire with extraordinary vehemence. Now begins the practice of blowing up of houses in Tower-street, those next the Tower, which at first did frighten people more than anything; but it stopped the fire where it was done, it bringing down the houses to the ground in the same places they stood, and then it was easy to quench what little fire was in it, though it kindled nothing almost. Paul's[6] is burned, and all Cheap-side. I wrote to my father this night, but the post-house being burned, the letter could not go.

September 5, 1666

About two in the morning my wife calls me up and tells me of new cries of fire, it being come to Barking Church, which is the bottom of our lane. I up, and finding it so, resolved presently to take her away, and did, and took my gold, which was about £2350, W. Hewer, and Jane, down by Proundy's boat to Woolwich; but, Lord! what a sad sight it was by moonlight to see the whole City almost on fire, that you might see it plain at Woolwich, as if you were by it. There, when I come, I find the gates shut, but no guard kept at all, which troubled me, because of discourse now begun, that there is plot in it, and that the French had done it. I got the gates open, and to Mr. Shelden's, where I locked up my gold, and charged my wife and W. Hewer never to leave the room without one of them in it, night or day. So back again, by the way seeing my goods well in the lighters at Deptford, and watched well by people. Home, and whereas I expected to have seen our house on fire, it being now about seven o'clock, it was not. I up to the top of Barking steeple, and there saw the saddest sight of desolation that I ever saw; everywhere great fires, oil-cellars, and brimstone,[7] and other things burning. I became afraid to stay there long, and therefore down again as fast as I could, the fire being spread as far as I could see it; and to Sir W. Pen's, and there eat a piece of cold meat, having eaten nothing since Sunday, but the remains of Sunday's dinner.

September 6, 1666

It was pretty to see how hard the women did work in the cannells, sweeping of water; but then they would scold for drink, and

6. St. Paul's Cathedral 7. sulfur

be as drunk as devils. I saw good butts of sugar broke open in the street, and people go and take handfuls out, and put into beer, and drink it. And now all being pretty well, I took boat, and over to Southwarke, and took boat on the other side the bridge, and so to Westminster, thinking to shift myself,[8] being all in dirt from top to bottom; but could not there find any place to buy a shirt or pair of gloves. A sad sight to see how the River looks; no houses nor church near it, to the Temple, where it stopped.

September 7, 1666

Up by five o'clock; and blessed be God! find all well; and by water to Paul's Wharf. Walked thence, and saw all the town burned, and a miserable sight of Paul's church, with all the roofs fallen, and the body of the quire fallen into St. Fayth's; Paul's school also, Ludgate, and Fleet-street, my father's house, and the church, and a good part of the Temple the like. This day our Merchants first met at Gresham College, which, by proclamation, is to be their Exchange. Strange to hear what is bid for houses all up and down here; a friend of Sir W. Rider's having £150 for what he used to let for £40 per annum. Much dispute where the Customhouse shall be; thereby the growth of the City again to be foreseen. I home late to Sir W. Pen's, who did give me a bed; but without curtains or hangings, all being down. So here I went the first time into a naked bed, only my drawers on; and did sleep pretty well: but still both sleeping and waking had a fear of fire in my heart, that I took little rest. People do all the world over cry out of the simplicity of my Lord Mayor in general, and more particularly in this business of the fire, laying it all upon him.

8. to change clothes

England's Glorious Revolution

By Will Durant and Ariel Durant

Will Durant and Ariel Durant explain that James II's goals of absolute power and a Catholic England so concerned the Protestant leaders that they formulated a strategy to help Dutch prince William III oust James II. The plan was both complex and risky, as it depended upon the inaction of both James's army and other European nations while William invaded. After William completed a successful invasion and James had fled to France, English leaders assembled a convention during which they offered the crown to William and his wife Mary, daughter of James II; the offer, which they accepted, came with conditions for their rule and restrictions on their power. Will Durant was a journalist and also a professor of Latin, French, and philosophy. He and his wife, Ariel Durant, wrote a popular multivolume work, The Story of Civilization, *which covers 110 centuries of world history.*

James, brooding in defeat [after losing a trial against several Protestant bishops], consoled himself with the infant to which the Queen had given birth on June 10, a month before her expected time. He would bring up this precious boy as a loyal and devoted Catholic. Day by day father and son, over every opposition and discouragement, would move a step nearer to the sacred goal—the old [absolute] monarchy living in concord with the old [Catholic] Church, in an England pacified and reconciled, in a Europe repenting its apostasy [abandonment of religion], and united again in the one true, holy, universal faith.

Perhaps it was the premature birth that brought disaster to the precipitate King. Protestant England agreed with James that this boy might continue the effort to restore Catholicism: it feared him for the same reason that the King loved him. It denied, at first, that this was the King's son; it accused the Jesuits of having brought in some purchased infant to the Queen's bed as part of a plot to keep the King's Protestant daughter Mary from inheriting the throne. It turned more and more to Mary as the hope of English Protestantism, and reconciled itself to another revolution to make her queen.

But Mary was now the wife of William III of Orange, Stadholder [chief magistrate] of the United Provinces; what would proud William say to being merely the consort of a queen? Why not offer him co-ordinate rule with Mary? After all, he too had royal English blood; his mother had been another Mary, daughter of Charles I. In any case William had no intention of playing consort to his wife. It was probably at his suggestion that Bishop [Gilbert] Burnet, who had exiled himself to the Continent on the accession of James, persuaded Mary to pledge her full obedience to William "in all things," whatever authority might devolve upon her. . . .

A Complex Strategy to Install William and Preserve English Protestantism

William, fighting Louis XIV for the preservation of Dutch independence and Protestantism, had hoped for a time to win his father-in-law to an alliance against a French King who was destroying the balance and liberties of Europe. When this hope faded, he had negotiated with those Englishmen who led the opposition to James. He had connived at the organization, on Dutch soil, of [James Scott, duke of] Monmouth's [unsuccessful 1685] expedition against the King, and had allowed it to depart unhindered from a Dutch port. He had reason to fear that James planned to disqualify him as a successor to the throne; and when a son was born to the King, the rights of Mary were obviously superseded. Early in 1687 William sent Everhard van Dykvelt to England to establish friendly contacts with Protestant leaders. The envoy returned with favorable letters from the Marquis of Halifax, the Earls of Shrewsbury, Bedford, Clarendon (son of the former Chancellor), Danby, Bishop Compton, and others. The letters were too vague to constitute clear treason, but they implied warm support for William as a contender for the throne.

In June, 1687, Kaspar Fagel, Grand Pensionary, issued a letter authoritatively stating William's views on toleration: the Stadholder desired freedom of religious worship for all, but opposed the abrogation of the Test Act confirming public office to adherents of the Anglican faith. This cautious pronouncement won him the support of prominent Anglicans. When the birth of a son to James apparently ended William's chances of succeeding James, the Protestant leaders decided to invite him to come and conquer the throne. The invitation (June 30, 1688) was signed by the twelfth Earl of Shrewsbury, the first Duke of Devonshire, the Earls of Danby and Scarborough, Admiral Edward Russell (cousin of the William Russell executed in 1683), Henry Sidney (brother of Algernon), and Bishop Compton. Halifax did not sign, saying that he preferred constitutional opposition; but many others, including Sunderland and John Churchill (both then in the service of James), sent William assurance of their support. The signers recognized that their invitation was treason; they deliberately took their lives in their hands, and dedicated their fortunes to the enterprise. Shrewsbury, a former Catholic converted to Protestantism, mortgaged his estates for forty thousand pounds, and crossed to Holland to help direct the invasion.

William could not act at once, for he was not sure of his own people, and he feared that any moment Louis XIV would renew his attack upon Holland. The German states also feared attack by France; nevertheless they raised no objection to William's invasion, for they knew that his ultimate aim was to check the Bourbon King [Louis XIV]. The Hapsburg governments of Austria and Spain forgot their Catholicism in their hatred of Louis XIV, and approved the deposition of a Catholic ruler friendly to France. Even the Pope gave the expedition his *nihil obstat* [official approval], so that it was by permission of Catholic powers that Protestant William undertook to depose Catholic James. Louis and James themselves precipitated the invasion. Louis proclaimed that the bonds of "friendship and alliance" existing between England and France would compel him to declare war upon any invader of England. James, fearing that this statement would further unify his Protestant subjects against him, denied the existence of such an alliance, and rejected the offer of French help. Louis let his anger get the better of his strategy. He ordered his armies to attack not Holland but Germany (September 25, 1688); and the States-General of the United Provinces, freed for a time from fear of the French, agreed to let William proceed on an expedition which might win England to alliance against France.

On October 19 the armada set forth—fifty warships, five hundred transports, five hundred cavalry, eleven thousand infantry,

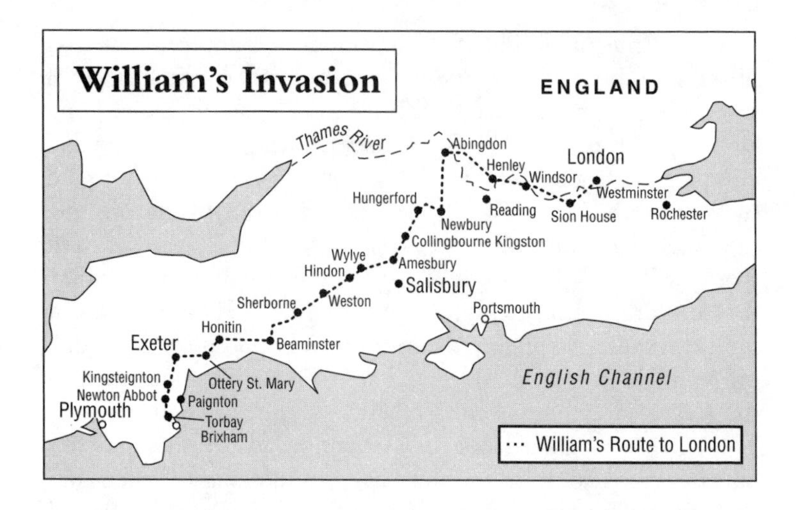

including many Huguenot [French Protestant] refugees from the French dragonnades. Driven back by winds, the fleet waited for a "Protestant breeze," and sailed again on November 1. An English squadron sent to intercept it was scattered by a storm. On November 5—the national holiday commemorating the Gunpowder Plot [an attempt by Catholics to blow up Westminster Palace when the king and Parliament were there]—the invaders landed at Torbay, an inlet of the Channel on the Dorsetshire coast. No resistance was encountered, but no welcome was received; the people had not forgotten Jeffreys and Kirke [officials who tortured and killed men involved in Monmouth's revolt]. James ordered his army, under command of Lord John Churchill, to assemble at Salisbury, and he himself joined it there. He found his troops so lukewarm in their allegiance that he could not trust them to give battle; he ordered a retreat. That night (November 23) Churchill and two other high officers of the King's army deserted to William with four hundred men. A few days later Prince George of Denmark, husband of James's daughter Anne, joined the spreading defection. Returning to London, the unhappy King found that Anne, with Churchill's wife, Sarah Jennings, had fled to Nottingham. The spirit of the once proud monarch broke under the discovery that both his daughters had turned against him. He commissioned Halifax to treat with William. On December 11 he himself left his capital. Halifax, back from the front, found the nation leaderless, but a group of peers made him president of a provisional government. On the thirteenth they received a message from James that he was in hostile hands at Faversham in Kent. They sent troops to rescue him, and on the sixteenth the humiliated King was back in Whitehall Palace. William, advancing toward London, sent some Dutch guardsmen with instructions to carry James to Rochester, and there let him escape. It was done; James fell into the trap laid for him, and quitted England for France (December 23). He would survive his fall by thirteen years, but he would never see England again.

The Convention Offers the Crown to William and Mary with Conditions

William reached London on December 19. He used his victory with characteristic firmness, prudence, and moderation. He put an end to the riots in which London Protestants had been pillaging and burning the houses of Catholics. At the request of the provisional government he summoned the lords, bishops, and former members of Parliament to meet at Coventry. The "Convention" that assembled there on February 1, 1689, declared that James had abdicated the throne by his flight. It offered to crown Mary as queen and accept William as her regent; they refused. It offered to crown William as king and Mary as queen; they accepted (February 13). But the Convention accompanied this offer with a "Declaration of Right," which was re-enacted by Parliament as the "Bill of Rights" on December 16, and (though not explicitly agreed to by William) became a vital part of the statutes of the realm:

> Whereas the late King James II . . . did endeavor to subvert and extirpate the Protestant religion, and the laws and liberties of this Kingdom:
>
> 1. By assuming and exercising a power of dispensing with, and suspending of, laws, and the execution of laws, without consent of Parliament; . . .
>
> 3. By . . . erecting a . . . "Court of Commission for Ecclesiastical Causes";
>
> 4. By levying money for and to the use of the Crown, by pretense of prerogative, for other time and in other manner than the same was granted by Parliament.

5. By raising and keeping a standing army . . . without consent of Parliament; . . .

7. By prosecutions in the Court of King's Bench for matters and causes cognizable only in Parliament . . .

All which are utterly and directly contrary to the known laws and statutes and freedom of this realm; . . .

Having therefore an entire confidence that . . . the Prince of Orange will . . . preserve them [the Parliament] from the violation of their rights which they have here asserted, and from all other attempts upon their religion, rights, and liberties, the . . . lords spiritual and temporal and commons, assembled at Westminster, do resolve that William and Mary, Prince and Princess of Orange, be and be declared King and Queen of England, France, and Ireland . . . and that the oaths hereafter mentioned be taken by all persons of whom the oaths of allegiance and supremacy might be required by law. . . .

"I, A.B., do swear that I do from my heart abhor, detest and abjure, as impious and heretical, this damnable doctrine . . . that princess excommunicated or deprived by the pope, or any authority of the see of Rome, may be deposed or murdered by their subjects, or any other whatsoever. And I do declare that no foreign prince, person, prelate, state, or potentate has, or ought to have any jurisdiction, power, superiority, . . . or authority . . . within this realm. So help me God."

. . . And whereas it hath been found by experience that it is inconsistent with the safety and welfare of this Protestant kingdom to be governed by a popish prince, or by any king or queen marrying a papist, the said lords spiritual and temporal, and commons, do further pray that it may be enacted that all and every person and persons that is, are, or shall be reconciled to, or shall hold communion with, the see or Church of Rome, or shall profess the popish religion, or shall marry a papist, shall be excluded and be forever incapable to inherit, possess, or enjoy the crown and government of this realm. . . .

The Revolution Preserves Institutions and Expands Commerce

This historic proclamation expressed the essential results of what Protestant England called the "Glorious Revolution": the explicit assertion of the legislative supremacy of Parliament, so long contested by four Stuart kings; the protection of the citizen against arbitrary governmental power; and the exclusion of Roman Catholics from holding or sharing the throne of England. Only next to these results in importance was the consolidation of governmental power in the landowning aristocracy; for the revolution had been initiated by great nobles and carried through with the landowning gentry as represented in the House of Commons; in effect, the "absolute" monarchy by "divine right" had been changed into a territorial oligarchy characterized by moderation, assiduity, and skill in government, co-operating with the princes of industry, commerce, and finance, and generally careless of the artisans and peasantry. The upper middle classes benefited substantially from the revolution. The cities of England recovered their freedom to be ruled by mercantile oligarchies. The merchants of London, who had shied away from helping James, lent £200,000 to finance William between his arrival in the capital and his first reception of parliamentary funds. That loan cemented an unwritten agreement: the merchants would let the landowners rule England, but the ruling aristocracy would direct foreign policy to commercial interests, and would leave merchants and manufacturers increasingly free from official regulation.

There were some inglorious elements in the Glorious Revolution. It seemed regrettable that England had had to call in a Dutch army to redress English wrongs, that a daughter should help oust her father from his throne, that the commander of his army should go over to the invader, and that the national Church should join in overthrowing a King whose divine and absolute authority it had sanctified against any act of rebellion or disobedience. It was regrettable that the supremacy of Parliament had to be vindicated by opposing freedom of worship. But the evil that these men and women did was interred with their bones; the good that they accomplished lived after them and grew. Even in establishing an oligarchy they laid the foundations of a democracy that would come with the broadening of the electorate.

They made the Englishman's home his castle, relatively secure against the "insolence of office" and "the oppressor's wrong." They contributed some part to that admirable reconciliation of order and liberty which is the English government today. And thy did all this without shedding a drop of blood—except the repeated nosebleeds of the harassed, helpless, deserted, witless King.

The Extent and Purpose of Government

By John Locke

John Locke, who lectured in philosophy at Oxford University in England, is the author of Essay Concerning Human Understanding. *In 1690, shortly after the Bill of Rights was drawn up during the Glorious Revolution, Locke published his* Essay Concerning the True Original Extent and End of Civil Government, *considered a milestone in the development of representative democracy. In the essay excerpted here, he argues that while people are free in a state of nature, they give up powers to form a society that will give them greater protection than they could acquire by themselves. According to Locke, a society rules by laws made by a legislative body, whose powers are derived from the people. He emphasizes that the people are the final judges of the trustworthiness of those who govern. Locke's essay supported the accomplishments of the Glorious Revolution and encouraged future leaders to take further steps toward representative government.*

To understand political power aright, and derive it from its original, we must consider what state all men are naturally in, and that is, a state of perfect freedom to order their actions, and dispose of their possessions and persons as they think fit, within the bounds of the law of Nature, without asking leave or depending upon the will of any other man.

A state also of equality, wherein all the power and jurisdiction is reciprocal, no one having more than another, there being nothing more evident than that creatures of the same species and rank, promiscuously born to all the same advantages of Nature, and the use of the same faculties, should also be equal one

Excerpted from *An Essay Concerning the True Original Extent and End of Civil Government*, by John Locke (London, 1690).

amongst another, without subordination or subjection, unless the lord and master of them all should, by any manifest declaration of his will, set one above another, and confer on him, by an evident and clear appointment, an undoubted right to dominion and sovereignty.

But though this be a state of liberty, yet it is not a state of licence; though man in that state have an uncontrollable liberty to dispose of his person or possessions, yet he has not liberty to destroy himself, or so much as any creature in his possession, but where some nobler use than its bare preservation calls for it. The state of Nature has a law of Nature to govern it, which obliges every one, and reason, which is that law, teaches all mankind who will but consult it, that being all equal and independent, no one ought to harm another in his life, health, liberty or possessions. . . .

Limitations on the Use of Nature's Goods

Now of those good things which Nature hath provided in common, every one hath a right (as hath been said) to as much as he could use, and had a property in all he could effect with his labour; all that his industry could extend to, to alter from the state Nature had put it in, was his. He that gathered a hundred bushels of acorns or apples had thereby a property in them; they were his goods as soon as gathered. He was only to look that he used them before they spoiled, else he took more than his share, and robbed others. And, indeed, it was a foolish thing, as well as dishonest, to hoard up more than he could make use of. If he gave away a part to anybody else, so that it perished not uselessly in his possession, these he also made use of. And if he also bartered away plums that would have rotted in a week, for nuts that would last good for his eating a whole year, he did no injury; he wasted not the common stock; destroyed no part of the portion of goods that belonged to others, so long as nothing perished uselessly in his hands. Again, if he would give his nuts for a piece of metal, pleased with its colour, or exchange his sheep for shells, or wool for a sparkling pebble or a diamond, and keep those by him all his life, he invaded not the right of others; he might heap up as much of these durable things as he pleased; the exceeding of the bounds of his just property not lying in the largeness of his posession, but the perishing of anything uselessly in it.

And thus came in the use of money; some lasting thing that men might keep without spoiling, and that, by mutual consent, men would take in exchange for the truly useful but perishable supports of life. . . .

Uniting into a Community for Security

Men being, as has been said, by nature all free, equal, and independent, no one can be put out of this estate and subjected to the political power of another without his own consent, which is done by agreeing with other men, to join and unite into a community for their comfortable, safe, and peaceable living, one amongst another, in a secure enjoyment of their properties, and a greater security against any that are not of it. . . .

For, when any number of men have, by the consent of every individual, made a community, they have thereby made that community one body, with a power to act as one body, which is only by the will and determination of the majority. For that which acts any community, being only the consent of the individuals of it, and it being one body, must move one way, it is necessary the body should move that way whither the greater force carries it, which is the consent of the majority, or else it is impossible it should act or continue one body, one community, which the consent of every individual that united into it agreed that it should; and so every one is bound by that consent to be concluded by the majority. . . .

Giving Up Powers to a Society

For in the state of Nature, a man has two powers. The first is to do whatsoever he thinks fit for the preservation of himself and others within the permission of the law of Nature. . . . The other power a man has in the state of Nature is the power to punish the crimes committed against that law. Both these he gives up when he joins in a private, if I may so call it, or particular political society, and incorporates into any commonwealth separate from the rest of mankind.

The first power—viz., of doing whatsoever he thought fit for the preservation of himself and the rest of mankind, he gives up to be regulated by laws made by the society, so far forth as the preservation of himself and the rest of that society shall require; which laws of the society in many things confine the liberty he had by the law of Nature.

Secondly, the power of punishing he wholly gives up, and engages his natural force, which he might before employ in the execution of the law of Nature, by his own single authority, as he thought fit, to assist the executive power of the society as the law thereof shall require. For being now in a new state, wherein he is to enjoy many conveniencies from the labour, assistance, and society of others in the same community, as well as protection from its whole strength, he is to part also with as much of his natural liberty, in providing for himself, as the good, prosperity, and safety of the society shall require, which is not only necessary but just, since the other members of the society do the like.

But though men when they enter into society give up the equality, liberty, and executive power they had in the state of Nature into the hands of the society, to be so far disposed of by the legislative as the good of the society shall require, yet it being only with an intention in every one the better to preserve himself, his liberty and property (for no rational creature can be supposed to change his condition with an intention to be worse), the power of the society or legislative constituted by them can never be supposed to extend farther than the common good, but is obliged to secure every one's property by providing against those three defects above mentioned that made the state of Nature so unsafe and uneasy. And so, whoever has the legislative or supreme power of any commonwealth, is bound to govern by established standing laws, promulgated and known to the people, and not by extemporary decrees, by indifferent and upright judges, who are to decide controversies by those laws; and to employ the force of the community at home only in the execution of such laws, or abroad to prevent or redress foreign injuries and secure the community from inroads and invasion. And all this to be directed to no other end but the peace, safety, and public good of the people. . . .

Legislative Power and Its Limits

Though in a constituted commonwealth standing upon its own basis and acting according to its own nature—that is, acting for the preservation of the community, there can be but one supreme power, which is the legislative, to which all the rest are and must be subordinate, yet the legislative being only a fiduciary power to act for certain ends, there remains still in the people a supreme power to remove or alter the legislative, when they find the legislative act contrary to the trust reposed in them. For all power given with trust for the attaining an end being limited by that end, whenever that end is manifestly neglected or opposed, the trust must necessarily be forfeited, and the power devolve into the hands of those that gave it, who may place it anew where they shall think best for their safety and security. . . .

The People Shall Be Judge

Here, it is like, the common question will be made: Who shall be judge whether the prince or legislative act contrary to their trust? This, perhaps, ill-affected and factious men may spread amongst the people, when the prince only makes use of his due prerogative. To this I reply, The people shall be judge; for who shall be judge whether his trustee or deputy acts well and according to the trust reposed in him, but he who deputes him and must, by having deputed him, have still a power to discard him when he fails in his trust? If this be reasonable in particular cases of private men, why should it be otherwise in that of the greatest moment, where the welfare of millions is concerned and also where the evil, if not prevented, is greater, and the redress very difficult, dear, and dangerous? . . .

The People Have a Right to Act as Supreme

To conclude. The power that every individual gave the society when he entered into it can never revert to the individuals again as long as the society lasts, but will always remain in the community; because without this there can be no community—no commonwealth, which is contrary to the original agreement; so also when the society hath placed the legislative in any assembly of men, to continue in them and their successors, with direction and authority for providing such successors, the legislative can never revert to the people whilst that government lasts; because, having provided a legislative with power to continue forever, they have given up their political power to the legislative, and cannot resume it. But if they have set limits to the duration of their legislative, and made this supreme power in any person or assembly only temporary; or else when, by the miscarriages of those in authority, it is forfeited; upon the forfeiture of their rulers, or at the determination of the time set, it reverts to the society, and the people have a right to act as supreme, and continue the legislative in themselves or place it in a new form, or new hands, as they think good.

THE HISTORY OF NATIONS

Chapter 4

Revolution, Reform, and Queen Victoria, 1760–1900

British Actions Stir American Colonial Resistance

BY WILL DURANT AND ARIEL DURANT

According to Will Durant and Ariel Durant, the British expected to use the American colonies for profit, but the Americans resisted British laws designed to regulate American merchants, farmers, and manufacturers and tax documents, tea, and many other products. American colonists united in boycotts and disobedience. When the conflicts intensified, opinion on both sides of the Atlantic was divided. Finally, King George III sent troops against the Americans, but his armies suffered defeats; when the French aided the Americans, the British lost the war. Will Durant was a journalist and a professor of Latin, French, and philosophy. He and his wife, Ariel Durant, wrote a popular multivolume work, The Story of Civilization, *which covers 110 centuries of world history.*

In 1750 the population of the English colonies in North America was approximately 1,750,000; the population of England and Wales was some 6,140,000. As the rate of growth in the colonies was much higher than in the mother country, it was only a matter of time when the offspring would rebel against the parent. . . .

The British Crown claimed authority to veto laws passed by the colonial assemblies. . . . In economic matters Parliament assumed the right to legislate for all the British Empire, and usually its acts favored the motherland at the expense of the colonies. Its aim was to make America a source of articles not readily produced in England, and a market for British manufactured goods. It discouraged the growth of colonial industries that would compete with England's. It forbade the colonists to manufacture cloth,

Excerpted from *Rousseau and Revolution*, by Will Durant and Ariel Durant (New York: Simon and Schuster, 1967).

hats, leather wares, or iron products; so the Earl of Chatham, otherwise so friendly to the colonies, declared that he would not allow a single nail to be made in America without the permission of Parliament. The colonies were forbidden to set up steel furnaces or rolling mills.

Restrictions on American Merchants

Many checks were put upon American merchants. They could ship goods only in British vessels; they could sell tobacco, cotton, silk, coffee, sugar, rice, and many other articles only to British dominions; they could import goods from the European Continent only after these had first been landed in England, had paid a port duty, and had been transferred to British vessels. To protect the export of English woolens to American colonies, colonial merchants were prohibited from selling colonial woolens outside the colony that had produced them. A heavy tax was laid by Parliament (1733) upon American imports of sugar or molasses from any but British sources. The colonists, especially in Massachusetts, evaded some of these regulations by smuggling, and by secret selling of American products to foreign nations, even to the French during the Seven Years' War. Of 1,500,000 pounds of tea imported yearly into the American colonies, only some ten per cent conformed to the requirement of passing through English ports. Much of the whiskey produced by the sixty-three distilleries of Massachusetts in 1750 used sugar and molasses smuggled in from the French West Indies.

In justification of the restrictions, the British pointed out that other European nations, to protect or reward their own people, laid similar restraints upon their colonies; that many American products enjoyed a virtual monopoly of the English market through their exemption from import dues; and that England deserved some economic return for the cost of the protection which her navy gave to colonial shipping, and which her armies gave to the colonists against the French and the Indians in America. The expulsion of French power from Canada, and of Spanish power from Florida, had freed the English from dangers that had long troubled them. England felt warranted in asking America to help her pay off the enormous debt—£140,000,000—which Great Britain had incurred in the Seven Years' War. The colonists replied that they had furnished twenty thousand troops for that war, and had themselves incurred a debt of £2,500,000.

American Resistance to the Stamp Act

In any case England decided to tax the colonies. In March 1765, [the king's minister George] Grenville proposed to Parliament that all colonial legal documents, all bills, diplomas, playing cards, bonds, deeds, mortgages, insurance policies, and newspapers be required to bear a stamp for which a fee would have to be paid to the British government. Patrick Henry in Virginia, Samuel Adams in Massachusetts, advised rejection of the tax on the ground that by tradition—Magna Carta, the Great Rebellion against Charles I, the "Bill of Rights"—Englishmen could justly be taxed only with their consent or the consent of their authorized representatives. How, then, could English colonials be taxed by a Parliament in which they had no representation? Britons answered that difficulties of travel and communication made American representation in Parliament impracticable; and they pointed out that millions of adult Englishmen had for centuries loyally accepted taxation by Parliament though they had had no vote in electing it; they felt what Americans should feel—that they were virtually represented in Parliament, because its members considered themselves as representing the whole British Empire.

The colonists were not convinced. Since Parliament had retained the power of taxing as the fulcrum of control over the king, so the colonies defended their exclusive right to tax themselves as the only alternative to financial oppression by men whom they had never seen, and who had never touched American soil. Lawyers evaded the requirement to use stamped documents; some newspapers carried a death's head where the stamp should have appeared; Americans began to boycott British goods; merchants canceled orders for British products, and some refused payment of their debts to England till the Stamp Act should be repealed. Colonial maidens pledged themselves to accept no suitors who would not denounce the Stamp Act. Popular resentment rose to the pitch of rioting in several cities; in New York the governor (appointed by the King [George III]) was hanged in effigy; in Boston the home of the lieutenant governor, Thomas Hutchinson, was burned down; the distributors of the stamps were forced, under threat of hanging, to resign their offices. Feeling the boycott, British merchants called for a repeal of the act; petitions were sent to the government from London, Bristol, Liverpool, and other cities, stating that without repeal many English manufacturers would be ruined; already thousands of workers had been dismissed because of lack of orders from America. Perhaps it was in recognition of these appeals that [William] Pitt, after a long illness, made a dramatic return to Parliament, and declared (January 14, 1766), "It is my opinion that this kingdom has no right to lay a tax upon the colonies." He ridiculed the "idea that the colonies are *virtually* represented in the House." When George Grenville interrupted and implied that Pitt was encouraging sedition, Pitt answered defiantly, "I rejoice that America has resisted."

New Disguised Taxes and Duties

On March 18 Lord [minister Charles] Rockingham persuaded Parliament to repeal the stamp tax. To appease "the King's Friends" he added to the repeal a "declaratory act" reaffirming the authority of the king, with the consent of Parliament, to make laws binding on the colonies, and the authority of Parliament to tax the British colonies. The Americans accepted the repeal, and ignored the declaratory act. Reconciliation now seemed possible. But in July the Rockingham ministry fell, and in the [Augustus] Grafton ministry that followed it the Chancellor of the Exchequer, Charles Townshend, renewed the attempt to make the colonies pay for the administrative and military forces needed to protect them against internal disorder or external attack. On May 13, 1767, he proposed to Parliament that new duties be laid upon glass, lead, paper, and tea imported into America. The revenue from these imports was to be used by the King to pay the salaries of the governors and judges appointed by him for America; any surplus would be directed to maintain the British troops there. Parliament approved. Townshend died a few months later.

The Americans resisted the new duties as disguised taxation. They had kept the royal troops and governors under control by making them largely dependent for their sustenance upon funds voted by the colonial assemblies; to surrender this power of the purse to the King would be to yield the direction of the American government to royal authority. The assemblies united in urging a renewed boycott of British goods. Efforts to collect the new duties were violently resisted. Lord [Frederick] North sought a compromise by canceling all the Townshend imports except for a threepence-per-pound duty on tea. The colonies relaxed their boycott, but resolved to drink only such tea as had been smuggled in. When three ships of the East India Company tried to land 298 chests of tea at Boston, half a hundred irate colonials, disguised as Mohawk Indians, boarded the vessels, overpowered the crews, and emptied the cargoes into the sea (December 16, 1773). Riots in other American ports frustrated further efforts to bring in the company's tea.

Divided Opinion Concerning War with the American Colonies

The rest of the story belongs mostly to America, but the part played in it by British statesmen, orators, writers, and public opinion forms a vital element in the history of England. Just as in America a numerous and active minority called for loyalty to the mother country and its government, so in England, while the public generally supported the martial measures of Lord North's ministry, a minority, represented in Parliament by [William Pitt, Earl of] Chatham, [Edmund] Burke, [Charles James] Fox, Horace Walpole, and [John] Wilkes, labored for peace on terms favorable to America. Some saw in this division of English opinion a revival of the opposition between Royalists and Parliamentarians in 1642. The Anglican Church fully supported the war against the colonies; so did the Methodists, following [John] Wesley's lead; but many other Dissenters regretted the conflict, for they remembered that a majority of the colonists had come from Dissenting groups. [Edward] Gibbon agreed with [Samuel] Johnson in condemning the colonies, but David Hume, nearing death, warned Britain that the attempt to coerce America would lead to disaster. The business interests veered to support of the King as war orders brought them profits. War, Burke mourned, "is indeed become a substitute for commerce.... Great orders for provisions and stores of all kinds ... keep up the spirits of the mercantile world, and induce them to consider the American war not so much their calamity as their resource."

The liberals feared that the war would strengthen the Tories against the Whigs, and the King against Parliament; one liberal, the Duke of Richmond, thought of moving to France to escape royal despotism. George III gave some excuse for such fears. He took full charge of the war, even of its military details; Lord [Frederick] North and the other ministers, often against their private judgment, obeyed the royal lead. The King felt that if the Americans succeeded England would face revolt in other colonies, and would finally be confined to its island. The Earl of

Chatham, however, warned Parliament that the forcible suppression of America would be a victory for the principles of Charles I and James II. On November 20, 1777, when British armies had suffered many defeats in America, and France was sending subsidies to the colonies, Chatham, coming to the House of Lords as if from the grave, heard with mounting impatience the ministerial "address from the throne," and rose to make one of the greatest speeches in the records of British eloquence [quoted in Houston Peterson, *Treasury of the World's Greatest Speeches*]. . . .

> *My lords, you cannot conquer America.* . . . You may swell every expense and every effort still more extravagantly; pile and accumulate every assistance you can buy or borrow; traffic and barter with every little pitiful German prince that sells and sends his subjects to the shambles . . . ; your efforts are forever vain and impotent—doubly so from this mercenary aid on which you rely, for it irritates, to an incurable resentment, the minds of your enemies. . . . If I were an American, as I am an Englishman, while a foreign troop was landed in my country, I never would lay down my arms—never—never—never!

Burke used all his powers of reasoning in the effort to dissuade Parliament and the ministry from a policy of force against America. From 1774 to 1780 he represented in Parliament the city of Bristol, whose merchants at first opposed war with America; he was also at this time a salaried agent of the state of New York. He did not, like Chatham, deny the right of Parliament to tax the colonies, and he did not support the appeal of the colonists to abstract theories of "natural right." He brought the question down to where hardheaded men of action could understand him: Was it practical to tax America? In his speech on American taxation (April 19, 1774) he condemned not only the Townshend Acts but the threepence tax on tea; he warned that if taxes were added to the industrial and commercial restrictions already laid upon America the colonists would persist in a revolt that would break up the nascent British Empire and tarnish the prestige of the Parliament.

Beaten on this issue, he renewed, on March 22, 1775, his plea for conciliation. He pointed out that trade with America had grown tenfold between 1704 and 1772, and he asked was it wise to disrupt, perhaps sacrifice, that commerce with war. He feared that war with the colonies would leave England open to attack by a foreign enemy; this happened in 1778. . . .

American Victories and French Help

Not the fervor of Chatham, Burke, and Fox, but the victories and diplomacies of the colonies persuaded the English people, and then their government, to thoughts of peace. [John] Burgoyne's surrender at Saratoga (October 17, 1777) was the turning point; for the first time England appreciated Chatham's warning, "You cannot conquer America." When France recognized the "United States of America," and joined in war against England (February 6, 1778), the judgment of French statesmen confirmed Chatham's, and the weight of French arms and of a restored French navy was added to the burden borne by the British nation. Lord North himself lost heart, and begged permission to resign; the King, loading him with gifts, bade him stay on.

Many prominent Englishmen now felt that only a government led by the Earl of Chatham could win the colonies back from the French alliance to union with England. But George would not hear of it. "I solemnly declare," he told North, "that nothing shall bring me to treat personally with Lord Chatham.". . .

On October 19, 1781, Lord [Charles] Cornwallis surrendered to Washington at Yorktown. "Oh, God, it is all over!" exclaimed Lord North, but the King insisted that the war must go on. In February and March, 1782, news came that Minorca had been taken by the Spaniards, and several West Indian islands by the French. Public meetings throughout England clamored for peace. North's majority in the Commons fell to twenty-two, to nineteen, to one—on a motion "that the House could no longer repose confidence in the present ministers" (March 15, 1782); this set an historic precedent for Parliament's procedure in forcing a change of ministry. On March 18 North wrote to George III a letter telling him, in effect, that both the royal policy toward America and the attempt to establish the supremacy of the king over Parliament had failed.

> Your Majesty is well apprized that in this country the Prince on the throne cannot, with prudence, oppose the deliberate resolution of the House of Commons. . . . The Parliament have uttered their sentiments, and

> their sentiments, whether just or erroneous, must ultimately prevail. Your Majesty . . . can lose no honor if you yield.

A Treaty of Peace

On March 20, 1782, after twelve years of patient service and submission, Lord North resigned. George III, his spirit broken, wrote a letter of abdication, but did not send it. He accepted a ministry of triumphant liberals: Rockingham, the Earl of Shelburne, Charles James Fox, Burke, and [Richard] Sheridan. When Rockingham died (July 1), [Willliam] Shelburne succeeded him as first lord of the treasury. Fox, Burke, and Sheridan, disliking Shelburne, resigned. Shelburne proceeded to arrange a treaty of peace (Paris, November 30, 1782; Paris and Versailles, January 20 and September 3, 1783) that surrendered Minorca and Florida to Spain, and Senegal to France, and acknowledged not only the independence of the American colonies but also their right to all the territory between the Alleghenies, Florida, the Mississippi, and the Great Lakes.

The English people had been eager for peace, but they resented the cession of so much terrain to the colonies.

The Agricultural and Industrial Revolutions

BY GEORGE MACAULAY TREVELYAN

According to George Macaulay Trevelyan, major changes in rural and urban England occurred simultaneously, both to the detriment of the lower classes. In the countryside, open fields, formerly worked by small farmers, were enclosed for greater efficiency, a change that benefited the large farmers. In the cities, families that had earned a livelihood in weaving and crafts industries saw their work taken over by rows of machines in large factories. Both the rural and urban poor lived in squalid conditions and poverty. Historian George Macaulay Trevelyan taught at Trinity College, Cambridge. He is the author of England Under the Stuarts, The Age of Shakespeare and the Stuart Period, *and* The English Revolution, 1688–1689.

When George III ascended the throne [in 1760] on the eve of the Industrial Revolution, the English labourer was in most cases a countryman. He enjoyed not a few of the amenities of the pleasant old-world life, and often some personal independence, and some opportunity of bettering his position. For a variety of reasons, real wages had been fairly good in the first part of the eighteenth century. The labourers and the small farmers had reason for the traditional pride that they felt as 'free-born Englishmen,' and they appear to have looked up to the gentry, more often than not, without envy or resentment. . . .

Reshaping the Farms into Enclosures

The revolution in agriculture between 1760 and 1840 transformed much land from wastes and open fields to the chess-

Excerpted from *British History in the Nineteenth Century: 1782–1901*, by George Macaulay Trevelyan (London: Longmans, Green and Company, 1924).

board of hedge and ditch that we know so well to-day. These were effected under the leadership of 'improving landlords.'...

The mouthpiece and inspirer of these men in the hey-day of their agricultural zeal was Arthur Young, at once the practical and literary leader of English country life during the period of its revolution. His patriotic idealism drew him into a crusade against the waste lands; he saw that, if properly enclosed and cultivated, they would yield far more than the gains made by the poor of the neighbourhood whose cattle wandered by right over these commons. He was no less zealous against the great open field of the midland village with its hundreds of tiny strips; he desired to see it hedged round into a score of fair-sized fields under farmers with enterprise and capital. Communal tillage was an anachronism, monstrously perpetuating into the age of enlightenment the methods by which Piers the Ploughman had toiled on the manors of John of Gaunt [duke of Lancaster in the fourteenth century].

Young saw his dreams realised. In whole districts the very landscape was changed according to his desire. The break-up of the old cautious peasant life helped the population to increase at a pace unknown during the long centuries of 'subsistence agriculture.' The enclosures helped England, by producing more corn and wealth, to survive the economic struggle with Napoleon. But unfortunately they had also another effect, which their chief author in the latter part of his life had the humanity to recognise and the manhood to proclaim. In 1801, Arthur Young wrote to tell his fellow-countrymen that: 'By nineteen out of twenty Enclosure Bills the poor are injured and most grossly.'...

The Enclosure System Makes Small Farmers Poor

The enclosures had increased the food supply and the national wealth; but the increased wealth had gone chiefly in rent to the landlord, in tithe to the parson, and to the pocket of the more fortunate of the big farmers. The lower middle class had become poor, and the poor had become paupers. Agricultural progress had been so handled as to bring disaster to the working agriculturist. This would have been avoided by leaving a larger number of small holders, and by enforcing the payment of a living wage by the farmer instead of throwing the farm hands as paupers upon the rates.

The pauperisation of rural England, the long-drawn-out disaster with which the nineteenth century opened, can only in part be ascribed to the mistakes accompanying the necessary enclosure of the land. It was equally due to the decadence of the cottage industries. As textile and other trades were year by year gathered round the new machinery and the new factories, the corresponding industries disappeared out of cottage after cottage and village after village, at the very time when efforts were being made in so many districts to convert common waste land and small holdings into large farms. The small yeoman or labourer, losing sometimes his own sources of income, sometimes those of his wife and children, and sometimes losing both together, was left in helpless dependence on the big farmer, who, just because the rural proletariat had nothing now to live on but the farm wage, was able to cut that wage down to the starvation rate. . . .

The danger of wholesale death by famine, with which rural England was faced in 1795, was averted by a remedy that perpetrated and increased the evils of the time,—the famous poor-rate in aid of wages. In May of that year the magistrates of Berkshire were summoned to meet at Speenhamland for the expressed object of fixing and enforcing a living wage for the county, in relation to the price of bread. It would no doubt have been hard to carry out during the period of violent price fluctuations between 1795 and 1815, but in principle this was the true remedy. If it had been adopted for Berkshire and for all England, it might have diverted our modern social history at its source into happier channels. It was the course pointed out by ancient custom and existing law. Unfortunately the magistrates, who had come to Speenhamland for this good purpose, were there persuaded not to enforce the raising of wages, but to supplement wages instead out of the parish rates. They drew up and published a scale, by which every poor and industrious person should receive from the parish enough to make up the deficiency of his wages to 3*s.* a week for himself, and for every other member of his family 1*s.* 6*d.* a week, when the loaf cost a shilling. As the loaf rose higher the dole was to rise with it. This convenient scale, vulgarly known as the 'Speenhamland Act,' was adopted by the magistrates in county after county, till, except in some of the northern shires, the labourers of all England were pauperised. 'Speenhamland' became a governing fact of English life until the Poor Law of 1834.

The result was that agricultural wages were kept unduly low. As the burden of maintaining the employee had been taken over by the parish and as labour was plentiful, the farmer had no motive to pay a higher wage. Too often wages fell and prices rose, until it was no longer possible to maintain even the wretched rate of subsistence which the Berkshire magistrates in 1795 had fixed on as the lowest permissible standard. Hollow-checked, ragged, housed in hovels, the peasantry of England degenerated year by year under the eyes of men who were doubling and trebling their rents, and who tried to silence [journalist William] Cobbett as an 'incendiary' because, when no one else dared, he pointed out the contrast. . . .

The labourers had nothing for which to save; they had no prospects; whatever they did, they were paupers for life. These conditions, and the corresponding conditions of factory life with its child labour, largely account for the sudden increase in a population which, so far as we know, had grown only very gradually since the Norman Conquest. The vast multiplication in the numbers of Englishmen was one of the causes of their misery. . . .

An Urban Revolution Occurs Alongside the Rural Revolution

Meanwhile, step by step with the rural revolution, advanced the urban revolution, similar in principle and in spirit, and at the outset similar in its social consequences. Just as the old theory of subsistence agriculture, associated with ancient rights, small properties and communal tillage, was being replaced by a new habit of mind that looked for the greatest net productivity of the national soil, on a basis of unfettered individual farming on the large scale—so in the towns the old theory of a 'limited' and 'well-regulated' trade, based on the local monopoly of a chartered few, subjecting themselves to a common set of rules about trade and apprenticeship, was being gradually abandoned for the new principle of open world-competition wherein all traders who could muster the capital and enterprise were invited to buy in the cheapest market and sell in the dearest, and to hire their labour wherever they liked and on what conditions each could secure. The change, in town as well as country, caused a wide cleavage of sympathy and of interest between classes which had previously shared, each in its degree, the common advantages of a fixed system of life and work; now that everyone scrambled for himself, the rich became richer and the poor poorer, and the law instead of attempting to redress the balance interfered heavily on the side of the employer. Such at least was the first phase of the new civilisation in England. . . .

The Impact of Iron and Coal

The social and intellectual conditions of the England of that day would not have been enough to initiate the Industrial Revolution without the presence on the spot of coal and iron. Both had long been known and used, but they had not yet been used together. . . . So long as wood remained the only fuel, the output of iron or steel was necessarily small, and so long as it remained small there could be no age of machinery. But in the middle of the eighteenth century, just when the English woodland was giving out, and the iron industry was beginning to leave our shores for the Scandinavian and North American forests, methods were devised to apply coal to the smelting process. This discovery led, by a chain of closely interrelated developments, to the whole urban revolution.

Iron-smelting moved to the North and Midlands to be near the coal. As the demand for coal grew, steam-engines, invented by James Watt in the early years of George III, were used to

During the Industrial Revolution, England's waterways were used to transport goods between industrial districts.

pump water from the mines. More iron, the result of more coal, in turn made it possible to produce more steam-engines, and men looked round for other ways to employ them, whether in locomotion or manufacture. In Watt's own lifetime his steam-engines were applied to the cotton industry. Already the need for more coal had produced not only steam-engines but English canals, and many years later it produced the steam railways. [James] Brindley's first canal and [George] Stephenson's first locomotive were both made to carry coal from the pit's mouth.

It was characteristic of England, as opposed to the France of the *ancien régime*, that some of our nobility took an active part in these developments. The Duke of Bridgewater employed Brindley and invested his own capital in the first canals. There were great noblemen who were also great coal owners, working their own mines, and thereby becoming in due course still greater noblemen.

The Textile Revolution

On the other hand, the changes in cotton and wool that followed hard on the changes in iron and coal were not patronised by the aristocracy, or even to any great extent by the merchant capitalists. The textile revolution was the work of a wholly new order of men, risen from the ranks by their energy in seizing the opportunities of the new industrial situation. A workman who had toiled at the hand-loom in his own cottage might borrow £100 to start as a small employer with the new machines. The more enterprising of the vanishing class of yeomen invested the price of their ancestral farms in a like venture. Such are the origins of not a few families who became honourably famous in the nineteenth century.

The first generation of these men had the defects as well as the merits of pioneers. A common type of 'millowner' in the days of the younger [member of Parliament William] Pitt was a hard-bitten North-country working-man, of no education and great force of character, taking little stock of his social or political relations with the outer world, allowing neither leisure nor recreation to himself or to his hands, but managing somehow to convert the original £100 that he borrowed into a solvent 'mill,' the prison-house of children, the hidden reef on which Napoleon's empire struck. As a rule, he bothered his head equally little about the children he employed and the foreign war in which he was to be a decisive factor—except in so far as they made or marred his own fortunes.

By the time the war came to an end, men and their manners were changing. A millowner of the second generation had been born and bred a bourgeois, but of a new and enterprising type. With more education and wider outlook than his grim old father, the young man looked about him for the uses, obligations and privileges of wealth, as they were understood in that generation. . . .

Cotton

The cotton industry, though not absolutely created by the new machinery, derived thence almost its whole importance. Between the accession of George III and the passing of the Reform Bill its output increased a hundred-fold. Already by 1806 cotton was said to supply a third of the total British exports. The industry was concentrated in South and Central Lancashire, because the port of Liverpool was convenient to a trade depending on the import of a raw cotton and the export of the manufactured article; because there it was near cheap coal; and because the climate of the damp Atlantic seaboard is peculiarly suitable to fine spinning.

The first mills, worked by water-power, were established on the upper reaches of the Pennine[1] streams. But throughout the long war with France, Watt's steam-engines were replacing water-power, and the industry was carried on by altogether more modern methods. This meant a change from small to large mills, real capitalist employers, great assemblies of working-people and an increase in the proportion of skilled mechanics,—circumstances all of which prepared the way for improved conditions of life in the future. The employees, now accumulated in one mill by hundreds instead of by scores, could not long fail to combine for economic and political action. The new type of large millowner had a secure financial position, more education and sometimes more enlightenment. Individuals of this class introduced factory conditions which inspectors in a later time could enforce as standards. And when the age of Factory Acts[2] came, it was easier to inspect properly one big mill than many small ones.

If the cotton industry showed England the way into some of the worst miseries of the industrial revolution, it also showed the way out, because it passed most rapidly through the period of

1. mountains near the border between England and Scotland 2. four Factory Acts—1833, 1844, 1847, 1850—each limiting the working hours of women and children

semi-capitalised and half-organised industry, with its mean cruelties, into full-blown capitalism where the workpeople, the masters and the State could readily take stock of each other.

Working Conditions in the Mills and Mines

But before the age of Factory Acts, the condition of women and children in both small and big mills was as a rule very wretched. Mothers and children worked from twelve to fifteen hours a day under insanitary conditions, without either the amenities of life which had sweetened and relieved the tedium of family work in the cottage, or the conditions which make factory life attractive to many women to-day. The discipline of the early factories was like the discipline of a prison. Small children were often cruelly treated to keep them awake during the long hours, which shortened their lives or undermined their health.

The men were in little better case. Often out of employment, they were forced to sell their wives and children into the slavery of the mills, while they themselves degenerated in squalid idleness. The hand-loom weavers had flourished until the early years of the nineteenth century, weaving the increased product of the new spinning mills. But the coming of the power-loom destroyed their prosperity; their wages fell, they went on to the rates as paupers, and drank the dregs of misery, until after long years their old-world employment altogether disappeared. . . .

Coal-mining was an ancient industry, but its development in the age of 'iron and coal' was prodigious, and a large part of the population now worked underground. Women were used there as beasts of burden, and children worked in the dark, sometimes for fourteen hours.[3] The men laboured under conditions that showed but little regard for health or human life. In Durham and Northumberland it was not the custom before 1815 to hold inquests on the victims of the innumerable accidents. Payment was not on a cash basis, owing to the 'truck' system [payment in goods instead of cash], and the oppression by the 'putties' or sub-

3. As late as 1842 the Royal Commission on Mines, which first threw light on the life of underground England, brought out such facts as these from a Lancashire woman: 'I have a belt round my waist and a chain passing between my legs, and I go on my hands and feet. The water comes up to my clog tops, and I have seen it over my thighs. I have drawn till I have the skin off me. The belt and chain is worse when we are in the family way.' It was also shown that children under five worked alone in the darkness.

contractors for labour. These things and the condition of the miners' cottages, which were generally owned by their employers, too often rendered the life of the miner of a hundred years ago 'brutish, nasty and brief.'...

The Neglect of Education

If the real meaning of the Industrial Revolution and the break-up of the apprentice system had been understood, men would have seen that education was no longer a luxury for the few, but a necessity for all members of the new society. Generations were to pass before this idea was acted upon by the State, as a corollary of the working-class enfranchisement of 1867. The first effect of the Industrial Revolution, and the misery and unrest that it caused among the poor, was to render education suspect as 'Jacobinical' [radical]. This notion was still prevalent in Parliament in 1807; the House of Commons took the compulsory element out of the Bill by which [Samuel] Whitbread proposed, somewhat on the Scottish model, to establish parish schools in England out of the rates. In the Lords the Bill, thus mutilated, was introduced by Lord Holland, but was rejected without a division, on the complaint of the Archbishop of Canterbury that it did not leave enough power to the clergy....

Religious rivalry, so disastrous in the legislative sphere, had a healthy effect on private benefaction, 'British' and 'National' schools multiplied, and the Church began to pull ahead, especially in rural districts. In 1818 as many as 600,000 children out of two million were attending schools of some sort. In the year of the Reform Bill, when Bell died, there were as many as 12,000 'National' schools....

The Benefits of Mechanics' Institutes

The cause of Adult Education received its first stimulus from the Industrial Revolution in the desire of mechanics for general scientific knowledge, and the willingness of the more intelligent part of the middle class to help to supply their demand. It was a movement partly professional and utilitarian, partly intellectual and ideal. Disinterested scientific curiosity was strong among the better class of workmen in the North. From 1823 onwards Mechanics' Institutes, begun in Scotland by Dr. [George] Birkbeck, spread through industrial England....

The success of these democratic Mechanics' Institutes, with

an annual subscription of a guinea, reminds us that there was one section of the working-men, the engineers and mechanics, who had already gained more than they lost by the Industrial Revolution.

Of that Revolution, the men who made and mended the machines were indeed the bodyguard. They were usually better paid than their fellow-workmen, they were on the average more intelligent, and they often took the lead in educational and political movements. They were less looked down upon by the employers, who had to consult them and to bow to their technical knowledge. They were in the forefront of progress and invention, and rejoiced in the sense of leading the new age. Such workmen were the Stephensons of Tyneside; there was nothing 'middle class' about the origins of the man who invented the locomotive, after having taught himself to read at the age of seventeen.

It is indeed easier to reconstruct the early history of the coal-miners and textile hands, than that of the mechanics and engineers, because the latter were scattered up and down the country. But any picture of the earliest and worst stage of the Industrial Revolution is too black if it omits the life of the mechanics. The motto of the coming age was 'self-help,' a doctrine that left behind many of the weaker and less fortunate; but at least there were from the first other classes besides employers and middlemen who reaped a large share of its benefits, and who grew to a larger manhood under the moral and intellectual stimulus of the individualist doctrine.

The Influence of Victoria and Albert

By Asa Briggs

Queen Victoria ruled from 1837 until her death in 1901. Asa Briggs describes the strengths and contributions of Queen Victoria and her husband, Prince Albert, both of whom were hard workers and bold in their promotion of high moral standards. After Albert died in 1861, Victoria was too demoralized to be a strong ruler, and the rise of political parties further eroded the power of the monarch. Asa Briggs, lecturer at the University of Oxford and the University of Leeds in England, was a member of the Institute for Advanced Study in Princeton, New Jersey. He is the author of History of Birmingham, Victorian People, *and* Friends of the People.

When Victoria came to the throne in 1837 at the age of 18 the monarchy was at a low ebb. There was little republican sentiment and much talk of 'altar, throne and cottage', but William IV's early popularity had withered away. Victoria's initial advantages were threefold—her youth, her sex, and her already clearly formed sense of duty. When George IV [1820–1830] and William IV [1830–1837] ascended the throne they had a past behind them; Victoria, whose succession to the throne had been far from certain, had only a future. Her sex, which might in different circumstances have been a handicap, enabled her to make a special appeal not only to the public but also to her prime minister, Melbourne. He was fascinated by the 'girl-Queen' and she by him, and the first phase of their 'partnership' between 1837 and 1839 was stimulating and happy for both of them. Moreover, from the start the Queen displayed great strength of character and responsibility. She wrote in her journal on the day of her accession that she would do her utmost to fulfil her duty to her country, and despite her youth

Excerpted from *The Age of Improvement: 1783–1867*, by Asa Briggs (New York: David McKay Company, Inc., 1959).

and lack of experience she immediately took it for granted that others would obey her. Her first triumph of character was over the experienced and worldly-wise Melbourne, whose occupations and habits she revolutionized. . . .

Victoria Marries Prince Albert

The position [of Melbourne] was altered, however, as a result of the Queen's marriage in February 1840, and after the influence of her husband had established itself—almost at once—Melbourne was inevitably pushed more and more into the background. It had long been the ambition of King Leopold of the Belgians, the Queen's uncle and one of her earliest *confidants*, to marry his niece to her cousin, Prince Albert of Saxe Coburg Gotha, and there had been much gossip about the match from 1837 onwards. Fortunately for Victoria, the marriage which had been planned was also a marriage of love. Albert, in her own words, 'completely won my heart', and the wedding, celebrated quietly in St. James's Palace, with no signs of enthusiasm in the country, began the happiest period of her life. Her husband was still six months under the age of 21 in 1840 and he was a far from popular figure with the aristocracy, the crowds, or the House of Commons—by a majority of 104 votes the annuity of £50,000 the government proposed to pay him was reduced to £30,000—but he was just as resolved as Victoria to take the task of government seriously and willing in so doing to sink 'his own *individual existence* in that of his wife'. Stiff and conservative, his first efforts were devoted to reinforcing the Queen's own desire to set an example of strict propriety at Court.

The difference between old ways and new was well brought out in an early clash of ideas with Melbourne about the nature of social morality. 'Character', Melbourne maintained, 'can be attended to when people are of no consequence, but it will not do when people are of high rank'. Albert cared far less about rank than industry and integrity, and besides being willing to work long hours with a Germanic thoroughness that [the "self-help philosopher" Samuel] Smiles could not have excelled, he displayed all those 'Victorian' virtues of character which Melbourne regarded as unnecessary in a man of his station. His 'seriousness' of purpose is witnessed by the causes to which he gave his full support. His first public speech was at a meeting on behalf of the abolition of slavery; he was a vigorous advocate of scientific research and education, of official patronage of art, and of reformed universities; he took an active interest in the work of the Society for Improving the Condition of the Labouring Classes, founded in 1844, and when criticized by Lord John Russell for attending one of its meetings replied firmly that he conceived 'one has a *Duty* to perform towards the great mass of the working classes (and particularly at this moment) which will not allow one's yielding to the fear for some possible inconvenience'; he helped to design and plan the building of a block of houses known as Prince Albert's 'model houses for families'; and last, but perhaps most important of all, he played such an important part in organizing the Great Exhibition of 1851 that if it had not been for his efforts, it is doubtful whether the Exhibition would have been held. In all these efforts Albert met with resistance and opposition, much of it centred in the country houses and the universities, places where old prejudices were strong and suspicions difficult to break down.

Albert had perforce to follow the dictates of self-help as much as [engineer George] Stephenson or [architect Joseph] Paxton, and on many doors which were open to them he had to knock loudly. Two years after the Queen had written in 1853 that the nation appreciated him and fully acknowledged what he had done 'daily and hourly for the country', he was being lampooned in the popular press and attacked in the clubs more than ever before. If there was any truth in the Queen's claim that he eventually succeeded in raising monarchy to 'the *highest* pinnacle of respect' and rendering it 'popular beyond what it *ever* was in this country', it was entirely as a result of his own exertions and courage. He had no deficiency of spirit. When times were blackest for him on the eve of the Crimean War, he could still write that he looked upon his troubles as 'a fiery ordeal that will serve to purge away impurities'.

Albert's Friendship with Peel

Friendship with [Sir Robert] Peel was as important to Albert as friendship with Melbourne had been to Victoria, and it helped in itself to set the tone of mid-Victorian England. Between 1841 and 1846 the Queen and her husband came to put their full trust in their great prime minister and the causes for which he stood—sound administration, strong government, and free trade. As early as 1843 the Queen wrote to the King of the Belgians praising

Peel as 'a great statesman, a man who thinks but little of party and never of himself'; after Peel's death she wrote that Albert felt the loss *'dreadfully'.* He feels 'he has lost a second father'.

There was something in common, indeed, between Peel and Albert, not only in their dislike of the noisy clamour of party but in their desire for practical improvement and their resentment of unthinking aristocracies. During the Crimean War Albert complained of the 'hostility or bitterness towards me' not only of the radicals but 'of the old High Tory or Protectionist Party on account of my friendship with the late Sir Robert Peel and of my success with the Exhibition', and the bitterness certainly went deep. If in the case of Peel the main taunt was one of betrayal of the landed interest, in the case of Albert it was one of never having belonged to it, of being un-English, of working by slow deliberation, not by instinct, of paying attention to the wrong things in the wrong way. In such a context of criticism even Albert's virtues could appear as vices. He was ridiculed in *Punch* for trying to act twenty different character parts; he was criticized in army messes for his zealous interference; he was attacked in Cambridge University for trying to do too much as Chancellor, not too little. He had won a hotly contested election for the Chancellorship in 1847, and it is easy to guess the reaction of Cambridge dons to his earnest desire to look at 'schemes of tuition' and examination papers on subjects in which he was particularly interested. His collection of information on every conceivable issue of public policy, his investigation of statistics, his preparation of memoranda, and his considerable European correspondence were all activities calculated to alienate aristocratic holders of power. So too was his stern insistence on the morality of the Court. There was an interesting incident in 1852 when the new prime minister, Lord Derby, submitted his list of names for household appointments and Albert

Queen Victoria on her wedding day

noted with horror that 'the greater part were the Dandies and Roués of London and the Turf'. The Prince cared little for aristocratic company or aristocratic pursuits—in 1861, the year of his death, for instance, he described Ascot [the horse races] as rendered 'much more tedious than usual by incessant rain'—and he did not attempt to hide his preference for the company of authors, scientists, social reformers, and pioneers of education. . . .

Victoria did not share all Albert's enthusiasms or even understand them. She cared little for the company of scientists, showed no interest in royal patronage of art, and in only few of her letters referred to literature. She delighted, however, in the Exhibition of 1851 and thrilled to the bravery of British troops in the Crimea. On thirty occasions she visited the Crystal Palace, noting in her *Journal* that she never remembered anything before that everyone was so pleased with as the Exhibition; during the war she wrote that 'the conduct of our *dear noble* Troops is *beyond praise'*, said that she felt as if 'they were *my own children'*, and objected to those critics of the military system who detracted from British victories by 'croaking'. Just because she genuinely shared such English sentiments and was not tempted, as Albert was, to seek for forms of intellectual expression, she was far more popular than he. She was not, of course, in any sense a democratic monarch responding to mass pressures or gaining publicity through the influence of mass communications, but she won loyalty and respect from the majority of the population, including the middle classes, many of whose qualities and limitations she shared. Perhaps the most vivid impression of her impact on English society can be gained from a perusal of newspaper reports [in the *Leeds of Mercury*] of her visits to the provinces in the 1850s. In 1858 she visited both Birmingham and Leeds. Everywhere there were great crowds 'who behaved as well in the streets as could any assemblage of the aristocracy at a Queen's drawing room'. The local newspapers, while praising the interest of the Prince Consort in science and industry, reserved their loudest praise for a queen who 'is as it were partner with the great and multitudinous people who do gladly obey her, joins with them in legislation, shares with them in government, and makes them to a great extent their own rulers'. They extolled her combination of 'feminine grace and royal dignity' and her lofty eminence above all party faction, but above all they argued that 'what consummates the whole is, that she is a wife and a mother of so lofty a purity and discharging her duties so well that she forms the brightest exemplar to the matrons of England'. . . .

Albert's Death Demoralizes Victoria

The death of the Prince Consort from typhoid fever in 1861 was a tragic blow to the Queen from which she never fully recovered. 'The loss of her husband', wrote Lady Lewis to her brother, Lord Clarendon, 'has changed her from a powerful sovereign (which she was with the knowledge and judgement of her husband to guide her opinions and strengthen her will) into a weak and desolate woman with the weight of duties she has not the moral and physical power to support'. Conventional condolences meant nothing to her, and only those who could find the right words to demonstrate their understanding of the extent of her loss were likely to touch any chord in her heart. Strangely enough, it was [Lord] Palmerston, with whom both she and the Prince had had so many differences and had fought such hectic battles, who found the correct phrase and wrote to her of the Prince as 'that perfect Being'.

From 1861 to [1867] the Queen was in the deepest retirement, resolved irrevocably that Albert's 'wishes—his plans—about everything are to be my law'. Although she found some consolation in the affairs of her family and its network of associations with other European courts, and although she spent many peaceful days at Balmoral, her favourite home, she wore mourning, shrank from large crowds, and feared formal social gatherings. She hated the thought of appearing in public as a 'poor, broken-hearted widow' and declared that she 'would as soon clasp the hand of the poorest widow in the land if she had truly loved her husband and felt for me, as I would a Queen, or any other in high position'. It was natural, though hard for her to bear, that the public could not appreciate the reason for her social abdication. In 1865 *Punch* printed a famous cartoon in which Paulina (Britannia) unveiled the covered statue and addressed Hermione (Victoria) with the words "Tis time! descend; be stone no more!' Two years later the Queen was still lost in an unfinished winter's tale and Bagehot could dismiss her and the Prince of Wales in the tersest of phrases as 'a retired widow and an unemployed youth'.

In time the Queen's age and experience were to produce new waves of loyalty and admiration, but the comment of Bagehot is the epitaph on the mid-Victorian period. What would have happened had the Prince Consort lived is a speculative puzzle which has fascinated many specialists in historical 'ifs'. Disraeli believed that 'if he had outlived some of our old stagers he would have given us, while retaining all constitutional guarantees, the blessings of absolute government'. It was a dubious estimate of future probabilities. For all Albert's belief (and that of Stockmar, his tutor) in strong government with a monarchy raised high above the noisy clamour of party and exercising unobtrusive but effective power, he was not able—nor was the Queen—to influence politics decisively even in the period of group politics from 1846 to 1859. . . .

The Decline of Royal Power

The rise of parties, particularly after the extension of the suffrage in 1867, was bound in the long run to limit royal power still further, and in the twentieth century 'strong government' could be provided only by organized party machines served by a neutral civil service and squeezing the monarchy out of politics altogether. Albert had believed that 'the exaltation of Royalty is possible only through the personal character of the sovereign. When a person enjoys complete confidence we desire for him more power and influence in the conduct of affairs', but even this worthy Victorian maxim has lost most of its political relevance in an age when issues are discussed not only in courts and cabinets but in party meetings and when 'public relations' count for as much as private rectitude in determining popular reactions.

What was left after 1861 was a series of royal prejudices, which increased in intensity in the last thirty years of Victoria's reign, and the moral force of monarchy, whenever the Queen cared to emphasize it. That the force counted for much is well brought out in the comment of the great historian, W.H. Lecky, on 'the profound feeling of sorrow and admiration' which greeted the news of her death. 'It shows', he said, 'that the vulgar ideals, the false moral measurements, the feverish social ambitions, the love of the ostentatious and the factitious, and the disdain for simple habits, pleasures and characters so apparent in certain conspicuous sectors of society, have not yet blunted the moral sense or prevented the moral perceptions of the great masses.'

The British Empire

BY JOHN W. YOUNG

The British Empire expanded in the late nineteenth century as England sought raw materials for industrial production and new markets for its goods. At its height, it included one-fourth of the world's population and one-fourth of the world's land. John W. Young describes the building of the British Empire and the loose and varied nature of its organization. The empire began to decline in the 1930s, and the process accelerated following World War II, when an increasing number of colonies demanded independence. John W. Young, who teaches politics at the University of Leicester in England, is the author of Britain and European Unity, 1945–1992 *and* Winston Churchill's Last Campaign.

The 1890s saw doubts not so much about Britain's current preeminence as about the ways to ensure a leading role through the next century. Queen Victoria's Diamond Jubilee in 1897 [a national celebration marking the 60th anniversary of Victoria's reign] marked the high point of national faith in an Empire which, covering a quarter of the globe and with over 400 million people (over half of them in India), was the largest ever seen and the essential source of Britain's greatness. It was the Empire which gave Britain, itself populated by only 42 million people, superiority in numbers over the combined Empires of Russia (130 million) and France (100 million), who were then seen as the most potent, likely threat to British security. It provided a focus for national pride, even a focus for national unity among the English, Scots, Welsh and Irish.

Building the Empire

The formal building of the Empire was driven by commercial, financial and strategic demands, though historians vigorously debate which was most vital and the precise reasons for annexation differed from possession to possession. It was a source of raw ma-

Excerpted from *Britain and the World in the Twentieth Century*, by John W. Young (London: Arnold, 1997).

terials and, especially in India's case, troops. It was also an outlet for settlement, trade and investment. Yet for all this it was not simply viewed by its creators as an exploitative enterprise. Missionary societies, rather than seekers after earthly glory, had often provided the spearhead of expansion and Victorians liked to see the Empire as part of a religious and 'civilising' mission, albeit by a racially superior people, in which the ideal of service (in the army, church or bureaucracy) played a vital role. Even in 1897, one of the Empire's greatest literary figures, Rudyard Kipling, could hint at doubts about how long it might survive: 'Lo all our pomp of yesterday, Is one with Nineveh and Tyre!' But most Britons showed no outward trace of such pessimism even if there was a sense of defensiveness and vulnerability in the very act of securing *formal* control over such a vast area. In mid-century, where possible, the British had preferred to exploit global trade through an *informal* system, where the activities of merchants were unimpeded by the territorial claims of other Great Powers. Formal control had been extended to certain areas by 1815, either to keep out competitors (as with the French in India and Canada) or to secure strategic points on shipping routes (such as Malta and Cape Colony).

The Costs of the Empire

However, such formal control had its costs, demanding governors, civil servants and military garrisons. This was true even though the British tried to run their possessions 'on the cheap', ruling indirectly via local elites, either through traditional channels of chiefs and princes, or through newly educated groups who staffed the lower levels of the civil service. In order to minimise discontent, a policy of 'divide and rule' was practised, local religious and social customs were preserved and major reforms were avoided. There was little attempt to tackle 'normal' levels of poverty, though assistance was given when famine and natural disaster caused particular distress; and by providing order, investment and trade the Empire did provide an important element of *mutual* gain for its members. Whilst education was improved and railways built, and whilst the Colonial Office tried to limit the exploitation of colonial peoples by British businessmen, there was no sophisticated policy of 'development' until the twentieth century. This low-cost system of rule helped to minimise taxes on British people and—backed by pro-Imperial propaganda, the

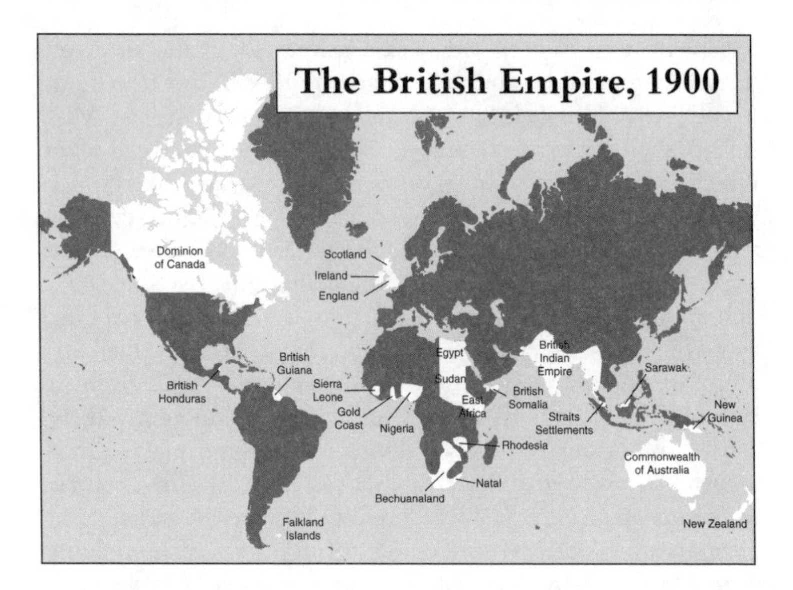

sense of awe which surrounded British rule, and the ultimate sanction of military force—kept the Empire in reasonable internal order. Thus India, for all its vast population, required less than 1500 British officials to govern it, and in peacetime before 1914 the total size of military forces in the colonies only reached about 320 000 (mostly in India, which had a British garrison of 70 000 and a native army of twice that number).

The Variety Within the Empire

The Empire was a scattered and ramshackle affair with many different forms of government, including crown colonies, protectorates and self-governing entities. India, a third of which was ruled by local princedoms, was itself a hotch-potch of languages, religions and peoples; elsewhere in East Asia, Britain ruled over Burma, the Malay states and the wealthy Chinese trading outlet of Hong Kong; in the Caribbean, the West Indies sugar islands had long since lost their profitability but their Afro-Caribbean population was not viewed as ready for self-government; in the Middle East, Britain's hold on Egypt relied on a military presence rather than a firm legal base; the settlement colonies of Canada, Cape Colony, Australia and New Zealand had been given a large degree of independence in domestic affairs but remained loyal to the Crown, partly because most of their population (except in Quebec and the Cape) was of recent British stock. White settlers in these 'Dominions', as they became known, had some of the highest living standards in the world and could rely on London to provide for their defence, a beneficial position which provoked increasing complaint from some in Britain. It led the Colonial Secretary, Joseph Chamberlain, to ask colonial leaders, at the Fourth Colonial Conference in August 1902, to provide greater financial assistance to 'the Weary Titan', especially to pay for the Royal Navy. By then the world had reached the end of the 20-year bout of expansion known as the 'New Imperialism', the most important aspect of which was the 'Scramble for Africa', in which the British had extended, formal control to much of East Africa and the wealthier, more densely populated areas of West Africa, such as the Gold Coast (later called Ghana) and Nigeria. Latin America, China and the Ottoman Empire continued to be exploited by 'informal' means, with British power in some parts of China verging on sovereign control. Egypt, with control of the Suez Canal, became an essential linchpin of Imperial security but, even together, the rest of the African colonies did not provide more than a few per cent of British trade and investment before 1914. They had been hastily seized, partly it seems as a pre-emptive measure against other European states, partly because of foreign commercial competition and protectionism, partly in the vain hope of achieving a position of complete security.

The Debate About Consolidation

Ministers and officials in London, concerned by the costs of Empire, by the need for good relations with other European states and the desire to preserve peace and stability (rather than profits), were often reluctant to extend formal control. However, their hand could be forced by their own local representatives, both political and military (the so-called 'men on the spot'), and formal Imperialism was goaded by commercial interests, by patriotic public opinion and by issues of prestige. Changes on the so-called 'periphery' (lands bordering the existing Empire) could also encourage expansion: tribal wars or dynastic instability might lead traders, for example, to demand that the British military enforce order. At the end of the Scramble, Britain had demonstrated its capability of offensive action and kept its lead over its competitors, grabbing more of Africa than anyone else. True, even this could be seen as a retreat, for where British businesses had in the past been able to exploit most of the world as a source of profit, now they concentrated attention on certain parts of the globe. The threat to Britain's belief in *laissez-faire* methods was further emphasised by the growth, in Europe during the Great Depression, of tariff barriers and what the British considered 'unfair' restrictive commercial practices. In response, British traders and investors themselves demanded that *laissez-faire* policies give way to government intervention to protect their interests and guarantee 'fair trade'. Feelings of vulnerability led Imperialists, in both the Conservative and Liberal parties, to consider diverse ideas to bind the Empire together and compete with such large, continental states as America and Russia. The idea of federation as a way to unite and strengthen individual colonies had already been seen in the formation of a Canadian government in 1867 (designed in part to counter the power of the archetypal federal country, the US); it was seen again with the formation of Australia in 1901. However, from the 1870s onwards the idea also grew, in intellectual and political circles, of a complete, Empire-wide federation. This was seen in books such as J.R. Selley's *The Expansion of England* (1884) and in pressure groups like the Imperial Federation Committee (1894). A more practical form of consolidation was the inauguration of government-level conferences between Britain and the settlement colonies, such as that which saw Chamberlain's 'Weary Titan' appeal. Nonetheless, whatever the signs of defensiveness and doubt in British policy, decline and fear can hardly be said to have dominated the nation's mind, and the country's leaders proved capable of determination, resilience and innovation in maintaining their leading position.

THE HISTORY OF NATIONS

Chapter 5

Modernism and War, 1900–1990

England Fights in World War I

BY HENRY PELLING

Henry Pelling describes the progress of World War I, 1914–1919. The British army was most active on the western front while the navy fought in the south Atlantic and the English Channel. Though British soldiers fought valiantly, they lost a few battles and suffered many casualties. In April 1917, America entered the war to retaliate against Germany, whose submarines had sunk American ships. The British held the front line while American troops and equipment moved into place. Finally, when German strength and morale had weakened, the war ended in November 1918. Henry Pelling taught history and politics at Queen's College, Oxford, England. He is the author of American Labor *and* The Challenge of Socialism.

Britain entered the war in a very fair state of preparation—at least, for a country which refused to maintain a large standing army. The navy, which was already mobilised, was ready for its immediate tasks, and the so-called Grand Fleet under Admiral Sir John Jellicoe was at once constituted and established at Scapa [chief British naval base off the coast of Scotland] to keep watch for any attempt at action by the German High Seas Fleet. The expeditionary force, at a strength of some 90,000, was sent to France under the command of General Sir John French, of Boer War fame; composed of skilled riflemen, it proved its worth in the fighting retreat of the French armies in front of Paris in late August and early September [1914]. After rearguard actions at Mons and Le Cateau, it thrust back at a gap in the enemy lines on the Marne, and thus helped to check the German advance and stabilise the line, which after the fall of Antwerp in October ran from the Channel ports to the French fortresses of the Alsace-Lorraine front, with a big salient in the

Excerpted from *Modern Britain: 1885–1955*, by Henry Pelling (Edinburgh: Thomas Nelson and Sons, 1960).

direction of Paris. But after further heavy fighting at Ypres in October and November there was little left of the original British expeditionary force: it could hold only 21 miles of line as against 430 held by the French. The 'contemptible' little British army, as the Kaiser was reported to have termed it, had proved its worth, but it could not continue to play a significant role without heavy reinforcement.

The hopes of the Western Allies at first turned to the eastern front, where the 'Russian steam-roller', descending on a thinly defended German frontier, was expected to advance with speed. But the Russian armies in the north had already been sent into reverse after a crushing defeat at the Battle of Tannenberg (28th August); and although an Austrian offensive against Poland failed with even heavier loss, German support enabled the eastern front to be stabilised. Further heavy fighting in November did not result in any important change before the onset of winter. The British Navy was meanwhile hunting down and destroying the few units of the German fleet that were on foreign stations; a minor German success at the Battle of Coronel off the Chilean coast was speedily avenged with the aid of reinforcements from the Grand Fleet at the Battle of the Falkland Isles. All save one of the German warships 'at large' had been eliminated by the end of 1914; but the main German fleet for the time being preferred not to venture a decisive combat. Various minor operations to occupy the German colonies were under way; but the only means of breaking the apparent deadlock in Europe seemed to be provided by the entry of Turkey into the war on the side of Germany and Austria in October.

Early Battles and Losses for the Allies

Meanwhile new British armies were being rapidly recruited and trained. The first of the wartime volunteers, together with the existing Territorial force of about 250,000 and contingents from the Dominions, were available for service early in 1915. . . .

Meanwhile the western front had settled down to an affair of trenches and barbed wire, and in the technical conditions of the time defensive operations obtained a considerable advantage. The arts of camouflage and deception were rudimentary, and while both sides had a few aircraft for reconnaissance, neither could achieve the type of air superiority which could prevent enemy observation. Heavy artillery bombardment could do something to prepare for an offensive, but it could not neutralise a well-entrenched and determined defence, which with a few machine-guns could take a heavy toll of advancing infantry. But the commanders on either side, and not least the British, were slow to appreciate these facts. The new British Army lost heavily in offensives at Neuve-Chapelle in March and at Festubert in May 1915, and Sir John French's insistence for prestige purposes on holding an exposed salient at Ypres caused a further heavy drain of casualties. At this time, however, reinforcements were more than making up for losses, and the British army in France grew to a total of twenty-one divisions in July. This increase in strength, coupled with the heavy commitments of the Germans on the Russian fronts, encouraged the Western Allies to launch a fresh offensive in September 1915. The Battle of Loos, as the struggle in the British sector was called, was virtually a defeat, partly at least owing to Sir John French's failure to throw in his reserves at the decisive moment. Shortly afterwards he was replaced by a corps commander, Sir Douglas Haig. In the east the Russians had by this time been forced to evacuate Poland and were standing entirely on the defensive; and Bulgaria was encouraged to enter the war on the German side and to join in an offensive against Serbia, which resulted in the entire occupation of that unhappy country. It was no great consolation that Italy had entered the war on the Allied side (May 1915), for the Italian forces could do little more than hold their own against the Austrians.

A War on Three Fronts and at Sea

The beginning of 1916 thus found three main fronts of war in existence—the eastern (Russia), the western (Britain and France), and the southern (Italy). By comparison with these the 'side-shows'—such as the Anglo-French position at Salonika in Greece and the British operations against Turkey in Mesopotamia—were of little importance. The war had already proved very costly to the French, who had had two million casualties; and the British, though still increasing the size of their armies, had lost half a million, including the bulk of the peacetime forces. The German command, with the advantage of the inner lines of communication, therefore determined to attack again in the west and in February launched a heavy attack against the French fortress of Verdun. The assault, which made very slow progress, was continued all through the spring and was broken off only in July, with Verdun still in French hands. By this time the British armies had built up considerably, and they were naturally expected to relieve the pressure on their allies by taking the offensive.

There ensued what became known as the Battle of the Somme [river in northern France]. Elaborate preparations for the offensive took place, but they were very obvious to the enemy. There was an artillery bombardment of the German positions, but this was inadequate, for the British forces were seriously short of artillery. After this the infantry were sent forward in broad daylight, and weighed down with 66 lb. of equipment each. According to the Official History this weight 'made it difficult to get out of a trench, impossible to move much quicker than a slow walk, or to rise and lie down quickly'. On the first day alone (1st July) the army lost 60,000 men; yet the attacks were renewed until October, and when they were done there was little to show for the vast effort. At a total cost of 420,000 British casualties, an advance of seven miles was made on a thirty-mile front, with no clear strategic advantage as a result. The German casualties, which were rather more than two to every three of the Allies', were inflated by the insistence of the German command on the recapture of all lost ground. One feature of the battle was the use of tanks, a British invention; but there were too few of them to make much difference to the outcome.

The pattern of developments on the eastern front in 1916 was not dissimilar from that of 1915: Russian successes against Austrian troops were followed by decisive German intervention to restore the situation. This time the initial Russian successes brought the Rumanians into the war on the Allied side, but it did not take long for the Germans to invade and occupy most of their country. At sea the war was largely developing into a German submarine offensive against Allied and neutral shipping. But in May 1916 a major fleet action was fought between the British and German navies in the North Sea. Known in Britain as the Battle of Jutland, it ended indecisively, with the German fleet retiring hastily to port after having inflicted much heavier casualties than it received. The British lost 115,025 warship tons and 6,945 men; the Germans lost 61,180 warship tons and 3,058 men. The German ships, ton for ton, were stronger and more heavily armed; their armour-piercing shells were better, their range-finding and fire-direction more efficient. All the same, the German fleet was no match for the *Queen Elizabeth* type of battleship; and its strength steadily deteriorated thereafter as its best officers and men were diverted to submarine warfare.

Attacks by German Submarines Bring America into the War

The German submarine threat had not been particularly serious in the first two years of the war, for there were at first few U-boats available. Moreover the British barrier of nets and mines across the Straits of Dover was a formidable obstacle, and the northern route was long and difficult. It was not at first customary for liners or merchant ships to be sunk without warning, but the practice gradually grew more frequent: it had considerable advantages in enabling the U-boat to escape detection and destruction. Unfortunately for the Germans, this development was strongly opposed by the neutral powers, and especially by the United States, which was supplying the Allies with many of the goods and materials of war. The sinking in May 1915 of the Cunard liner *Lusitania,* with the loss of 100 American lives, was followed by vigorous diplomatic activity, and although the United States did not intervene with armed force the Germans were obliged to promise not to sink merchant ships without warning.

By the end of 1916 the German morale had been sapped by the continuous struggle on so many war fronts for over two years. The naval blockade by the Allies was reducing living standards and threatening to cause starvation to the population. The German command was therefore inclined to desperate measures in order to secure an early decision of the war. Prominent among these was the abandonment of attempts to placate the neutrals, and the beginning of unrestricted submarine warfare in February 1917. This was in the belief that it was more important to strike immediate blows at Britain than to keep America out of the war. Already from October 1916 the monthly toll of Allied shipping had been over 300,000 tons; by April 1917 it rose to 875,000. But in April the United States entered the war; and thereafter the position gradually improved, partly as a result of American and Japanese naval assistance, partly by the introduction of the convoy system, and partly by the construction of further elaborate mine barriers across the North Sea and elsewhere.

Also early in 1917 the German command decided to forestall further offensives on the western front by a retreat to a carefully prepared defensive line, known to the Germans as the Siegfried

Line, but called by the Allies the Hindenburg Line. It lay some twenty-five miles behind the existing front. This decision was of great value to the German army, for when General Nivelle, the new French commander, organised a joint attack by British and French troops in April, his plans were soon frustrated by the new defence in depth. Although the British won Vimy Ridge, a useful strategic point in front of Arras [city in northern France], the failure of the French led to mutinies in the French Army and the replacement of Nivelle by Pétain, the defender of Verdun. And Pétain, in view of the state of the army, decided to stay on the defensive until 'the Americans and the tanks' should be available in large numbers. Haig, left to himself, then launched the long and bitter hundred-day offensive of Passchendaele (July-November)—an offensive in Flanders designed to reach the Channel ports, but in fact quickly bogged down in an agony of mud and rain with a loss of 300,000 men to the British Army. . . .

It was obvious early in 1918 that the Allies had but to hold the western front in order to win the war, for the American contribution in men and materials alike would be enormous if it had time to develop. The Germans on the other hand, with the aid of reinforcements from the eastern front, were impelled to attack in order to seek a decision before it was too late. The

The crew of a German U-boat monitors the waters near the British Isles during World War I.

British Army in March 1918 was not as large as a year earlier, owing to the heavy losses of 1917 and the commitments in Italy and elsewhere. Consequently the German offensive of March and April found the British front thinly held. The attack threw General Gough's Fifth Army into retreat across the Somme and almost into complete dissolution. The crisis led for the first time to a unity of the French and British commands: Haig accepted Foch as Commander-in-Chief over himself and Pétain. A further offensive against the First Army in Flanders produced the pitch of extremity that occasioned Haig's famous General Order of the Day:

> There is no other course open to us but to fight it out! Every position must be held to the last man: there must be no retirement. With our backs to the wall and believing in the justice of our cause, each one of us must fight to the end.

Under this inspiration the defence held on, and the attack weakened, only to be resumed on the French front in May. The Germans took Soissons and were within thirty-seven miles of Paris; but again they were held, and this time American troops, in action for the first time in considerable numbers, played a part in the battle. A further German assault on the French front in July led to a penetration over the Marne, but again it came to a standstill. Thereafter the initiative passed to the Allies.

German Strength and Morale Weakened

It was to Haig's credit that he at once realised how far the German strength had been weakened by their costly offensive. In August he set on foot a series of skilful attacks on weak sections of the enemy front, which rapidly led to a turning of the main fortifications. From September onwards it was clear that the German Army was on the verge of defeat. That month saw a successful American operation on another western sector; the collapse of Bulgaria, which had lost its stiffening of German troops; and the opening of a new full-scale offensive under Foch's direction. Foch sought to combine two gigantic pincer-jaws—a Franco-American attack between Rheims and Verdun and a British attack in Flanders, aimed at Lille. The offensive had hardly begun when Ludendorff, the German commander, demanded the formation of a new German government which would undertake peace negotiations. The blockade had been taking its toll: short of fuel and food, the German people readily succumbed to illness, and their morale was low. On 5th October Prince Max of Baden, who formed the new government, informed President Wilson of America that he was willing to treat for peace. Wilson demanded a responsible government instead of 'military masters and monarchical autocrats'. On 29th October a mutiny broke out among the seamen of the High Seas Fleet when they were ordered to sea; on the 31st Turkey surrendered after heavy defeats in Palestine at the hands of Allenby, the British commander. On 4th November Austria capitulated, her armies in Italy having been routed at the Battle of Vittorio Veneto. In the face of growing revolution at home the Kaiser abdicated on 9th November; and the armistice was signed on the morning of the 11th. Its terms indicated that in fact it was a capitulation: it involved the immediate evacuation of occupied territory and also of the left bank of the Rhine, as well as bridgeheads across the river; and the fleet was to be surrendered.

The cost of the war to Britain in casualties was three-quarters of a million killed and almost one and three-quarter million wounded. Another two hundred thousand men from the Empire were killed, and twice as many wounded. The total military enlistments for Britain were over six million; for the Empire, altogether about nine and a half million. The figures themselves conveyed something of the enormous effort and sacrifice involved.

The Protestant-Catholic Conflict in Northern Ireland

By Bentley B. Gilbert

Bentley B. Gilbert traces the worsening conflicts in Ireland between the Easter Rebellion of 1916 and the late 1970s. In the early 1900s, factions in southern Ireland wanted independence from the British Empire, but many in northeastern Ireland wanted to remain under British rule. The British put down the 1916 insurrection in Dublin by force, but in 1920 they divided Ireland into two countries, both of which remained under British rule. The north accepted this act, but the south rejected it and continued to fight for complete independence. In 1921, the Irish Free State was set up, making the south a self-governing country. Conflict continued between those who supported this arrangement and those who wanted the north to join the south in independence from Britain. This conflict was especially intense within Northern Ireland, where Protestants generally supported British rule and Catholics favored independence. After the failure of the 1921 compromise, conflict between Protestants and Catholics gradually accelerated into civil war. By the 1970s, according to Gilbert, opposing sides had solidified their positions to the point that the chances for reconciliation seemed few. Bentley B. Gilbert, who taught history at the University of Cincinnati in Ohio, is the author of British Social Policy, 1914–1939 *and* David Lloyd George: A Political Life.

Perhaps the most tragic and invincible problem in the United Kingdom in the period [from 1918 to 1980], a conundrum that seems not only without solution but without hope, [was] the civil war in Northern Ireland. Even as astute a politician as [Prime Minister David] Lloyd George had been

Excerpted from *Britain Since 1918*, by Bentley B. Gilbert (New York: St. Martin's Press, 1980).

unable to solve it, only to sweep it under the rug. Lloyd George's unstable compromise in 1921, had meant surrender to the Protestants of the North while giving disguised independence—in effect the right to claim independence—to 26 counties of the South. He had abandoned the landowning unionist magnates of the South who had destroyed his attempts at settlement after the [1916] Easter Rebellion. But in order to gain Tory support for this sacrifice, a bargain the party had been unwilling to make either in 1914 or 1916, he was forced to institutionalize Protestant ascendancy in the North. The Better Government of Ireland Act, the Fourth Home Rule Act, gave the power not to the inhabitants of six of the nine counties of Ulster but to a party machine which for nearly 50 years held unquestioned control of the Northern Irish administration. Politics in the North ignored the overriding issues of the rest of the United Kingdom, unemployment, welfare, capital and labour—even though the area suffered devastating unemployment—and centered entirely on the matter, as it was put, of 'maintaining the constitution'. Northern Irish politics were consistent if not stable. In the 47 years between 1921 and 1968, during which Britain experienced 14 changes of Prime Minister, Northern Ireland had four, all of the same party. Of these four, two presided for a period of 39 years. There were many similarities to post-reconstruction one-party rule in the American South.

A Segregated Society

Like the American South also, Northern Ireland was a segregated society in which the lines dividing Protestant and Catholic extended far beyond religion, into housing, schooling and commerce. Each side enshrined its own peculiar sort of atavistic tribalism in secret organizations, public ceremonies and commemorations of past victories, a form of living history. With political power firmly in the hands of the two-thirds of the population who were Protestant there was plenty of evidence of discrimination against Catholics in school financing, employment, and gerrymandering of local government districts and having provided adequate grievances, the Protestants could justifiably argue that the Catholic population of Northern Ireland was less than entirely loyal to the settlement of 1920 [which partitioned the country]. There were continual provocations to disturbance on each side and serious riots in 1935 with lesser ones in 1959.

Briefly the advent of the fourth Prime Minister in Northern Ireland's history, Captain Terence O'Neill in 1963, and of Harold Wilson in Britain in 1964, offered hope of reconciliation between Protestants and Catholics. Public opinion polls even suggested that a large number of Catholics were willing to accept the constitutional division of Ireland and to work for better conditions for themselves within the existing framework. At the same time there were signs of friendliness between the governments at Dublin and Belfast [capitals of South and North, respectively]. O'Neill was the first Northern Irish Prime Minister not of the generation of the Troubles and the treaty. In January and February 1965 the Prime Ministers of North and South made much publicized calls at each other's capitals and in 1966 Wilson returned the remains of Roger Casement who had been hanged in Pentonville Prison following the Easter Rebellion 50 years before.

There was at last some movement. But as many historians have noted, oppression seems most unendurable when the possibility for its amelioration appears. Moreover there was from the United States the exemplary success of the civil rights movement which brought much improvement to the condition of the blacks in the American South. In the middle-sixties a coalition of moderate Catholics, some liberal Protestants, and a substantial number of students from Queens University, had formed the North Ireland Civil Rights Association. The Association goals were constitutional, securing an end to gerrymandering of local authority districts, equal funding for Catholic housing and school projects, and countering the rhetoric of Protestant extremists. Particularly violent among these was the Free Presbyterian Minister, Ian Paisley, who had already begun to speak out against the rather mild reforms that Captain O'Neill had proposed since taking office.

A Stalemate Develops in Three Phases

The story of the tragic stalemate in North Ireland falls easily into three phases. The first extended from June 1968, when the Civil Rights Association undertook its first large public demonstration in Dungannon, typically over housing, to January 1969. During this period Catholic moderates demonstrated in most major Ulster towns and were generally opposed by Protestant hard-liners whose spokesman, and usually also leader, was Ian Paisley. Police intervention was limited to occasional arrests and beating of

Catholics. The issues however were only those of civil and economic discrimination against Catholics and violence, so far, was not lethal.

The second phase began on 1 January 1969 with vicious attacks by Protestant thugs upon marchers who had set out to walk from Belfast to Londonderry. By the time the demonstrators, many seriously hurt, reached Londonderry, a city which itself was virtually a Northern Irish Protestant shrine, the community was in an uproar. The badly disorganized police were attacking the Catholic Bogside section of the town while the citizens in the Bogside defended themselves with rocks, petrol bombs, and barricades. During this period, which lasted until the autumn of 1969, the entire character of the struggle changed from a demand for Catholic equality carried forward by young, largely middle-class demonstrators, to a general war between Catholic and Protestant working classes of the larger towns in which the issues changed to simple racial hatred combined with a fairly consistent demand for the unification of North and South, in effect for British withdrawal from the North. The second phase also saw the breakdown of political control, the hardening of public opinion against Prime Minister O'Neill's moderate policies, and the demoralization of the Royal Ulster Constabulary who lost any semblance of power over the Protestant mobs with whom, in any case, they usually sympathized. The result, in August 1969, was the replacement of the Royal Ulster Constabulary for peace-keeping purposes by the British Army. Three months earlier, in May 1969, O'Neill had resigned.

As heavy reinforcements of British troops arrived in Northern Ireland to strengthen the three battalions already there, a shift in authority from Belfast to London took place. The manifest impotence of the police to protect to Catholics, which had made the introduction of troops necessary in the first place, revealed to all the weakness of Northern Ireland's government. On 1 April 1972, direct rule from London superseded the authority of the Stormont Parliament which had governed Ireland since 1921.

However, well before the introduction of direct rule, by the end of 1969, the third phase had begun. Northern Ireland had become a battleground between British troops and a sinister new force, the professional terrorists of the Provisional Wing of the Irish Republican Army. The Provisionals of the seventies traced their ancestry back to DeValera's[1] anti-treaty forces of 1922, that is to the portion of the original Irish Republican Army of the Troubles which had refused to accept the partition treaty brought back from London in December 1921 by Arthur Griffith and Michael Collins and which in 1922 had risen against the government of the new Irish Free State. For half a century after their defeat the IRA remained an illegal but visible conspiracy, devoted to the unification of the island, denouncing the governments of both North and South, and committing from time to time acts of terrorism in both Ireland and Britain. The Provisionals in the North represented yet another breakaway group which had seceded from the 'official' IRA based in Dublin when the latter turned more and more toward Marxist political agitation while giving up violence.

Civil War Prevails

The present phase of Northern Ireland's civil war, then, continues to be the battle between the Provisionals and the British troops whose appearance at first had been welcomed by the Catholic ghettos. Undoubtedly the IRA was present during the early civil rights marches but attained ascendancy only by taking advantage of attacks of Protestants on peaceful demonstrators and later, after the Londonderry march, by helping to resist Protestant invasions of Catholic housing areas. As such they were able to present themselves as the only protectors of the Catholic population and to replace the demand for civil rights within the context of a Northern Ireland with the ancient cry of United Ireland. By the beginning of the decade of the seventies civil rights for Catholics, if it meant recognition by Catholics of the separation of North and South, had virtually disappeared as a demand and with it had gone, unhappily, any possibility of the peaceful reconciliation which had seemed briefly possible in the sixties. The Protestants refused to discuss civil rights if it meant discussing also the unification of North and South and the Catholics would discuss nothing else.

The termination of Home Rule and the imposition of direct government from London carried with it the implication that Northern Ireland was incapable of governing itself. Consequently, even though one may suspect that many North Irish

1. Eamon DeValera was political head of the Irish Republic.

Protestants cared little whether the Parliament at Stormont sat or not, demands for a return to local self-government began to be heard among politicians almost immediately. Britain's problem was that it could not simply return power to the exclusively Protestant political machine that had run Northern Ireland for half a century. Somehow Catholic participation would have to be ensured. But since 1969 no Catholic politician could survive in the North who did not recognize the sentiment among his constituents for some sort of political connection with the South, a topic upon which Protestants were immovable.

Politicians Caught Between Two Poles

Among the several of [Prime Minister] Edward Heath's failed initiatives was the attempt, beginning in the spring of 1973, to reconstruct the Northern Irish administration with the statutory inclusion (power sharing) of Catholics, at all levels of government while providing also for the formation of at least an embryonic Council of Ireland which would recognize the unity of the island. Although an assembly and an executive council were in fact elected they were unable to function and the Protestants of Northern Ireland on 15 May 1974, proclaimed a general strike which virtually paralyzed the six counties. As a result power was reclaimed by the [Prime Minister Harold] Wilson government. Britain has been caught in the vice on one side of intransigent Protestantism which sees the English connection first of all as the symbol of freedom from Catholic domination and on the other side of an IRA terrorism which will accept nothing but total unification. (Not surprisingly, like the Protestant militants, the Provisional IRA also rejected the tentative power sharing proposals and the Council of Ireland.) Between these two poles lies surely the majority of the population of both North and South, which may favour privately either separation or unification but which most of all wants to see the killing stopped. Meanwhile on the sidelines exists a hapless Irish government in Dublin, well aware that the IRA gunmen represent in the long run as grave a threat to itself as to the British, but which is unable to take action against them without seeming to favour partition.

Thus for over a decade violence and disorder have been the rule in Northern Ireland, arrests by British soldiers are countered by bombings of troop carriers and sniping, with occasional outrages in Great Britain and most recently by the murder of Earl

Mountbatten. The tragedy in the situation seems to be that for the political authorities in Britain there are no options. Proposals for concessions to the Catholics in the North break against the hard wall of the Northern Irish Protestant siege mentality. On the other hand the Provisional IRA has no interest in a stable and contended Irish population within the present Northern Irish constitutional framework. Negotiations among the few remaining moderate leaders, Catholic or Protestant, are repudiated by the rank and file, as occurred in the power sharing experiments of 1973–74 and in the constitutional convention of 1975–76. And in ten years a generation has grown up in civil war with new sacrifices to celebrate and a new calendar of saints and devils to revere and hate.

"Their Finest Hour": England's Determination During World War II

By Winston Churchill

After the fall of France during World War II, Britain's Prime Minister Winston Churchill made the following famous speech to the House of Commons on June 18, 1940. In the speech, which was later broadcast to the nation, he reviewed one by one the strengths of the army, navy, and air force, concluding that British military strength, with help from the Dominion, was adequate to meet Hitler's aggression. He reminded his audiences of the stakes involved and hoped that history one day would say of the nation, "This was their finest hour." Winston Churchill was prime minister from 1940 to 1945 and from 1951 to 1955. He is the author of The Second World War *and winner of the Nobel Prize for literature.*

The disastrous military events which have happened during the past fortnight have not come to me with any sense of surprise. Indeed, I indicated a fortnight ago as clearly as I could to the House that the worst possibilities were open; and I made it perfectly clear then that whatever happened in France would make no difference to the resolve of Britain and the British Empire to fight on, "if necessary for years, if necessary alone." During the last few days we have successfully brought off the great majority of the troops we had on the line of communication in France; and seven-eighths of the troops we have sent to France since the beginning of the war—that is to say, about 350,000 out of 400,000 men—are safely back in this

Excerpted from Winston Churchill's speech before the House of Commons, June 18, 1940.

country. Others are still fighting with the French, and fighting with considerable success in their local encounters against the enemy. We have also brought back a great mass of stores, rifles and munitions of all kinds which had been accumulated in France during the last nine months.

The Strength of the Army

We have, therefore, in this Island today a very large and powerful military force. This force comprises all our best-trained and our finest troops, including scores of thousands of those who have already measured their quality against the Germans and found themselves at no disadvantage. We have under arms at the present time in this Island over a million and a quarter men. Behind these we have the Local Defense Volunteers, numbering half a million, only a portion of whom, however, are yet armed with rifles or other firearms. We have incorporated into our Defense Forces every man for whom we have a weapon. We expect very large additions to our weapons in the near future, and in preparation for this we intend forthwith to call up, drill and train further large numbers. Those who are not called up, or else are employed during the vast business of munitions production in all its branches—and their ramifications are innumerable—will serve their country best by remaining at their ordinary work until they receive their summons. We have also over here Dominions armies. The Canadians had actually landed in France, but have now been safely withdrawn, much disappointed, but in perfect order, with all their artillery and equipment. And these very high-class forces from the Dominions will now take part in the defense of the Mother Country. . . .

The Strength of the Navy

It seems to me that as far as seaborne invasion on a great scale is concerned, we are far more capable of meeting it today than we were at many periods in the last war and during the early months of this war, before our other troops were trained, and while the B.E.F. [British Expeditionary Force] had proceeded abroad. Now, the Navy have never pretended to be able to prevent raids by bodies of 5,000 or 10,000 men flung suddenly across and thrown ashore at several points on the coast some dark night or foggy morning. The efficacy of sea power, especially under modern conditions, depends upon the invading force being of large size.

It has to be of large size, in view of our military strength, to be of any use. If it is of large size, then the Navy have something they can find and meet and, as it were, bite on. Now, we must remember that even five divisions, however lightly equipped, would require 200 to 250 ships, and with modern air reconnaissance and photography it would not be easy to collect such an armada, marshal it, and conduct it across the sea without any powerful naval forces to escort it; and there would be very great possibilities, to put it mildly, that this armada would be intercepted long before it reached the coast, and all the men drowned in the sea or, at the worst blown to pieces with their equipment while they were trying to land. We also have a great system of minefields, recently strongly reinforced, through which we alone know the channels. If the enemy tries to sweep passages through these minefields, it will be the task of the Navy to destroy the mine-sweepers and any other forces employed to protect them. There should be no difficulty in this, owing to our great superiority at sea. . . .

The Strength of the Air Force

This brings me, naturally, to the great question of invasion from the air, and of the impending struggle between the British and German Air Forces. It seems quite clear that no invasion on a scale beyond the capacity of our land forces to crush speedily is likely to take place from the air until our Air Force has been definitely overpowered. In the meantime, there may be raids by parachute troops and attempted descents of airborne soldiers. We should be able to give those gentry a warm reception both in the air and on the ground, if they reach it in any condition to continue the dispute. But the great question is: Can we break Hitler's air weapon? Now, of course, it is a very great pity that we have not got all Air Force at least equal to that of the most powerful enemy within striking distance of these shores. But we have a very powerful Air Force which has proved itself far superior in quality, both in men and in many types of machine, to what we have met so far in the numerous and fierce air battles which have been fought with the Germans. In France, where we were at a considerable disadvantage and lost many machines on the ground when they were standing round the aerodromes, we were accustomed to inflict in the air losses of as much as two and two-and-a-half to one. In the fighting over Dunkirk, which was a sort of no-man's-land, we undoubtedly beat the German Air Force, and

With optimism and determination, Winston Churchill led the British people through the darkest days of World War II.

gained the mastery of the local air, inflicting here a loss of three or four to one day after day. Anyone who looks at the photographs which were published a week or so ago of the re-embarkation, showing the masses of troops assembled on the beach and forming an ideal target for hours at a time, must realize that this re-embarkation would not have been possible unless the enemy had resigned all hope of recovering air superiority at that time and at that place.

In the defense of this Island the advantages to the defenders will be much greater than they were in the fighting around Dunkirk. We hope to improve on the rate of three or four to one which was realized at Dunkirk; and in addition all our injured machines and their crews which get down safely—and, surprisingly, a very great many injured machines and men do get down safely in modern air fighting—all of these will fall, in an attack upon these Islands, on friendly soil and live to fight another day; whereas all the injured enemy machines and their complements will be total losses as far as the war is concerned. . . .

Dangers Ahead, but Hope of Victory

There remains, of course, the danger of bombing attacks, which will certainly be made very soon upon us by the bomber forces of the enemy. It is true that the German bomber force is superior in numbers to ours; but we have a very large bomber force also, which we shall use to strike at military targets in Germany without intermission. I do not at all underrate the severity of the ordeal which lies before us; but I believe our countrymen will show themselves capable of standing up to it, like the brave men of Barcelona, and will be able to stand up to it, and carry on in spite of it, at least as well as any other people in the world. Much will depend upon this; every man and every woman will have the chance to show the finest qualities of their race, and render the highest service to their cause. For all of us, at this time, whatever our sphere, our station, our occupation or our duties, it will be a help to remember the famous lines:

> He nothing common did or mean.
> Upon that memorable scene.

I have thought it right upon this occasion to give the House and the country some indication of the solid, practical grounds upon which we base our inflexible resolve to continue the war. There are a good many people who say, "Never mind. Win or lose, sink or swim, better die than submit to tyranny—and such a tyranny." And I do not dissociate myself from them. But I can assure them that our professional advisers of the three Services unitedly advise that we should carry on the war, and that there are good and reasonable hopes of final victory. We have fully informed and consulted all the self-governing Dominions, these great communities far beyond the oceans who have been built up on our laws and on our civilization, and who are absolutely free to choose their course, but are absolutely devoted to the ancient Motherland, and who feel themselves inspired by the same emotions which lead me to stake our all upon duty and honor. We have fully consulted them, and I have received from their Prime Ministers, Mr. Mackenzie King of Canada, Mr. Menzies of Australia, Mr. Fraser of New Zealand, and General Smuts of South Africa—that wonderful man, with his immense profound mind, and his eye watching from a distance the whole panorama of European affairs—I have received from all these eminent men, who all have Governments behind them elected on wide franchises, who are all there because they represent the will of their people, messages couched in the most moving terms in which they endorse our decision to fight on, and declare themselves ready to share our fortunes and to presevere to the end. That is what we are going to do. . . .

During the first four years of the last war the Allies experienced nothing but disaster and disappointment. That was our constant fear: one blow after another, terrible losses, frightful dangers. Everything miscarried. And yet at the end of those four years the morale of the Allies was higher than that of the Germans, who had moved from one aggressive triumph to another, and who stood everywhere triumphant invaders of the lands into which they had broken. During that war we repeatedly asked ourselves the question: How are we going to win? and no one was able ever to answer it with much precision, until at the end, quite suddenly, quite unexpectedly, our terrible foe collapsed before us, and we were so glutted with victory that in our folly we threw it away. . . .

Much Is at Stake

What General Weygand called the Battle of France is over. I expect that the Battle of Britain is about to begin. Upon this battle depends the survival of Christian civilization. Upon it depends our own British life, and the long continuity of our institutions and our Empire. The whole fury and might of the enemy must very soon be turned on us. Hitler knows that he will have to break us in this Island or lose the war. If we can stand up to him, all Europe may be free and the life of the world may move forward into broad, sunlit uplands. But if we fail, then the whole world, including the United States, including all that we have known and cared for, will sink into the abyss of a new Dark Age made more sinister, and perhaps more protracted, by the lights of perverted science. Let us therefore brace ourselves to our duties, and so bear ourselves that, if the British Empire and its Commonwealth last for a thousand years, men will still say, "This was their finest hour."

World War II

By Robert Edwin Herzstein

Robert Edwin Herzstein explains England's role in World War II. Since England and its allies were unprepared, Hitler easily conquered Poland, Denmark, Norway, France, and other western European nations. Left alone to hold against Hitler, Britain used its fighter planes to defend the homeland and its navy to protect its sea routes. The combined strength of the American and British navies prevailed over the German and Italian armies, but, according to Herzstein, the war left terrible destruction. Robert Edwin Herzstein taught history at the University of South Carolina. He is the author of Adolph Hitler and the German Trauma, 1913–1945 *and* Roosevelt and Hitler: Prelude to War.

Within a month after the German attack on Poland began (September 1, 1939), the Polish armies were encircled and destroyed. Germany held the western half of the defunct republic, and the eastern half was occupied by Russian troops. Hitler hoped at this point, October 6, 1939, to arrange a peace settlement with the French and British, for fighting was almost nonexistent in the west. The Germans behind their vulnerable new "West Wall," the French holding their supposedly impregnable Maginot Line, and the British across the North Sea measured one another carefully. The long and lethal deadlock of trench warfare which so often immobilized armies in World War I had created the belief that a strong defensive position was almost unassailable, and the swift Polish campaign taught the French little about the risks they might run as passive victims of open mobile warfare. For six months the French and British waited, hoping that a sea blockade would weaken Germany and end the war. This was ironic, for in the decade before the outbreak of fighting a French colonel and a British military historian and theoretician had put forth dynamic theories of tank and aerial warfare. The Allies might have made good use of these ideas in 1939. Charles de Gaulle and Basil Liddell-Hart saw the striking offensive capabilities of an independent armored force. They realized that in the next great war the advantage would lie not with the defense, as it apparently had in the war of 1914–1918, but with a daring, mechanized offense. German officers such as General von Manstein and Adolf Hitler himself took advantage of these French and British teachings.

The German Army Attacks

The Germans built up reserves of necessary military commodities. Their chemists had learned how to produce synthetic nitrates, quinine, rubber, and gasoline, and their war strength steadily increased throughout the winter of 1939–1940. On April 9 they struck again, and again they found their chosen opponents unready and distracted. A lightning thrust into Denmark and an air- and sea-borne invasion of Norway delivered these two countries into their power within a few weeks.

One month after the blow at Denmark and Norway they struck France, the Netherlands, Belgium, and Luxembourg (May 10, 1940). Some aid was furnished by spies and German sympathizers within these states, but the victory was achieved primarily by speed, strength, and ruthlessness. Holland was crushed in less than a week, largely by air-borne paratroopers dropped at vital communications centers. The Belgian army, despite the arrival of some French and British support, was split, surrounded, and forced to capitulate on May 28, 1940.

Not strength and swiftness alone, but the inspired use of mechanized divisions as well, explained the German victories. Germany's economy was geared to a lightning, or *Blitzkrieg* campaign. Production quotas were determined on the basis of the needs of the campaign at hand. Although Germany had not yet armed in depth in 1939 and 1940, the adaptability of its war-oriented industries made possible the rapid concentration of certain types of offensive weapons in a crucial area.

The French had prepared for a war of siege and were bewildered by a war of movement. When the famed Maginot Line was outflanked in the Ardennes area between May 10 and May 22 and an army of giant tanks and mechanized infantry crossed the Meuse River to sweep across northern France on their way to the French channel ports, the Allied forces in northeastern France and Belgium were trapped. At this point, General Maxime

Weygand became commander-in-chief of the French forces, and the fabled hero of Verdun, Marshal Henri-Philippe Pétain, entered the government as vice-premier. Neither Weygand nor Pétain was able to halt the Nazi tide. Uncertain which way the German columns would turn, outfought, outgeneraled, and broken in morale, several Allied armies in the northeast found themselves cut off from France's remaining forces. The Germans sliced through France, speeding down the Somme Valley to the sea. With Belgium isolated and conquered and communications with Paris cut, the British Expeditionary Force recoiled upon Dunkirk on the North Sea coast. All heavy equipment had to be abandoned, but most of the men were saved by a mass evacuation completed June 4. For the shattered French divisions, however, no line of escape was open. On June 10, one month after the German drive had commenced in the west, Italy declared war and invaded southern France. On June 17 the French high command asked for an armistice, and on June 25 the fighting ceased. Two-thirds of France was held by the Germans.

Britain Left Alone to Defend Against Hitler

By the end of June 1940, Great Britain stood alone against a continent where Hitler was master. Not since Napoleon's day had one despot controlled such a wide European empire or commanded such awesome military superiority. Continental seacoast, harbors, and bases from Norway to Spain were in German hands. Gibraltar might be assailed from the rear with Spanish collaboration. Italy threatened the Mediterranean sea routes; Italian armies in Libya and Ethiopia were preparing to invade Egypt, close the Suez Canal, and even attack Aden. The threat to British supply routes to London, Southampton, Liverpool, and Glasgow was more immediate and dangerous, for German air power might block the shipping lanes. Even if ships could get through, supplies might run out. The Scandinavian countries, the Netherlands, France, and French North Africa had provided three-fourths of Britain's imports of iron ore and paper, from half to three-fourths of the butter and eggs, and a major proportion of other vital commodities. With the Germans controlling the sources of these items, the British had to look abroad and provide ships for the long haul from Canada, the United States, South America, and Australia. In World War I, German U-boats had cut British shipping and imports to a margin so narrow that in 1917 only a six weeks' supply of food and raw materials remained in reserve. With many more strategic harbors available for submarines and surface raiders, and with advanced bases and fields for aerial attack and reconnaissance, it seemed almost certain that Hitler would isolate, cripple, and starve Britain where [Emperor of Germany] Kaiser William II had failed.

It had taken the Germans only four weeks to crush Poland, a state of 34 million people. They overcame the resistance of Norway, Denmark, the Netherlands, Belgium, and France, with a combined population exceeding 60 million, in eight weeks. Could Great Britain, alone and vulnerable, expect to survive? The British themselves did not know the answer, but they faced the emergency with extraordinary courage and confidence. On May 10, 1940, the day the Netherlands and Belgium were attacked, the Chamberlain ministry resigned, and the energetic Winston Churchill became prime minister of a coalition war cabinet. Under his forceful and inspiring leadership the British prepared to fight for their national existence.

British Advantages

Three circumstances favored the British defense. In the first place, the Germans were not prepared to attempt an immediate invasion of the British Isles at the most favorable moment, after France fell. The suddenness of their success threw their armies out of gait. They had prepared for land, not for naval or amphibious, operations, and they could not cross the English Channel while the British fleet remained intact. Second, the Germans' submarine fleet was limited, and they were unable to open at once the ruinous undersea warfare against British shipping for which, ironically, they now possessed superfluous bases. Third, German air power, still superior to all opposition, had been developed primarily to operate in combination with the ground forces and functioned less effectively when used as an independent arm of attack. The British, on the other hand, though late in arming, had since 1938 specialized in fighter planes which could close swiftly with the German bombers when the latter were far from their bases and lacked a defensive escort.

Adolf Hitler once said, "On the land I am a hero, on the sea a coward." He also had little appreciation of the needs of modern aerial warfare. Neither [German military leader Hermann

London endured heavy bombing and widespread death and destruction at the hands of the Germans.

Wilhelm] Goering nor Hitler consistently pursued one single aim in the Battle of Britain. The decision to bombard British industries and cities came about in part because of Hitler's rage over minor British bombardments of a few German towns.

In ten weeks the attackers lost nearly twenty-four hundred aircraft to the defenders' eight hundred. British Spitfire and Hurricane fighters, directed by secret methods of detection and communication, provided an answer to German mass bombing. After October 1940 the German fighter and anti-radar attacks weakened, and winter skies and cloudy weather helped to shroud the stricken land. Britain survived, but at the cost of many gallant pilots, thousands of civilian casualties, and the damage or destruction of one British home in five.

Britain Protects Sea Routes

World War II was a historic example of a struggle between land power and sea power, for Britain and the United States [America entered World War II in December 1941] maintained control of most of the ocean routes, while German and Italian forces were limited more and more inexorably to the land. Whenever they crossed salt water, the Axis [Germany, Japan, Italy, and Germany's eastern European satellites] armies exposed their supply lines to attack. The fact dictated British and, later, Anglo-American strategy. The weakest sectors of the German-Italian battlefront were those held by the Italian troops in Libya and Ethiopia. Second were the Italian islands in the Mediterranean, Sicily and Sardinia, which had likewise to be supplied by ship. Third was the Italian peninsula, for Italy ordinarily imported oil, coal, and wheat by sea, and the long coastline was vulnerable to naval invasion in war. These three concentric and exposed zones were assailed in turn by the British and Allied forces.

The Germans, Italians, and Japanese were not wholly deficient in sea power. Germany could control the Baltic Sea and part of the North Sea; Italy could interrupt the shipping lanes in the Mediterranean; Japan dominated the coastal routes of the Far East to the East Indies. But none of these powers depended for its day-to-day existence, as Great Britain did, on keeping the high seas open. Japan did not attack British positions in the Far East until early in 1942, by which time Germany's great opportunity of 1940 had long since passed. The Axis was a false alliance, containing little trust and less joint planning.

To deal British trade and prestige a deadly blow, an enemy had only to close some of the bottlenecks. The straits of Dover, Gibraltar, Suez, Aden, or Singapore under hostile guns would seriously dislocate British naval power and commercial economy. German planes, submarines, and long-range cannon might seal the English Channel. A thrust through Spain (with or without the consent of the Nationalist regime the Axis nations had helped into power there) might close the Straits of Gibraltar. Pantelleria, a small island between Sicily and Tunisia, had been heavily fortified by the Italians to bisect the Mediterranean, and an attack upon Egypt and Aden from the new Italian conquest, Ethiopia, might close both ends of the Red Sea. Finally, a Japanese descent upon Singapore would curtail sea traffic to the Far East and cut off China. But Japan was not at war with Britain until the end of 1941.

When the fall of France placed continental Europe under German control, the British cabinet did not hesitate, in the midst of the Battle of Britain, to ship an armored division all the way around Africa to reinforce the defenses of the Suez Canal. The spring of 1941 found British expeditionary forces pressing a steady campaign against the Italian East African empire. No longer able to supply the army marooned in Ethiopia, because the British were astride the communication route through Suez, Mussolini saw his proud conquest crumble. Eritrea, Italian Somaliland, and Ethiopia fell before British attacks between March and May 1941. An Italian attempt to reach Egypt through Libya in 1940 was hurled back. Renewed with German aid in 1941, it was repulsed a second time. The difficulty of supplying their African forces across the mid-Mediterranean helped to explain these Axis failures, and in April 1941 the Germans drove at Suez more directly. Pressing into the Balkans, they overran Yugoslavia and Greece and seized the island of Crete with air-borne divisions (April–May 1941).

Meanwhile, the British, to forestall a land drive through Constantinople and Turkey and so to Suez, occupied French Syria, Iraq, and Iran (May–September 1941). Sea power had once more frustrated land and air power, and air attack failed to redress the balance. Though the Germans had dispatched their specially trained and equipped Afrika Korps to Libya and the British were driven back almost to the gates of Alexandria, the outcome was delayed, not averted. At El Alamein in October 1942 the British under [Bernard L.] Montgomery defeated the Germans and Italians under [Erwin] Rommel. The Axis forces fell back upon French Tunis, where they confronted the additional Allied forces that had landed in Algeria and Morocco in November. In May 1943, the last German resistance in Tunisia collapsed. Allied forces controlled all Africa, and the Mediterranean was reopened to their shipping. The slow but relentless pressure of sea power was turning the scale, and German and Italian forces were confined thenceforth to "Fortress Europe." . . .

The End of the War and Its Destruction Assessed

The German surrender on May 7, 1945, ended hostilities in Europe and left the British and American governments free to concentrate their forces in the Pacific. British, American, and Chinese divisions had destroyed three Japanese armies in Burma by May 5. By June, United States forces, in desperate fighting, captured Okinawa, providing bombing planes with a base 325 miles from Japan.

Japan's morale was already weakening when three terrible

blows ended its will to resist. On August 6, 1945, a single atomic bomb, secretly prepared by Allied scientists, was dropped on Hiroshima, destroying three-fifths of the city. On August 8, Soviet Russia declared war on Japan, as it had agreed to do at the three-power Yalta Conference earlier in the year, and commenced a powerful invasion of Manchuria. On August 9, a second atomic bomb leveled Nagasaki. The Japanese cabinet decided to abandon the struggle and capitulated on August 14. United States forces landed in Japan two weeks later, and formal terms of surrender were signed at Tokyo on September 2.

The war that raged from September 1939 to August 1945 wrought such tragic destruction of lives and property that cold statistics cannot begin to convey its impact. Fifty-seven nations became engaged in the struggle, and their armed forces at peak strength exceeded 90 million. Six years of fighting caused the deaths of an estimated 15 million soldiers, sailors, and airmen. But death also struck behind the firing lines. Long-range bombing planes devastated inland cities. Of the millions of workers conscripted by Germany from conquered countries, many died as pawns in the lethal conflict. More millions died or were put to death in concentration camps, including 6 million Jews murdered by the Nazis. The number of civilian deaths resulting from the war cannot be estimated with any accuracy; it probably surpassed the military fatalities, raising the total number of deaths to more than 50 million.

World War II not only lasted longer and ranged more widely than World War I; it also destroyed four times as many lives and ten times as much wealth. Military expenditures by the combatant governments and property damage resulting from the hostilities were calculated when the fighting ceased at $1,500 billion. Spent wisely, such a sum could have provided housing, schools, and hospitals for a quarter of the world's population, a comparison that suggests the magnitude of the tangible wealth sacrified.

But there were also intangible costs. In peace, according to an ancient saying, sons bury their fathers; in war fathers bury their sons. There were the canceled hopes of 50 million people, many of them young, who died prematurely and unnecessarily. There was the grief of parents, widows, and children. There was a weakened reverence for the sanctity of human life and for human decency and dignity. These are values that cannot be calculated and losses that cannot be measured.

THE HISTORY OF NATIONS

Chapter 6

Recent Challenges

England's Domestic Agenda

By Tony Blair

Tony Blair has been the prime minister of Britain since 1997 when, as the Labor Party candidate, he took over the government after many years of conservative rule. In the following excerpts from a speech delivered in February 2001 at the beginning of his second term, he cites the accomplishments of the Labor government during his first term, the problems that remain to be solved, and his plans to solve them. Blair focuses on the need for greater employment opportunities for middle- and lower-income families. He cites the need for more health care workers and police, improvements in education, and reform of the criminal justice system. Blair was a lawyer, a member of Parliament, and leader of the Labor Party before becoming prime minister.

There are still big challenges ahead before this country has a dynamic economy, first-class public services, safe streets and decent communities. Life is a real struggle for many people, uncertain, insecure and under constant pressure, and that goes for middle class as well as lower income families. We as a government should acknowledge this openly. Even though we are proud of our record, we are not entitled to claim the job is done. What we are entitled to claim is we have made a good start.

Even if manufacturing has been through tough times, the economy is stable, inflation is the lowest in Europe and interest rates are half of what they were in the 1980s and 1990s. Primary schools have seen a change in results. Though violent crime is still rising, overall crime is down. Even if three million children still live in poverty, that is a million fewer than in May 1997 thanks to the measures that have been put in place. Even with the fuel duty rising, taxes overall are still well below our main Euro-

Excerpted from Tony Blair's speech to the people of the United Kingdom, February 8, 2001.

pean Union competitors and living standards are up over 10% from four years ago. . . .

Issues Relating to Middle- and Lower-Income Families

As a nation, we are wasting too much of the talents of too many of the people. The mission of any second term must be this: to break down the barriers that hold people back, to create real upward mobility, a society that is open and genuinely based on merit and the equal worth of all. To build on solid economic foundations a decent education for all and a criminal justice system modernized so that it targets the hard-core criminal.

Such a society can only be based on a radical extension of opportunity, matched by a true sense of responsibility. The talent of the people has to be set free, not from the 1980s problems of too much state interference, but from problems [former Prime Minister Margaret] Thatcher failed to tackle. These include the bonds of second-rate jobs and poor rewards for middle and lower income families, insufficient reach of the new technology to all parts of the country, regional industrial decline, broken down communities.

These barriers hold people back. These are the things we have only made a start in improving. Their removal is the only way of clearing the path to a society in which everyone, not just a few, get the chance to succeed. But none of it can happen without us choosing as a nation to make it happen. The foundations of a strong economy have been put in place as a result of the choices we have made. Britain is now getting its economic confidence back.

We have built the foundations for full employment with the success of the New Deal and our welfare reforms. Today there are one million more jobs and unemployment has fallen significantly in all parts of the country. Youth unemployment is down by over 80%. People who had no reason to get up in the morning can now earn a living. But we had to levy the windfall tax on the privatized utilities to get it. In the last four years, we have shown that school standards can improve. Infant class sizes have fallen sharply. Primary schools' results are up dramatically thanks to teachers embracing the literacy and numeric strategies. The latest Ofsted report shows that more than eight out of ten schools are improving their teaching. Numerous school refurbishment projects have been funded. There are 7,000 more than in 1998 and more than 2,000 more teacher trainees than this time last year.

Progress in Health Care and Crime Fighting

The first proper regime of inspection and national standards are in place. Both inpatient and outpatient waiting lists are being brought down. The average wait for inpatient treatment is now less than three months, although far too many still wait too long. There are 16,000 new nurses and nearly 5,000 more doctors. We are creating new medical schools and recruiting another 20,000 nurses as part of the NHS [National Health Service] Plan. There are 33 major hospital developments underway in England alone and five are already open. We have new services and faster treatment for cancer services, but there is still much more that will go into producing first class health service.

Crime is down 10% since 1997. Domestic burglary is down 21%. But violent crime is still rising and that is the next big challenge. We have invested in big crime reduction plans throughout the country. Police numbers have been on a downward trend since 1993. Now, as a result of new investment the number is rising. Our new crime-fighting fund has provided resources for another 9,000 additional police recruits. We have laid the foundations of a new constitution that include a Scottish parliament, a national assembly in Wales, an assembly in Northern Ireland and a mayor for London. We are also working to strengthen Europe's defense within NATO. . . .

I believe we have laid the foundations for a fairer society that extends opportunity and lifts people out of poverty.

Those are the foundations. Now we have to make the next steps based on new choices and challenges. Though hardened by the setbacks of government, though more realistic about how long it takes to change big institutions, we remain bold in our ambitions for the country. Ambitious to rise to new challenges like how we spread prosperity to all parts of Britain and harness new technology, how we invest and reform public services so they become dynamic and responsive to the needs of the public, how we build a welfare state based on work for those who can and security for those who can't.

We will set a new policy agenda that includes the ways in which we intend to meet these challenges. Our two main focuses are education and crime. These follow on from the health and transport plans last year and will mean that in the four main public service areas we will have carefully worked-out strategies over

RECOGNITION OF THE PUBLIC SECTOR

At a time when successful business leaders are most admired, Jackie Ashley urges the government to recognize the value of public workers who manage schools, hospitals, and the rail service.

Sometimes, the best people to run things—schools, hospitals, even rail services—are the people who have spent a lifetime doing just that, but who need more encouragement, more money, training and freedom to do better. The public services are still full of intelligent, hard-working and often idealistic people who aren't chasing a big home and a BMW as the most important things in life. The hurt of public sector unions is not always prejudice; it is often a cool recognition of how things really are.

One of the biggest questions for the second term is the extent to which the government recognises that, in the end, business should get on with its business, and the public sector continue to be an independent, self-confident zone of public life—reformed, outward-looking, but not constantly denigrated as second best to the real heroes, the entrepreneurs. The ministers at the sharp end know this in their hearts. There are many former teachers, lecturers, local government officers and health service employees in the new government, and now is their moment. They must, for the sake of the country as well as the Labour Party, stand up for the honour and reputation of public service against the naive post-Thatcher belief that business techniques are the answer to everything.

Jackie Ashley, "Stand Up for the Public Sector," *New Statesman (1996)*. 130(June 25, 2001): 8.

the next few years. The education plan will cover forward education policy and in particular signal an overhaul of the comprehensive system. A crime plan will include reforms of every aspect of the criminal justice system. A document on industrial policy and the knowledge economy will outline how we will empower people to cope with change and spread prosperity to every region and community in Britain. The budget will then set out the next economic and fiscal steps in our program of economic change.

In the next five years, we are going to more than double the number of specialist schools to 1500. We will offer schools three new specialisms: engineering, science, business and enterprise. The business and enterprise schools will develop strong business and entrepreneurial links and encourage many more to enter the fields of business and industry. I want to see more, not less, partnership between public and private sectors in the provision of public services.

For all the talk of an enterprise culture, we are still a long way from getting there. We need to reform radically not just the relationship between business and government but how we encourage small businesses and how taxation affects the business environment. And I do not believe we can carry on with a criminal justice system that is often, despite the hard work of those that operate it, uncoordinated, ineffective and hopelessly out of date.

Two Themes: Opportunity and Responsibility

Two themes run through this entire agenda: opportunity and responsibility. Both are about people and their individual development and potential. Human capital is the key to economic advancement in a knowledgeable economy. Individual responsibility is the key to social order. Both depend on developing the full potential of all people to provide a more mobile society and a more flexible economy.

Opening up economy and society to merit and talent is the true radical second term agenda. In the past, the idea of meritocracy has been attacked. But creating a society that is meritocratic is not wrong; it is insufficient. It needs to recognize talent in all its forms, not just intelligence. And it needs to be coupled with a platform that recognizes the equal worth of all our citizens.

But breaking down the barriers to success and allowing

people's innate ability to shine through is an indispensable part of building a decent and prosperous country. It cannot be achieved with the government standing back and allowing a Darwinian survival of the fittest. It requires an active government ensuring a fair playing field and investing in our people and in our public services to release the potential of all.

How far we are from a society of true equal opportunity, is a measure of how far a radical New Labor Government has to go. The foundations are laid. The land of opportunity is not yet built. But I am more certain now than in May 1997, it can and it will be.

The Changing Power of the British State

By Martin Walker

One of Tony Blair's reforms as prime minister has been the decentralization of power in Great Britain. Martin Walker reviews the recent devolution of power to Scotland and Wales and the sovereignty already relinquished to the European Union. The major issue confronting Blair, according to Walker, is if and when Britain will give up its pound currency and adopt the euro, the currency of the European Union. Walker is former bureau chief for the Guardian *newspaper in Moscow, Washington, and Brussels. He is the author of* America Reborn: A Twentieth-Century Narrative in Twenty-Six Lives *and the novel* The Caves of Perigord.

Tony Blair is dismantling the British state as it has existed since the 18th century. Is his new Britain a fair trade for the old? . . .

Blair's second election victory was far from impressive. He won just 40.8 percent of the vote, but thanks to Britain's winner-take-all electoral system, his party secured nearly twice as many seats in Parliament as the Conservatives and Liberal-Democrats combined, even though their total share of the vote was just over 50 percent. The unusually low turnout of voters (below 60 percent) reflected a widespread political apathy; Blair won the support of only one potential voter in four, well below the 32 percent of the potential vote that Margaret Thatcher won in her 1983 landslide. These are dismal figures, and a far less imposing mandate than the commanding masses of Labor members of Parliament would suggest.

Yet Blair relies on this dubious mandate for the fulfillment of his grand project to modernize Britain. . . .

The signal commitment of Blair's second term is to offer all the English regions a referendum on whether they want to follow the example of Scotland and Wales and have their own elected assemblies. They are to be offered powers over transportation policies, including those for roads, airports, and public transportation; over land use and development planning; and over economic development, with a yet-to-be-defined authority to raise taxes for local investments. The formal proposal is still being drafted at this writing, but rough calculations suggest that the national government, which currently spends some 40 percent of GDP, will surrender a 2.5 to 5 percent share of GDP to the new regional assemblies.

Past Changes in Regional Power

Blair is not proposing simply to turn back the clock to the pre-Thatcher years [Margaret Thatcher was prime minister from 1979–1990]. The English provinces have not enjoyed powers such as these since the great days of Victorian Britain, when the flourishing industrial cities of the north built their palatial town halls, when Glasgow and Manchester vied for the title of second city of the empire, and when to be lord mayor of Birmingham was to aspire, like [politician] Joseph Chamberlain, to be prime minister and to raise a grand political dynasty. The provincial powers were eroded, first, by the pre-1914 welfare state, with its high taxes to finance old-age pensions and unemployment insurance, and then by the extraordinary centralizing effect of two world wars. To begin redressing the balance of power from London to the regions is to reverse what seemed an implacable trend of the 20th century. But to return the powers of self-government and home rule to Scotland and Wales, with even the limited powers to tax so far entrusted to the Scottish Assembly, is to begin dismantling the British state as it has existed since the dawn of the 18th century.

In her groundbreaking book *Britons* (1992), the historian Linda Colley analyzes the way that a new, militant, Protestant British patriotism was deliberately forged in the 18th century after the 1707 Act of Union with Scotland. She suggests that the current processes of democratic devolution reflect the way that "God has ceased to be British and Providence no longer smiles. . . . Whether Great Britain will break down into separate Welsh, Scottish, and English states or whether, as is more likely, a more federal Britain will emerge as part of an increasingly federal Europe, remains to be seen. What seems indisputable is that a substantial rethinking of what it means to be British can no longer be evaded."

Britain's Relations with Europe

Blair made it known that he had read Colley's book with profit and attention. He shares her view that almost every question about the future of Britain hinges on the development of its relations with Europe. Europe—or, rather, the backlash within the Conservative Party against her anti-Europe campaigns—destroyed the political career of Margaret Thatcher. Divisions over Europe then broke the government of her successor, John Major. The British Parliament has already surrendered a great deal of its sovereignty, including the power to legislate, to European institutions. The European Court of Justice is, for most practical purposes, Britain's Supreme Court. Having deliberately avoided a written constitution for centuries, Britain has now incorporated the European Charter of Human Rights into the national law. British foreign policy, accustomed since 1941 to functioning within the context of the transatlantic alliance, has now also to accommodate the constraints of Europe's new Common Foreign and Security Policy.

The great political question of the next five years of Blair's government is whether Britain, by embracing the euro [the new currency of the European Union], will go on to surrender its sovereignty over the economy and entrust to the European Central Bank the power to set interest rates and determine the money supply. The powers to declare war and peace and to regulate the coinage have traditionally defined sovereignty. The process of European integration is now far enough advanced to have encroached mightily on both.

A Referendum on the Euro

Blair has promised a referendum within the next two years on whether to abandon the pound and adopt the euro. He suggests that the choice should be made essentially on the economic merits of the case. But the arguments cut both ways. The British economy has done remarkably well of late while remaining outside the euro zone; that the new currency, as managed by the European Central Bank, has lost some 30 percent of its value against the dollar over the past 18 months is hardly reassuring. And yet,

60 percent of British exports now go to the other 14 members of the European Union. The Union's imminent enlargement to some 26 or more members through the incorporation of Central and Eastern Europe will create a single market of 520 million consumers in the world's largest economic bloc. That adds to the attraction of the euro, and to the suspicion that the impending change may represent an opportunity Britain cannot afford to miss.

But to couch the argument solely in economic terms is willfully to miss the point, and Blair is suspected of doing so because he remains so nervous about the constitutional questions. By forcing a resolution, the referendum on the euro will end half a century of vacillation over Europe. It is not a choice Britain relishes having to make. The referendum is also an intensely high-risk course for Blair to adopt, since opinion polls show a consistent majority of two to one against the euro. Blair knows that he is playing with psychological fire: The British nation's identity was born in opposition to Europe. The most treasured national myths, from the defeat of the Spanish Armada in 1588 to the defiance of Hitler in 1940, from "Britannia Rules the Waves" to the "Thin Red Line," celebrate achievements against other European powers. Building a worldwide empire was itself an act of turning the national back on Europe. The wider world beyond Europe still beckons, and the instinctive sense that Britain has more in common with its reliable American ally remains strong.

Still, given Blair's political skills and his gift for careful preparation, only the boldest pundit would bet against his success. The opinion polls suggest that almost as large a majority thinks adopting the euro to be inevitable as says it intends to vote no. Scare stories quote foreign businessmen warning that Japanese and American investments will shun an isolated Britain. At London dinner tables there is endless gossip about the deals Blair will make, from backing Rupert Murdoch's expansion into lucrative European broadcasting to privatizing the BBC [British Broadcasting Corporation] to secure the support of media barons. Opponents warn darkly of the vast sums the City of London and French and German corporations are prepared to pour into pro-euro propaganda. American diplomats in the salons and on talk shows argue that a Britain fully engaged in a united Europe will have far more influence in Washington than an isolated offshore island ever could.

The role of the powerful Chancellor of the Exchequer, Gordon Brown, is much debated. He is credited with checking Blair's instinct to hold the referendum on the euro back in the prime minister's first honeymoon period, in 1997, and his ambition to succeed Blair burns hot to the touch. Blair's own ambitions, given that he is a young 50, provoke intense speculation. Some claim to have heard Bill Clinton's private prediction that Blair will step down after winning the referendum and go to Brussels to replace Romano Prodi as president of the European Commission. A victory on the euro would be a nice prize to bring along. Others close to Blair say he intends to match Thatcher by winning a third election. Nobody really knows, which is half the fun. The next two years of British politics promise to be riveting psychodrama, a feverish prologue to the historic referendum.

Thatcher vs. Blair on Modern Britain

The referendum campaign will also see a personal duel between the two most gifted and compelling British politicians of the last half-century, Thatcher and Blair, a battle without quarter between the two great modernizers of the British state. It promises to be an almost oedipal encounter, between the woman who restored the national fortunes and the national pride, and the heir who knew what he wanted to do with the transformed nation she had bequeathed him. Blair's twin projects, to decentralize Britain and to Europeanize it, are anathema to Thatcher. Yet the striking feature of the past 20 years in Britain is how much the Thatcher-Blair years dovetail into each other and become a single tumultuous period of wholesale change that has swept aside the old postwar Britain of welfare state and decolonization, "One Nation" and creeping decline.

Britain is not just a different country now; it is three or four or five different countries. Scotland and Wales have become far more than nostalgic names on maps, and provincial England is poised to follow their path toward home rule. London, with its elected mayor, has become one of the great city-states of the global economy.

Foreign Policy for a New Era

By *Newsweek*

Since the terrorist attacks on America, Prime Minister Tony Blair has articulated a vision of foreign policy based on the idea of international community achieved through a combination of pragmatic strategy and humanitarian effort. According to the editors of Newsweek, *this vision first began to evolve during the NATO intervention in Kosovo in 1999, in which the threat of greater military force was used to achieve peace. Following September 11, Blair used diplomacy to garner international support for the war against terror while also calling for a humanitarian effort to rebuild war-torn Afghanistan.*

With the military campaign in Afghanistan going well, Blair's mind is on the aftermath.[1] Magnanimity in victory, he explains, requires us to do more than roust out terrorism. We must help make right a decade of Western neglect and heedlessness and rebuild a failed state. Afghanistan deserves what he calls a "fresh start," not only because that's the right thing to do but because it's in our own self-interest. "I know some people think this is a utopian idea," says Blair. "But I actually find it pretty much realpolitik, from where I'm sitting anyway."

Blair's Vision Breaks with Tradition

There you have it, vague as it may sound. The Blair Doctrine. It's impossible to imagine any other contemporary European statesman arguing for such a missionary foreign policy. It's nearly as hard to imagine Britain doing it, at least before Blair. His brand of prag-

1. In October 2001, a U.S.-led military effort began against the Al Qaeda terrorist group and the Taliban government of Afghanistan in retaliation for the September 11 attacks on America. By the end of the year, the United States had achieved victory over Al Qaeda and the Taliban in Afghanistan.

matic moralism represents such a radical break from tradition as to amount, almost, to a revolution—a vision of a new world order that couples Thatcherite toughness [referring to the conservative former prime minister Margaret Thatcher] with the moral values of Christian socialism. However improbably, Blair has his own [liberal] Labour Party embracing the use of military might—and his conservative rivals accepting humanitarian intervention.

When it comes to translating vision into reality, Britain's peripatetic prime minister is in a pretty good place these days. George W. Bush may be commander in chief of the military campaign in Afghanistan. But Blair is its evangelist in chief. His indefatigable globe-trotting diplomacy has united an impressively broad coalition behind the war. Of any leader, Blair has been by far the most articulate and persuasive in explaining and justifying the war, not only to the West but to the rest of the world as well. And now he is stumping just as hard for the nation-building and Marshall Plan–like reconstruction that he believes must follow. [The Marshall Plan was George C. Marshall's program for rebuilding Europe after World War II.]. . .

He has grown to become a force in his own right, part conscience of the West but more important a pragmatic exponent of a new globalized, post–cold-war world order. That's what he means when he speaks of September 11—a "cruelty beyond our comprehension"—as a turning point. Blair is more than a voice for just wars and humanitarian interventionism, as he was in Bosnia and Kosovo and Sierra Leone. These days, he is pioneering nothing less than a wholesale rethink about international relations and the meaning of national interests. For Blair, the world is a community, where problems even in a faraway place like Afghanistan can abruptly become your own. If recent events have proved anything, says Peter Mandelson, a member of Parliament and a close friend of Blair's, it's that "we cannot isolate risks or instability." Foreign Secretary Jack Straw puts it another way. "Terrorists are strongest where states are weakest," he says, making the case for nation-building in Afghanistan—and setting the stage for a challenge that could be harder to pull off than the war. . . .

The Importance of Humanitarian Intervention

Blair has always been in the vanguard of humanitarian interventionism. In 1999, still relatively new to his job, Blair alone among

19 NATO leaders pushed hard to plan for a ground war in Kosovo, even before the bombing campaign began.[2] He pushed so hard, in fact, that at one point his friend Bill Clinton bluntly told him to back off, believing any such move would be political poison. (Clinton, of course, had had the experience of having 18 of his troops killed in action in Somalia—an ignominy that Blair has yet to live through.) Yet it was Blair who almost singlehandedly got NATO to change its losing tactics in the Kosovo air war. Flying to Washington on the eve of the alliance's 50th anniversary, he convinced Clinton during a private dinner that the war could not be confined to high-altitude bombing in Kosovo, that it had to be carried to Belgrade if it were not to be lost. The White House was reluctant—but just weeks later Slobodan Milosevic capitulated. . . .

Amid speculation in the press that U.S. troops in Afghanistan weren't going to hang around for peacekeeping or humanitarian purposes, it was a clear signal that Britain was gearing up for the long haul, in contrast to the United States. Blair denied the subsequent round of stories about a "rift" between Washington and London. But the fact remains that he is ahead of the Bush administration in important ways.

To cite but a few: ever since the first week in October 2001 Blair's war team has been warning Washington, to little avail, that the coalition needed to downsize the role of the Northern Alliance in any future Afghan government. Sensitive to the need to publicize evidence against Osama bin Laden [the leader of Al Qaeda], Blair had his staff prepare what amounted to an indictment, presented it to Parliament and put it on the Internet. The Bush administration has not shown much of an appetite for nation-building. The British, on the other hand, as early as Oct. 10 briefed reporters on a massive reconstruction plan that would take five to 10 years and cost at least $20 billion.

The Importance of Community

Where does that world view come from? As he describes it, Kosovo was the crucible. Ever the perpetual student, Blair then devoured books about the benighted Balkans, just as he now de-

2. In 1999 hostilities intensified between ethnic Albanians, who sought an independent Kosovo, and Serbians led by Slobodan Milosevic. A NATO bombing campaign eventually forced the Serbs to retreat.

vours the Quran and writings about Afghanistan. "Kosovo was very, very important to me," he says. "I was absolutely convinced that unless we sorted it out, we were going to have huge problems in Europe." He said as much in a groundbreaking address delivered on April 22, 1999, in Chicago, titled "The Doctrine of International Community." He had written the talk on the flight to America with a small group of advisers. One, David Milliband, remembers: "That was the first time he articulated the idea of community—and that foreign policy and domestic policy cannot be put in separate boxes." We can't turn our backs on conflicts and human-rights violations in other countries, Blair said. We need a new framework in which to consider the new, borderless world: "Just as within domestic politics, the notion of community—the belief that partnership and cooperation are essential to the advancement of self-interest—is coming into its own; so it needs to find its international echo."

Even then, the brave new world Blair envisioned was taking human shape. With his wife, Cherie, he would soon visit Macedonia, teeming with Muslim refugees whom most of the rest of the world watched on television. He was shaken by what he saw and heard; Cherie was in tears. Flying on to Bucharest, Blair raged in a speech to the Romanian Parliament: "I felt an anger so strong, a loathing of what Milosevic stands for so powerful, that I pledged to [those refugees], as I pledge to you now, that Milosevic and his hideous racial genocide will be defeated."

A switch had been turned on in Blair that would not easily be turned off, not least because such issues resonate so deeply with Blair's innermost and longstanding personal convictions. His doctrine of international community grew out of Blair's Oxford days, and his exposure to the works of a Scottish philosopher named John Macmurray. Macmurray postulated that the individual was defined by his relationship to the community—inverting [economist] Adam Smith's precept that people acting out of self-interest ultimately benefit society as a whole. . . .

Perhaps a Vision Whose Time Has Come

Blair's "not a philosopher," notes his biographer John Rentoul. He may speak (and act) out of conviction, but his policies (and politics) are well grounded in pragmatism—"what works," as Blair himself puts it. NATO vs. Milosevic worked, he says, and not just because the allies were in the right. Victory was won in Kosovo because of its strategy and tactics, bringing the air war to Belgrade and signaling that NATO was prepared to send in ground troops. He was "absolutely right to push for a ground-troops plan. If we had had one sooner, Milosevic would have given in sooner," says a senior British military commander. Says Blair himself: "A lot of people thought that I took a far too forward position on Kosovo. I believe [mine] was the right assessment."

Blair brings the same certitude to the war on terror. Returning from his first visit to New York and Washington after September 11, Blair delivered yet another speech, this time to his party faithful. "Understand what we are dealing with," he said of bin Laden and Al Qaeda. "Listen to the calls of those passengers on the planes. Think of the children, told they were going to die. Think of the screams and the anguish of the innocent as those hijackers drove at full throttle planes laden with fuel into buildings where tens of thousands worked. If they could have murdered not 7,000 but 70,000, does anyone doubt they would have rejoiced? There is no compromise possible with such people, no meeting of minds. Just a choice: defeat it or be defeated by it. We can't do it all. Neither can the Americans. But the international community could, together, if it chose to."

The rhetoric struck some as extravagant. "Totally over the top," says one Tory M.P. [member of Parliament] But even he, a member of the shadow cabinet, applauds Blair's conduct in the war on terror—and supports "in principle" the prime minister's vision of the international community as a force for good. That admirable comity may not last, but it speaks to the power of Blair's vision—and suggests that it may indeed be a vision whose time has come.

Hope for the Irish Peace Process

By Brian Lennon

Achieving peace in Northern Ireland is still a challenge for both the British and the Irish, but the Good Friday agreement signed in 1998 has made progress possible. Brian Lennon describes the Good Friday agreement and assesses recent changes by the Protestant Unionists and the Catholic Republicans. The Republicans have started decommissioning weapons, the Unionists have agreed to sit on the Police Board, and both sides are occasionally talking face to face. Brian Lennon works with Community Dialogue in Northern Ireland. He is the author of Catholics and the Future of Northern Ireland.

As part of an ecumenical group from Northern Ireland, I visited San Francisco about 10 years ago. After we had made a presentation, a young man asked why I was so opposed to the violence being committed by the Irish Republican Army. I repeated the arguments I had given in my talk: that violence in our context was morally wrong, that murdering policemen in Northern Ireland would do nothing to persuade the British to withdraw but would increase divisions between Catholics and Protestants and that violence destroyed the moral fabric of the Catholic community. Further, after more than 400 years living on the island (longer than whites have been in America), perhaps Unionists had a right to live in Ireland, and since both the United Kingdom and Ireland had joined the European Community in 1973, talk of independent states in Europe was somewhat anachronistic. At the end of the conversation the young man said, "Well, I will continue to do my bit to support the struggle."

At the time I was furious. I wanted him to meet the relatives of those who had been murdered. I wanted him to know their

Excerpted from "Is the End Near in Northern Ireland?" by Brian Lennon, *America*, December 3, 2001.

suffering. I wanted him to realize that while it takes a millisecond to kill somebody, it takes years and often generations to deal with the aftermath. Had I met the young man after Sept. 11, his response might have been different.

The Sept. 11 attack was shocking. It came shortly after three members of Sinn Fein [a Nationalist party] had been arrested in Colombia in an area controlled by leftist rebels. What were they doing there? Was the I.R.A. [Irish Republican Army] in league with the rebels? Was it training them? The incident was a deep embarrassment to Sinn Fein in the United States. The Sept. 11 attack added to a cold wind currently being experienced by Irish Republicans. An even colder wind seemed to be threatening the 1998 Good Friday agreement.

On Oct. 8 Unionists offered two motions in the Northern Ireland Assembly to expel Sinn Fein from the government on the grounds that the I.R.A. had not commenced decommissioning [weapons]. Following the inevitable failure of the motion because it could not attract cross-community support, David Trimble, leader of the Ulster Unionists, announced he was pulling his ministers out of the government, thereby precipitating its collapse.

Yet, as so often in the past, the Northern Ireland peace process has risen from the ashes of despair to a new optimism. On Oct. 22 Gerry Adams [president of Sinn Fein] called on the I.R.A. to start the process of decommissioning. The following day they did so. General John De Chastelain, whose commission has been charged under the agreement with overseeing decommissioning, announced that a "significant event" had taken place. Unionists opposed to the agreement quickly pointed out that his words had been carefully chosen: they did not specify that a significant number of weapons had been decommissioned. But David Trimble, leader of the Ulster Unionist Party, recognized the move for what it was—perhaps the most significant event since the signing of the [Good Friday] agreement on April 10, 1998. It meant that at last the I.R.A. was starting the process of going out of business, that Republicans were committing themselves to politics, that the old policy of the "armalite and the ballot box" was changing irrevocably to the ballot box alone.

Two Viewpoints: Unionist and Republican

The agreement had been in trouble for some time. At a recent residential meeting organized by Community Dialogue—the group with whom I work—a young Unionist youth worker said he wakes up every morning with a knot of anger in his belly because the Republicans have won everything, "and they have done it through violence." The young man's comment reflects the deep anger in the Unionist community. Part of this is due simply to change. In the past, things seemed much clearer. The I.R.A. was trying to kill the security forces, the security forces were trying to arrest them and everyone knew where they stood. Then the I.R.A. declared a cease-fire, the agreement was signed and Republicans ended up holding the ministries for education and health in the new government. There was a palpable gasp in the Northern Ireland Assembly when Martin McGuinness was named minister for education: a leading I.R.A. man is in charge of the education of our children! For their part, Republicans are either genuinely puzzled or outright dismissive of this Unionist response. They see themselves, with some merit, as having made enormous sacrifices. They have given up the "armed struggle," even though it was central to their philosophy. They have accepted the setting up of a new Northern Ireland Assembly, and they have taken their place as ministers in a government whose ultimate authority is derived from Westminster [in London]. All this has been immensely difficult for them. Further, although they have failed to get what they would see as satisfactory police reform, they have remained involved in the process.

The 1998 Good Friday Agreement

Despite the many difficulties, the peace process is alive, if not well. The agreement set up a variety of political institutions within Northern Ireland, between Northern Ireland and the Republic, and between the United Kingdom and the Dublin government. All of these were designed to reflect one core political reality: there are two groups in Northern Ireland. Each has the power to block the other from running Northern Ireland, and the consent of both is required if these institutions are to work. In other words, the only way we can go forward is together; and the only way we can do this is through politics, not through armed struggle.

In Northern Ireland the agreement set up the Northern Ireland Assembly. All major decisions required cross-community support. The assembly appoints a 10-person executive, whose seats are distributed on the basis of party strength within the assembly.

This meant that Unionists held five (Ulster Unionist Party three, Democratic Unionist Party two) and Nationalists five (Social Democratic and Labor Party three, Sinn Fein two). The idea was that the normal practice of cabinet government would apply.

In fact this did not work. Ian Paisley's D.U.P [Democratic Unionist Party] said they would not share government with Sinn Fein, and they refused to attend meetings of the executive at which Sinn Fein was present. They did, however, take part in committee meetings attended by Sinn Fein. Nonetheless the executive produced a government budget—the first time this has ever happened in Northern Ireland. This was a great achievement. The assembly also had a series of committees that shadowed ministers, and these also worked well. All this was a sign of

New Construction in Belfast

Barry White reports that a new Ramada hotel has opened in Belfast, Northern Ireland. Construction such as this symbolizes that the international community has enough confidence in the peace process to invest its money.

Two Northern Irelands were in the news last week [August 13, 2001]. Dominating the front pages: the battered peace process, forever caught in the punch-up between good news and bad. Back on the business pages, a different story unfolded. A luxury Ramada hotel opened its doors in Belfast—part of a sustained construction boom that belies the city's skewed image as a war zone alight with burning police Land Rovers. Real-estate prices continued to climb, well ahead of inflation; retail rents were rising faster in Belfast than anywhere else in Britain except London. A Confederation of British Industry survey found that Northern Ireland was one of only two places in the United Kingdom that would not lose jobs in 2001.

Barry White, "Give Peace a Chance," *Newsweek International,* August 20, 2001.

the vast amount of agreement that exists among the people of Northern Ireland.

Since the 1998 agreement, there have also been new government measures designed to combat discrimination and to give new human rights protection. Nationalists broadly welcomed these initiatives; Unionists for the most part opposed them.

The agreement failed to deal with policing, and the matter was referred to the Patten Commission. Both the S.D.L.P. [Social Democrat and Labor Party, a Nationalist party] and Sinn Fein opposed the British proposals on the grounds that they failed to implement Patten's recommendations. However, this fall [2001] the S.D.L.P. accepted the amended British proposals and appointed representatives to the Police Board. Sinn Fein continued to reject it. Unionists saw the police reforms as a betrayal of the sacrifices made by the Royal Ulster Constabulary in fighting terrorism, but they also eventually agreed to nominate representatives to the board. For the first time, therefore, Nationalists and Unionists will together be taking responsibility for policing. The absence of Sinn Fein is a major limitation on this achievement. . . .

The Role of the United States

The U.S. government under President Clinton made a significant contribution to the peace process. U.S. involvement helped the doves within the Republican movement argue that there was a better way than violence. It also encouraged Unionists to start making their case on the world stage, a project at which they have for the most part been singularly unsuccessful. (The most startling recent example of bad public relations was the blockading of schoolchildren in the Ardoyne, organized by Loyalists this summer and fall [2001].)

The United States can still help Northern Ireland by pressing Republicans to continue decommissioning, by making expertise available for party political development, by funding community initiatives and by investment. (Northern Ireland remains a good prospect, with an educated, English-speaking workforce within the European Union, together with a good infrastructure.) Besides, it would be contradictory if the United States, while obviously focussed on defending itself against terrorism, did not continue to help lay a solid foundation for peace in Northern Ireland, thereby finally ending at least one centuries-long conflict.

New Hope for the Peace Process

David Trimble responded to the I.R.A.'s decision to commence decommissioning by agreeing to come back into government with Sinn Fein. Eighty percent of his party's executives supported his decision. But because two of his assembly members, Peter Weir and Pauline Armitage, voted against him, he failed to get sufficient cross-community support to be reappointed as first minister. In the end he was rescued by the Alliance Party—which has always refused to be either Unionist or Nationalist—redesignating itself as Unionist. This device flew in the face of a central clause of the agreement—insisted on during the 1998 negotiations by Nationalists—that all major decisions would have cross-community support, but the manoeuvre worked: the government is back in business. The appointment of David Trimble as first minister and Mark Durkan of the S.D.L.P. as deputy first minister received a standing ovation from Sinn Fein assembly members. That is a change, and it is good news.

Unsolved Racial Problems

Arun Kundnani

In the following selection, Arun Kundnani describes the growing racial tensions in the towns of northern England. He contends that a history of growing unemployment, poverty, racism, and segregation have led to increasing isolation and desperation among the Asian population, which led to police riots in the summer of 2001. Arun Kundnani is a writer for Race and Class, *a quarterly publication of the Institute of Race Relations that focuses on issues of racism in economic injustice around the world.*

From April to July 2001, the northern English towns of Oldham, Burnley and Bradford saw violent confrontations between young Asians and the police, culminating in the clashes of 7–9 July in Bradford in which 200 police officers were injured. The clashes were prompted by racist gangs attacking Asian communities and the failure of the police to provide protection from this threat. In the scale of the damage caused and the shock they delivered to the nation, the 2001 riots were the worst riots in Britain since the Handsworth, Brixton and Tottenham uprisings of 1985.

The fires that burned across Lancashire and Yorkshire through the summer of 2001 signalled the rage of young Pakistanis and Bangladeshis of the second and third generations, deprived of futures, hemmed in on all sides by racism, failed by their own leaders and representatives and unwilling to stand by as, first fascists, and then police officers, invaded their streets. Their violence was ad hoc, improvised and haphazard. It was no longer the organised community self-defence of 1981, when Asian youth burnt down the Hambrough Tavern in Southall, where fascists had gathered, or when twelve members of the Bradford Black United Youth League were arrested for preparing petrol bombs to counter violent fascist incursions into their community. And whereas the 1981 and 1985 uprisings against the police in Brixton, Handsworth, Tottenham and Toxteth had been the violence of a community united—black and white—in its anger at the 'heavy manners' of the police, the fires this time were lit by the youths of communities falling apart from within, as well as from without; youths whose violence was, therefore, all the more desperate. It was the violence of communities fragmented by colour lines, class lines and police lines. It was the violence of hopelessness. It was the violence of the violated.

Mechanization and Globalisation Cause Unemployment

Colonialism has been interwoven with the history of the northern mill towns since the beginning of the industrial revolution. Cotton-spinning—on which the towns' early success was based—was a technology, borrowed from India, which became central to the emergence of northern England as the 'factory of the world'. Cotton grown in the plantations of the Caribbean, the US deep South, or the fields of Bengal was brought to Lancashire and Yorkshire to be spun into cloth and sold back at profit to the empire. This was a global trade before globalisation.

By the 1960s, the mills were investing in new technologies which were operated twenty-four hours a day to maximise profit. The night shifts, which were unpopular with the existing workforce, soon became the domain of the Pakistani and Bangladeshi workers who were now settling in the mill towns. But as the machinery developed, the need for labour diminished, and such labour as was needed could be got for less elsewhere. The work once done cheaply by Bangladeshi workers in the north of England could now be done even more cheaply by Bangladeshi workers in Bangladesh.

As the mills declined, entire towns were left on the scrapheap. White and black workers were united in their unemployment. The only future now for the Asian communities lay in the local service economy. A few brothers would pool their savings and set up a shop, a restaurant or a take-away. Otherwise there was minicabbing, with long hours and the risk of violence, often racially motivated. With the end of the textile industry, the largest employers were now the public services but discrimination kept most of these jobs for whites.

By the end of the twentieth century, a generation had lived with soaring rates of unemployment, reaching around 50 per cent, for example, among young Asians in Oldham. Across the Pennine hills, from Oldham, Burnley, Accrington, Blackburn and Preston to Bradford and Leeds, a string of Pakistani and Bangladeshi communities were among Britain's most impoverished 1 per cent, communities that had sunk well below the radar of a Blair administration that was more concerned with the welfare of members of the Asian millionaires' club.

Segregation in Housing and Education

The textile industry was the common thread binding the white and Asian working class into a single social fabric. But with its collapse, each community was forced to turn inwards on to itself. The depressed inner-city areas, lined with old 'two-up-two-down' terraced houses which had been built for mill-worker families, were abandoned by those whites that could afford to move out to the suburbs. Those that could not afford to buy themselves out took advantage of discriminatory council housing policies which allocated whites to new housing estates cut off from Asian areas. Out of Bradford's large stock of council housing, just 2 per cent had been allocated to Asians. . . . It was 'white flight' backed by the local state. The geography of the balkanised northern towns became a chessboard of mutually exclusive areas.

Segregation in housing led to segregation in education. In some districts, school catchment areas contained near 100 per cent populations of just one ethnic group. In others, where catchment areas ought to have produced mixed intakes, the mechanism of parental choice allowed white parents to send their children to majority-white schools a little further away. What resulted were Asian ghetto schools in which expectations of failure were common: poor results could be explained away by 'cultural problems'. Asian girls would be married off anyway, so why bother? The minority of teachers willing to tackle these issues found themselves struggling against a mass of institutionalised preconceptions. With mainstream schooling mired in a culture of failure, some Asian parents looked to 'faith schools'—which would offer education within an Islamic framework—as a way of raising standards for their children's education.

A generation of whites and Asians was now growing up whose only contact with each other was through uncertain glances on the street or through the pages of local newspapers. Mutual distrust festered. The local press, drawing on dubious police statistics, did their bit to promote the idea that young Asians were thugs hellbent on attacking whites at random. The regular racist violence against Asians was marginalised, while Asian crime on whites was sensationalised and misinterpreted as racially motivated. The segregation of communities, the roots of which lay in institutional racism, came to be perceived as 'self-segregation'—the attempt by Asians to create their own exclusive areas or 'no-go areas' because they did not want to mix with whites. It was a self-fulfilling prophecy.

A New Generation Unprotected by Police and Community Leaders

By the 1990s, a new generation of young Asians, born and bred in Britain, was coming of age in the northern towns, unwilling to accept the second-class status foisted on their elders. When racists came to their streets looking for a fight, they would meet violence with violence. And with the continuing failure of the police to tackle racist gangs, violent confrontations between groups of whites and Asians became more common. Inevitably, when the police did arrive to break up a melee, it was the young Asians who bore the brunt of police heavy-handedness. As such, Asian areas became increasingly targeted by the police as they decided that gangs of Asian youths were getting out of hand. The real crime problems faced by Asian communities—not only racist incursions but the growing epidemic of heroin abuse—were ignored. Among young Asians, there grew a hatred of a police force that left them vulnerable to racism, on the one hand, and, on the other, criminalised them for defending themselves.

But this new generation had also been sold short by its own self-appointed community leaders. The state's response to earlier unrest had been to nurture a black elite which could manage and contain anger from within the ranks of black communities. Where a middle class existed, it was co-opted; where one did not, it was created. A new class of 'ethnic representatives' entered the town halls from the mid-1980s onwards, who would be the surrogate voice for their own ethnically-defined fiefdoms. They entered into a pact with the authorities; they were to cover up and gloss over black community resistance in return for free rein in preserving their own patriarchy. It was a colonial arrangement which prevented community leaders from making radical criticisms, for fear that funding for their pet projects would be jeopardised. The authorities hoped that if they threw some money at the bigwig blacks, they would stop complaining. And the community leaders proved them right.

Anti-Racism Confused with Ethnic Recognition

The result was that black communities became fragmented, horizontally by ethnicity, vertically by class. Different ethnic groups were pressed into competing for grants for their areas. The poor and the still poorer fought over the scraps of the paltry regeneration monies that the government made available to keep them quiet. Money that did come in was spent, after empty 'community consultation exercises', on projects that brought little benefit, particularly to the increasingly restive youths. Worst of all, the problem of racism came to be redefined in terms of ethnic recognition so that to tackle racism was to fund an ethnic project, any ethnic project, no matter how dubious. As Sivanandan put it, 'equal opportunities became equal opportunism'.

The confusion between anti-racism and ethnic recognition spread to the schools, too, where teaching other people's culture came to be perceived as the best strategy to overcome segregation. Unfortunately, the Asian 'culture' taught to whites did little to give them a meaningful appreciation of Asian life, based as it was on hackneyed formulae of samosas and saris. And since white working-class children were perceived as having no culture, their parents soon started to complain of favouritism to Asians in the classroom. Competition over ethnic funding was thus joined by competition over classroom time. Genuine education about other people, their histories and their straggles, was replaced with the grim essentialism of identity politics. A generation grew up who were not given the tools to understand how their own towns and cities had become increasingly divided by race.

Furthermore, as cultural protectionism replaced anti-racism, the cultural development of Asian communities was itself stunted. The community leadership tried to insulate their clans from the wider world, which they saw only as a threat to the patriarchical system on which their power depended. Internal critics were considered disloyal. Thus the dirty linen of the Asian communities—the deep-seated gender inequality, the forced marriages, the drug problems—was washed neither in public nor in private.

Police Excess and Racism

In the end, it was the benighted arrogance of the police that provoked the youths into uprising. When the police responded to white racists going on a rampage through the Asian area of Glodwick in Oldham by donning riot gear, arresting Asians and attempting to disperse the increasingly angered crowds of local residents, it lost any claim to be defending 'the rule of law'. Rather, it was an invading army. And Asian youths responded to it as such, using stones, burning cars and petrol bombs to drive the police, dogs and vans and all, off their streets. It took the police six hours to regain control of the area. Similar events would later ignite Burnley and Bradford.

Yet in the aftermath of the riots, there was scant attention paid to the racism of the police. Just two years previously, in the wake of the publication of the Macpherson report, chief constables had made soul-searching admissions that their forces were riddled with racism. But the possibility that institutional racism had now contributed to the riots was not a view that was aired. Instead, the prime minister and home secretary gave their full backing to the police, even offering to provide new toys—water cannons—if they wanted them. Just as [former Prime Minister Margaret] Thatcher had wanted to see the riots under her regime only as outbreaks of criminality, not as the fractures produced by her own political programme, so too [Prime Minister Tony] Blair spoke of 'thuggery', refusing to look beyond a narrow law-and-orderism, refusing to see in the riots the reflection of his own failed ambitions to tackle 'social exclusion'.

The Asians Are Blamed

Following in the government's path, a hundred other voices rushed to condemn the rioters, while little was heard from young mill-town Asians themselves. The community leaders blamed a lack of discipline, a decline in Muslim values, and the undue influence of western values which, to them, was a threat to their own authority. The Asian middle class in the rest of Britain, forgetting that their own secure place in society came about because of those who had taken to the streets in the seventies and eighties, blamed the 'village mentality' of Asian communities not as lucky as their own. The World Council of Hindus mixed class snobbery with communalism to publicly disown the Muslim rioters, hoping to make clear to whites that Hindus should not be tarnished with the same brush. Asian solidarity had died.

The popular press first blamed 'outside agitators', then blamed the community leaders who had failed in their allotted role: to control 'their people'. Then it was the inherent separatism of Islamic culture that was to blame—these people did not want to integrate; they were 'self-segregating'. A people that had been systematically cut off, shunned, dispossessed and left to rot, was now blamed for refusing to mix. There was talk of 'forced integration', perhaps a return to busing Asian schoolchildren into white areas, the hated system used in the 1960s when fears grew that too many Asians were attending the same Southall schools. There was talk of new restrictions on immigration—involving English-language tests—which would remove the right to family union. The far-Right British National Party was the only beneficiary from this cacophony of disdain. It distributed leaflets around Britain calling for a boycott of Asian businesses.

A generation of Asians, discarded for their class, excluded for their race, stigmatised for their religion, ghettoised and forgotten, has found its voice—but is yet to be heard.

Appendix: England's Monarchs

Kent
Ethelbert, 560–616

Northumbria
Ethelfrith, 593–617
Edwin, 617–633
Oswald, 635–642
Oswy, 642–670
Ecgfrith, 670–685

Mercia
Penda, 626–655
Ethelbald, 716–757
Offa II, 757–796
Cenulf, 796–821

Wessex
Ine, 688–726
Egbert, 802–839
Ethelwulf, 839–858
Ethelbald, 858–860
Ethelbert, 860–866
Ethelred, 866–871

England
Alfred, 871–899
Edward, 899–924
Ethelstan, 924–939
Edmund, 939–946
Edred, 946–955
Edwig, 955–959
Edgar, 959–975
Edward, 975–978
Ethelred 978–1016
Edmund, 1016
Canute, 1017–1035
Harold, 1035–1040
Harthacanute, 1040–1042
Edward, 1042–1066
Harold, 1066
William I, 1066–1087
William II, 1087–1100
Henry I, 1100–1135
Stephen, 1135–1154
Henry II, 1154–1189
Richard I, 1189–1199
John, 1199–1216
Henry III, 1216–1272
Edward I, 1272–1307
Edward II, 1307–1327
Edward III, 1327–1377
Richard II, 1377–1399
Henry IV, 1399–1413
Henry V, 1413–1422
Henry VI, 1422–1461
Edward IV, 1461–1483
Edward V, 1483
Richard III, 1483–1485
Henry VII, 1485–1509
Henry VIII, 1509–1547
Edward VI, 1547–1553
Mary, 1553–1558
Elizabeth I, 1558–1603
James I, 1603–1625
Charles I, 1625–1649
Interregnum, 1649–1660
Charles II, 1660–1685
James II, 1685–1688

William III and Mary,
1689–1702
Anne, 1702–1714
George I, 1714–1727
George II, 1727–1760
George III, 1760–1820
George IV, 1820–1830
William IV, 1830–1837
Victoria, 1837–1901
Edward VII, 1901–1910
George V, 1910–1936
Edward VIII, 1936
George VI, 1936–1952
Elizabeth II, 1952–

CHRONOLOGY

ca. 2000–1800 B.C.
Stonehenge is built.

43
Roman soldiers invade England.

45
London is established as a trading center.

ca. 122–126
Hadrian's wall is built.

410
Roman soldiers withdraw from England.

449
Angles, Saxons, and Jutes invade England.

597
Pope Gregory I sends St. Augustine to Kent.

ca. 650
The northern and southern Scottish kingdoms unite.

731
Venerable Bede writes *Ecclesiastical History.*

789
Viking invasions begin, landing at Portland.

795
Danish invasions begin.

825
Egbert takes control of Kent, Sussex, Surrey, and Essex.

838
Viking Lindisforne defeats Egbert.

851
Viking troops storm London.

871
Alfred becomes king.

892
King Alfred begins the *Anglo-Saxon Chronicle.*

ca. 1000
The epic poem *Beowulf* is written.

1066
Norman duke William the Conqueror invades England.

1068–1075
William suppresses revolts in the west, midlands, and north.

1086–1087
William compiles the *Doomsday Book*, recording landholders and livestock.

1095–1291
The Crusades, Christian expeditions to the Holy Land, occur.

1164
The Constitution of Clarendon defines church-state relations.

1179
Common law evolves under Henry II.

1215
The Magna Carta restricts the rights of kings.

1220–1260
Salisbury cathedral is built.

1290
Edward I expels Jews.

1295
The first Parliament with elected representatives meets.

1337
The Hundred Years' War begins.

ca. 1341–1342
Poet Geoffrey Chaucer is born.

1348–1349
The bubonic plague kills thousands of people.

1370
Mystery (miracle) plays are performed in Chester and Coventry.

1381
Peasants revolt over taxes.

1390
An act stipulating eight justices for each county is passed.

1399
Richard II exiles Henry of Bolingbroke.

1405
The first morality plays are performed.

1415
Henry V defeats French forces at Agincourt.

1455
The Wars of the Roses begin.

1485
Tudor accession begins with Henry VII when Henry Tudor wins victory at Bosworth Field.

1532
Henry VIII takes control of the church and appoints the archbishop of Canterbury.

1536
Henry VIII dissolves monasteries and confiscates property.

1537
Thomas Cromwell orders every parish to have an English Bible.

1542–1547
Witchcraft is made a capital offense.

1549
Parliament orders the *Book of Common Prayer* to be used in church services.

1553
Mary, daughter of Henry VIII, ascends the throne.

1554
Queen Mary marries Philip of Spain, threatening Spanish domination of England.

1558
Elizabeth, daughter of Henry VIII, ascends the throne.

1559
Royal injuctions enforce re-introduction of the *Book of Common Prayer.*

1563
Thirty-nine articles are passed, imposing Protestantism on the Church of England.

1564
William Shakespeare is born.

1569
Mary, Queen of Scots, flees to England, galvanizing discontent in the north.

1576
The first public theater, called the Theatre, is built by Richard Burbage.

1577–1580
Francis Drake circumnavigates the globe.

1587
Mary Stuart, formerly Queen of Scots, is executed.

1588
The Spanish Armada is defeated.

1590s
Shakespeare is established as a great dramatist.

1600
A charter is granted to the East India Company.

1601
The Poor Laws create a tax to help the "deserving poor."

1603
Stuart accession begins with James I.

1604
The Hampton Court conference orders a new translation of the Bible.

1605
The Gunpowder Plot, the celebrated attempt to murder James I, takes place.

1606
James I grants a charter for Virginia colonies.

1611
The King James Bible is published.

1625
James I dies; Charles I becomes king.

1629–1640
Charles I rules without Parliament.

1639
A trading post is established in India.

1642–1648
Civil wars erupt in England.

1649
Charles I is executed.

1649–1653
Parliament rules England as a commonwealth.

1650
The first coffeehouse is built in Oxford.

1653–1659
England becomes a Protectorate under Oliver and Richard Cromwell.

1660

The Restoration of Charles II occurs; the Royal Society for the study of science and literature is established.

1665

The bubonic plague kills between 70,000 and 100,000 people.

1666

The great fire of London destroys homes and churches.

1673

The first of the Test Acts excludes Catholics from military and civil office.

1678

The Popish Plot, a rumor of a plot to murder Charles II and establish absolutist, Catholic government, occurs; Christopher Wren completes fourteen new churches to replace those destroyed in the great fire of 1666.

1685

Charles II dies; James II becomes king.

1687

Issac Newton publishes *Mathematical Principles.*

1688

The archbishop and six bishops are tried for protesting James II's order that the Declaration of Indulgence be read from every pulpit; Prince William of Orange invades England; the Glorious Revolution ousts James II.

1689

The Bill of Rights is adopted; William is crowned William III with wife, Mary.

1689–1702

Parliament and the English upper classes enact the Revolutionary Settlement drawn up when William and Mary were crowned.

1694

The Bank of England is given a charter.

1701
Newspapers and pamphlets devoted to arguing religious and war policy are developed.

1702
Anne, daughter of James II, ascends the throne.

1711
Joseph Addison and Richard Steele begin the *Spectator*, a daily news journal.

1714
The Hanover accession begins with George I.

1716
The Septennial Act is passed, giving members of Parliament seven-year terms.

1741
George F. Handel completes his *Messiah*.

1750–1760
Turnpikes are built.

1753
Hardwicke's Marriage Act, designed to prevent hurried marriages by requiring publication of banns, is introduced.

1756–1763
The Seven Years' War occurs; India and Canada become colonies.

1759–1761
The Worsley-Manchester canal is built.

1760–1793
1611 Enclosure Acts, requiring hedging around agricultural fields, are passed.

1765
The Stamp Act, a tax on official paper that is bitterly resented by American colonists, is introduced.

1768
The spinning jenny, a multiple-spindle machine for spinning wool or cotton, is invented.

1769

James Cook claims Australia for England; James Watt patents the steam engine.

1773

The Boston Tea Party, the dumping of tea into Boston Harbor to protest the tax on tea, occurs.

1775–1783

The American War of Independence occurs, ending in Britain's defeat.

1801

The first census of England and Wales takes place.

1803

The Napoleonic War begins.

1805

Horatio Nelson defeats French and Spanish fleets in the Battle of Trafalgar, during which Nelson is killed.

1815

Napoléon is defeated in the Battle of Waterloo; the Congress of Vienna arranges settlement after Napoléon's defeat; the Corn Laws prohibit all foreign grain imports after the domestic price fell.

1829

The first paid uniformed police force is introduced.

1832

The First Reform Bill extends franchise to some middle-class men.

1833

The Factory Act sets limits on the employment of children.

1837

Victoria ascends the throne.

1838

Chartism, a movement to extend franchise to working-class men, begins.

1840
New Zealand is annexed; Victoria marries Prince Albert.

1846
The Corn Laws are repealed.

1848
The General Board of Health is established.

1851
The Great Exhibition of English inventions takes place.

1854–1856
The Crimean War with Russia occurs, ending in a British and French victory.

1859
Charles Darwin publishes *On the Origin of Species.*

1867
The Second Reform Bill extends franchise, adding 1.12 million people to the electorate.

1870
The Education Act divides England into school districts and provides for improved national education.

1884
The Third Reform Bill enfranchises nearly all males.

1888
The Football (soccer) League, with twelve clubs, is established.

1897
Victoria's Diamond Jubilee occurs; the British Empire is at its height; the Workman's Compensation Act establishes compensation for industrial accidents.

1914–1919
World War I occurs, with heavy British losses sustained on the western front in 1916 and 1917.

1918
The Fourth Reform Act enfranchises some women.

1919

The Treaty of Versailles ends World War I.

1919–1920

The war between the Irish Republican Army (IRA) and British government forces occurs, ending in "Bloody Sunday" on November 21, 1920.

1920

The League of Nations is established; British Communist Party is formed.

1926

The British Broadcasting Company (BBC) becomes a public corporation.

1928

The Equal Franchise Act extends franchise to all women over twenty-one.

1931

Parliament approves the Commonwealth of Nations.

1936

Edward VIII abdicates the throne to marry an American divorcée.

1939–1945

World War II occurs.

1940

The German air assault on London, the Blitz, begins.

1940–1945

Winston Churchill, an outstanding war leader, serves as prime minister.

1945

Atomic bombs are dropped on Hiroshima and Nagasaki; the United Nations is founded in San Francisco.

1946

The National Health Service Act becomes law (it is enacted in 1948).

1948–1951

The Marshall Plan aids European financial recovery after World War II.

1958

The Campaign for Nuclear Disarmament begins in response to the 1957 British H-bomb test.

1964

The Independent Television Act extends licensing and regulating of television companies.

1973

England joins the European Union (EU).

1982

Britain fights the Falklands War with Argentina.

2001

England is one of three EU countries that chooses not to adopt the euro, the common European currency.

For Further Research

General Histories

Winston Churchill, *History of the English Speaking People*. Vols. 1–12. London: BPC, 1971.

John Richard Green, *A Short History of the English People*. Rev. Alice Stopford Green. New York: American, 1916.

Robert Edwin Herzstein, *Western Civilization*. Boston: Houghton Mifflin, 1975.

W.E. Lunt, *History of England*. 4th ed. New York: Harper, 1956.

John Osborne and the Editors of *Life, Britain*. New York: Time, 1961.

Arnold Toynbee, *A Study of History*. New York: Oxford University Press, 1947.

George Macaulay Trevelyan, *History of England*. New York: Longmans, Green, 1926.

R.J. White, *The Horizon Concise History of England*. New York: American Heritage, 1971.

F. Roy Willis, *Western Civilization: An Urban Perspective*. Vol. 2. New York: D.C. Heath, 1973.

Histories of Periods

Maurice Ashley, *England in the Seventeenth Century*. New York: Barnes & Noble, 1978.

———, *Great Britain to 1688: A Modern History*. Ann Arbor: University of Michigan Press, 1961.

G.E. Aylmer, *A Short History of Seventeenth-Century England*. New York: New American Library, 1963.

John W. Derry, *A Short History of Nineteenth-Century England*. New York: New American Library, 1963.

Margaret Drabble, *For Queen and Country: Britain in the Victorian Age.* New York: Seabury, 1979.

Leon Garfield, *The House of Hanover: England in the Eighteenth Century.* New York: Seabury, 1976.

R.W. Harris, *A Short History of Eighteenth-Century England.* New York: New American Library, 1963.

Alfred F. Haveghurst, *Twentieth-Century Britain.* 2nd ed. New York: Harper and Row, 1962.

C. Walter Hodges, *The Battlement Garden: Britain from the Wars of the Roses to the Age of Shakespeare.* London: Andre Deutsch, 1979.

David Howarth, *1066: The Year of the Conquest.* New York: Viking, 1977.

Percival Hunt, *Fifteenth-Century England.* Pittsburgh: University of Pittsburgh Press, 1962.

W.D. Hussey, *British History, 1815–1939.* Cambridge, England: Cambridge University Press, 1971.

T.L. Jarman, *A Short History of Twentieth-Century England.* New York: New American Library, 1963.

Laura Marvel, ed., *Elizabethan England.* San Diego: Greenhaven, 2002.

A.R. Myers, *England in the Late Middle Ages.* New York: Penguin, 1971.

John B. Owen, *The Eighteenth Century: 1714–1815.* Totowa, NJ: Rowman and Littlefield, 1975.

I.A. Richmond, *Roman Britain.* New York: Penguin, 1963.

K.B. Smellie, *Great Britain Since 1688.* Ann Arbor: University of Michigan Press, 1962.

Doris Mary Stenton, *English Society in the Early Middle Ages.* New York: Penguin, 1965.

Dorothy Whitelock, *The Beginnings of the English Society.* New York: Penguin, 1954.

G.W.O. Woodward, *A Short History of Sixteenth-Century England*. New York: New American Library, 1963.

John W. Young, *Britain and the World in the Twentieth Century*. London: Arnold, 1997.

Histories of Events or Topics

David Anderson, *The Spanish Armada*. New York: Hampstead, 1988.

Geoffrey Ashe in association with Debrett's Peerage, *The Discovery of King Arthur*. Garden City, NY: Anchor/Doubleday, 1985.

Arthur Bryant, *Spirit of England*. London: Collins, 1982.

Elizabeth Burton, *The Pageant of Elizabethan England*. New York: Charles Scribner's Sons, 1958.

Christopher Chippindale, *Stonehenge Complete*. Ithaca, NY: Cornell University Press, 1983.

Leonard Cottrell, *The Great Invasion*. New York: Coward-McCann, 1958.

Leonard W. Cowie, *Plague and Fire: London, 1665–66*. New York: G.P. Putnam's Sons, 1970.

———, *The Trial and Execution of Charles I*. London: Wayland, 1972.

Eric de Mare, *London's River: The Story of a City*. New York: Macmillan, 1964.

David C. Douglas, *William the Conqueror*. Berkeley and Los Angeles: University of California Press, 1964.

Leonard Everett Fisher, *The Tower of London*. New York: Macmillan, 1987.

Elizabeth Hallam, ed., *The Wars of the Roses: From Richard II to the Fall of Richard III at Bosworth Field—Seen Through the Eyes of Their Contemporaries*. New York: Weidenfeld & Nicolson, 1988.

J.F.C. Harrison, ed., *Society and Politics in England, 1780–1960*. New York: Harper & Row, 1965.

Dorothy Hartley, *Lost Country Life*. New York: Pantheon, 1979.

Kristy McLeod, *Drums and Trumpets: The House of Stuart*. New York: Seabury, 1977.

Helen Hill Miller, *Captains from Devon: The Great Elizabethan Seafarers Who Won the Oceans for England*. Chapel Hill, NC: Algonquin, 1985.

Wallace Notestein, *The English People on the Eve of Colonization*. New York: Harper & Row, 1954.

Richard Ollard, *This War Without an Enemy: A History of the English Civil Wars*. New York: Atheneum, 1976.

Nikolaus Pevsner, *The Englishness of English Art*. New York: Penguin, 1956.

Marjorie and C.H.B. Quennell, *A History of Everyday Things in England*. Vols. 1–4. Rev. Christine Hole. London: B.T. Batsford, 1952–1953.

Conyers Read, *The Tudors: Personalities and Practical Politics in the Sixteenth Century*. New York: Henry Holt, 1936.

L.F. Salzman, *English Trade in the Middle Ages*. Oxford, England: Clarendon, 1931.

Stephen W. Sears, *The Horizon History of the British Empire*. New York: American Heritage, 1973.

Lytton Strachey, *Eminent Victorians*. New York: G.P. Putnam's Sons, n.d.

Philip A.M. Taylor, ed., *The Industrial Revolution in Britain: Triumph or Disaster?* Lexington, MA: D.C. Heath, 1970.

George Macaulay Trevelyan, *Illustrated English Social History*. Vols. 1–3. London: Longmans, Green, 1944.

Amabel Williams-Ellis and F.J. Fisher, *The Story of English Life*. New York: Coward-McCann, 1963.

INDEX